MIPS RISC Architecture

Gerry Kane
Joe Heinrich

Prentice Hall, Englewood Cliffs, New Jersey 07632

Published by Prentice-Hall, Inc.
A Simon & Schuster Company
Englewood Cliffs, New Jersey 07632

The publisher offers discounts on this book when ordered
in bulk quantities. For more information, write:

> Special Sales/Professional Marketing
> Prentice-Hall, Inc.
> Professional & Technical Reference Division
> Englewood Cliffs, New Jersey 07632

MIPS is a registered trademark of MIPS Computer Systems.
RISCompiler and RISC/os are Trademarks of MIPS Computer Systems, Inc.
UNIX is a Trademark of AT&T Bell Laboratories.
Ada is a registered trademark of the U.S. Government (Ada Joint Program Office).
VADS and Verdix are registered trademarks of the Verdix Corporation.
APSO and GVAS are trademarks of the Verdix Corporation.

FCC Note to User Information

Warning—This machine generates, uses, and can radiate radio frequency energy and if not installed and used in accordance with the instruction manual, may cause interference to radio communications. It has been type tested and found to comply with the limits for a Class A computing device pursuant to Subpart J of Part 15 of FCC Rules, which are designed to provide reasonable protection against such interference when operated in a commercial environment. Operation of this equipment in a residential area is likely to cause interference in which case the user at his own expense will be required to take whatever measures may be required to correct the interference.

Canadian Department of Communication
Notice to User

This digital apparatus does not exceed the Class A limits for radio noise emissions from digital apparatus as set out in the radio interference regulations of the Canadian Department of Communications.

Le present appareil numerique n'emet pas de bruits radioelectriques depassant les limites applicables aux appareils numeriques de classe A prescrites dans le reglement sur le brouillage radioelectrique edicte par le Ministere des Communications du Canada.

MIPS Computer Systems, Inc.
930 Arques Ave.
Sunnyvale, CA 94086.

Customer Service Telephone Number:
USA and Canada: (800) 443–MIPS

Printed in the United States of America

10 9 8 7 6 5 4 3 2 1

ISBN 0-13-590472-2

Prentice-Hall International (UK) Limited, *London*
Prentice-Hall of Australia Pty. Limited, *Sydney*
Prentice-Hall Canada Inc., *Toronto*
Prentice-Hall Hispanoamericana, S.A., *Mexico*
Prentice-Hall of India Private Limited, *New Delhi*
Prentice-Hall of Japan, Inc., *Tokyo*
Simon & Schuster Asia Pte. Ltd., *Singapore*
Editora Prentice-Hall do Brasil, Ltda., *Rio de Janeiro*

Acknowledgements

Special thanks to **Earl Killian** (from whose specification the vast majority of this revision is derived), **Steven Przybylski**, **Keith Garrett**, **Peter Davies**, and **Charlie Price**, all of whom made themselves available time and time again as resources. Thanks also to **Larry Weber**, **Jill Mullan**, **Ken Klingman**, **Karen Sielski**, **Tom Riordan**, **Norman Yeung**, **Amir Nayyerhabibi**, **Muhammad Helal**, **Ashish Dixit**, **Andy Keane**, **Bobri Roberts**, and **Dane Elliot** — and everyone else whom we have failed to list, who helped us along the way. On the editorial front, thanks to **Robin Cowan**, of The Cowan Conglomerate, Ltd., for her insightful advice, together with **Karen Gettman** and **Karen Bernhaut**, of Prentice Hall, for helping to shepherd this book from nascence to publication.

About This Book

This book is the primary reference manual for the MIPS RISC Architecture. On the one hand it describes the user instruction set (the ISA), together with extensions to this ISA; on the other it describes specific implementations of this architecture as exemplified by the R2000, R3000, R4000, and R6000 (collectively known as the R-Series) processors. Since growth is dynamic, it is probably inevitable that there will be further extensions, enhancements, and implementations of this architecture.

The R-Series processors are available from the following manufacturers:

Integrated Device Technology, Inc.
3236 Scott Boulevard
P.O. Box 58015
Santa Clara, CA 95052–8015
Tel: (408) 727–6116
Telex: 887766
Fax: (408) 988–3029

LSI Logic Corporation
1551 McCarthy Blvd.
Milpitas, CA 95035
Tel: (408) 433–8000
Telex: 171.641
Fax: (408) 433–7447
Attn: MIPS Division

MIPS Computer Systems, Inc.
930 Arques Avenue
Sunnyvale, CA 94086–3650
Tel: (408) 720–1700
Telex: 510 601 5346
Fax: (408) 720–9809

NEC Eelectronics
401 Ellis Street
P.O. Box 7241
Mountain View, CA
Tel: (415) 960 -6000
Attn: Microprocessor Marketing

NEC Corporation
NEC Building
7–1, Shiba 5–chome, Minatoku
Tokyo 108–01, Japan
Tel: (03)–3454–1111
Telex: 22686
Fax: (03)–3798–6959

NEC Electronics Europe
Oberrather Str.4
4000 Dusseldorf 30, West Germany
Tel: (0211)–650301
Telex: 8589960
Fax: (0211)–6503327

Performance Semiconductor Corporation
610 E. Weddell Drive
Sunnyvale, CA 94089
Tel: (408) 734–9000
Fax: (408) 734–0258
Attn: Microprocessor Marketing

Siemens Components, Inc.
2191 Laurelwood Road
Santa Clara, CA 95054
Tel: (408) 980–4506
Fax: (408) 980–4510
Attn: Integrated Circuit Division

Siemens AG, Semiconductor Division
Marketing Microprocessor Products
Balanstrasse 73
POB 801709
D–8000 Munich 80
Tel: (–89) 4144–0
Telex: 52108–0
Fax: (–89) 4144–2689

Sony Corporation
10833 Valley View Street
Cypress, CA 90630–0016
Component Products Company
Tel: (714) 229–4270
Fax: (714) 229–4271

Sony Corporation
4–10–18, Takanawa
Minato–ku, Tokyo,108 Japan
Products Marketing Dept. III
Semiconductor Div.
Component Marketing Gp.
Tel: (03) 3448–3425
Fax: (03) 3448–7458

Organization

This book is organized into two major sections: Chapters 1 through 6 describe the characteristics of the CPU and Chapters 7 through 9 describe the FPU. The Appendices that follow contain the instruction sets for each, along with specific detailed information about programming, compatibility and scheduling hazards.

The contents of each chapter are summarized in the list below.

Chapter 1, RISC Architecture: An Overview, describes the general characteristics and concepts of reduced instruction set computers.

Chapter 2, CPU Architecture Overview, describes the general characteristics and capabilities of the processor. It also provides a programming model which describes how data is represented in the CPU registers and in memory and also provides a summary of the CPU registers.

Chapter 3, CPU Instruction Set Summary, provides a summary description of the CPU's instruction set.

Chapter 4, Memory Management System, describes the virtual memory system supported by the CPU's System Control Coprocessor.

Chapter 5, Caches, describes the cache implementations in the R-Series processors.

Chapter 6, Exception Processing, describes the events that cause exceptions and the sequences that occur during processing of the exceptions.

Chapter 7, FPU Overview, describes the general characteristics and capabilities of the FPU. This chapter also provides a summary of FPU registers and describes how data is represented in its registers.

Chapter 8, FPU Instruction Set Summary & Instruction Pipeline, provides a summary description of the FPU instruction set and a discussion of instruction overlapping.

Chapter 9, Floating Point Exceptions, describes how the FPU supports the IEEE standard floating point exceptions.

Appendix A provides a detailed description of the format and operation of each CPU instruction.

Appendix B provides a detailed description of the format and operation of each FPU instruction.

Appendix C describes machine language programming tips that can simplify implementation of commonly required tasks.

Appendix D describes assembly language programming techniques and provides guidelines for writing programs for use with the MIPS assembler.

Appendix E describes how the FPU supports the IEEE floating point standard and provides programming tips that can simplify implementation of standard operations not implemented by the FPU.

Appendix F describes scheduling constraints to be recognized when programming.

Contents

1

RISC Architecture: An Overview

2

MIPS Processor Architecture Overview

3

CPU Instruction Set Summary

4

Memory Management System

5

Caches

6
Exception Processing

7
FPU Overview

8
FPU Instruction Set Summary & Instruction Pipeline

9
Floating-Point Exceptions

A
CPU Instruction Set Details

B
FPU Instruction Set Details

C
Machine Language Programming Tips

D
Assembly Language Programming

E
IEEE Standard 754 Floating-Point Compatibility Issues

F
Scheduling Hazards

Index

Tables

Figures

1
RISC Architecture:
An Overview

MIPS RISC architecture delivers dramatic cost/performance advantages over computers based on traditional architectures. This advantage is the result of a development methodology that demands optimization across many disciplines including custom VLSI, CPU organization, system-level architecture, operating system considerations, and compiler design. The trade-offs involved in this optimization process typify, and indeed are the essence of, RISC design. Although most of this book is devoted to describing the MIPS RISC architecture, this chapter provides a context for that description by examining some of the underlying concepts that characterize RISC architectures in general.

Scope

RISC design is a methodology still somewhat in its infancy, enduring the usual growing pains as it strives for maturity. Because of the complexity of the subject and its dynamic state, a thorough and comprehensive discussion is beyond the scope of this book. A concise discussion of RISC is made more difficult by the nature of the design techniques — they involve myriad trade-offs and compromises between software/hardware, silicon area/compiler technology, component process technology/system software requirements, and so on. Therefore, this chapter provides only a brief overview of RISC concepts and their implementation so that the MIPS architecture can be better understood and appreciated.

Architecture versus Implementation

When discussing MIPS RISC products, an important distinction must be made between application architecture, and the hardware implementation of that architecture.

For our purposes, the term *application architecture* refers to the instruction set, the physical components and timing, etc., to which all hardware implementations must adhere, and to which applications must limit themselves. *Implementation* refers to specific hardware designs using this application architecture, as presently embodied by the R-Series (R2000, R3000, R4000, and R6000) processors.

To emphasize the distinction between architecture and implementation in this book, we have set specific descriptions of *applications* and *implementations* apart as shown in the examples below:

Implementation Note:

> This is an example of a section containing information that is **hardware implementation-specific.**

Application Note:

> This is an example of a section containing information that is **application-specific.**

Application and implementation notes contain information of interest to an experienced user.

This book focuses on the MIPS RISC instruction set architecture (ISA) with reference, where necessary, to specific hardware implementations. The ISA specifies User-mode operation; Kernel-mode operations and operation by the System Control Processor (CP0, described in Chapters 2, 3, and 4) are defined by the specific hardware implementation. There is not a one-to-one correlation between the MIPS architecture and its implementation; rather, the MIPS architecture is carefully decoupled from specific hardware implementations, leaving implementors free to design their own hardware within the framework of the ISA definition. For instance, there may be other hardware implementations beyond the R4000 and R6000 processors.

Another example of implementation being decoupled from architecture is provided by the System Control Coprocessor (CP0). CP0 is physically incorporated on the processor chip, but the definition of its actual implementation is outside the scope of the application architecture; in other words, its implementation is independent of the architecture within which it operates. R-Series processors all have separate implementations of CP0, with some overlap.

MIPS ISA and Extensions

Although the architecture has evolved in response to a shifting compromise between software and hardware resources in the computer system, this evolution maintains object-code compatibility for programs that execute in User mode (see Chapter 4 for a description of operating modes). The R-Series processors all implement the ISA for User-mode programs; this guarantees that User-mode programs conforming to the ISA will execute on any MIPS hardware implementation. Accordingly, since the ISA encompasses the entire User-mode instruction set, applications should be compiled to the MIPS ISA, which is applicable across the entire body of MIPS processors. In this way, applications retain compatibility with all MIPS processors.

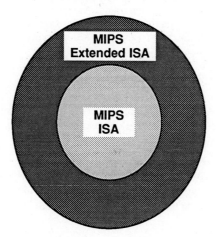

Figure 1–1. Relationship Between the MIPS ISA and its Extensions

The MIPS R4000 and R6000 processors implement an extension to the ISA, which is used mostly for Kernel-mode and hardware-specific programs; the relationship between the ISA and its extension is shown in Figure 1–1. The R4000/R6000 extension includes:

- more instructions (see Chapters 2, 3 and Appendix A)
- hardware interlocks (see Chapter 3)

It should be noted that the R4000 also implements the MIPS 64-bit architecture — however this is not covered in the present book.

Application Note:

> Extensions to the ISA are *not* intended for, nor are they especially useful for, third-party application software, ordinary UNIX™ commands, or any place in which binary compatibility is relevant. Thus, the Application Binary Interface (ABI), which resides with the ISA, continues to be used by most UNIX programmers.
>
> Using the knowledge that UNIX and other operating system kernels often have separate versions for different hardware platforms, ISA extensions are targeted at several areas. Using these extensions, wired-down code space can be shrunk, new multiprocessor instructions can be used, and some common in-kernel code sequences can be improved. Embedded system kernels and some applications (especially Ada) shrink substantially and run noticably faster. Programs intended for use only on MIPS R4000/R6000 processors may be recompiled if desired; some types of floating-point-intensive programs may gain performance.
>
> Finally, Dynamically Shared Objects (DSOs) that allow ISA-specific routines to be used with applications that meet an approved ABI, are provided .

What Is RISC?

Historically, the evolution of computer architectures has been dominated by families of increasingly complex processors. Under market pressures to preserve existing software, Complex Instruction Set Computer (CISC) architectures evolved by the gradual accretion of microcode and increasingly elaborate operations. The intent was to supply more support for high-level languages and operating systems, as semiconductor advances made it possible to fabricate more complex integrated circuits. It seemed self-evident that architectures *should* become more complex as these technological advances made it possible to hold more complexity on VLSI devices.

In recent years, however, Reduced Instruction Set Computer (RISC) architectures have implemented a much more sophisticated handling of the complex interaction between hardware, firmware, and software. RISC concepts emerged from statistical analysis of how software actually uses the resources of a processor. Dynamic measurement of system kernels and object modules generated by optimizing compilers show an overwhelming predominance of the simplest instructions, even in the code for CISC machines. Complex instructions are often ignored because a single way of performing a complex operation rarely matches the precise needs of high-level language and system environments. RISC designs eliminate the microcoded routines and turn the low-level control of the machine over to software.

This approach is not new. But its application is more universal in recent years thanks to the prevalence of high-level languages, the development of compilers that can optimize at the microcode level, and dramatic advances in semiconductor memory and packaging. It is now feasible to replace machine microcode ROM with faster RAM, organized as an instruction cache. Machine control then resides in the instruction cache and is, in effect, customized on the fly. The instruction stream generated by system- and compiler-generated code provides a precise fit between the requirements of high-level software and the capabilities of the hardware.

Reducing or simplifying the instruction set is not the primary goal of the architectural concepts described here — it is a side effect of the techniques used to obtain the highest performance possible from available technology. Thus, the term *Reduced Instruction Set Computers* is a bit misleading: it is the push for performance that really drives and shapes RISC designs. Therefore, let us begin by defining performance.

Performance

Processor performance is the time required to accomplish a specific task (or program, or algorithm, or benchmark) and is expressed as the product of three factors:

Time per Task = **C** * **T** * **I**
where: **C** = *Cycles per Instruction*
              T = *Time per Cycle (clock speed)*
              I = *Instructions per Task*

Performance can be improved by reducing any of these three factors. RISC-type designs strive to improve performance by minimizing the first two factors. However, changes that reduce the cycles/instruction and time/cycle factors tend to increase the instructions/task factor. Most of the criticisms leveled at RISC have targeted this latter tendency; in response, optimizing compilers and other techniques have been developed.

The sections that follow discuss each of the three performance-related factors listed above, and describe some of the techniques used in RISC-type designs to minimize each factor.

Time per Instruction

The time required to execute an instruction is the product of the first two factors (C and T) in the equation developed in the preceding section. These two factors are complementary: increasing the clock speed (reducing the time per cycle) decreases the amount of work that can be accomplished within a cycle. Thus, fast clock rates (short cycle times) tend to increase the number of cycles required to perform an instruction as illustrated in Figure 1–2:

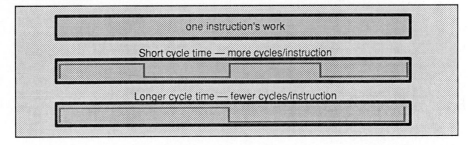

Figure 1–2. Relationship Between Cycle Length and Task Completion

In most processors, it makes little difference whether cycle time is short and instructions require many cycles, or cycle time is long with instructions requiring few cycles — it's the total time/instruction (time/cycle X cycles/instruction) that is significant. Typically, the cycle time is chosen to allow execution of the most simple operations (or suboperations) in a single cycle, and execution of other, more complex operations in multiple cycles. Thus, the instruction stream in a typical CISC processor might look like that shown in Figure 1–3:

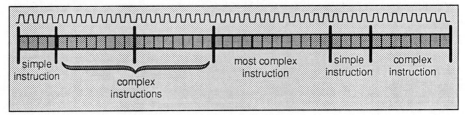

Figure 1–3. Typical CISC Instruction Stream

Executing the simple instructions in Figure 1–3 requires four cycles, whereas executing the more complex instructions require either eight or twelve cycles. At first glance this approach seems to achieve a rather efficient utilization of time: simple instructions are executed quickly and more complicated instructions are given additional time to execute. Each instruction is given just the amount of time it needs — no more and no less. Unfortunately this technique has a very damaging drawback that makes it unsuitable for RISC-type designs: it greatly complicates the use of instruction pipelines. Instruction pipelines are an essential technique used to reduce the cycles/instruction factor; however, any gain a pipeline provides would be negated by an instruction set in which the cycles/instruction factor is variable.

The advantages of instruction pipelines and the impact they have on the design of instruction sets are discussed in the following sections.

Cycles per Instruction (C)

If the work each instruction performs is simple and straightforward, the time required to execute each instruction can be shortened and the number of cycles reduced. The goal of RISC designs has been to achieve an execution rate of one instruction per machine cycle (multiple-instruction-issue designs now seek to increase this rate to more than one instruction per cycle). Techniques that help achieve this goal include:

- instruction pipelines
- load and store (load/store) architecture
- delayed load instructions
- delayed branch instructions

Instruction Pipelines

One way to reduce the number of cycles required to execute an instruction is to overlap the execution of multiple instructions. Instruction pipelines divide the execution of each instruction into several discrete portions and then execute multiple instructions simultaneously. The instruction pipeline technique can be likened to an assembly line — the instruction progresses from one specialized stage to the next until it is complete (or *issued*) — just as an automobile moves along an assembly line. (This is in contrast to the nonpipeline, microcoded approach, where all the work is done by one general unit and is less capable at each individual task.) For example, the execution of an instruction might be subdivided into four portions, or clock cycles, as shown in Figure 1–4:

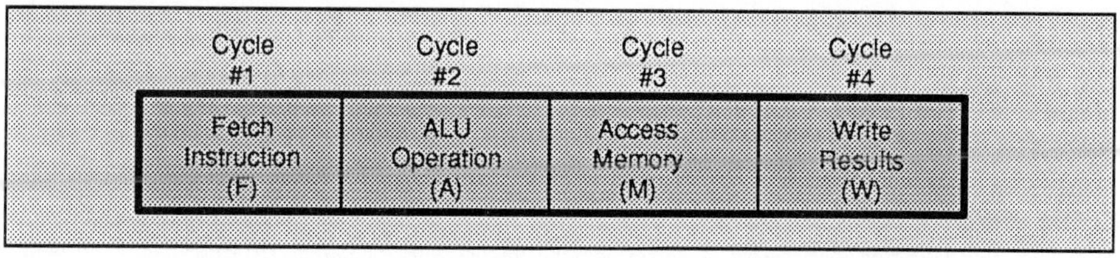

Cycle #1	Cycle #2	Cycle #3	Cycle #4
Fetch Instruction (F)	ALU Operation (A)	Access Memory (M)	Write Results (W)

Figure 1–4. Functional Division of a Hypothetical Pipeline

An instruction pipeline can *potentially* reduce the number of cycles/instruction by a factor equal to the depth of the pipeline. For example, in Figure 1–5 each instruction still requires a total of four clock cycles to execute. However, if a four-level instruction pipeline is used, a new instruction can be initiated at each clock cycle and the effective execution rate is one cycle per instruction.

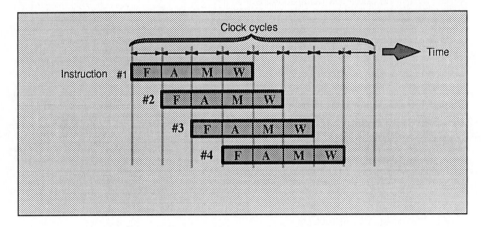

Figure 1–5. Multiple Instructions in a Hypothetical Pipeline

The previous paragraph stated that a pipeline can *potentially* reduce the number of cycles/instruction by a factor equal to the depth of the pipeline. Fulfilling this potential requires the pipeline always be filled with useful instructions and nothing delay the advance of instructions through the pipeline. These requirements impose certain demands on the architecture. For example, consider the earlier example of a serially-executing instruction stream in which each instruction can require a different number of clock cycles. Figure 1–6 illustrates how this same instruction stream would look as it proceeds through the pipeline.

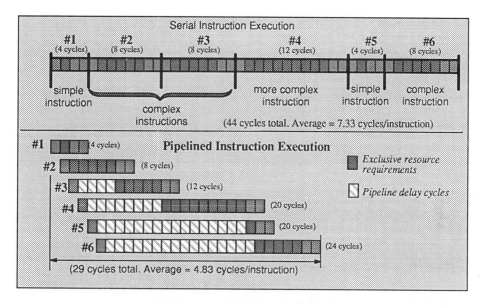

Figure 1–6. Serial and Pipeline Instruction Streams

In this example, the darkly shaded cycles indicate where the instructions require the use of the same resources (for example, ALU, shifters, or registers). Competition for these resources blocks the progress of instructions through the pipeline and causes delay cycles to be inserted for many of the instructions until the required resources become available. The pipeline technique shortens the average number of cycles/instruction in this example, but the gains are greatly reduced by the delay cycles that must be added.

The negative effect of variable execution time is actually much worse than the preceding example might indicate. Management of an instruction pipeline requires proper and efficient handling of events such as branches, exceptions, or interrupts, which can completely disrupt the flow of instructions. If the instruction stream includes a variety of different instruction lengths together with a mixture of delay and normal cycles, pipeline management becomes very complex. Additionally, such a varied, complex instruction stream makes it almost impossible for a compiler to schedule instructions to reduce or eliminate delays. Consequently, a primary goal of RISC designs is to define an instruction set where execution of most, if not all, instructions requires a uniform number of cycles and, ideally, achieves a minimum execution rate of one instruction for each clock cycle.

Load/Store Architecture

The discussion of the instruction pipeline illustrates how each instruction can be subdivided into several discrete parts which permit the processor to execute multiple instructions in parallel. For this technique to work efficiently, the time required to execute each instruction subpart should be approximately equal. If one part requires an excessive length of time, there is an unpleasant choice: either halting the pipeline (inserting wait or ''stall'' cycles), or making all cycles longer to accommodate this lengthier portion of the instruction.

Instructions that perform operations on operands in memory tend to increase either the cycle time or the number of cycles/instruction. Such instructions require additional time for execution to calculate the addresses of the operands, read the required operands from memory, calculate the result, and store the results of the operation back to memory. To eliminate the negative impact of such instructions, RISC designs implement a load and store (load/store) architecture in which the processor has many registers, all operations are performed on operands held in processor registers, and main memory is accessed only by load and store instructions. This approach produces several benefits:

- reducing the number of memory accesses eases memory bandwidth requirements
- limiting all operations to registers helps simplify the instruction set
- eliminating memory operations makes it easier for compilers to optimize register allocation — this further reduces memory accesses and also reduces the instructions/task factor.

All of these factors help RISC designs approach their goal of executing one cycle/instruction. However, two classes of instructions hinder achievement of this goal — load instructions and branch instructions. The following sections discuss how RISC designs overcome obstacles raised by these classes of instructions.

Delayed Load Instructions

Load instructions read operands from memory into processor registers for subsequent operation by other instructions. Because memory typically operates at much slower speeds than processor clock rates, the loaded operand is not immediately available to subsequent instructions in an instruction pipeline. This data dependency is illustrated in Figure 1–7.

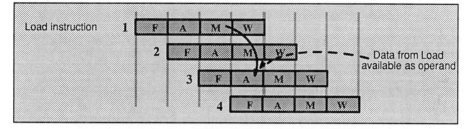

Figure 1–7. Data Dependency Resulting From a Load Instruction

In this illustration, the operand loaded by instruction 1 is not available for use in the A cycle (ALU, or Arithmetic/Logic Unit operation) of instruction 2. One way to handle this dependency is to delay the pipeline by inserting additional clock cycles into the execution of instruction 2 until the loaded data becomes available. This approach obviously introduces delays that would increase the cycles/instruction factor.

In many RISC designs the technique used to handle this data dependency is to recognize and make visible to compilers the fact that all load instructions have an inherent latency or *load delay*. Figure 1–7 illustrates a load delay or latency of one instruction. The instruction that immediately follows the load is in the *load delay slot*. If the instruction in this slot does not require the data from the load, then no pipeline delay is required.

If this load delay is made visible to software, a compiler can arrange instructions to ensure that there is no data dependency between a load instruction and the instruction in the load delay slot. The simplest way of ensuring that there is no data dependency is to insert a No Operation instruction (NOP, see Appendix D) to fill the slot, as shown in Figure 1–8.

```
Load    R1,A
Load    R2,B
NOP             <— this instruction fills the delay slot
Add     R3,R1,R2
```

Figure 1–8. Inserting a NOP in the Load Delay Slot

Although filling the delay slot with NOP instructions eliminates the need for hardware-controlled pipeline stalls in this case, it still is not a very efficient use of the pipeline stream since these additional NOP instructions increase code size and perform no useful work. (In practice, however, this technique need not have much negative impact on performance.)

A more effective solution to handling the data dependency is to fill the load delay slot with a useful instruction. Good optimizing compilers can usually accomplish this, especially if the load delay is only one instruction. Figure 1–9 illustrates how a compiler might rearrange instructions to handle a potential data dependency:

```
# Consider the code for C := A+ B; F := D
   Load    R1,A
   Load    R2,B
   Add     R3,R1,R2   <── this instruction stalls because R2 data is not available
   Load    R4,D
   ...        ...

# An alternative code sequence (where delay length = 1)
   Load    R1,A
   Load    R2,B
   Load    R4,D
   Add     R3,R1,R2   <── no stall since R2 data is available
   ...        ...
```

Figure 1–9. Arranging a Nondependent Instruction in the Load Delay Slot

Since the Add (Add R3,R1,R2) instruction does not depend on the availability of the data from the third Load instruction (Load R4,D), the delay slot (for Load R2,B) can be filled with a usable instruction (Load R4,D) and the pipeline can be fully utilized.

Delayed Branch Instructions

Branch instructions usually delay the instruction pipeline because the processor must calculate the effective destination of the branch and fetch that instruction. When a cache access requires an entire cycle, and the fetched branch instruction specifies the target address, it is impossible to perform this fetch (of the destination instruction) without delaying the pipeline for at least one pipe stage (one cycle). Conditional branches can cause further delays because they require the calculation of a condition, as well as the target address. Figure 1–10 illustrates a delay of one pipeline stage while the instruction at the destination address is calculated and fetched:

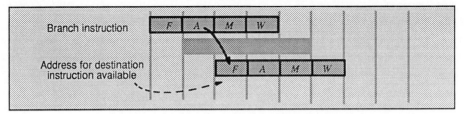

Figure 1–10. Pipeline Delay During Branch Operation

Instead of stalling the instruction pipeline to wait for the instruction at the target address, RISC designs typically use an approach similar to that used with Load instructions: Branch instructions are delayed and do not take effect until after one or more instructions immediately following the Branch instruction have been executed. The instruction or instructions in this branch delay slot are always executed, as illustrated in the Figure 1–11.

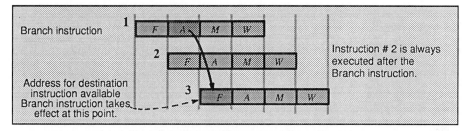

Figure 1–11. Filling a Branch Delay Slot

With this approach, the inherent delay associated with branch instructions is made visible to the software, and compilers attempt to fill the branch delay slot with useful instructions. This task is usually not too difficult if there is only a single-instruction delay — as is the case shown in Figure 1–12.

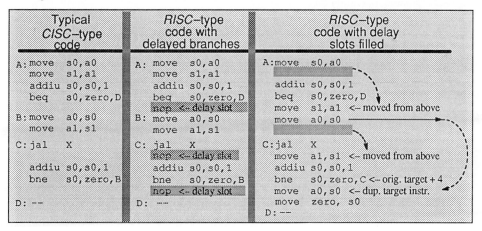

Figure 1–12. Single-Instruction Branch Delay

If the branch delay slot cannot be filled with any useful instructions, NOP instructions can be inserted to keep the instruction pipeline filled. Usually, however, a compiler can fill the slot with useful instructions. The preceding example illustrates two different techniques used to fill the slot:

- Often, an instruction that occurs before the branch can be executed after the branch without affecting the logic or the branch instruction itself. Thus, in Figure 1–12, the Move S1,A1 and Move A1,S1 instructions can be moved from their original positions to the delay slots without changing the logic of the program.

- The original target instruction of the BNE instruction was the Move A0,S0 instruction at label *B:*. In the example, this instruction is duplicated in the delay slot following the BNE instruction and the target of the BNE instruction is changed to be the instruction at label *C:*. This technique increases the static number of instructions by two, and only increases the dynamic instruction count by two also.

Time per Cycle (T)

The time required to perform a single machine cycle is determined by factors such as:

- instruction decode time.
- instruction operation time.
- instruction access time (memory bandwidth).
- architectural simplicity.

Many of the same design approaches that reduce the number of cycles/instruction also help reduce the time/cycle. For example, dividing up instruction execution into several discrete stages to implement the instruction pipeline can also result in reducing the time required to execute a cycle.

Instruction Decode Time

The time required to decode instructions is partly related to the number of instructions in the instruction set and the variety of instruction formats supported. Thus, simple, uniform RISC instruction sets minimize the instruction decode circuitry and time requirements. For example, if the instruction formats are uniform, with consistent use of bit fields within the instructions, the processor can decode multiple fields simultaneously to speed the process. In addition to providing instructions only to perform simple tasks, RISC designs also reduce the number of options such as addressing modes to further reduce the number of possible instruction formats.

Instruction Operation Time

For CISC architectures, instruction operation time is usually measured in multiples of cycles. RISC designs strive to complete an instruction per cycle and to make that cycle time as short as possible (second generation MIPS RISC processors target a completion rate of more than one instruction per cycle). Many of the techniques discussed earlier under the category of reducing the number of cycles/instruction also help reduce instruction operation time. For example, the time required for register-to-register operations is much less than the time needed to operate on memory operands. Thus, the load/store architectural approach described earlier also helps reduce the cycle time.

Instruction Access Time (Memory Bandwidth)

The time needed to access (fetch) an instruction is largely dependent upon the speed of the memory system and often becomes the limiting factor in RISC-type designs because of the high rate at which instructions can be executed. While the load/store architecture (discussed earlier in this chapter) common to RISC designs helps reduce memory bandwidth requirements, achieving a completion rate of one instruction/cycle is impossible unless the memory system can deliver instructions at the cycle rate of the processor. A variety of techniques are used to obtain the required memory bandwidth needed to support the high-performance RISC designs. Two common techniques are:

- Supporting hierarchical memory systems using high-speed cache memory to provide the primary, reusable pool of instructions and data that are frequently accessed by the processor.
- Supporting separate caches for instructions and data to double the effective cache-memory bandwidth.

The use of separate caches for data and instructions has an additional benefit beyond decreasing the access time: the contiguity of a separate set of instructions or data is typically much greater than that of a mixture of instructions and data. Therefore, for most programs, data and instructions held in separate caches are more likely to be reusable than if a common, shared cache is used.

Another technique that helps minimize the time required to fetch an instruction is to require uniform length instructions (a fixed number of bits), and that these instructions always be aligned on a regular boundary. For example, many RISC processors define all instructions to be 32 bits wide and require that they be aligned on word boundaries. This approach eliminates the possibility of a single instruction extending across a word boundary (requiring multiple fetches) or across a memory management boundary (requiring multiple address translations). For more information on MIPS caches, please see Chapter 5.

Overall Architectural Simplicity

The general simplicity of RISC architectures allows streamlining of the entire machine organization. As a result, the overhead to each instruction can be reduced and the clock cycle can be shortened as designers are able to focus on optimizing a small number of critical processor features. The general simplicity of the machine also allows the use of more aggressive semiconductor process technologies in the manufacture of the processor, which in turn provide the potential for faster performance.

Instructions per Task (I)

This factor of the performance equation is where RISC designs are most vulnerable and has been the source of most of the criticism directed at RISC designs. Since RISC processors implement the more complex operations performed by CISC processors by using a series of simple instructions, the total number of instructions needed to perform a given task tends to increase as the complexity of the instruction set decreases. Therefore, a given program or algorithm written using the instruction set for a RISC processor tends to have more instructions than the same task written using the instruction set for a CISC processor.

Advances in RISC techniques have done much to mitigate this negative tendency and, for many algorithms, the dynamic instruction count for good RISC processors is not significantly different than for CISC processors. The primary techniques that help reduce the instructions/task factor are optimizing compilers and operating system support.

Optimizing Compilers

Reliance on high-level languages (HLLs) has been increasing for many years while the importance of assembly language programming has diminished. This trend has led to an emphasis on the use of efficient compilers to convert high-level language instructions to machine instructions. Primary measures of compiler efficiency are the compactness of the code it generates and the execution time of that code. Modern optimizing compilers have evolved to provide increased efficiency in the high-level-language-to-machine-language translation.

Nothing about optimizing compilers is inherently RISC-oriented; many of the techniques these compilers use were developed before the current generation of RISC architectures arrived and are applied to RISC and CISC machines alike. There is, however, a symbiotic relationship between optimizing compilers and RISC architectures. Compilers do their best optimization with RISC architecture; RISC-type computers, in many cases, rely on compilers to obtain their full performance capabilities.

During the development of more efficient compilers, an analysis of instruction streams revealed that most time was spent executing simple instructions and performing load and store operations — the more complex instructions were used much less. It was also discovered that compilers produced code that was often a narrow subset of processor architecture: complex instructions and features were, in practice, not used by compilers.

It might seem illogical that people writing compilers would end up ignoring the most powerful instructions and using the simpler ones, but it occurs because the powerful instructions are hard for a compiler to use or because the instructions don't precisely fit the high-level language requirements. A compiler works better with instructions that perform simple, well-defined operations with minimal side effects. Since these characteristics are typical of a RISC instruction set, there is a natural match between RISC architectures and efficient, optimizing compilers. This match makes it easier for compilers to choose the most effective sequences of machine instructions to accomplish the tasks described by a high-level language.

Optimizing Techniques

An examination of some of the techniques compilers use to optimize programs makes the match between compilers and RISC architectures more apparent.

- *Register allocation.* The compiler allocates processor registers to hold frequently used data and thus reduce the number of load/store operations. Figure 1–13 illustrates how careful register allocation can reduce the number of instructions required to perform a task:

```
# task is A:= B + C
    Load   R1,B
    Load   R2,C
    Add    R3,R1,R2
    Store  R3,A

# If A, B, and C are allocated to registers
    Add    Ra,Rb,Rc
```

Figure 1–13. Register Allocation as an Optimizing Technique

In this example, the two Load instructions are eliminated when the required values are available in registers, and the Store instruction is not needed since the compiler will hold the result of the Add in a register for future use.

- *Redundancy elimination.* The compiler looks for opportunities to reuse results and thus eliminate redundant computations.

- *Loop optimization.* A compiler optimizes loop operations by recognizing variables and expressions that don't change during a loop and then moving them outside the loop.

- *Replacing slow operations with faster ones.* A compiler searches for situations where slow operations, such as special cases of a multiply or divide, can be replaced with faster operations, such as shift and add instructions.

- *Strength reduction.* This technique consists of replacing resource-expensive operations with cheaper ones. For example, multidimensional arrays are often indexed using a combination of several multiplication and addition operations. Strength reduction might simplify the index calculation by using a previously calculated address and a simple addition operation.

- *Pipeline scheduling.* The compiler schedules and reorganizes instructions to ensure that pipeline delay slots are filled with useful instructions as described in earlier sections on load and branch delays.

None of the techniques described above are uniquely linked to RISC architectures. However, the simplicity of a RISC machine makes it inherently easier for a compiler to discover optimization opportunities and implement these optimizations with a clear view of their effects.

Optimization Levels

The development of optimizing compilers has produced its own terminology. This section describes those terms commonly used to categorize the various levels of optimization performed by compilers. The optimization techniques used can be divided into four levels according to their scope and degree of difficulty:

- *Peephole optimization* attempts to make improvements in code size or performance within a narrow context. An example of this level is replacing slower operations with faster ones.

- *Local optimization* makes decisions based on views of multiple-instruction sequences. An example of this level is to examine sequences of instructions to determine the best prolog/epilog to use as the entry/exit code for a function. Other examples include keeping values in registers over short periods of time, and eliminating branch instructions that have another branch instruction as a target.

- *Global optimization* optimizes program control flow by enhancing branch and loop structures and by performing strength reduction.

- *Inter-procedural optimization.* This level is rarely performed because techniques such as allocating register assignments to maximize their life between procedures, merging procedures, and converting appropriate procedures to in-line code to reduce overhead are just being developed.

Operating System Support

The performance gains obtained by providing support for operating systems are often subtle and not as easily defined or measured as with some of the other RISC techniques. While CISC architectures typically provide elaborate support for operating systems, the RISC approach emphasizes *appropriate* support. The appropriateness is based on a rigorous evaluation of the performance gains that can be obtained by the support of any particular function. The guiding principles are to avoid unnecessary complexity unless justified by statistics of actual usage, and to simplify and streamline operations required most frequently by operating systems.

The learning path here parallels the one traveled during exploration of compiler efficiencies — trying to put features supporting high-level languages into hardware often frustrated compiler writers. Similarly, putting special features into hardware to support operating systems does not always match the real needs of operating systems. With compilers, it was learned that the special instructions intended to simplify support of high-level languages were not often used by compilers. Similarly, it has been found that special hardware features for operating systems may also miss their mark. Often, the most efficient way of supporting an operating system is to provide raw speed with simple, minimal controls.

The sections that follow illustrate some of the subtle ways in which RISC-type designs can supply appropriate operating system support to enhance performance without adding unacceptable complexity to the hardware:

Virtual Memory System

Translation Lookaside Buffers (TLBs) provide the virtual-to-physical address translation that is essential in implementing a powerful operating system.

Implementation Note:

> While nothing about TLBs is RISC-specific, the chip area gained by overall simplification of the processor *can* be used to implement on-chip TLBs. For instance, in the R2000/R3000/R4000 implementations, an on-chip TLB enhances performance by eliminating cycle(s) that otherwise might be required to transfer the virtual address to an external TLB.

Modes and Protection

Operating systems require some mechanisms for controlling user access to system and processor resources. CISC processors often provide a variety of operating modes and protection mechanisms. However, multiple modes and protection schemes can add complexity to the hardware, and experience teaches that there is seldom a complete match between these mechanisms and operating system requirements. The present RISC approach supplies *limited* control and protection mechanisms: the MIPS architecture uses a kernel/privileged, user/unprivileged method of differentiation, and the R4000 adds Supervisor mode to User and Kernel modes.

Interrupts and Traps

Many CISC processors provide extensive hardware support for responding to interrupts and traps by saving a large amount of state information and generating numerous vector addresses to which control is transferred in response to exceptions. This support adds complexity to the hardware but does not necessarily simplify the task of the operating system. For example, many operating systems do not need or use their numerous distinct exception vector addresses; instead, they first execute a common interrupt handler that does the work to determine the specific processing needed for the exception. The operating system itself might then determine what state information (if any) needs to be saved. This approach results in simplified hardware and lets the appropriate complexity be provided by the operating system as needed.

Special-Function Instructions

There has been no mention of special instructions to simplify and support operating system activities. Once again, the rule of simplicity and appropriateness argues against the inclusion of special instructions. Even in cases where significant time is spent in an operating system, the bulk of time is spent executing general code rather than performing special functions. Thus, it is more efficient to let the operating system use standard, simple, nonspecialized instructions to perform all of its functions.

The RISC Design Process

The RISC design process is, at best, an iterative process that uses feedback to tune the design. For example, MIPS Computer Systems started with the knowledge of earlier RISC efforts, most significantly the Stanford University MIPS research work, and with the optimizing compilers developed from that effort. Based on that previous experience, a base-level instruction set was proposed, and measurements were taken from simulations of code compiled with the existing optimizers. Proposals for additions to the instruction set were carefully weighed to verify that they *actually* improved performance. Specifically, MIPS used the rule that any instruction added for performance reasons had to provide a verifiable one percent performance gain over a range of applications, or the instruction was rejected.

The result of this approach is an instruction set that is very well-tuned for high-level language use. Every instruction is either structurally necessary (such as Restore From Exception) or can naturally be generated by compilers. This stands in contrast to many other machines, even ones also labeled RISC, that often have user-level instructions or instruction mode combinations that are very difficult to reach from compiled languages.

These same stringent requirements were applied to the many different memory-management alternatives that were proposed and simulated before the final design for the CPU was chosen. All functions and features that complicated the design had to be empirically proven to enhance performance within the complete system before they might be included.

Hidden Benefits of RISC Design

Some of the important benefits that result from the RISC design techniques are not attributable to the architectural characteristics adopted to enhance performance but are a result of the overall reduction in complexity: the simpler design allows both chip area resources and human resources to be applied to features that enhance performance.

Shorter Design Cycle

The architectures of RISC processors can be implemented more quickly: it is much easier to implement and debug a streamlined, simplified architecture with no microcode than a complex, microcoded architecture. CISC processors have such a long design cycle that they are often not fully debugged until the technology in which they were designed is obsolete. The shorter time required to design and implement RISC processors lets them make use of the best available technologies.

Smaller Chip Size

The simplicity of RISC processors also frees scarce chip-area resources for performance-critical structures like larger register files, TLBs, coprocessors, and fast multiply-divide units. Such additional resources help these processors obtain an even greater performance edge.

User (Programmer) Benefits

Somewhat surprisingly, simplicity in architecture also helps the user:

- The uniform instruction set is easier to use.
- There is a closer correlation between instruction count and cycle count making it much easier to measure the true impact of code optimization activities.
- Programmers can have a higher confidence in hardware correctness.

Advanced Semiconductor Technologies

Finally, as new VLSI implementation technologies are developed, they are always introduced with tight limits on the number of transistors that fit on each chip. The simplicity of RISC architecture allows it to be implemented in far fewer transistors than CISC architectures. The result is that the first computers capable of exploiting the new VLSI technologies (for example, VLSI ECL, VLSI GaAs) have been using and will continue to use RISC architectures. Therefore, RISC processors can always use the most advanced technologies and reap the performance benefits before those technologies become usable by CISC processors.

2
MIPS Processor
Architecture Overview

This chapter provides an architectural overview of the following aspects of the R-Series (R2000, R3000, R4000, and R6000) processors:

- CPU registers
- CP0 registers
- instruction set
- programming model
- Memory Management Unit (MMU)

The R2000 and R3000 each consist of two tightly coupled processors implemented on a single chip.

- The first processor is a full 32-bit RISC CPU.
- The second processor is the system control coprocessor (CP0), containing a 64-entry fully-associative TLB, and control registers which support a virtual memory subsystem and separate data and instruction caches.

Figure 2–1 shows a functional block diagram of the R2000 and R3000 processor architecture. The R2000 and R3000 also support external coprocessors, such as the R2010 and R3010 Floating-Point Units (FPUs), which are connected to the R2000 and R3000 respectively.

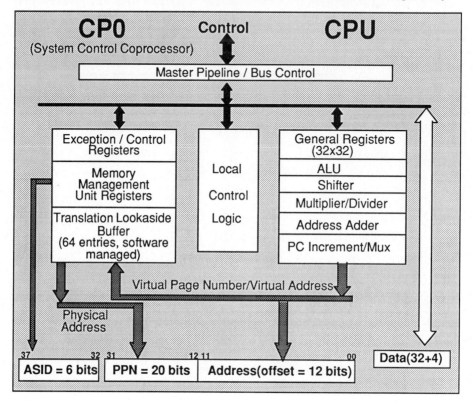

Figure 2–1. R2000/R3000 Functional Block Diagram

The R4000 is similar to the R2000/R3000 processors. It contains a 48-entry fully-associative on-chip TLB, mapped with two pages per entry; separate on-chip primary data and instruction caches; an optional off-chip secondary cache; and an on-chip FPU.

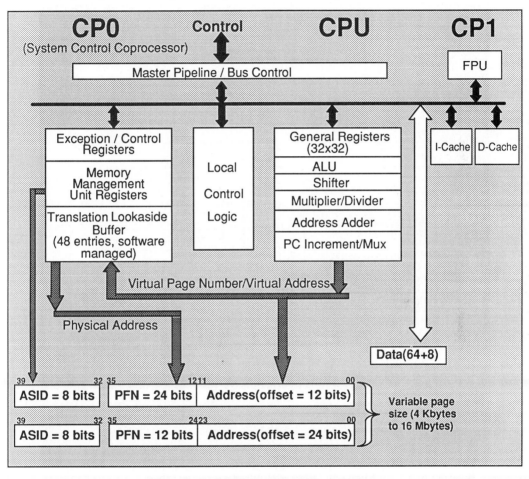

Figure 2–2. R4000 Functional Block Diagram

The R6000 differs from the previously described processors by implementing an on-chip 6-bit-wide TLB Slice which contains 16 entries — 8 data and 8 instructions in the R6000, 16 combined in R6000A. This TLB Slice produces a 6-bit prediction of the virtual-to-physical address translation. The full TLB, which is in a reserved portion of the off-chip secondary cache, is accessed only if a cache miss occurs.

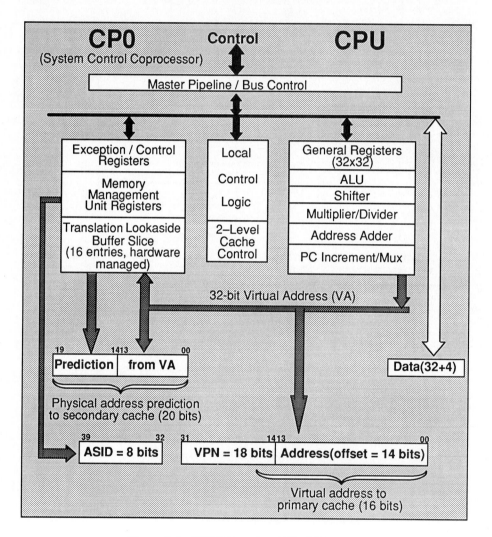

Figure 2–3. R6000 Functional Block Diagram

Processor Features

This section briefly describes the 32-bit programming model, MMU, and caches in the R-Series processors. A more detailed description is given in succeeding sections.

- **Full 32-bit Operation.** The R-Series processors contain 32 general-purpose 32-bit registers; all instructions and addresses are 32 bits. R6000 registers also contain 4 bits of parity.

- **Efficient Pipelining.** The processor pipeline design results in an execution rate that approaches one instruction per cycle. Pipeline stalls and exceptional events are handled precisely and efficiently.

- **MMU.** The R2000/R3000/R4000 processors use an on-chip TLB to provide fast address translation for virtual-to-physical memory mapping of the 4-Gbyte virtual address space. The R6000, which has a 16-entry on-chip TLB Slice, stores its TLB entries in a reserved area of off-chip secondary cache.

- **Cache Control.** The R2000/R3000 processors provide a high-bandwidth memory interface which handles separate external instruction and data caches ranging in size from 4 Kbytes to 64 Kbytes each. I- and D-caches are both accessed during a single CPU cycle. The R4000 primary instruction and data caches reside on-chip, and can hold from 8 Kbytes to 32 Kbytes; the off-chip secondary cache can hold from 128 Kbytes to 4 Mbytes. The R6000 CPU has two external primary caches (data and instruction, similar to R2000/R3000), along with an external secondary cache that can hold both instructions and data. The R6000 primary instruction cache size ranges from 16 Kbytes to 64 Kbytes, while the primary data cache size is fixed by software at 16 Kbytes. The secondary cache can hold either 512 Kbytes or 2 Mbytes. All R2000/R3000/R4000 (and most R6000) cache control logic is on the processor chip.

- **Coprocessor Interface**. The CPU generates all addresses and handles memory interface control for up to three additional tightly coupled external coprocessors. In practice, CP1 is effectively reserved for the FPU.

Implementation Note:

In theory, more than one external coprocessor can be used with the R6000 CPU, but as presently implemented the R6000 only supports CP1. The R4000 supports CP0 and CP1, both of which are on-chip.

CPU Registers

The CPU provides 32 general purpose 32-bit registers, a 32-bit Program Counter (PC), and two 32-bit registers that hold the results of integer multiply and divide operations. Figure 2–4 shows the CPU registers, which are described in detail later in this chapter.

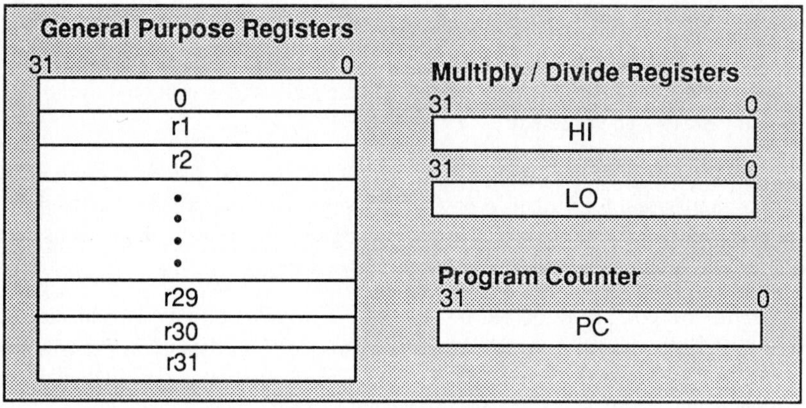

Figure 2–4. CPU Registers

A Program Status Word (PSW) register does not exist; its functions are provided by the *Status* and *Cause* registers incorporated within CP0. CP0 registers are described later in this chapter.

CPU Instruction Set Overview

Each CPU instruction is 32 bits long. As shown in Figure 2–5, there are three instruction formats: immediate (I-type), jump (J-type), and register (R-type). Provision of these three instruction formats simplifies instruction decoding; more complicated (and less frequently used) operations and addressing modes can be synthesized by the compiler, using sequences of these simple instructions.

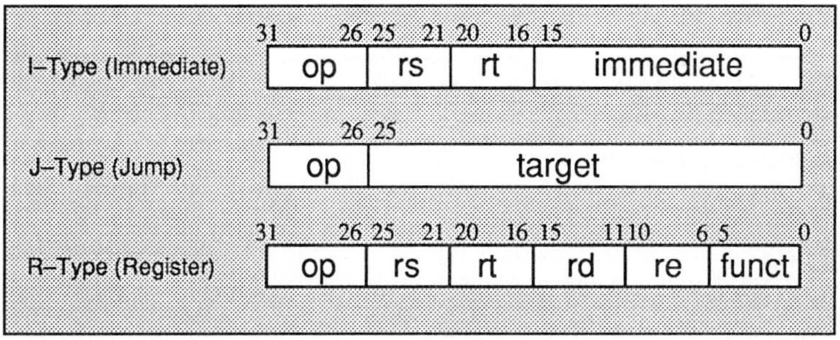

Figure 2–5. CPU Instruction Formats

The instruction set can be divided into the following groups:

- **Load/Store** instructions move data between memory and general registers. They are all I-type instructions, since the only addressing mode supported is base register plus 16-bit, signed immediate offset.

- **Computational** instructions perform arithmetic, logical, and shift operations on values in registers. They occur in both R-type (both the operands and the result are registers) and I-type (one operand is a 16-bit immediate) formats.

- **Jump and Branch** instructions change the control flow of a program. Jumps are always to a paged absolute address formed by combining a 26-bit target with 4 bits of the Program Counter (J-type format) or 32-bit register addresses (R-type format). Branches have 16-bit offsets relative to the program counter (I-type). Jump and link instructions save a return address in register 31.

- **Coprocessor** instructions perform operations in the coprocessors. Coprocessor load and store instructions are I-type. Coprocessor computational instructions have coprocessor-dependent formats (see the FPU instructions in Chapter 8).

- **Coprocessor 0** instructions perform operations on CP0 registers to manipulate the memory management and exception handling facilities of the processor.

- **Special** instructions perform a variety of tasks, including movement of data between special and general registers, system calls, and breakpoint. These instructions are always R-type.

A more detailed summary is provided in Chapter 3 and a complete description of each instruction is given in Appendix A.

Table 2–1 lists the instruction set (ISA) common to all MIPS R-Series processors; Table 2–2 lists instructions that are an extension to the ISA, and as such are implemented on the R4000 and R6000.

Table 2–1. CPU Instruction Set (ISA)

OP	Description	OP	Description
Load/Store Instructions		**Multiply/Divide Instructions**	
LB	Load Byte	MULT	Multiply
LBU	Load Byte Unsigned	MULTU	Multiply Unsigned
LH	Load Halfword	DIV	Divide
LHU	Load Halfword Unsigned	DIVU	Divide Unsigned
LW	Load Word		
LWL	Load Word Left	MFHI	Move From HI
LWR	Load Word Right	MTHI	Move To HI
		MFLO	Move From LO
SB	Store Byte	MTLO	Move To LO
SH	Store Halfword		
SW	Store Word	**Jump and Branch Instructions**	
SWL	Store Word Left	J	Jump
SWR	Store Word Right	JAL	Jump And Link
Arithmetic Instructions (ALU Immediate)		JR	Jump to Register
		JALR	Jump And Link Register
ADDI	Add Immediate	BEQ	Branch on Equal
ADDIU	Add Immediate Unsigned	BNE	Branch on Not Equal
SLTI	Set on Less Than Immediate	BLEZ	Branch on Less than or Equal to Zero
SLTIU	Set on Less Than Immediate Unsigned	BGTZ	Branch on Greater Than Zero
		BLTZ	Branch on Less Than Zero
ANDI	AND Immediate	BGEZ	Branch on Greater than or Equal to Zero
ORI	OR Immediate		
XORI	Exclusive OR Immediate	BLTZAL	Branch on Less Than Zero And Link
LUI	Load Upper Immediate	BGEZAL	Branch on Greater than or Equal to Zero And Link
Arithmetic Instructions (3-operand, R-type)		**Coprocessor Instructions**	
ADD	Add	LWCz	Load Word to Coprocessor
ADDU	Add Unsigned	SWCz	Store Word from Coprocessor
SUB	Subtract	MTCz	Move To Coprocessor
SUBU	Subtract Unsigned	MFCz	Move From Coprocessor
SLT	Set on Less Than	CTCz	Move Control to Coprocessor
SLTU	Set on Less Than Unsigned	CFCz	Move Control From Coprocessor
AND	AND	COPz	Coprocessor Operation
OR	OR	BCzT	Branch on Coprocessor z True
XOR	Exclusive OR	BCzF	Branch on Coprocessor z False
NOR	NOR		
Shift Instructions		**Special Instructions**	
SLL	Shift Left Logical	SYSCALL	System Call
SRL	Shift Right Logical	BREAK	Break
SRA	Shift Right Arithmetic		
SLLV	Shift Left Logical Variable		
SRLV	Shift Right Logical Variable		
SRAV	Shift Right Arithmetic Variable		

Table 2–2. Extensions to the ISA

OP	Description	OP	Description
	Load/Store Instructions		**Exception Instructions**
		TGE	Trap if Greater Than or Equal
LL	Load Linked	TGEU	Trap if Greater Than or Equal Unsigned
SC	Store Conditional	TLT	Trap if Less Than
SYNC	Sync	TLTU	Trap if Less Than Unsigned
		TEQ	Trap if Equal
	Jump and Branch Instructions	TNE	Trap if Not Equal
BEQL	Branch on Equal Likely	TGEI	Trap if Greater Than or Equal Immediate
BNEL	Branch on Not Equal Likely	TGEIU	Trap if Greater Than or Equal
BLEZL	Branch on Less than or Equal to Zero Likely		Unsigned Immediate
BGTZL	Branch on Greater Than Zero Likely	TLTI	Trap if Less Than Immediate
BLTZL	Branch on Less Than Zero Likely	TLTIU	Trap if Less Than Unsigned Immediate
BGEZL	Branch on Greater than or Equal to Zero Likely	TEQI	Trap if Equal Immediate
BLTZALL	Branch on Less Than Zero And Link Likely	TNEI	Trap if Not Equal Immediate
BGEZALL	Branch on Greater than or Equal to Zero And Link Likely		**Coprocessor Instructions**
BCzTL	Branch on Coprocessor z True Likely	LDCz	Load Double Coprocessor
BCzFL	Branch on Coprocessor z False Likely	SDCz	Store Double Coprocessor

Table 2–3 lists the CP0 instructions. CP0 instructions are dependent upon hardware implementation; the R2000, R3000, R4000, and R6000 CP0 instructions are nearly identical, except for those which reflect differences in TLB and cache design.

Table 2–3. CP0 Instructions

Op	Description	Processor		
		R2000/R3000	R4000	R6000
MTC0	Move to CP0	Yes	Yes	Yes
MFC0	Move from CP0	Yes	Yes	Yes
RFE	Restore from Exception	Yes	No	Yes
TLBR	Read Indexed TLB Entry	Yes	Yes	No
TLBWI	Write Indexed TLB Entry	Yes	Yes	No
TLBWR	Write Random TLB Entry	Yes	Yes	No
TLBP	Probe TLB for Matching Entry	Yes	Yes	No
LWR*	Flush Cache Entry	No	No	Yes
LWL*	Load from Cache	No	No	Yes
SWR*	Invalidate Cache Entry	No	No	Yes
SWL*	Store to Cache	No	No	Yes
ERET	Exception Return	No	Yes	No
CACHE	Cache Operation	No	Yes	No

*These instructions require a special mode bit be set to perform this operation — as opposed to their normal function.

Programming Model

This section describes the organization of data in registers and memory, and the available set of general registers. It also gives a summary description of all CPU registers.

Data Formats and Addressing

The CPU defines a 64-bit doubleword, a 32-bit word, a 16-bit halfword and an 8-bit byte. The byte ordering is configurable in either *Big-endian* or *Little-endian* format.

Figures 2–6 and 2–7 show the ordering of bytes within words and the ordering of words within multiple-word structures for the Big-endian and Little-endian conventions.

Endianness refers to the location of byte 0 within a multi-byte structure. When configured as a Big-endian system, byte 0 is the most significant (leftmost) byte, thereby providing compatibility with MC 68000® and IBM 370® conventions. This configuration is shown in Figure 2–6.

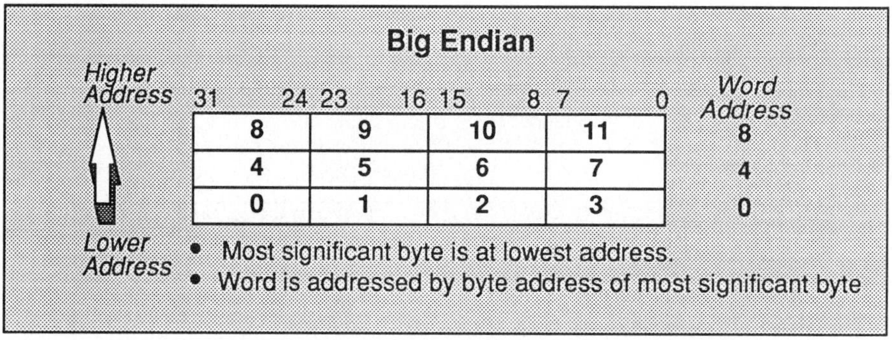

Figure 2–6. Addresses of Bytes within Words: Big-endian Byte Alignment

When configured as a Little-endian system, byte 0 is always the least significant (rightmost) byte, which is compatible with iAPX® x86 and DEC VAX® conventions. This configuration is shown in Figure 2–7.

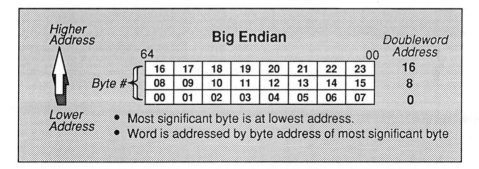

Figure 2–7. Addresses of Bytes within Words: Little-endian Byte Alignment

In this book, bit 0 is always the least significant (rightmost) bit, thus bit designations are always Little Endian (although no instructions explicitly designate bit positions within words).

Figures 2–8 and 2–9 show byte alignment in doublewords.

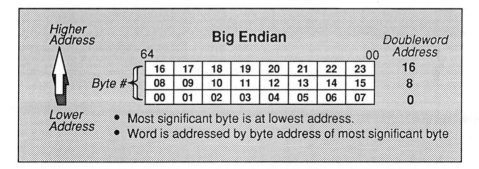

Figure 2–8. Addresses of Bytes within Doublewords: Big-endian Byte Alignment

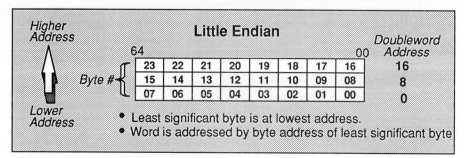

Figure 2–9. *Addresses of Bytes within Doublewords: Little-endian Byte Alignment*

The CPU uses byte addressing, with alignment constraints, for halfword, word, and doubleword accesses. Halfword accesses must be aligned on an even byte boundary (0, 2, 4...); word accesses must be aligned on a byte boundary divisible by four (0, 4, 8...), and doubleword accesses on a byte boundary divisible by eight (0, 8, 16...).

Implementation Note:

> Doubleword objects can only be loaded from and stored to R6010 and R4000 Floating-Point Units.

As shown in Figures 2–6 and 2–7, the address of a multiple-byte data item is the address of the most significant byte on a Big-endian configuration, or the address of the least significant byte on a Little-endian configuration.

Special instructions are provided for addressing words that are not aligned on 4-byte (word) boundaries: LWL, LWR, SWL, SWR. These instructions are used in pairs to provide addressing of misaligned words with one additional instruction cycle over that required for aligned words. For each of the two endianness conventions, Figure 2–10 shows the bytes that are accessed when addressing a misaligned word with byte address 3.

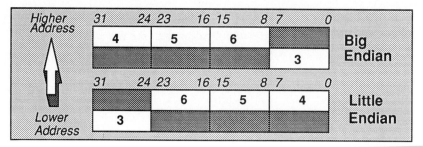

Figure 2–10. *Misaligned Word: Byte Addresses*

CPU General Purpose Registers

Figure 2–11 shows the CPU registers. There are 32 general registers, each consisting of a single 32-bit word. These 32 general registers are treated symmetrically, with two exceptions: *r0* is hardwired to a value of zero and *r31* is the link register for Jump And Link instructions.

Register *r0* can be specified as a target register for any instruction when the result of the operation is discarded. The register maintains a zero value under all conditions when used as a source register.

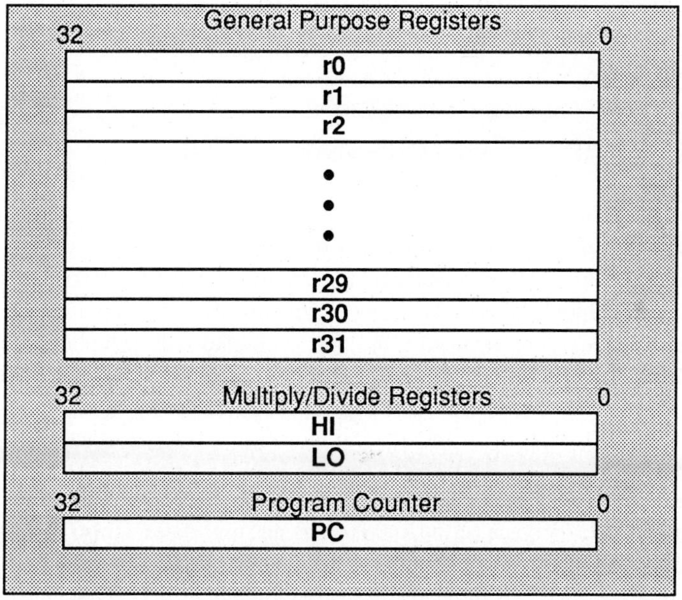

32	General Purpose Registers	0
	r0	
	r1	
	r2	
	•	
	•	
	•	
	r29	
	r30	
	r31	

32	Multiply/Divide Registers	0
	HI	
	LO	

32	Program Counter	0
	PC	

Figure 2–11. CPU Registers

Special Registers

The R-Series processor defines three special registers whose use or modification is implicit with certain instructions. These special registers are:

- *PC*   Program Counter
- *HI*   Multiply/Divide register higher word
- *LO*   Multiply/Divide register lower word

The two Multiply/Divide registers (*HI*, *LO*) store the doubleword, 64-bit result of integer multiply operations and the quotient (in *LO*) and remainder (in *HI*) of integer divide operations.

In addition, CP0 has a number of special purpose registers that are used in conjunction with the memory management system and during exception processing. Refer to Chapter 4 for a description of the memory management registers and to Chapter 6 for a discussion of the exception handling registers.

System Control Coprocessor (CP0)

The CPU can operate with up to four tightly-coupled coprocessors (designated CP0 through CP3). Coprocessor unit number one (CP1) is reserved for the floating-point coprocessor, while units two and three are reserved for future definition by MIPS. CP0 is incorporated on the CPU chip and supports the virtual memory system together with exception handling. The virtual memory system is implemented with either an on-chip TLB (R2000/R3000/R4000) or TLB Slice and in-cache TLB (R6000), and the group of programmable registers shown in Figures 2–12 through 2–14. The numeral accompanying each register refers to the register number, as shown in Table 2–4.

CP0 translates virtual addresses into physical addresses, and manages exceptions and transitions between kernel, supervisor (in the R4000 only), and user states. It also controls the cache subsystem and provides diagnostic control and error recovery facilities. In some processors, a generic system timer facility is provided for interval timing, time-keeping, process accounting, and time-slicing (see the *Count* and *Compare* registers in Chapters 4 and 6, respectively). The numeral accompanying each register refers to the register number.

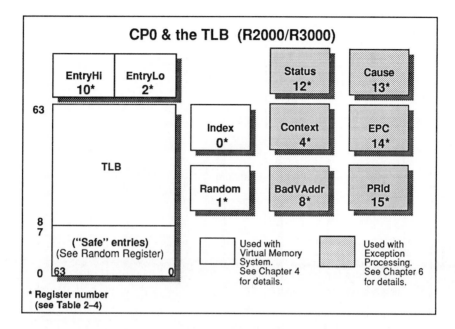

Figure 2–12. The R2000/R3000 CP0 Registers

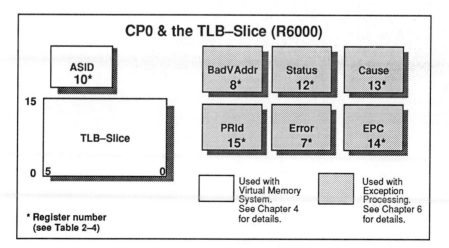

Figure 2–13. The R6000 CP0 Registers

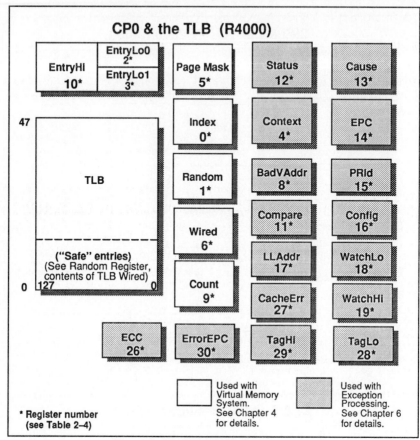

Figure 2–14. The R4000 CP0 Registers

System Control Coprocessor (CP0) Registers

The CP0 registers shown in Figures 2–12 through 2–14 manipulate the memory management and exception handling capabilities of the CPU. Table 2–4 provides a brief description of each register. Refer to Chapter 4 for a detailed description of the registers associated with the virtual memory system and to Chapter 6 for descriptions of the exception processing registers.

Table 2–4. System Control Coprocessor (CP0) Registers

Number	Register	Description
0	Index	Programmable pointer into TLB array (on-chip TLB only)*
1	Random	Pseudo-random pointer into TLB array (read only) (on-chip TLB only)*
2	EntryLo	Low half of TLB entry (R2000 and R3000 only)
2	EntryLo0	Low half of TLB entry for even VPN (R4000 only)
3	EntryLo1	Low half of TLB entry for odd VPN (R4000 only)
4	Context	Pointer to kernel virtual PTE table (on-chip TLB only)*
5	PageMask	TLB Page Mask (R4000 only)
6	Wired	Number of wired TLB entries (R4000 only)
7	Error	Parity control/status register (R6000 only)
8	BadVAddr	Bad virtual address
9	Count	Timer Count (R4000 only)
10	EntryHi	High half of TLB entry (on-chip TLB only)*
10	ASID	Address Space identifier (in-cache TLB only)*
11	Compare	Timer Compare (R4000 only)
12	SR	Status Register
13	Cause	Cause of last exception
14	EPC	Exception Program Counter
15	PRId	Processor Revision Identifier
16	Config	Configuration Register (R4000 only)
17	LLAddr	Load Linked Address (R4000 only)
18	WatchLo	Memory reference trap address low bits (R4000 only)
19	WatchHi	Memory reference trap address high bits (R4000 only)
20–25	————	*unused*
26	ECC	S-cache ECC and Primary Parity (R4000 only)
27	CacheErr	Cache Error and Status register (R4000 only)
28	TagLo	Cache Tag register (R4000 only)
29	TagHi	Cache Tag register (R4000 only)
30	ErrorEPC	Error Exception Program Counter (R4000 only)
31	————	*unused*

*On-chip = R2000, R3000 and R4000; in-cache = R6000

Memory Management System

The R2000/R3000 processors have a physical addressing range of 4 Gbytes (32 bits); the R4000 and R6000 have a physical addressing range of 64 Gbytes (36 bits). However, since most systems implement a physical memory smaller than 4 Gbytes, all four CPUs provide a logical expansion of memory space by translating addresses composed in a large virtual address space into available physical memory addresses. The virtual address space is divided into 2 Gbytes for users and 2 Gbytes for the kernel.

The Translation Lookaside Buffer (TLB)

Virtual memory mapping is assisted by a TLB. The R2000/R3000/R4000 on-chip TLB and R6000 on-chip TLB Slice provide very fast virtual memory access and are well matched to the requirements of multitasking operating systems. Descriptions of each version are as follows:

- The R2000/R3000 fully-associative on-chip TLB contains 64 entries, each of which maps to a 4-Kbyte page, with controls for read/write access, cacheability, and process identification.

- The R4000 fully-associative on-chip TLB contains 48 entries, each of which maps to a pair of variable-size pages, ranging from 4 Kbytes to 16 Mbytes.

- The R6000 uses a 16-entry on-chip TLB Slice, 8 for instruction and 8 for data for the R6000, and 16 combined in R6000A; the page size is 16 Kbytes.

Operating Modes

The R2000, R3000, and R6000 CPUs have two operating modes: *User* mode and *Kernel* mode; the R4000 has an additional mode, called *Supervisor*. The CPU normally operates in User mode until an exception is detected forcing it into Kernel mode. It remains in Kernel mode until a Restore From Exception *(RFE)* instruction is executed (the R4000 uses the ERET instruction). The manner in which memory addresses are translated or *mapped* depends on the operating mode of the CPU. Chapter 4 describes the MMU and Operating modes in greater detail.

R2000/R3000 Pipeline Architecture

The execution of a single R2000/R3000 instruction consists of five primary steps or *pipe stages,* as shown in Figure 2–15: Instruction Fetch (IF), Read (RD), Arithmetic/Logic Unit operation (ALU), Memory Access (MEM), Register Write-back (WB). Each cycle is further divided into separate phases, named phase one ($\phi1$) and phase two ($\phi2$).

IF	$\phi1$	Uses the micro-TLB to translate instruction virtual address to physical address (after branch decision in ALU $\phi1$).
IF	$\phi2$	Sends the physical address to the instruction cache.
RD	$\phi1$	Returns instruction from the instruction cache, whereupon tags are compared and parity is checked.
RD	$\phi2$	Reads the register file. If a branch, then calculates branch target address. Latches coprocessor condition input.
ALU	$\phi1+\phi2$	Bypasses operands from other pipeline stages and calculates add, logical, shift, etc., results. Shifts store data and starts integer multiply/divide, or floating-point operation.
ALU	$\phi1$	If a branch, decides whether the branch is to be taken or not. If a load or store, then calculates virtual address.
ALU	$\phi2$	If a load or store, translates virtual address to physical using TLB.
MEM	$\phi1$	If a load or store, sends physical address to data cache.
MEM	$\phi2$	If a load or store, returns data from data cache. Compares tags and checks parity, and extracts byte for loads. If an MTCz or MFCz instruction, then transfers data to or from coprocessor.
WB	$\phi1$	Writes the register file.

Each step requires approximately one CPU cycle, as shown in Figure 2–15 (parts of some operations overlap another cycle while other operations require only half a cycle).

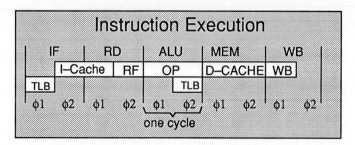

Figure 2–15. R2000/R3000 Instruction Execution Sequence

The R2000/R3000 processors use a five-stage pipeline to achieve an instruction execution rate approaching one instruction per CPU cycle. Thus, execution of five instructions at the same time results in instruction overlapping as shown in Figure 2–16.

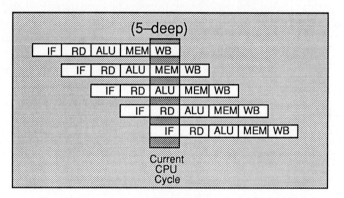

Figure 2–16. R2000/R3000 Instruction Overlapping

This pipeline operates efficiently because different CPU resources (address and data bus accesses, ALU operations, register accesses, and so on) are used on a noninterfering basis.

R6000 Pipeline Architecture

The execution of a single R6000 instruction consists of five primary steps:

I   Fetch instruction from instruction cache.

R/A   Read register file, bypass results from other stages, use ALU to calculate results or virtual address for loads and stores.

D   Load or store: read or write primary data cache.

N   Detect primary cache misses and resolve exceptions. On load, send data from data cache to processor.

W   Write register file.

Each of these steps require approximately one CPU cycle as shown in Figure 2–17.

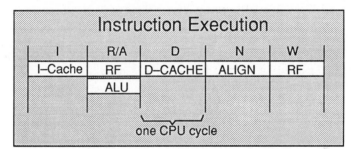

Figure 2–17. R6000 Instruction Execution Sequence

The R6000 uses a five-stage pipeline; thus, execution of five instructions at the same time are overlapped as shown in Figure 2–18.

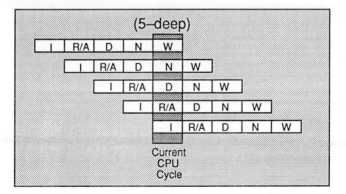

Figure 2–18. R6000 Instruction Overlapping

R4000 Pipeline Architecture

The execution of a single R4000 CPU instruction consists of eight primary steps, as shown in Figure 2–19.

IF Instruction Fetch First. Virtual address is presented to the I-cache and TLB.

IS Instruction Fetch Second. I-cache outputs the instruction and the TLB generates the physical address.

RF Register file. Three activities occur in parallel:
- instruction is decoded and check made for interlock conditions
- instruction tag check is made
- operands are fetched from the register file.

EX Instruction execute. One of three activities can occur:
- if the instruction is a register-to-register operation, the ALU performs the arithmetic or logical operation
- if the instruction is a load or store, the data virtual address is calculated
- if the instruction is a branch, the branch target virtual address is calculated and branch conditions are checked.

DF Data Cache First. Virtual address is presented to the D-cache and TLB.

DS Data Cache Second. D-cache outputs the instruction and the TLB generates the physical address.

TC Tag check. Tag check is performed for loads and stores.

WB Write back. Instruction result is written back to register file.

The R4000 uses an 8-stage pipeline; thus, execution of 8 instructions at a time are overlapped as shown in Figure 2–19.

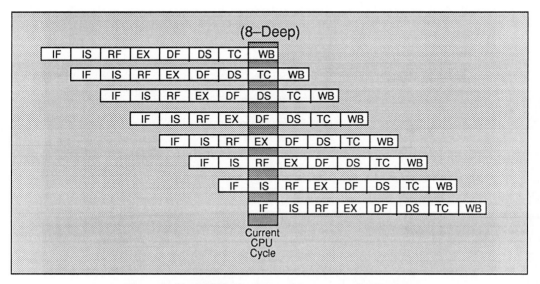

Figure 2–19. R4000 Pipeline and Instruction Overlapping

Memory System Hierarchy

The high performance capabilities of the processor demand system configurations incorporating techniques that are frequently employed in large, mainframe computers but seldom encountered in systems based on more traditional microprocessors.

A goal of RISC machines is to achieve an instruction completion rate of one instruction per CPU cycle, or better. MIPS R-Series processors achieve this goal by means of a compact and uniform instruction set, a deep instruction pipeline (as described above), and careful adaptation to optimizing compilers. Many of the advantages obtained from these techniques can, however, be negated by an inefficient memory system.

Figure 2–20 illustrates memory in a simple microprocessor system. In this system, the CPU outputs addresses to memory, reads instructions and data from memory, and writes data to memory. The memory space is completely undifferentiated: instructions, data, and I/O devices are all treated the same. In such a system, the primary factor limiting performance is memory bandwidth.

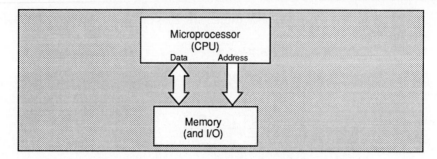

Figure 2–20. A Simple Microprocessor Memory System

Figure 2–21 illustrates a memory system that supports the significantly greater memory bandwidth required to take full advantage of the processor performance capabilities.

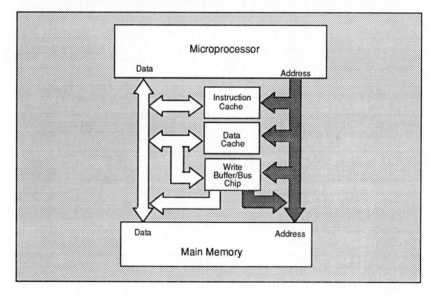

Figure 2–21. Example of a System with High-Performance Memory and Write Buffer

The key features of a system using high-performance memory are:

- **Cache Memory.** Local, high-speed memory (called *cache* memory) holds instructions and data that are repetitively accessed by the CPU (for example, within a program loop), reducing the number of references that must be made to the slower-speed main memory. The caches supported by MIPS processors can be much larger; while a small cache can improve performance of some programs, significant improvements for a wide range of programs require large caches.

- **Separate Caches for Data and Instructions.** Even with high-speed caches, memory speed can still be a limiting factor because of the fast cycle time of a high-performance microprocessor. MIPS processors support separate caches for instructions and data, alternating accesses of the two caches during each CPU cycle. Thus, the processor can obtain data and instructions at the cycle rate of the CPU, using caches constructed with commercially available static RAM devices.

- **Write Buffer.** To ensure data consistency, data written to data caches must also be written to main memory. To relieve the CPU of this responsibility (and the inherent performance burden) the R2000 and R3000 processors support an interface to an external write buffer. The R4000 and R6000 do not need external write buffers.

3
CPU Instruction Set Summary

This chapter provides an overview of the CPU instruction set by summarizing each instruction category in a table. Refer to Appendix A for individual descriptions of each CPU instruction.

Instruction Formats

Each CPU instruction consists of a single word (32 bits) aligned on a word boundary. There are three instruction formats, as shown in Figure 3–1. Coprocessor instructions are implementation-dependent; see Appendix A for their definition. This approach simplifies instruction decoding, since the compiler can synthesize more complicated (and less frequently used) operations and addressing modes.

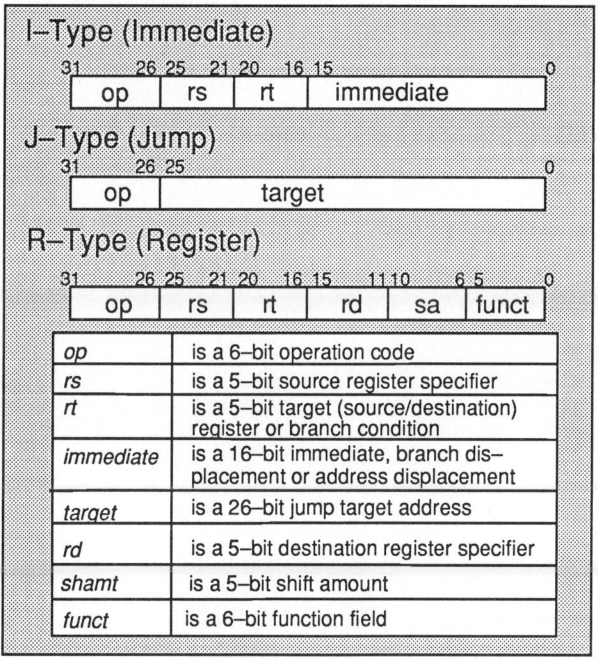

I–Type (Immediate)

31 26	25 21	20 16	15 0
op	rs	rt	immediate

J–Type (Jump)

31 26	25 0
op	target

R–Type (Register)

31 26	25 21	20 16	15 11	10 6	5 0
op	rs	rt	rd	sa	funct

op	is a 6–bit operation code
rs	is a 5–bit source register specifier
rt	is a 5–bit target (source/destination) register or branch condition
immediate	is a 16–bit immediate, branch displacement or address displacement
target	is a 26–bit jump target address
rd	is a 5–bit destination register specifier
shamt	is a 5–bit shift amount
funct	is a 6–bit function field

Figure 3–1. CPU Instruction Formats

Instruction Notation Conventions

In this document, all variable (not fixed) subfields in an instruction format — such as *rs, rt, immediate*, and so on — are shown in lowercase italic characters.

For the sake of clarity, an alias is sometimes used for a variable subfield in the formats of specific instructions. For example, LWC is an alias for *rs* in the format for load and store instructions. Such an alias is always lowercase italic, since it refers to an unfixed, variable subfield.

Two instruction subfields, *op* and *function*, have fixed 6-bit values for specific instructions; these values are given uppercase Roman mnemonic names in this document. For example, *op* = LB in the Load Byte instruction; *op* = SPECIAL and *function* = ADD in the Add instruction.

In some cases, a single field has both fixed and variable subfields, so the name contains both upper- and lowercase characters. For example, LWCz (Load Coprocessor z) represents 4 different 6-bit opcodes, each composed of the fixed 4-bit subfield LWC concatenated with the variable 2-bit subfield z, which designates one of the four coprocessors.

Listings of the bit encodings for the fixed fields of all instructions are located at the end of Appendix A; individual bit encodings accompany each instruction.

Load and Store Instructions

Load/Store instructions move data between memory and the general registers. They are all immediate (I-type) instructions. The only addressing mode that load/stores directly support is *base register plus 16-bit signed immediate offset.*

Implementation Note:

> All load operations have a latency of one instruction. This single-instruction *load delay slot* is an architectural feature of MIPS R-Series processors; all ISA implementations attempt to execute the instruction following a load before the load result is available.
>
> In R2000/R3000 implementations, the hardware does not interlock, so any data loaded from memory into a register is not available until the second instruction after the load instruction (and use of the target register in the load delay slot is undefined). An exception to this is the target register for the Load Word Left and Load Word Right instructions, which may be the same register as that used for the destination of the load instruction immediately preceding. (Refer to Instruction Pipeline at the end of this chapter for a detailed discussion of load instruction latency.)
>
> In the R4000/R6000 implementations, the instruction immediately following a load can use the contents of the loaded register. In such cases, hardware interlocks require additional real cycles; consequently, scheduling load delay slots is still desirable — although not absolutely required for functional code.

The load/store instruction opcode determines the access type which indicates the size of the data item to be loaded or stored as shown in Figure 3–2. Regardless of access type or byte-numbering order (endianness), the address specifies the byte with the smallest byte address in the addressed field. For a Big-endian configuration, it is the most significant byte; for a Little-endian configuration, it is the least significant byte.

Application Note:

> Two special load/store instructions are provided as extensions to the MIPS ISA: Load Linked and Store Conditional. These instructions are used in carefully coded sequences to provide one of several synchronization primitives, including test-and-set, bit-level locks, semaphores, and sequencers/event counts.

The bytes that are used within the addressed doubleword can be determined from the access type and the three low order bits of the address, as shown in Figure 3–2. Certain combinations of access type and low order address bits never occur; only the combinations shown in Figure 3–2 are permissible — any other combinations cause address error exceptions. Table 3–1 lists the load and store instructions defined by the ISA; Table 3–2 lists the instructions which are extensions to the ISA.

Access Type (Value)	Low Order Address Bits 2 1 0	Bytes Accessed			
		Big Endian 63 ———— 0		Little Endian 63 ———— 0	
(doubleword) 7	0 0 0	0 1 2 3 4 5 6 7		7 6 5 4 3 2 1 0	
		Byte		Byte	
(word) 3	0 0 0	0 1 2 3		3 2 1 0	
	1 0 0	4 5 6 7		7 6 5 4	
(triple–byte) 2	0 0 0	0 1 2		2 1 0	
	0 0 1	1 2 3		3 2 1	
	1 0 0	4 5 6		6 5 4	
	1 0 1	5 6 7		7 6 5	
(halfword) 1	0 0 0	0 1		1 0	
	0 1 0	2 3		3 2	
	1 0 0	4 5		5 4	
	1 1 0	6 7		7 6	
(byte) 0	0 0 0	0		0	
	0 0 1	1		1	
	0 1 0	2		2	
	1 1 0	3		3	
	1 0 0	4		4	
	1 1 0	5		5	
	1 0 1	6		6	
	1 1 1	7		7	

Figure 3–2. Byte Specifications for Loads/Stores

Table 3–1. Load and Store Instruction Summary

Instruction	Format and Description	op	base	rt	offset
Load Byte	*LB rt,offset(base)* Sign-extend 16-bit *offset* and add to contents of register *base* to form address. Sign-extend contents of addressed byte and load into register *rt*.				
Load Byte Unsigned	*LBU rt,offset(base)* Sign-extend 16-bit *offset* and add to contents of register *base* to form address. Zero-extend contents of addressed byte and load into register *rt*.				
Load Halfword	*LH rt,offset(base)* Sign-extend 16-bit *offset* and add to contents of register *base* to form address. Sign-extend contents of addressed halfword and load into register *rt*.				
Load Halfword Unsigned	*LHU rt,offset(base)* Sign-extend 16-bit *offset* and add to contents of register *base* to form address. Zero-extend contents of addressed halfword and load into register *rt*.				
Load Word	*LW rt,offset(base)* Sign-extend 16-bit *offset* and add to contents of register *base* to form address. Load contents of addressed word into register *rt*.				
Load Word Left	*LWL rt,offset(base)* Sign-extend 16-bit *offset* and add to contents of register *base* to form address. Shift addressed word left so that addressed byte is leftmost byte of a word. Merge bytes from memory with contents of register *rt* and load the result into register *rt*.				
Load Word Right	*LWR rt,offset(base)* Sign-extend 16-bit *offset* and add to contents of register *base* to form address. Shift addressed word right so that addressed byte is rightmost byte of a word. Merge bytes from memory with contents of register *rt* and load the result into register *rt*.				
Store Byte	*SB rt,offset(base)* Sign-extend 16-bit *offset* and add to contents of register *base* to form address. Store the least significant byte of register *rt* at addressed location.				
Store Halfword	*SH rt,offset(base)* Sign-extend 16-bit *offset* and add to contents of register *base* to form address. Store the least significant halfword of register *rt* at addressed location.				
Store Word	*SW rt,offset(base)* Sign-extend 16-bit *offset* and add to contents of register *base* to form address. Store the contents of register *rt* at addressed location.				
Store Word Left	*SWL rt,offset(base)* Sign-extend 16-bit *offset* and add to contents of register *base* to form address. Shift contents of register *rt* left so that the leftmost byte of the word is in the position of the addressed byte. Store the bytes containing the original data into corresponding bytes at addressed byte.				
Store Word Right	*SWR rt,offset(base)* Sign-extend 16-bit *offset* and add to contents of register *base* to form address. Shift contents of register *rt* right so that the rightmost byte of the word is in the position of the addressed byte. Store the bytes containing the original data into corresponding bytes at addressed byte.				

Table 3–2. Load and Store Instruction Extensions

Instruction	Format and Description	op	base	rt	offset
Load Linked	*LL rt,offset(base)* Sign-extend 16-bit *offset* and add to contents of register *base* to form address. Sign-extend contents of addressed word and load into register *rt*.				
Store Conditional	*SC rt,offset(base)* Sign-extend 16-bit *offset* and add to contents of register *base* to form address. Store contents of register *rt* at addressed location.				
Sync	*SYNC* Complete any load or store fetched before current instruction, before any load or store after this instruction will be allowed to start.				

Computational Instructions

Computational instructions perform arithmetic, logical, and shift operations on values in registers. They occur in both register (R-type) format, in which both operands are registers, and immediate (I-type) format, in which one operand is a 16-bit immediate. There are four categories of computational instructions:

- ALU Immediate instructions, summarized in Table 3–3
- Three-Operand Register-Type instructions, summarized in Table 3–4
- Shift instructions, summarized in Table 3–5
- Multiply/Divide instructions, summarized in Table 3–6

Table 3–3. ALU Immediate Instruction Summary

Instruction	Format and Description	op	rs	rt	immediate
ADD Immediate	*ADDI rt,rs,immediate* Add 16-bit sign-extended *immediate* to register *rs* and place the 32-bit result in register *rt*. Trap on 2's-complement overflow.
ADD Immediate Unsigned	*ADDIU rt,rs,immediate* Add 16-bit sign-extended *immediate* to register *rs* and place the 32-bit result in register *rt*. Do not trap on overflow.
Set on Less Than Immediate	*SLTI rt,rs,immediate* Compare 16-bit sign-extended *immediate* with register *rs* as signed 32-bit integers. Result = 1 if *rs* is less than *immediate*; otherwise result = 0. Place result in register *rt*.
Set on Less Than Immediate Unsigned	*SLTIU rt,rs,immediate* Compare 16-bit sign-extended *immediate* with register *rs* as unsigned 32-bit integers. Result = 1 if *rs* is less than *immediate*; otherwise result = 0. Place result in register *rt*.
AND Immediate	*ANDI rt,rs,immediate* Zero-extend 16-bit *immediate*, AND with contents of register *rs* and place the result in register *rt*.
OR Immediate	*ORI rt,rs,immediate* Zero-extend 16-bit *immediate*, OR with contents of register *rs* and place the result in register *rt*.
Exclusive OR Immediate	*XORI rt,rs,immediate* Zero-extend 16-bit *immediate*, exclusive OR with contents of register *rs* and place the result in register *rt*.
Load Upper Immediate	*LUI rt,immediate* Shift 16-bit *immediate* left 16 bits. Set least significant 16 bits of word to zeros. Store the result in register *rt*.

Table 3–4. Three-Operand Register-Type Instruction Summary

Instruction	Format and Description	op	rs	rt	rd	sa	function
Add	*ADD rd,rs,rt* Add contents of registers *rs* and *rt* and place the 32-bit result in register *rd*. Trap on 2's-complement overflow.						
Add Unsigned	*ADDU rd,rs,rt* Add contents of registers *rs* and *rt* and place the 32-bit result in register *rd*. Do not trap on overflow.						
Subtract	*SUB rd,rs,rt* Subtract contents of registers *rt* from *rs* and place the 32-bit result in register *rd*. Trap on 2's-complement overflow.						
Subtract Unsigned	*SUBU rd,rs,rt* Subtract contents of registers *rt* from *rs* and place the 32-bit result in register *rd*. Do not trap on overflow.						
Set on Less Than	*SLT rd,rs,rt* Compare contents of register *rt* to register *rs* as signed 32-bit integers. Result = 1 if *rs* is less than *rt*; otherwise result = 0.						
Set on Less Than Unsigned	*SLTU rd,rs,rt* Compare contents of register *rt* to register *rs* as unsigned 32-bit integers. Result = 1 if *rs* is less than *rt*; otherwise result = 0.						
AND	*AND rd,rs,rt* Bitwise AND the contents of registers *rs* and *rt*, and place the result in register *rd*.						
OR	*OR rd,rs,rt* Bitwise OR the contents of registers *rs* and *rt*, and place the result in register *rd*.						
Exclusive OR	*XOR rd,rs,rt* Bitwise exclusive OR the contents of registers *rs* and *rt*, and place the result in register *rd*.						
NOR	*NOR rd,rs,rt* Bitwise NOR the contents of registers *rs* and *rt*, and place the result in register *rd*.						

Table 3–5. Shift Instruction Summary

Instruction	Format and Description	op	rs	rt	rd	sa	function
Shift Left Logical	*SLL rd,rt,sa* Shift the contents of register *rt* left by *sa* bits, inserting zeros into the low order bits. Place the 32-bit result in register *rd*.						
Shift Right Logical	*SRL rd,rt,sa* Shift the contents of register *rt* right by *sa* bits, inserting zeros into the high order bits. Place the 32-bit result in register *rd*.						
Shift Right Arithmetic	*SRA rd,rt,sa* Shift the contents of register *rt* right by *sa* bits, sign-extending the high order bits. Place the 32-bit result in register *rd*.						
Shift Left Logical Variable	*SLLV rd,rt,rs* Shift the contents of register *rt* left. The low order 5 bits of register *rs* specify the number of bits to shift left; insert zeros into the low order bits of *rt* and place the 32-bit result in register *rd*.						
Shift Right Logical Variable	*SRLV rd,rt,rs* Shift the contents of register *rt* right. The low order 5 bits of register *rs* specify the number of bits to shift right; insert zeros into the high order bits of *rt* and place the 32-bit result in register *rd*.						
Shift Right Arithmetic Variable	*SRAV rd,rt,rs* Shift the contents of register *rt* right. The low order 5 bits of register *rs* specify the number of bits to shift right; sign-extend the high order bits of *rt* and place the 32-bit result in register *rd*.						

Table 3–6. Multiply/Divide Instruction Summary

Instruction	Format and Description	op	rs	rt	rd	sa	function
Multiply	*MULT rs,rt* Multiply the contents of registers *rs* and *rt* as 2's-complement values. Place the 64-bit result in special registers *HI* and *LO*.
Multiply Unsigned	*MULTU rs,rt* Multiply the contents of registers *rs* and *rt* as unsigned integers. Place the 64-bit result in special registers *HI* and *LO*.
Divide	*DIV rs,rt* Divide the contents of register *rs* by *rt*, treating operands as 2's -complement values. Place the 32-bit quotient in special register *LO* and the 32-bit remainder in *HI*.
Divide Unsigned	*DIVU rs,rt* Divide the contents of register *rs* by *rt*, treating operands as unsigned values. Place the 32-bit quotient in special register *LO* and the 32-bit remainder in *HI*.
Move From HI	*MFHI rd* Move the contents of special register *HI* to register *rd*.
Move From LO	*MFLO rd* Move the contents of special register *LO* to register *rd*.
Move To HI	*MTHI rd* Move the contents of register *rd* to special register *HI*.
Move To LO	*MTLO rd* Move the contents of register *rd* to special register *LO*.

The number of cycles required for multiply/divide operations is implementation-dependent. The MFHI and MFLO instructions are interlocked so that any attempt to read them before prior operations have completed will cause execution of these instructions to be delayed until the operation finishes. For each implementation, Table 3–7 gives the number of cycles required between a MULT, MULTU, DIV or DIVU operation, and a subsequent MFHI or MFLO operation, to resolve an interlock or stall.

Table 3–7. Multiply/Divide Instruction Cycle Timing

Implementation (Processor)	Cycles Required			
	MULT	MULTU	DIV	DIVU
R2000	12	12	35	35
R3000	12	12	35	35
R4000	10	10	69	69
R6000	17	18	38	37

Jump and Branch Instructions

Jump and branch instructions change the control flow of a program. All jump and branch instructions occur with a one instruction delay: that is, the instruction immediately following the jump or branch is always executed while the target instruction is being fetched from storage. See the section describing the Delayed Instruction Slot at the end of this chapter for a detailed discussion of the delayed jump and branch instructions.

Both jumps and jump-and-links use the jump (J-type) instruction format for subroutine calls. In this format, the 26-bit target address is shifted left two bits, and combined with the high order four bits of the current program counter to form a 32-bit absolute address.

Returns, dispatches, and large cross-page jumps use the register (R-type) instruction format (for JR and JALR), which takes a 32-bit byte address contained in a register.

Branches have 16-bit signed offsets relative to the program counter (I-type). Jump-and-link and branch-and-link instructions save a return address in register 31.

Tables 3–8 and 3–9 summarize those CPU jump and branch instructions that are shared by all MIPS R-Series processors; Table 3–10 summarizes branch instructions that are reserved for the R4000 and R6000.

Table 3–8. Jump Instruction Summary

Instruction	Format and Description	op	target			
Jump	*J target* Shift the 26-bit *target* address left two bits, combine with high order four bits of the PC, and jump to the address with a 1-instruction delay.					
Jump And Link	*JAL target* Shift the 26-bit *target* address left two bits, combine with high order four bits of the PC, and jump to the address with a 1-instruction delay. Place the address of the instruction following the delay slot in *r31* (*Link* register).					
Instruction	**Format and Description**	op	rs	rt	rd	sa function
Jump Register	*JR rs* Jump to the address contained in register *rs*, with a 1-instruction delay.					
Jump And Link Register	*JALR rs, rd* Jump to the address contained in register *rs*, with a 1-instruction delay. Place the address of the instruction following the delay slot in register *rd*.					

In Tables 3–9 and 3–10, the following constraints are observed:

- Branch target. All branch instruction target addresses are computed by adding the address of the instruction in the delay slot and the 16-bit *offset* (shifted left two bits and sign-extended to 32 bits). All branches occur with a delay of one instruction.

- Conditional branch (Table 3–10). If the conditional branch is not taken, the instruction in the delay slot is nullified.

Table 3–9. Branch Instruction Summary

Instruction	Format and Description
Branch on Equal	*BEQ rs,rt,offset* [op | rs | rt | offset] Branch to target address if register *rs* is equal to register *rt*.
Branch on Not Equal	*BNE rs,rt,offset* Branch to target address if register *rs* is not equal to register *rt*.
Branch on Less than or Equal Zero	*BLEZ rs,offset* Branch to target address if register *rs* is less than or equal to zero.
Branch on Greater Than Zero	*BGTZ rs,offset* Branch to target address if register *rs* is greater than zero.
Branch on Less Than Zero	*BLTZ rs,offset* [REGIMM | rs | sub | offset] Branch to target address if register *rs* is less than zero.
Branch on Greater than or Equal Zero	*BGEZ rs,offset* Branch to target address if register *rs* is greater than or equal to zero.
Branch on Less Than Zero And Link	*BLTZAL rs,offset* Place address of instruction following the delay slot in register *r31* (Link register). Branch to target address if register *rs* is less than zero.
Branch on Greater than or Equal Zero And Link	*BGEZAL rs,offset* Place address of instruction following the delay slot in register *r31* (Link register). Branch to target address if register *rs* is greater than or equal to zero.

The following instructions are extensions to the ISA and valid only if used on the R4000 or R6000 processors; a reserved instruction exception is generated if these instruction are used on an R2000 or R3000 processor.

Table 3–10. Branch Instruction Summary (Extensions to the ISA)

Instruction	Format and Description
Branch on Equal Likely	BEQL rs,rt,offset `op  rs  rt  offset` Branch to target address if register rs is equal to register rt.
Branch on Not Equal Likely	BNEL rs,rt,offset Branch to target address if register rs is not equal to register rt.
Branch on Less Than or Equal to Zero Likely	BLEZL rs,offset Branch to target address if register rs is less than or equal to zero.
Branch on Greater Than Zero Likely	BGTZL rs,offset Branch to target address if register rs is greater than zero.
Branch on Less Than Zero Likely	BLTZL rs,offset `REGIMM  rs  sub  offset` Branch to target address if register rs is less than zero.
Branch on Greater Than or Equal to Zero Likely	BGEZL rs,offset Branch to target address if register rs is greater than or equal to zero.
Branch on Less Than Zero And Link Likely	BLTZALL rs,offset Place address of instruction following the delay slot in register r31 (Link register). Branch to target address if register rs is less than zero.
Branch on Greater Than or Equal to Zero And Link Likely	BGEZALL rs,offset Place address of instruction following the delay slot in register r31 (Link register). Branch to target address if register rs is greater than or equal to zero.

Special Instructions

Special instructions (different from the SPECIAL opcode) allow the software to initiate traps, and are always R-type. Special instructions that are valid for all MIPS R-Series processors are shown in Table 3–11; special instructions that are extensions to the ISA (and reserved for the R4000 and R6000) are given in Tables 3–12 and 3–13.

Table 3–11. Special Instructions

Instruction	Format and Description	SPECIAL	rs	rt	rd	sa	function
System Call	*SYSCALL* Initiates system call trap, immediately transferring control to exception handler.
Breakpoint	*BREAK* Initiates breakpoint trap, immediately transferring control to exception handler.

The following trap and trap immediate instructions, shown in Tables 3–12 and 3–13, are valid only if used on R4000 and R6000 processors; a reserved instruction exception will be generated if these instructions are used on an R2000 or R3000.

Table 3–12. Trap Instructions (ISA Extensions)

Instruction	Format and Description	SPECIAL	rs	rt	rd	sa	function
Trap if Greater Than or Equal	*TGE rs,rt* Trap exception occurs if register *rs* is greater than or equal to register *rt*.
Trap if Greater Than or Equal Unsigned	*TGEU rs,rt* Trap exception occurs if register *rs* is greater than or equal to register *rt*.
Trap if Less Than	*TLT rs,rt* Trap exception occurs if register *rs* is less than register *rt*.
Trap if Less Than Unsigned	*TLTU rs,rt* Trap exception occurs if register *rs* is less than register *rt*.
Trap if Equal	*TEQ rs,rt* Trap exception occurs if register *rs* is equal to register *rt*.
Trap if Not Equal	*TNE rs,rt* Trap exception occurs if register *rs* is not equal to register *rt*.

Table 3–13. Trap Immediate Instructions (ISA Extensions)

Instruction	Format and Description	REGIMM	rs	rt	immediate
Trap if Greater Than or Equal Immediate	*TGEI rs,immediate* Trap exception occurs if register *rs* is greater than or equal to *immediate*				
Trap if Greater Than or Equal Unsigned Immediate	*TGEIU rs,immediate* Trap exception occurs if register *rs* is greater than or equal to *immediate*				
Trap if Less Than Immediate	*TLTI rs,immediate* Trap exception occurs if register *rs* is less than *immediate*.				
Trap if Less Than Unsigned Immediate	*TLTIU rs,immediate* Trap exception occurs if register *rs* is less than *immediate*.				
Trap if Equal Immediate	*TEQI rs,immediate* Trap exception occurs if register *rs* is equal to *immediate*.				
Trap if Not Equal Immediate	*TNEI rs,immediate* Trap exception occurs if register *rs* is not equal to *immediate*.				

Coprocessor Instructions

Coprocessor instructions perform operations in their respective coprocessors. Coprocessor loads and stores are I-type, and coprocessor computational instructions have coprocessor-dependent formats. Table 3–14 summarizes the coprocessor instructions valid on all MIPS R-Series processors; Table 3–15 summarizes those instructions defined as extensions to the ISA and valid only on the R4000 and R6000 processors.

Table 3–14. Coprocessor Instruction Summary

Instruction	Format and Description
Load Word to Coprocessor	*LWCz rt,offset(base)* `op` `base` `rt` `offset` Sign-extend 16-bit *offset* and add to contents of register *base* to form address. Load contents of addressed word into coprocessor register *rt* of coprocessor unit z.
Store Word from Coprocessor	*SWCz rt,offset(base)* Sign-extend 16-bit *offset* and add to contents of register *base* to form address. Store contents of coprocessor register *rt* from coprocessor unit z at addressed memory word.
Move To Coprocessor	*MTCz rt,rd* `COPz` `sub` `rt` `rd` `0` Move contents of CPU register *rt* into coprocessor register *rd* of coprocessor unit z.
Move From Coprocessor	*MFCz rt,rd* Move contents of coprocessor register *rd* of coprocessor unit z into CPU register *rt* .
Move Control To Coprocessor	*CTCz rt,rd* Move contents of CPU register *rt* into coprocessor control register *rd* of coprocessor unit z.
Move Control From Coprocessor	*CFCz rt,rd* Move contents of control register *rd* of coprocessor unit z into CPU register *rt* .
Coprocessor Operation	*COPz cofun* `COPz` `CO` `cofun` Coprocessor unit z performs an operation. The state of the CPU is not modified by a coprocessor operation.
Branch on Coprocessor z True	*BCzT offset* `COPz` `BC` `br` `offset` Compute a branch target address by adding the address of the instruction in the delay slot and the 16-bit *offset* (shifted left two bits and sign extended to 32 bits). Branch to the target address (with a delay of one instruction) if coprocessor unit z condition line is true.
Branch on Coprocessor z False	*BCzF offset* Compute a branch target address by adding the address of the instruction in the delay slot and the 16-bit *offset* (shifted left two bits and sign extended to 32 bits). Branch to the target address (with a delay of one instruction) if coprocessor unit z condition line is false.

The following instructions are valid only if used on R4000 and R6000 processors; a reserved instruction exception is generated if these instruction are used on an R2000 or R3000.

Table 3–15. Coprocessor Instruction Summary (Extensions to the ISA)

Instruction	Format and Description
Load Doubleword to Coprocessor	*LDCz rt,offset(base)* `op` `base` `rt` `offset` Sign-extend 16-bit *offset* and add to contents of register *base* to form address. Load contents of addressed doubleword into coprocessor registers *rt* and *rt+1* of coprocessor unit z.
Store Doubleword from Coprocessor	*SDCz rt,offset(base)* Sign-extend 16-bit *offset* and add to contents of register *base* to form address. Store contents of coprocessor registers *rt* and *rt+1* from coprocessor unit z at addressed memory word.
Branch on Coprocessor z True Likely	*BCzTL offset* `COPz` `BC` `br` `offset` Compute a branch target address by adding the address of the instruction in the delay slot and the 16-bit *offset* (shifted left two bits and sign extended to 32 bits). Branch to the target address (with a delay of one instruction) if coprocessor unit z condition line is true. If conditional branch is not taken, the instruction in the branch delay slot is nullified.
Branch on Coprocessor z False Likely	*BCzFL offset* Compute a branch target address by adding the address of the instruction in the delay slot and the 16-bit *offset* (shifted left two bits and sign extended to 32 bits). Branch to the target address (with a delay of one instruction) if coprocessor unit z condition line is false. If conditional branch is not taken, the instruction in the branch delay slot is nullified.

System Control Coprocessor (CP0) Instructions

Coprocessor 0 instructions perform operations on the System Control Coprocessor (CP0) registers to manipulate the memory management and exception handling facilities of the processor. Table 3–16 summarizes the available instructions that work with CP0. All of these instructions are implementation dependent; for instance, TLBR, TLBWI, TLBWR, and TLBP are reserved as R2000/R3000/R4000 instructions. When used on the R6000, setting the *MM* bit in the *Status* register changes the meaning of LWL, LWR, SWL, and SWR from load and store instructions to memory management instructions.

Table 3–16. System Control Coprocessor (CP0) Instruction Summary

Instruction	Format and Description
Move To CP0	*MTC0 rt,rd* COP0 | sub | rt | rd | 0 Load the contents of CPU register *rt* into register *rd* of CP0.
Move From CP0	*MFC0 rt,rd* Load the contents of CP0 register *rd* into CPU register *rt*.
Read Indexed TLB Entry	*TLBR* **R2000/R3000/R4000 only** COP0 | CO | function Load *EntryHi* and *EntryLo* registers with TLB entry pointed at by the *Index* register.
Write Indexed TLB Entry	*TLBWI* **R2000/R3000/R4000 only** Load TLB entry pointed at by the *Index* register with the contents of the *EntryHi* and *EntryLo* registers.
Write Random TLB Entry	*TLBWR* **R2000/R3000/R4000 only** Load TLB entry pointed at by the *Random* register with the contents of the *EntryHi* and *EntryLo* registers.
Probe TLB for Matching Entry	*TLBP* **R2000/R3000/R4000 only** Load the *Index* register with the address of the TLB entry whose contents match the *EntryHi* and *EntryLo* registers. If no TLB entry matches, set the high order bit of the Index register.
Restore From Exception	*RFE* **R2000/R3000/R6000 only** Restore the previous interrupt mask and mode bits of the *Status* register into the current status bits. Restore the old status bits into the previous status bits.
Return from Exception	*ERET* **R4000 only** Return from exception, interrupt, or error trap.

Table 3–16. System Control Coprocessor (CP0) Instruction Summary (cont.)

Instruction	Format and Description	op	base	rt	offset
Flush	*LWR offset(base)* **R6000 only** Sign-extend 16-bit *offset* and add to contents of register *base* to form address. If cache line at specified address is dirty, write it to memory and set the cache line state to clean.				
Invalidate	*SWR offset(base)* **R6000 only** Sign-extend 16-bit *offset* and add to contents of register *base* to form address. Invalidate specified cache line.				
Load From Cache	*LWL rt,offset(base)* **R6000 only** Sign-extend 16-bit *offset* and add to contents of register *base* to form address. Contents of cache at address are loaded into register *rt*.				
Store to Cache	*SWL rt,offset(base)* **R6000 only** Sign-extend 16-bit *offset* and add to contents of register *base* to form address. Contents of register *rt* are stored at address in cache.				
Cache	*Cache sub,offset(base)* **R4000 only** CACHE base sub offset Virtual address is formed from addition of *offset* and *base*, and this virtual address is translated into a physical address using the TLB. Sub-opcode *sub* specifies a cache operation for this address.				

Delayed Instruction Slot

The MIPS RISC architecture uses a number of internal techniques that enable the execution of all instructions in a single cycle; however, two categories of instructions have special requirements that could disturb the smooth flow of instructions through the pipeline:

- Load instructions have a delay, or latency, of one cycle before the data being loaded is available to another instruction.

- Jump and branch instructions have a delay of one cycle while they fetch the instruction and the target address if the branch is taken.

One method for dealing with the delay inherent with these instructions is to stall the flow of instructions through the pipeline whenever a load, jump, or branch instruction is executed. However, in addition to the negative impact this method would have on instruction throughput, it also complicates the pipeline logic, exception processing, and system synchronization.

Application Note:

For branches and jumps, all R-Series processors delay one cycle (have a delay slot).

For loads, R2000 and R3000 processors also have a delay slot. R4000 and R6000 processors do not need this load delay slot because the hardware interlocks if there is a data dependency.

Scheduling load delay slots is still desirable, although not absolutely required, for functional code.

Delayed Loads

Figure 3–3 shows three instructions in the R2000/R3000 pipeline. Instruction 1 (I1) is a Load instruction. The data from the load is not available until the end of the I1 MEM cycle — too late to be used by I2 during its ALU cycle, but available to I3 in its ALU cycle. Therefore, software must ensure that I2 does not depend on the data being loaded by I1. Usually, a compiler can reorganize instructions so that something useful is executed during the delay slot or. If no other instruction is available, a No Operation (NOP) instruction is inserted in the slot.

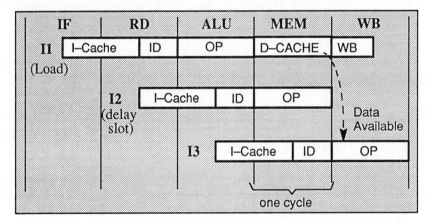

Figure 3–3. Load Instruction Delay Slot

Delayed Jumps and Branches

Figure 3–4 also shows three instructions in the R2000/R3000 pipeline. Instruction 1 (I1) is a Branch instruction, and must calculate the branch target address, which is not available until the beginning of the ALU cycle of I1 — too late for the I-cache access of I2 but available to I3 for its I-cache access. The instruction in the delay slot (I2) always executes before the branch or jump actually occurs.

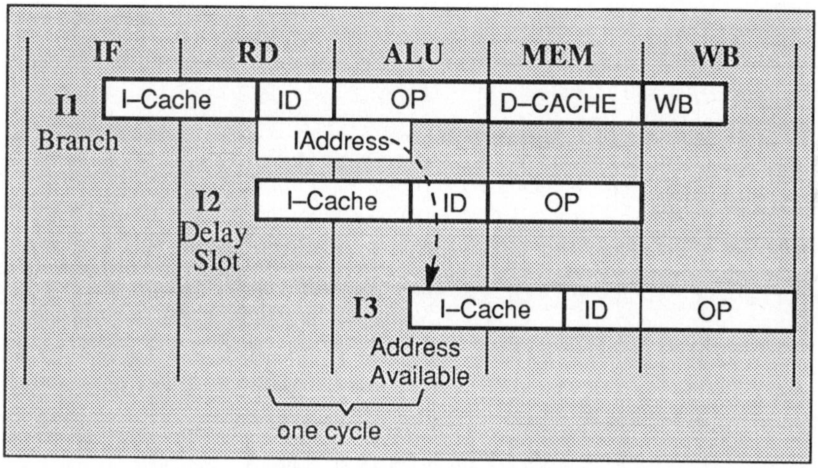

Figure 3–4. The Jump/Branch Instruction Delay Slot

An assembler has several ways to use the branch delay slot productively:

- It can insert an instruction that logically precedes the branch instruction in the load delay slot since the instruction immediately following the jump/branch effectively belongs to the block preceding the transfer instruction.

- It can replicate the instruction that is the target of the branch/jump into the load delay slot, provided no side effects occur if the branch falls through.

- It can move an instruction up from below the branch into the load delay slot, provided that no side effects occur if the branch is taken.

- If no other instruction is available, it can insert a NOP instruction in the delay slot.

4
Memory Management System

A MIPS R-Series processor provides a full-featured memory management unit (MMU) that uses either:

- an on-chip Translation Lookaside Buffer (TLB) in the R2000, R3000, and R4000, or

- an on-chip TLB Slice in the R6000 to make a prediction of the physical address, together with an off-chip TLB stored in the secondary cache.

Both MMUs provide very fast virtual memory accesses. This chapter describes the operation of the TLB and TLB Slice, and the CP0 registers that provide the software interface to the TLB. The memory mapping scheme which translates virtual addresses to physical addresses, is also described in detail.

Memory System Architecture

The virtual memory system logically expands CPU physical memory space by translating addresses composed in a large virtual address space into physical memory space.

The number of bits in a physical address is defined as PSIZE. For R2000 and R3000 processors, PSIZE is equal to 32 bits. Virtual address mapping uses 4-Kbyte pages (lower 12 bits of address, or *address offset*); thus, mapping affects only the most significant 20 bits of a 32-bit virtual address, the *virtual page number* (VPN). The 12-bit offset is passed along unchanged, as shown in Figure 4–1. Table 4–1 lists the virtual and physical address sizes (in bits), together with page sizes, for each processor.

Table 4–1. Virtual, Physical, and Page Sizes

Processor	VSIZE	PSIZE	Page Size
R2000	32	32	4 Kbytes
R3000	32	32	4 Kbytes
R4000	32	36	4 Kbytes to 16 Mbytes
R6000	32	36	16 Kbytes

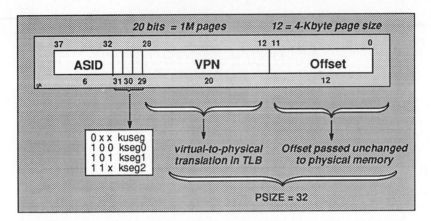

Figure 4–1. R2000/R3000 Virtual Address Format

For R4000 processors, PSIZE is equal to 36 bits, with a variable-size VPN and offset, as shown in Figure 4–2. Page sizes are run from 4 Kbytes (12-bit offset) to 16 Mbytes (24-bit offset).

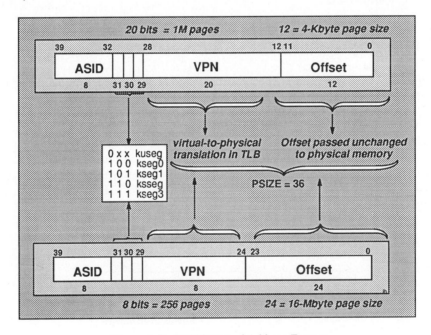

Figure 4–2. R4000 Virtual Address Format

For R6000 processors, PSIZE is equal to 36 bits, with an 18-bit VPN and a 14-bit offset, as shown in Figure 4–3. Pages are 16 Kbytes (14-bit offset).

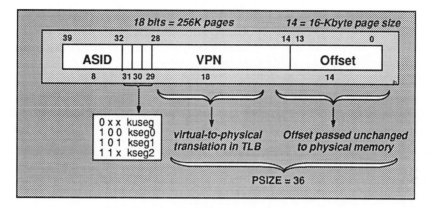

Figure 4–3. R6000 Virtual Address Format

The virtual address is extended with an Address Space Identifier (ASID) to reduce the frequency of TLB flushing when switching context. The size of the ASID field is 6 bits in R2000 and R3000 processors, and 8 bits in R4000 and R6000 processors. The R2000, R3000, and R4000 ASID is contained in the CP0 *EntryHi* register; the R6000 ASID is contained in the CP0 *ASID* register. Both registers are described in this chapter.

Operating Modes

This section describes the three operating modes of the R-Series processors:

- User mode
- Supervisor Mode (R4000 only)
- Kernel mode

Two of these modes are provided by all MIPS R-Series processors: *Kernel* mode, which is analogous to the "supervisory" mode provided by many machines, and *User* mode, in which nonsupervisory programs are executed. The R4000 provides a third, intermediate mode, called *Supervisor* mode.

The CPU enters Kernel mode whenever an exception is detected and it remains in Kernel mode until a Restore From Exception (RFE) instruction is executed (the R4000 uses ERET instead of RFE).

User Mode Virtual Addressing (R-Series)

In User mode, a single, uniform virtual address space (*kuseg*) of 2 Gbytes (2^{31} bytes) is available, as shown in Figure 4–4. Each virtual address is tagged (extended) with either a 6-bit (R2000/R3000) or 8-bit (R4000/R6000) Address Space Identifier (ASID) field to form unique virtual addresses for up to 64 (R2000/R3000) or 256 (R4000/R6000) user processes. By assigning each process an ASID, the system is able to maintain TLB state across context switches. All references to *kuseg* are mapped through the TLB, and cache use is determined by bit settings within the TLB entry for each page. All valid User mode virtual addresses have the most significant bit cleared to 0; any attempt to reference an address with the most significant bit set while in the User mode causes an Address Error exception. (See Chapter 6.)

The 2-Gbyte User segment starts at address zero, 0x0000 0000. The TLB maps all references to *kuseg* identically from all modes, and controls cache accessibility. (The *N* bit in a TLB entry determines whether the reference is cached; see Figure 4–12.) The current user process resides in *kuseg*. Figure 4–4 shows User mode address space.

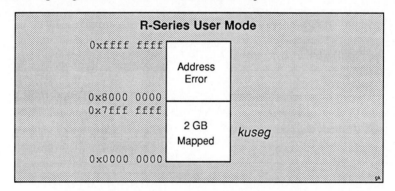

Figure 4–4. MIPS User Mode Address Space

Supervisor-Mode Virtual Addressing (R4000)

Supervisor mode, as shown in Figure 4–5, is available on the R4000 processor only. Supervisor mode is intended for those layered operating system implementations where a "true kernel" runs in R4000 Kernel mode, and the rest of the operating system runs in Supervisor mode. When bits $KSU = 01$, bit $EXL = 0$, and bit $ERL = 0$ in the *Status* register (see Chapter 6 for a description of the *Status* register), the processor is executing in Supervisor mode and two distinct virtual address spaces are simultaneously available, *suseg* and *sseg*.

- *suseg*. When the most significant bit of the virtual address is cleared, the virtual address space, labelled *suseg*, covers the full 2^{31} bytes (2 Gbytes) of the current user address space. The virtual address is extended with the contents of the ASID field to form unique virtual addresses. This mapped space starts at virtual address 0x0000 0000 and runs up to 0x8000 0000.

- *sseg*. When the most significant three bits of the virtual address are 110, the virtual address space selected is the 2^{29}-byte (512-Mbyte) supervisor virtual space labelled *sseg*. The virtual address is extended with the contents of the ASID field to form unique virtual addresses. This mapped space begins at virtual address 0xc000 0000 and runs up to 0xe000 0000.

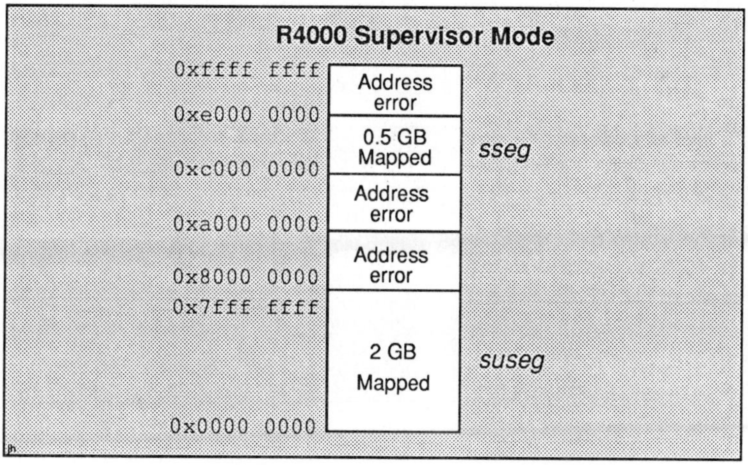

Figure 4–5. MIPS R4000 Supervisor Mode Address Space

Kernel-Mode Virtual Addressing (R2000, R3000 and R6000)

When R2000, R3000 or R6000 processors are operating in Kernel mode, four distinct virtual address spaces are simultaneously available. Three are dedicated to the kernel (the fourth is *kuseg*, User-mode space) and differentiated by the high order bits of the virtual address:

- *kseg0*. When the most significant three bits of the virtual address are 100, the virtual address space selected is the 2^{29}-byte (512-Mbyte) kernel physical space labelled *kseg0*. References to *kseg0* are not mapped through the TLB; the physical address selected is defined by subtracting 0x8000 0000 from the virtual address. Caches are always enabled for accesses to these addresses.

- *kseg1*. When the most significant three bits of the virtual address are 101, the virtual address space selected is the 2^{29}-byte (512-Mbyte) kernel physical space labelled *kseg1*. References to *kseg1* are not mapped through the TLB; the physical address selected is defined by subtracting 0xa000 0000 from the virtual address. Caches are always disabled for accesses to these addresses, and physical memory (or memory-mapped I/O device registers) are accessed directly.

- *kseg2*. When the most significant two bits of the virtual address are 11, the virtual address space selected is the 2^{30}-byte (1-Gbyte) kernel virtual space labelled *kseg2*. The virtual address is extended with the contents of the ASID field to form unique virtual addresses.

Figure 4–6 shows the boundaries of the four segments defined in this mode.

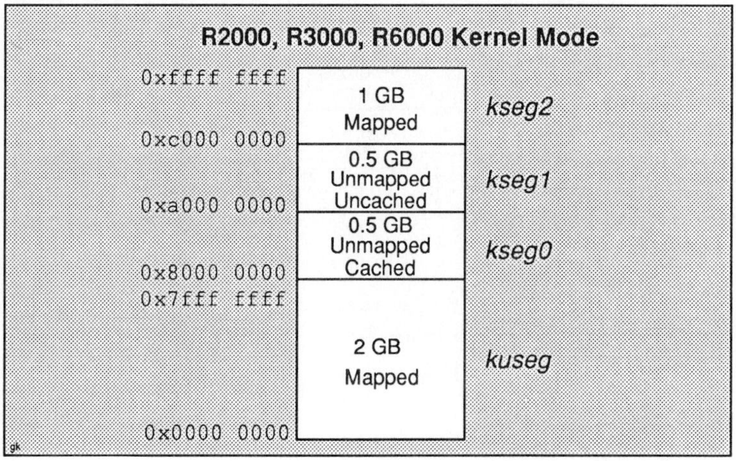

R2000, R3000, R6000 Kernel Mode

0xffff ffff	1 GB Mapped	kseg2
0xc000 0000	0.5 GB Unmapped Uncached	kseg1
0xa000 0000	0.5 GB Unmapped Cached	kseg0
0x8000 0000 / 0x7fff ffff	2 GB Mapped	kuseg
0x0000 0000		

Figure 4–6. MIPS R2000/R3000/R6000 Kernel Mode Address Space

Kernel-Mode Virtual Addressing (R4000)

When an R4000 processor is operating in Kernel mode (bits $KSU = 00$, or bit $EXL = 1$, or bit $ERL = 1$, in the *Status* register) the virtual address space of 2^{32} bytes (4 Gbytes) is divided into five regions, differentiated by high order bits of the virtual address.

- *kuseg*. When the most significant bit of the virtual address is cleared, the virtual address space selected covers the full 2^{31} bytes (2 Gbytes) of the current user address space labelled *kuseg*. The virtual address is extended with the contents of the ASID field to form unique virtual addresses.

- *kseg0*. When the most significant three bits of the virtual address are 100, the virtual address space selected is the 2^{29}-byte (512-Mbyte) kernel physical space labelled *kseg0*. References to *kseg0* are not mapped through the TLB; the physical address selected is defined by subtracting 0x8000 0000 from the virtual address. Cacheability and coherency are controlled by the K0C field of the *Config* register.

- *kseg1*. When the most significant three bits of the virtual address are 101, the virtual address space selected is the 2^{29}-byte (512-Mbyte) kernel physical space labelled *kseg1*. References to *kseg1* are not mapped through the TLB; the physical address selected is defined by subtracting 0xa000 0000 from the virtual address. Caches are disabled for accesses to these addresses, and physical memory (or memory-mapped I/O device registers) are accessed directly.

- *ksseg*. When the most significant three bits of the virtual address are 110, the virtual address space selected is the 2^{29}-byte (512-Mbyte) supervisor virtual space labelled *ksseg*. The virtual address is extended with the contents of the ASID field to form unique virtual addresses.

- *kseg3*. When the most significant three bits of the virtual address are 111, the virtual address space selected is the 2^{29}-byte (512-Mbyte) kernel virtual space labelled *kseg3*. The virtual address is extended with the contents of the ASID field to form unique virtual addresses.

Figure 4–7 shows the boundaries of the five segments defined in this mode.

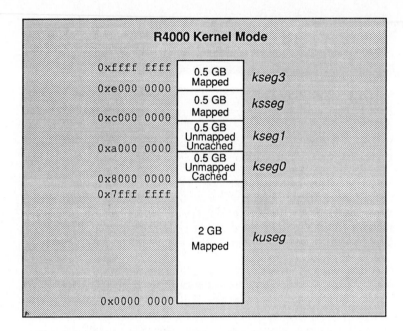

Figure 4–7. MIPS R4000 Kernel Mode Address Space

Virtual Memory and the TLB

Mapped virtual addresses are translated into physical addresses using a TLB, located either on-chip (in the R2000/R3000/R4000 implementation) or off-chip in a secondary cache (in the R6000).

R2000/R3000/R4000 TLBs

The R2000/R3000 TLB is a fully associative on-chip memory device that holds 64 entries to provide mapping of 64 4-Kbyte pages. The R4000 on-chip TLB holds 48 entries that provide mapping to 48 odd/even page pairs of sizes variable from 4 Kbytes to 16 Mbytes. When address mapping is indicated, each TLB entry is simultaneously checked for a match with the extended virtual address.

R6000 TLB

The R6000 TLB is located off-chip in a reserved area of the two-way set associative secondary cache. Unlike the other R-Series processors, the R6000 has virtual tag primary caches that support some MMU functions and does not need to make a full virtual-to-physical translation for each access. Also unlike the fully-associative on-chip TLBs of the R2000, R3000, and R4000 that are consulted on each access to memory, the in-cache TLB of the R6000 is only consulted when virtual address cache tags do not match on a memory access.

There are 64 32-word cache lines reserved for TLB entries in each set of the two-way set associative cache. For each cache line in the R6000 in-cache TLB, the corresponding virtual address cache tag holds the VPN and ASID fields. The data portion of the cache line contains 32 physical translations, covering a region of 512 Kbytes (32 16-Kbyte pages).

Coprocessors

The CPU supports up to four coprocessors, with certain limitations:

- an R6000 can use only one external coprocessor (CP1), in present implementations

- the R4000 supports only CP0 and CP1, both of which are on-chip.

CP0 is implemented as an integral part of the CPU, and supports address translation, exception handling, and other privileged operations. It also contains the registers shown in Figures 4–8, 4–9, and 4–10, plus one of the following TLBs:

- 64-entry TLB (R2000/R3000)

- 48-entry TLB (R4000)

- 16-entry TLB Slice (8 instruction, 8 data in R6000; 16 combined in R6000A)

The sections that follow describe how each of the TLB-related registers is used. (CP0 functions and registers associated with exception handling are described in Chapter 6.) The numeral accompanying each CP0 register in Figures 4–8, 4–9, and 4–10 refers to the register number, as described in Table NO TAG of Chapter 2.

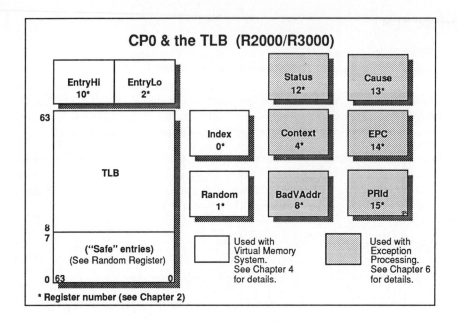

Figure 4–8. The R2000/R3000 CP0 Registers and the TLB.

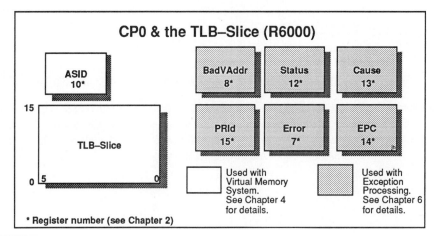

Figure 4–9. The R6000 CP0 Registers and the TLB Slice.

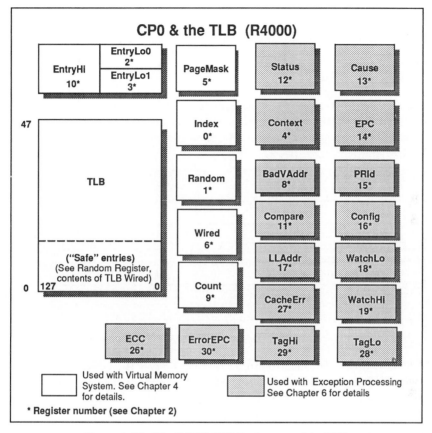

Figure 4–10. The R4000 CP0 Registers and the TLB.

TLB Entries

This section describes the format of the TLB entries for each of the R-Series processors.

R2000/R3000 TLB Entry Format

An R2000/R3000 TLB entry is 64 bits wide; Figure 4–11 shows the entry format. Each field of a R2000/R3000 TLB entry has a corresponding field in the *EntryHi/EntryLo* register pair described in the following section. Refer to Figure 4–12 for a description of the R2000/R3000 TLB entry fields.

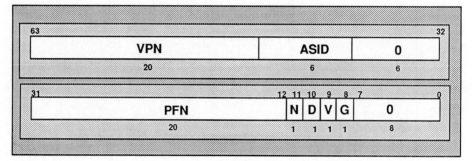

Figure 4–11. Format of an R2000/R3000 TLB Entry

The *EntryLo* register is the natural form of a Page Table Entry (PTE); however, since PTEs are always loaded by system software and not by the hardware, an operating system can use another format for memory-resident PTEs.

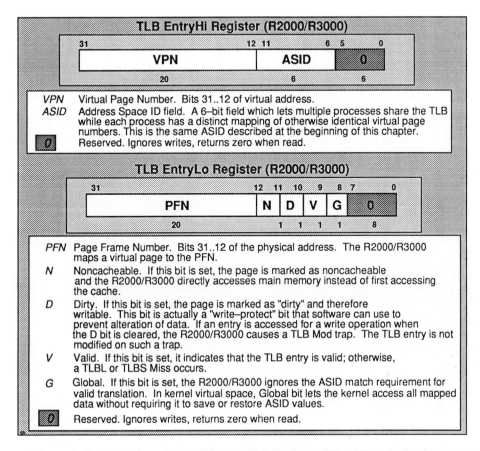

Figure 4–12. Fields in an R2000/R3000 TLB Entry (EntryHi and EntryLo Registers)

R4000 TLB Entry Format

Figure 4–13 shows an R4000 TLB entry. The entry stores 98 bits which, allowing for future expansion, are held in a 128-bit framework. Each field of an entry has a corresponding field in the *EntryHi*, *EntryLo0/1*, or *PageMask* registers, as shown in Figure 4–14.

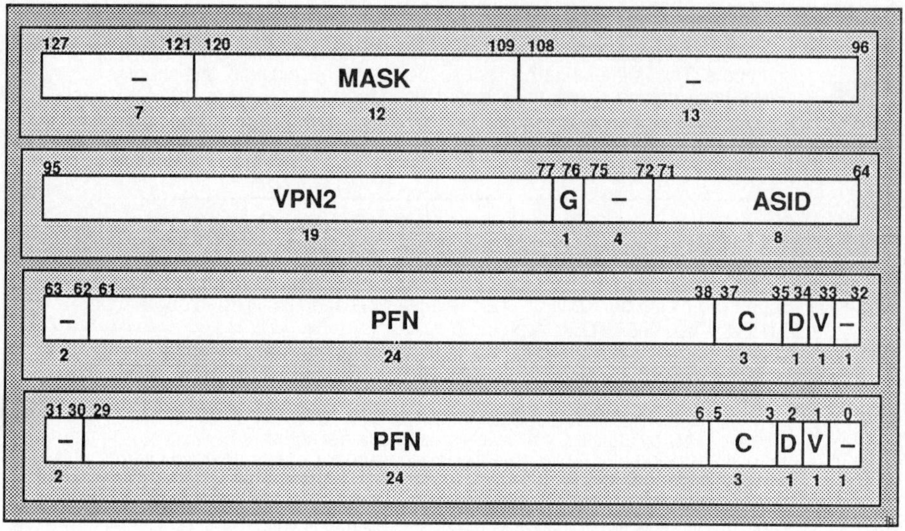

Figure 4–13. Format of an R4000 TLB Entry

The format of the R4000 *EntryHi*, *EntryLo0*, *EntryLo1*, and *PageMask* registers are nearly the same as the 98-bit TLB entry (the TLB uses the *Global* field, bit 76, which is reserved in the *EntryHi* register).

PageMask Register (R4000)

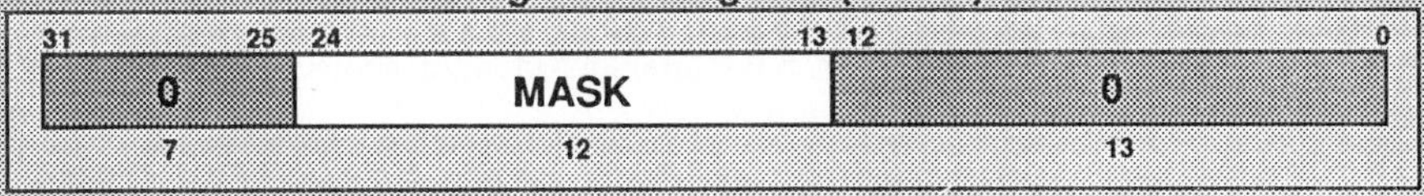

31	25 24		13 12		0
0		MASK		0	
7		12		13	

MASK	Page comparison mask
0	Reserved. Currently ignores writes, returns zero when read.

EntryHi Register (R4000)

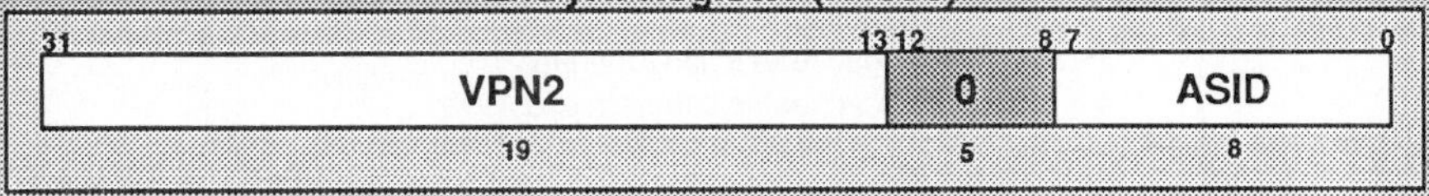

31	13 12	8 7	0
VPN2	0	ASID	
19	5	8	

VPN2	Virtual Page Number divided by two (maps to two pages)
ASID	Address Space ID field. An 8-bit field which lets multiple processes share the TLB while each process has a distinct mapping of otherwise identical virtual page numbers. This is the same ASID described at the beginning of this chapter.
0	Reserved. Ignores writes, returns zero when read.

EntryLo0 & EntryLo1 (R4000)

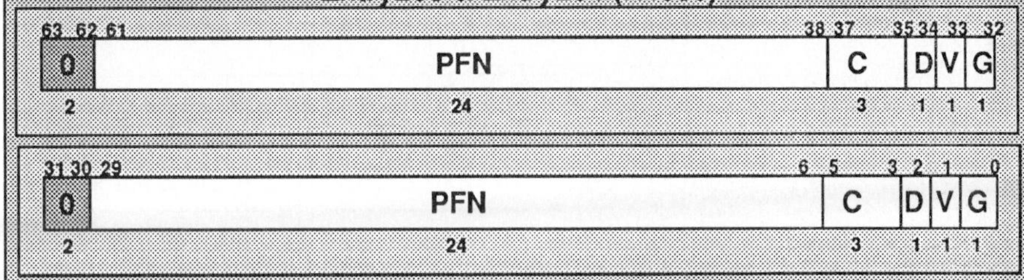

63 62 61		38 37	35 34 33 32
0	PFN	C	D V G
2	24	3	1 1 1

31 30 29		6 5	3 2 1 0
0	PFN	C	D V G
2	24	3	1 1 1

PFN	Page Frame Number. Upper bits of the physical address
C	Specifies the cache algorithm to be used; see Table 4–2.
D	Dirty. If this bit is set, the page is marked as "dirty" and therefore writable. This bit is actually a "write–protect" bit that software can use to prevent alteration of data.
V	Valid. If this bit is set, it indicates that the TLB entry is valid; otherwise, a TLBL or TLBS Miss occurs.
G	Global. If this bit is set in both Lo0 and Lo1, then ignore the ASID
0	Reserved. Ignores writes, returns zero when read.

Figure 4–14. Fields of an R4000 TLB Entry

The cache algorithm (C) bits specify whether references to the page should be cached; if cached, the algorithm selects between several cache coherency algorithms. Table 4–2 shows the algorithms selected by decoding the C bits (further information about the cache coherency algorithms is contained in Table 4–3).

Table 4–2. Cache Algorithm Bit Values

C Bit Value	Algorithm
0	reserved
1	reserved
2	uncached
3	cacheable noncoherent
4	cacheable coherent exclusive
5	cacheable coherent exclusive on write
6	cacheable coherent update on write
7	reserved

R6000 and R6000A TLB Entry Formats

The R6000/R6000A TLBs are held in a reserved portion of secondary cache; Figure 4–15 shows the formats of R6000 and R6000A TLB entries.

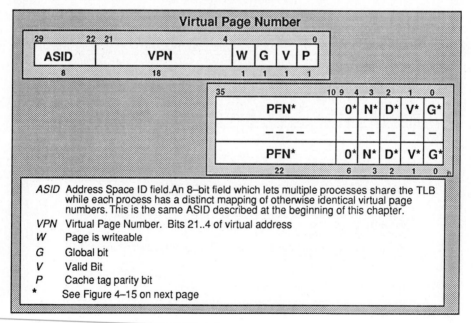

Figure 4–15. The R6000 and R6000A TLB Entries

Physical Page Number

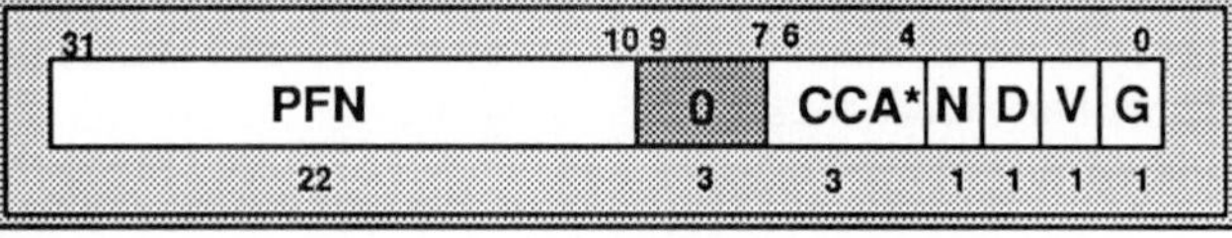

```
        31                        10 9   7 6     4          0
       ┌────────────────────────┬─────┬─────┬─┬─┬─┬─┐
       │          PFN           │  0  │CCA* │N│D│V│G│
       └────────────────────────┴─────┴─────┴─┴─┴─┴─┘
                  22               3     3   1 1 1 1
```

PFN	Page Frame Number. Bits 35..14 of the physical address
CCA*	Cache Coherency Algorithm (see Table 4–3). These bits are in R6000A only; they are zero in the R6000.
N	Noncacheable. If this bit is set, the page is marked as noncacheable and the CPU directly accesses main memory instead of the cache.
D	Dirty. If this bit is set, the page is marked as "dirty" and therefore writable. This bit is actually a "write–protect" bit that software can use to prevent alteration of data. If an entry is accessed for a write operation when the D bit is cleared, the CPU causes a TLB Mod trap. The TLB entry is not modified on such a trap.
V	Valid. If this bit is set, it indicates that the TLB entry is valid; otherwise, a TLBL or TLBS Miss occurs.
G	Global. If this bit is set, the CPU ignores the ASID match requirement for valid translation. In kernal virtual space, Global bit lets the kernel access all mapped data without requiring it to save or restore ASID values.
0	Reserved. Ignores writes, returns zero when read.

Figure 4–15. The R6000 and R6000A TLB Entry (cont.)

Table 4–3 shows the bit encoding for the *CCA* field (bits 6..4) in the R6000A TLB entry.

Table 4–3. CCA Field Encoding for R6000A TLB Entry

Cache Coherency Algorithmn Field Encoding				
Value	Attribute	Load Miss	Store Miss	Store Hit Shared
0	Reserved			
1	Reserved			
2	Noncacheable	Noncoherent Read Word	Noncoherent Write Word	Noncoherent Write Word
3	Cacheable Noncoherent	Noncoherent Read Block	Noncoherent Read Block	Noncoherent Write Word
4	Cacheable Coherent Exclusive	Coherent Read Block Exclusive	Coherent Read Block Exclusive	Coherent Write Word
5	Cacheable Coherent Shared	Coherent Read Block Shared	Coherent Read Block Exclusive	Coherent Write Word
6	Cacheable Coherent Update	Coherent Read Block Shared	Coherent Read Block Exclusive	Coherent Write Word
7	Reserved			

EntryHi, EntryLo, EntryLo0, EntryLo1, and PageMask Registers

These registers provide the data pathway through which the TLB is read, written, or probed. When address translation exceptions occur, these registers are loaded with relevant information about the address that caused the exception.

EntryHi Register (CPU Register 10)

The *EntryHi* register is a read/write register used to access an on-chip TLB (R2000, R3000, and R4000 processors). In addition, the *EntryHi* register contains the ASID used to match the virtual address with a TLB entry when virtual addresses are presented for translation.

The *EntryHi* register also holds the contents of the high order bits of a TLB entry when performing TLB read and write operations. When either a TLB refill, TLB invalid, or TLB modified exception occurs, the *EntryHi* register is loaded with the Virtual Page Number (VPN) and the ASID of the virtual address that failed to have a matching TLB entry.

EntryHi is accessed by the TLBP, TLBW, TLBWI, and TLBR instructions. Figures 4–12 and 4–14 show the format of this register.

EntryLo (2), EntryLo0 (2), and EntryLo1 (3) Registers

On R2000 and R3000 processors, the *EntryLo* register is a 32-bit read/write register used to access an on-chip TLB; *EntryLo* holds the low order 32 bits of a TLB entry when performing TLB read and write operations. On R4000 processors, *EntryLo* consists of two registers: *EntryLo0* for even virtual pages and *EntryLo1* for odd virtual pages. Figures 4–12 and 4–14 show the format of these registers.

PageMask Register (5)

The *PageMask* register, used only in the R4000, is a read/write register for reading from or writing to the on-chip TLB; it implements a variable page size by holding a per-entry comparison mask. TLB read and write operations use this register as a source or destination; when virtual addresses are presented for translation, the corresponding bits in the TLB specify which of the virtual address bits 24..13 participate in the comparison. Figure 4–14 shows the format of the *PageMask* register.

Table 4–4 gives MASK values for the full range of R4000 page sizes. When MASK is not one of these values, the operation of the TLB is undefined.

Table 4–4. MASK Values for Page Sizes

Page size	Bit											
	24	23	22	21	20	19	18	17	16	15	14	13
4 Kbytes	0	0	0	0	0	0	0	0	0	0	0	0
16 Kbytes	0	0	0	0	0	0	0	0	0	0	1	1
64 Kbytes	0	0	0	0	0	0	0	0	1	1	1	1
256 Kbytes	0	0	0	0	0	0	1	1	1	1	1	1
1 Mbyte	0	0	0	0	1	1	1	1	1	1	1	1
4 Mbytes	0	0	1	1	1	1	1	1	1	1	1	1
16 Mbytes	1	1	1	1	1	1	1	1	1	1	1	1

ASID Register (10)

The *ASID* register is a R/W register on the R6000; the ASID value is held in the low eight bits (0..7) of the register, and 0 is held in the remainder of the register. The R6000 *ASID* register placement, register 10, is the same as the R2000, R3000 and R4000 *EntryHi* register.

Figure 4–16 shows the format of the *ASID* register.

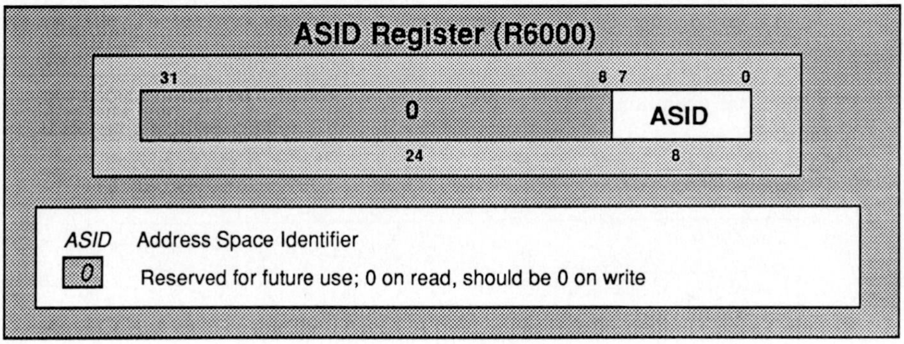

Figure 4–16. The ASID Register

Index Register (0)

The *Index* register, which is used in the R2000, R3000, and R4000 implementations, is a 32-bit, read/write register which contains six bits that index an entry in the on-chip TLB. The high order bit of the register shows the success or failure of a TLB Probe (TLBP) instruction (described at the end of this chapter).

The *Index* register also specifies the TLB entry that is affected by the TLB Read (TLBR) and TLB Write Index (TLBWI) instructions. Figure 4–17 shows the format of the *Index* register.

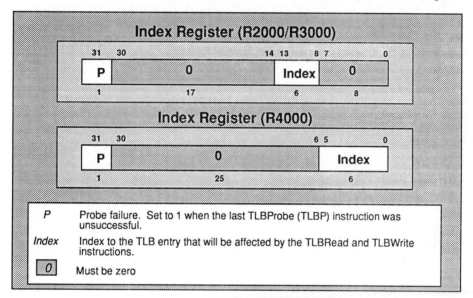

Figure 4–17. The Index Register

Random Register (1)

The *Random* register, which is used in the R2000, R3000, and R4000 implementations, is a read-only register of which six bits are used to index an entry in the on-chip TLB.

On R2000 and R3000 processors, the value of this register decrements on each machine clock cycle, whether or not the processor executes an instruction. On R4000 processors, this register decrements for each instruction executed. The values range between:

- a lower bound set by the number of TLB entries reserved for exclusive use by the operating system (8 on R2000 and R3000, and the contents of the *Wired* register on R4000 processors), and

- an upper bound set by the total number of TLB entries. For R2000 and R3000 processors the upper bound is 63; for R4000 processors the upper bound is 47.

The *Random* register specifies the entry in the TLB affected by the TLB Write Random instruction, TLBWR. The register does not need to be read for this purpose; however, the register is readable to verify proper operation of the processor.

To simplify testing, the *Random* register is set to the value of the upper bound upon system reset. On the R4000, this register is also set to the upper bound when the *Wired* register is written. The format of the *Random* register is shown in Figure 4–18.

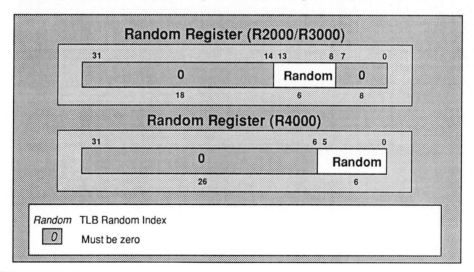

Figure 4–18. The Random Register

Wired Register (6)

The *Wired* register is an R4000 read/write register that specifies the boundary between the wired (fixed, nonreplaceable entries that cannot be overwritten) and random entries of the TLB. For R2000 and R3000 processors, this boundary is fixed at 8 and the *Wired* register is not available.

The *Wired* register is set to zero upon system reset. Writing this register also sets the *Random* register to the value of its upper bound (see *Random* Register, above).

Figure 4–19 shows the format of the *Wired* register.

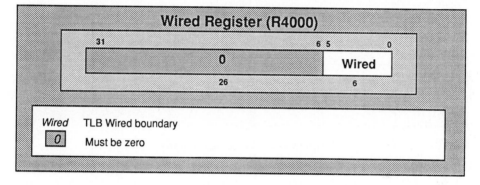

Figure 4–19. The Wired Register

Count Register (9)

The *Count* register is implemented on R4000 processors only, and acts as a timer, increment-ing at a constant rate whether or not an instruction is executed, retired, or any forward progress is made. The rate at which the *Count* register is incremented is dependent upon its implemen-tation; on R4000 processors this register increments at half the maximum instruction issue rate.

This register can be read or written; it can be written for diagnostic purposes or system initiali-zation to synchronize two processors operating in lock-step.

Figure 4–20 shows the format of the *Count* register.

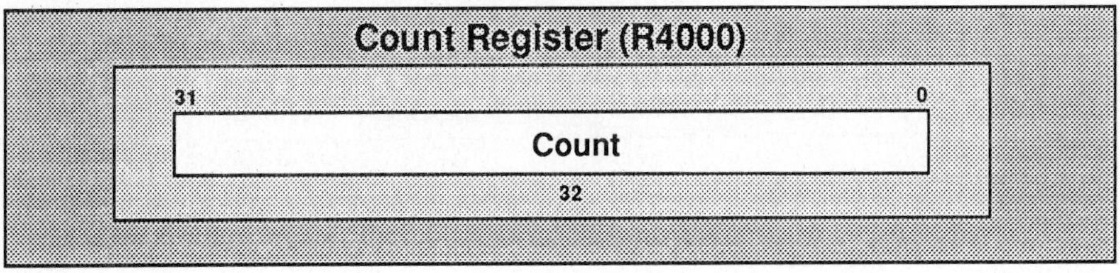

Count Register (R4000)

31	0
Count	
32	

Figure 4–20. The Count Register

Virtual Address Translation

This section describes the MIPS R-Series implementations of virtual-to-physical address translation.

R2000/R3000 Implementation

During virtual-to-physical address translation, the R2000/R3000 processors compare the ASID and the highest 20 bits (VPN) of the virtual address to the contents of the TLB. Figure 4–21 illustrates the TLB address translation process.

A virtual address matches a TLB entry when the VPN field of the virtual address equals the VPN field of the entry, and either the Global (G) bit of the TLB entry is set, or the ASID field of the virtual address (as held in the *EntryHi* register) matches the ASID field of the TLB entry. While the Valid (V) bit of the entry must be set for a valid translation to take place, it is not involved in the determination of a matching TLB entry.

If a TLB entry matches, the physical address and access control bits (N, D, and V, see Figure 4–12 for their descriptions) are retrieved from the matching TLB entry. Otherwise, a TLB or User TLB (UTLB) miss exception occurs. If the access control bits (D and V) indicate that the access is not valid, a TLB modification or TLB miss exception occurs. If the N bit is set, the physical address that is retrieved is used to access main memory, bypassing the cache.

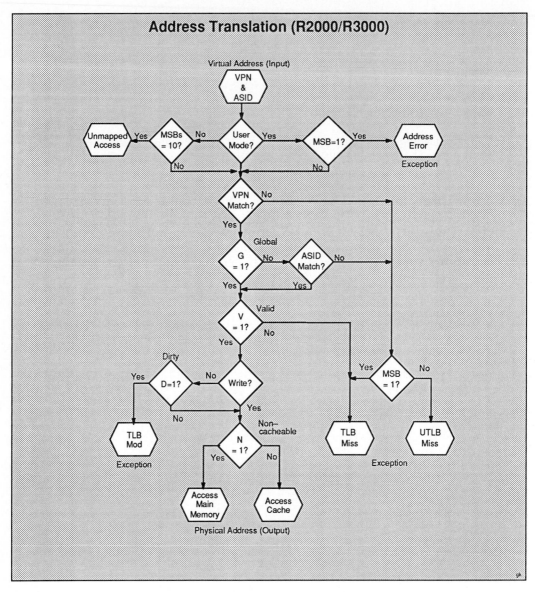

Figure 4–21. R2000/R3000 TLB Address Translation

R4000 Implementation

During virtual-to-physical address translation, the R4000 CPU compares the ASID and, depending upon the page size, the highest 8-to-20 bits (VPN) of the virtual address to the contents of the TLB. Figure 4–22 illustrates the TLB address translation process.

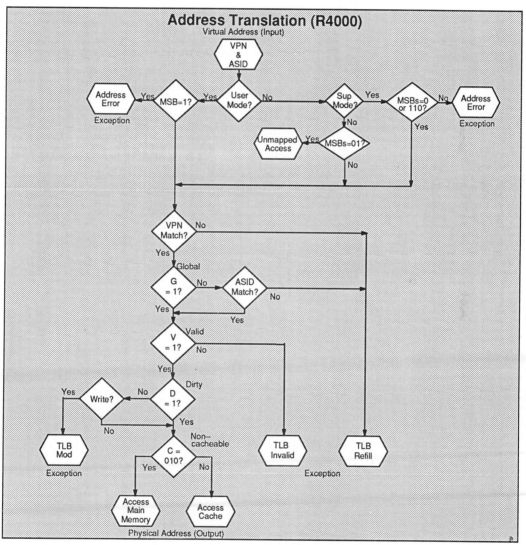

Figure 4–22. R4000 TLB Address Translation

A virtual address matches a TLB entry when the VPN field of the virtual address equals the VPN field of the entry, and either the *G* bit of the TLB entry is set or the ASID field of the virtual address (as held in the *EntryHi* register) matches the ASID field of the TLB entry. While the *V* bit of the entry must be set for a valid translation to take place, it is not involved in the determination of a matching TLB entry.

If a TLB entry matches, the physical address and access control bits (C, D, and V) are retrieved from the matching TLB entry. Otherwise, a TLB miss exception occurs. If the access control bits (D and V) indicate that the access is not valid, a TLB modification or TLB miss exception occurs. If the C bits equal binary 010, the physical address that is retrieved is used to access main memory, bypassing the cache.

R6000 Implementation

The R6000 TLB is in a reserved portion of the secondary cache, and is updated by software. Unlike the fully associative on-chip TLBs used in the R2000, R3000, and R4000 implementations (which are consulted on each access to memory), the R6000 retains some MMU information in the primary cache tags so the in-cache TLB is consulted only when virtual-address cache tags do not match on a memory access, or there is an unmapped access to *kseg0* or *kseg1*. For each cache line in the in-cache TLB, the corresponding virtual-address cache tag holds the VPN and ASID fields to determine the virtual address mapped by the set of TLB entries. Figure 4–23 illustrates the TLB address translation process.

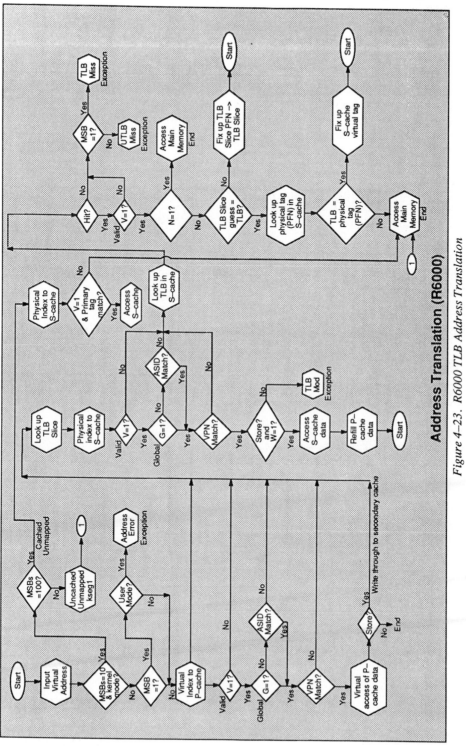

Figure 4–23. R6000 TLB Address Translation

Address Translation (R6000)

TLB Instructions

The instructions that the CPU provides for working with the TLB are listed in Table 4–5 and described briefly below. These instructions are valid only for processors with an on-chip TLB (R2000, R3000, and R4000). The R6000 uses the SCACHE, LCACHE, FLUSH, and IN-VALIDATE instructions to modify the TLB.

Table 4–5. TLB Instructions

Op Code	Description
TLBP	Translation Lookaside Buffer Probe
TLBR	Translation Lookaside Buffer Read
TLBWI	Translation Lookaside Buffer Write Index
TLBWR	Translation Lookaside Buffer Write Random

Translation Lookaside Buffer Probe (TLBP). The *Index* register is loaded with the address of the TLB entry whose contents match the contents of the *EntryHi* register. If no TLB entry matches, the high order bit of the *Index* register is set. The architecture does not specify the operation of memory references associated with the instruction immediately after a TLBP instruction, nor is the operation specified if more than one TLB entry matches.

Translation Lookaside Buffer Read (TLBR). This instruction loads the *EntryHi* and *EntryLo* registers with the contents of the TLB entry specified by the contents of the *Index* register.

Translation Lookaside Buffer Write Index (TLBWI). This instruction loads the specified TLB entry with the contents of the *EntryHi* and *EntryLo* registers. The contents of the *Index* register specify the TLB entry.

Translation Lookaside Buffer Write Random (TLBWR). This instruction loads a pseudo-randomly-specified TLB entry with the contents of the *EntryHi* and *EntryLo* registers. The contents of the *Random* register specify the TLB entry.

5
Caches

Cache Designs

The time needed to access (fetch) an instruction is largely reliant upon the speed of the system memory. This access time often becomes the limiting factor in RISC-type designs, because of the high rate at which instructions can execute. Achieving a completion rate of one instruction/cycle is impossible unless the memory system delivers instructions at the cycle rate of the processor. As mentioned in Chapter 1, a variety of techniques can furnish the required memory bandwidth needed to support high-performance RISC designs. Two commonly used techniques are listed below.

The first technique uses high-speed cache memory to provide a primary pool of reusable instructions and data that are accessed more frequently by the processor. Figure 5–1 shows the functional position of cache memory in such a hierarchical memory system.

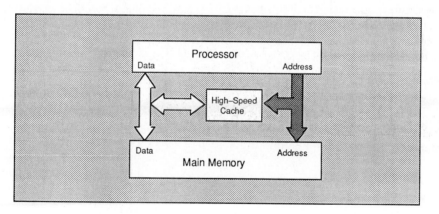

Figure 5–1. Functional Position of a Cache in a Hierarchical Memory System

A second technique uses separate caches for instructions (I-cache) and data (D-cache) to double the effective cache-memory bandwidth. The access time of the cache-memory devices can be the limiting factor for processor throughput; use of separate caches allows the processor simultaneous access to instruction cache and data cache.

Figure 5–2 illustrates a memory system with separate caches for instructions and data.

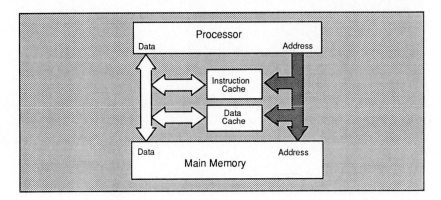

Figure 5–2. System with a Dual-Cache Memory System

The use of separate caches for instructions and data has an additional benefit beyond increasing the bandwidth: caches can be tailored to suit the individual instruction and data reference patterns. This is the reason, for instance, that the R6000 has different line lengths for the I-cache and the D-cache.

Separate caches have an additional benefit: separate instruction and data streams reduce the likelihood of contention for specific sets that can occur in direct-mapped caches. By splitting a direct-mapped unified in cache in two, a form of associativity is introduced that reduces the poor performance resulting from frequent references to different addresses that map onto the same set.

MIPS Cache Memory

MIPS processors are normally configured with separate instruction and data caches (as shown in Figure 5–2), and in some cases employ a secondary cache as well. A configuration can also have variable cache sizes, within the implementation-dependent minimum and maximum cache size limits listed in Table 5–1.

Table 5–1. MIPS Processor Cache Sizes

Implementation	Minimum Cache Size	Maximum Cache Size
R2000 (I- or D-cache)	4 Kbytes	64 Kbytes
R3000 (I- or D-cache)	4 Kbytes	256 Kbytes
R4000 (I-cache)	8 Kbytes	32 Kbytes
R4000 (D-cache)	8 Kbytes	32 Kbytes
R4000 (Secondary cache)	128 Kbytes	4 Mbytes
R6000 (I-cache, primary)	16 Kbytes	64 Kbytes
R6000 (D-cache, primary)	16 Kbytes	16 Kbytes
R6000 (Secondary cache)	512 Kbytes	2 Mbytes

When a processor has both an instruction cache and a data cache, the two caches need not be the same size. R4000 processors have I- and D-caches on-chip, and consequently are fixed in size for a given implementation. R6000 processors use a combined instruction-and-data second-level cache, which is two-set associative containing either 512 Kbytes or 2 Mbytes. The primary cache size is determined by logic outside the R6000 processor chip.

Pseudocode descriptions of the cache are given below, using the following implementation-dependent pseudocode variables:

- CACHESIZE, the number of words in the cache
- CACHEBITS, the base-two log of the number of bytes in the cache.

CACHESIZE and CACHEBIT values are given in Table 5–2.

Table 5–2. Pseudocode Descriptions of Cache Configurations

Cache Size (in bytes)	CACHESIZE (words)	CACHEBITS
4 K	1024	12
8 K	2048	13
16 K	4096	14
32 K	8192	15
64 K	16384	16
128 K	32768	17
256 K	65536	18
512 K	131072	19
1 M	262144	20
2 M	524288	21
4 M	1048576	22

R4000 and R6000 processors use a single tag for multiple data words; the set of data words and their accompanying tag is called a *cache line*. R4000 and R6000 processors use the following implementation-dependent variables:

- LINESIZE, the number of words in a cache line

- LINEBITS, the base-two log of the number of bytes in a cache line.

The values for these variables are listed in Table 5–3.

Table 5–3. Cache Line Definitions

Line Size (in bytes)	LINESIZE (in words)	LINEBITS
16	4	4
32	8	5
64	16	6
128	32	7
256	64	8

R2000 Caches

The R2000 instruction and data caches are:

- write-through
- direct-mapped
- indexed with a physical address
- checked with a physical tag
- organized with 1-word (4-byte) cache line
- refilled with a data block of 1 word (4 bytes) on a cache miss.

Separate caches are accessed for cached instruction and data fetches. For R2000 processors, instruction and data cache lines consist of:

- a single 32-bit word
- a cache tag
- a valid bit

The data field is protected by four bits of parity and the tag field is protected by three bits of parity. The low order bits of the physical address select a single cache line (direct mapped). A cache *hit* occurs when the cache tag matches the physical address and the valid bit is set. On a cache *miss,* the processor reads one word from memory and refills the cache.

Word stores to cached addresses write both the data cache and memory (a write-through cache) and cannot miss. Partial-word stores to cached addresses, such as those generated by SB, SH, and sometimes SWL/SWR instructions, unconditionally invalidate the addressed cache line (write around). Figure 5–3 shows the format of the R2000 cache word.

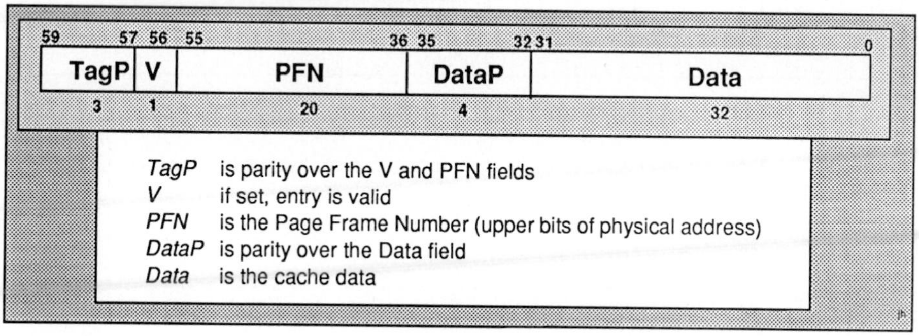

59 57	56	55 36	35 32	31 0
TagP	**V**	**PFN**	**DataP**	**Data**
3	1	20	4	32

TagP   is parity over the V and PFN fields
V   if set, entry is valid
PFN   is the Page Frame Number (upper bits of physical address)
DataP   is parity over the Data field
Data   is the cache data

Figure 5–3. Format of R2000 Cache Word

R3000 Caches

The R3000 instruction and data caches are:

- write-through

- direct-mapped

- indexed with a physical address

- checked with a physical tag

- organized with 1-word (4-byte) cache line

- refilled selectably with data blocks of either 4 words (16 bytes), 8 words (32 bytes), 16 words (64 bytes), or 32 words (128 bytes) on a cache miss.

The R3000 caches are similar to those of the R2000, having the following two additional configuration options, both of which are selected when the processor is reset.

If *store partial* mode is selected, partial-word stores take two cycles. First the addressed cache line is read; then, on a cache hit, updated data is written into the cache and a full-word write is sent to memory. On a miss the cache is not modified and the partial-word write is sent to memory.

If *multi-word refill* mode is selected, a cache miss is read from main memory, and the CACHEREFILL number of words is written into the cache, (where CACHEREFILL can be set to 4, 8, 16, or 32 words).

Figure 5–4 shows the format of the R3000 cache word.

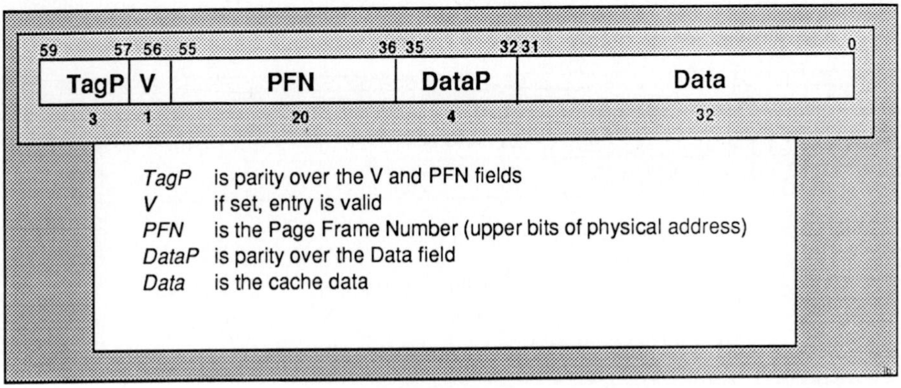

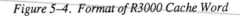

59 57	56	55 36	35 32	31 0
TagP	V	PFN	DataP	Data
3	1	20	4	32

TagP is parity over the V and PFN fields
V   if set, entry is valid
PFN   is the Page Frame Number (upper bits of physical address)
DataP is parity over the Data field
Data is the cache data

Figure 5–4. Format of R3000 Cache Word

MIPS RISC Architecture

R4000 Caches

The R4000 has an on-chip primary cache system consisting of separate instruction and data caches, and the R4000 can support an optional off-chip secondary cache as well. This configuration is shown in Figure 5–5.

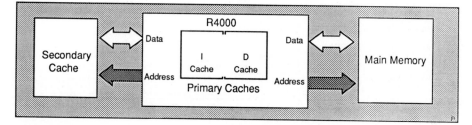

Figure 5–5. R4000 Cache System

R4000 Primary Instruction Cache

The R4000 primary instruction cache is:

- direct-mapped

- indexed with a virtual address

- checked with a physical tag

- organized with either a 4-word (16-byte) or 8-word (32-byte) cache line

- refilled selectably with data blocks of either 4 words (16 bytes) or 8 words (32 bytes) on a cache miss.

The R4000 primary instruction cache is organized as blocks of data assigned a 25-bit tag. The tag holds a 24-bit physical address and a single valid bit. Byte parity is used on the instruction data, and a single parity bit is used for the tag. The format of a 32-byte primary instruction cache line is shown in Figure 5–6.

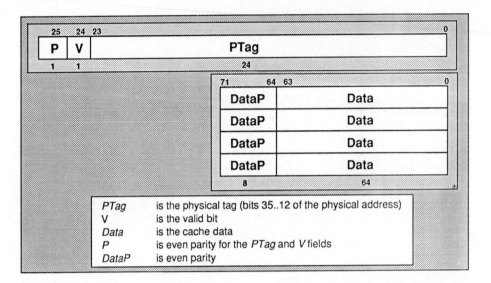

Figure 5–6. Format of R4000 Primary Instruction Cache Line

R4000 Primary Data Cache

The R4000 primary data cache is:

- write-back

- direct-mapped

- indexed with a virtual address

- checked with a physical tag

- organized with either a 4-word (16-byte) or 8-word (32-byte) cache line

- refilled selectably with data blocks of either 4 words (16 bytes) or 8 words (32 bytes) on a cache miss.

The R4000 primary data cache is organized as blocks of data with a 27-bit tag. The tag holds a 24-bit physical address, a 2-bit cache line state, and a write-back bit. Byte parity is used for data protection: a single parity bit is used for the tag and the write-back bit has its own parity bit.

Figure 5–7 shows the format of a 32-byte primary data cache line.

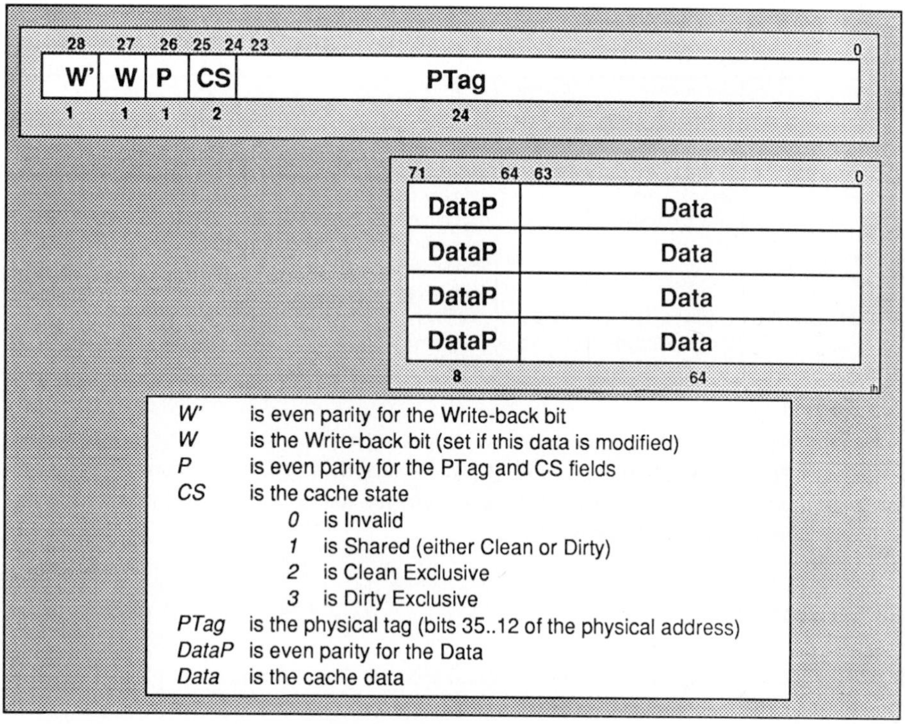

28	27	26	25 24	23	0
W'	W	P	CS	PTag	
1	1	1	2	24	

71	64	63	0
DataP		Data	
DataP		Data	
DataP		Data	
DataP		Data	
8		64	

W'	is even parity for the Write-back bit
W	is the Write-back bit (set if this data is modified)
P	is even parity for the PTag and CS fields
CS	is the cache state
	0 is Invalid
	1 is Shared (either Clean or Dirty)
	2 is Clean Exclusive
	3 is Dirty Exclusive
PTag	is the physical tag (bits 35..12 of the physical address)
DataP	is even parity for the Data
Data	is the cache data

Figure 5–7. Format of R4000 Primary Data Cache Line

In all R4000 processors, the *W* (write-back) bit, not the cache state, indicates when the primary cache contains modified data that must be written back to memory or the secondary cache.

In R4000 processors without a secondary cache, two states indicate whether the cache line is valid (*Invalid* and *Dirty Exclusive*). In R4000 processors with a secondary cache, four states (*Invalid, Shared, Clean Exclusive*, and *Dirty Exclusive*) control whether load or store operations need to access the secondary cache for coherency purposes. These four states are described in Table 5–4.

Table 5–4. R4000 Cache Coherency States

Primary State	Secondary States	Action On Load	Action On Store
Invalid	All	Miss	Miss
Shared	Shared Dirty Shared Dirty Exclusive	None	Read secondary cache tag. If Dirty Exclusive, set primary state to Dirty Exclusive; otherwise if coherency algorithm is Update On Write, then send update and set secondary cache state to Dirty Shared; otherwise send invalidate and set primary and secondary states to Dirty Exclusive.
Clean Exclusive	Clean Exclusive	none	Set data and secondary cache states to Dirty Exclusive.
	Dirty Exclusive	none	Set data cache state to Dirty Exclusive.
Dirty Exclusive	Dirty Exclusive	none	none

When the primary cache is filled from the secondary cache, the secondary cache state is mapped into primary cache state by folding the *Shared* and *Dirty Shared* secondary states into the *Shared* primary state. The *Dirty Exclusive* primary state allows the primary cache to be written without a secondary access.

R4000 Secondary Cache

R4000 processors support an optional external secondary cache which can be configured at chip reset a either one joint cache, or separate I-cache and D-cache. This secondary cache is:

- write-back

- direct-mapped

- indexed with a physical address

- checked with a physical tag

- organized with either a 4-word (16-byte), 8-word (32-byte), 16 -word (64-byte), or 32-word (128-byte) cache line

- refilled selectably with data blocks of either 4 words (16 bytes), 8 words (32 bytes), 16 words (64 bytes), or 32 words (128 bytes) on a cache miss.

This 25-bit tag holds a 19-bit physical address, a 3-bit cache line state, and a 3-bit primary cache index. The tag is protected by a 7-bit error correction code, and contains bits 35..17 of the physical address.

Figure 5–8 shows the format of the R4000 secondary-cache line.

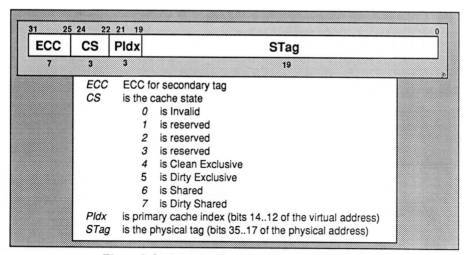

Figure 5–8. Format of R4000 Secondary Cache Line

The cache state (*CS* bits) indicates whether

- the cache line data and tag are valid,

- the data is at least potentially present in the caches of other processors (*Shared* versus *Exclusive*)

- the processor is responsible for updating main memory (*Clean* versus *Dirty*).

The R4000 primary caches must be a subset of the secondary cache. R4000 processors maintain this subset property by checking and invalidating the primary caches if necessary, when a secondary cache line is replaced. The PIdx field allows the processor to locate those primary cache blocks, indexed in the primary cache by a virtual (not physical) address, that may contain data from this secondary cache block.

A second function of the PIdx field is to detect a cache alias. If the physical address tag matches during a data reference to the secondary cache (S-cache), but the PIdx field does not match the appropriate bits in the virtual address, the reference was made from a different virtual address than the one that created the S-cache line. Since this could create a cache alias, the processor signals this condition by taking a Virtual Coherency exception (see Chapter 6).

R6000 Caches

The R6000 has a two-level cache system that includes two primary caches (for data and instructions), and a single secondary cache which holds both instructions and data. This cache organization is shown in Figure 5–9.

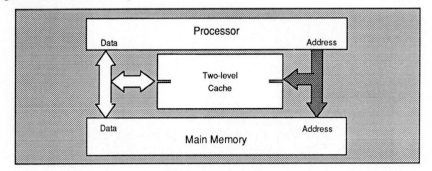

Figure 5–9. R6000 Cache

R6000 Primary Caches

The R6000 primary data cache is:

- write-through
- direct-mapped
- indexed with a virtual address
- checked with a virtual tag
- organized with a 2-word (8-byte) cache line
- refilled with data blocks of 2 words (8 bytes) on a cache miss.

The R6000 primary instruction cache is:

- direct-mapped
- indexed with a virtual address
- checked with a virtual tag
- organized with a 8-word (32-byte) cache line
- refilled with data blocks of 8 words (32 bytes) on a cache miss.

The R6000 primary instruction and data caches have separate parity for each byte. Associated with each line is a 30-bit primary cache tag. The virtual address selects a single cache line (direct mapped).

The tag holds:

- an 8-bit address space identifier (ASID)

- an 18-bit virtual page number (VPN)

- 4 1-bit values denoting writable, global, valid, and tag parity values.

The format of a 32-byte primary instruction cache line is shown in Figure 5–10.

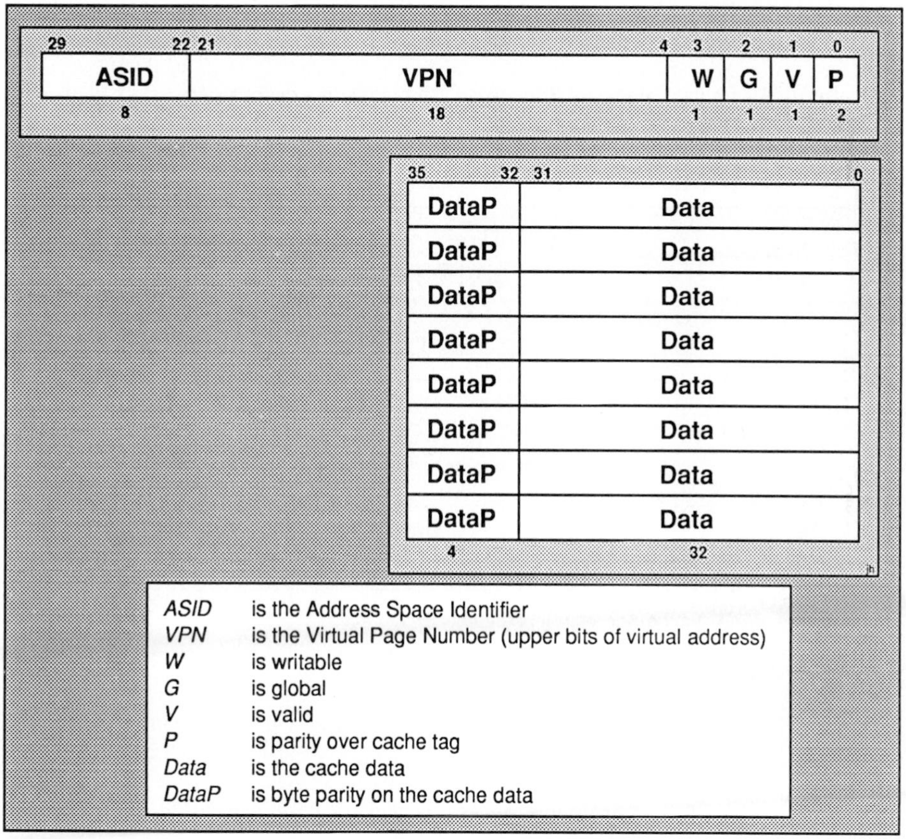

Figure 5–10. Format of R6000 Primary Instruction Cache Line

The first-level instruction and data caches hold the virtual cache tags. Reuse of virtual addresses, including the reassignment of ASIDs, may require software to invalidate the contents of the instruction and data caches.

R6000 Secondary Cache

The R6000 secondary cache is:

- write-back
- 2-way set associative
- indexed with a physical address
- checked with a virtual and physical tags
- organized with a 32-word (128-byte) cache line
- refilled with data blocks of 32 words (128 bytes) on a cache miss.

The R6000 secondary cache holds both instructions and data, with a per-word dirty bit. Associated with each line are 30 additional bits of secondary cache tag, as shown in Figure 5–11.

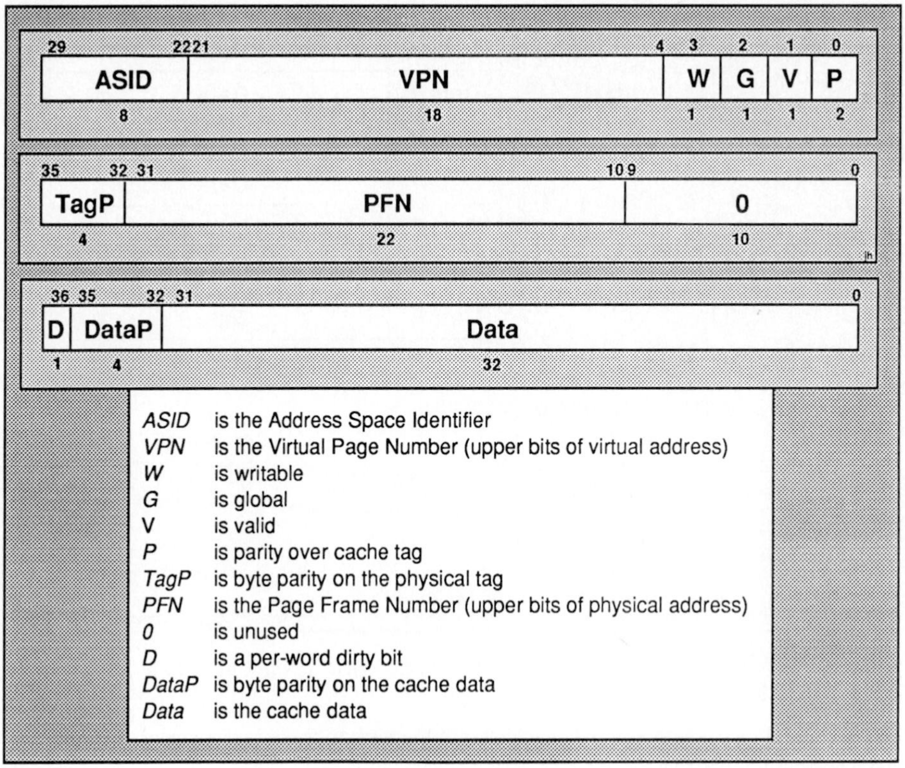

29 22 21		4 3	2	1	0
ASID	VPN	W	G	V	P
8	18	1	1	1	2

35 32 31	10 9	0
TagP	PFN	0
4	22	10

36 35 32 31	0
D	DataP	Data
1	4	32

ASID	is the Address Space Identifier
VPN	is the Virtual Page Number (upper bits of virtual address)
W	is writable
G	is global
V	is valid
P	is parity over cache tag
TagP	is byte parity on the physical tag
PFN	is the Page Frame Number (upper bits of physical address)
0	is unused
D	is a per-word dirty bit
DataP	is byte parity on the cache data
Data	is the cache data

Figure 5–11. Format of R6000 Secondary Cache Line

The secondary cache consists of two associative sets. Each may contain either 256 Kbytes or 1 Mbyte of data, for a total cache size of either 512 Kbytes or 2 Mbytes. The high 32 Kbytes of this 512-Kbyte/2-Mbyte space is reserved for the in-cache Translation Lookaside Buffer (TLB) and physical tags. Physical addresses that would otherwise access this portion of the cache are mapped instead to another 32-Kbyte area of the cache.

The secondary cache is indexed with a physical address and both virtual and physical tags are stored. A match on the virtual tag indicates a cache hit; a mismatch on the virtual tag indicates either a cache miss or an incorrect virtual-to-physical address translation. The physical tags are then used to detect virtual address aliasing and are checked after translating the virtual-to-physical address using the in-cache TLB.

When the virtual-to-physical memory mapping is changed (including the reassignment of ASIDs), software must flush the contents of the secondary cache virtual tags. A subsequent reference to the same physical address causes the virtual tag to regenerate.

6

Exception Processing

This chapter describes how MIPS R-Series processors handle exceptions and also describes those CP0 registers that are used during exception processing. For a description of the remaining CP0 registers, please see Chapter 4.

When the CPU detects an exception, the normal sequence of instruction execution is suspended; the processor exits User mode and is forced into Kernel mode where it can respond to the abnormal or asynchronous event. All events that initiate exception processing are described in this chapter. Table 6–1 lists the exceptions that the CPU recognizes.

The CPU exception handling system efficiently handles machine exceptions, including Translation Lookaside Buffer (TLB) misses, arithmetic overflows, I/O interrupts, and system calls. All of these events interrupt normal execution flow; the CPU aborts the instruction causing the exception and also aborts all subsequent instructions in the pipeline which have begun execution. The CPU then performs a direct jump into a designated exception handler routine.

Implementation

When an exception occurs, the CPU loads the Exception Program Counter (*EPC*) with a restart location where execution may resume after the exception has been serviced. The restart location in the *EPC* is the address of the instruction that caused the exception or, if the instruction was executing in a branch delay slot, the address of the branch instruction immediately preceding the delay slot.

Table 6–1. CPU Exception Types

Name	Cause Code	Description
Reset	–	The reset exception aborts the current execution stream and starts executing at the reset vector. A separate vector is provided for this exception.
Soft Reset	–	(R4000 only) The soft reset exception aborts the current execution stream and starts executing at the reset vector. Soft Reset is used to reinitialize the processor without going through the entire Reset hardware sequence.
NMI	–	(R4000 only) This is a nonmaskable interrupt requested by external logic. Since the Reset vector is used for this interrupt, the system must reset after this exception.
TLB Refill	TLBL/TLBS	The referenced address did not match any TLB entry. A separate vector is provided for this exception. On R4000 processors, this vector is used for all virtual address spaces when the *Status* register *EXL* bit is 0; for the R2000, R3000, and R6000, this exception is used only for references to the user address space from either Kernel or User mode. (See TLB Refill Exception in this chapter for explanation of TLBL and TLBS.)
TLB Invalid	TLBL/TLBS	Virtual address reference that matches an invalid TLB entry. (See TLB Refill Exception in this chapter for explanation of TLBL and TLBS.)
TLB Modified	Mod	An attempt to write to a virtual address that did not have *D* bit set in the corresponding TLB entry.
Bus Error	IBE/DBE	An external interrupt signaled by bus interface circuitry. A bus error is signaled for events such as bus time-out, bus parity errors, and invalid memory addresses or access types. (See Bus Error Exception in this chapter for explanation of IBE and DBE.)
Address Error	AdEL/AdES	An attempt is made to load, fetch, or store a word not aligned on a word boundary, or load or store a halfword not aligned on a halfword boundary, or load or store a doubleword not aligned on a doubleword boundary, or to reference a privileged virtual address. (See Address Error Exception in this chapter for explanation of AdEL and AdES.)
Integer Overflow	Ov	An add or subtract operation causes 2's-complement overflow.
Trap	Tr	A trap operation was executed with a true condition.
System Call	Sys	Execution of a SYSCALL instruction.
Breakpoint	Bp	Execution of a BREAK instruction.
Coprocessor Unusable	CpU	Execution of a coprocessor instruction for which the corresponding coprocessor-usable bit was not set.
Floating-Point Exception	FPE	(R4000 only) One of several floating-point exceptions. See Chapter 9.
Interrupt	Int	One of several interrupt conditions. See the *Cause* register.
Machine Check	MC	(R6000 only) Fatal parity error detected.
Uncached LDC1/SDC1	NCD	(R6000 only) LDC1/SDC1 to an uncached address.
Virtual Coherency	VCEI/VCED	(R4000 only) Different virtual indexes used in primary cache for the same physical location.
Cache error	-	(R4000 only) Parity error in primary cache, or ECC error in secondary cache.
Watch	WATCH	(R4000 only) Reference to *WatchHi*/*WatchLo* address.

The Exception Handling Registers

The CP0 registers listed in numerical order below contain information that is related to exception processing. The software examines these registers during exception processing to determine the cause of an exception and the state of the CPU at the time of an exception. Each of these registers is described in detail in the sections that follow.

- *Context* register, (CP0 register number 4)

- *Error* register, (CP0 register number 7)

- *BadVAddr* (Bad Virtual Address) register, (CP0 register number 8)

- *Compare* register, (CP0 register number 11)

- *Status* register, (CP0 register number 12)

- *Cause* register, (CP0 register number 13)

- *EPC* (Exception Program Counter) register, (CP0 register number 14)

- *PRId* (Processor Revision Identifier) register, (CP0 register number 15)

- *Config* register, (CP0 register number 16)

- *LLAdr* (Load Linked Address) register, (CP0 register number 17)

- *WatchLo* (Memory Reference Trap Address Low) register, (CP0 register number 18)

- *WatchHi* (Memory Reference Trap Address High) register, (CP0 register number 19)

- *ECC* register, (CP0 register number 26)

- *CacheErr* (Cache Error and Status) register, (CP0 register number 27)

- *TagLo* (Cache Tag) register, (CP0 register number 28)

- *TagHi* (Cache Tag) register, (CP0 register number 29)

- *ErrorEPC* (Error Exception Program Counter) register, (number 30)

Two other CP0 registers, the *Index* register (number 0) and the *Random* register (number 1), implement the virtual memory management system and contain information of interest when handling exceptions related to virtual memory errors. Refer to Chapter 4 for a description of these two registers.

Context Register (CP0 Register 4)

The *Context* register is a read/write register containing a pointer into a kernel virtual Page Table Entry (PTE) array. It is used in the TLB refill handler, which loads TLB entries for normal User-mode references. The *Context* register is used only for an on-chip TLB (R2000, R3000, and R4000) and is not valid for R6000 implementations.

The *Context* register duplicates some of the information provided in the *BadVAddr* register, but provides information in a form that may be more useful for a software TLB exception handler.

The *Context* register can hold a pointer into the PTE. The operating system sets the PTE base field in the register, as needed. Normally, the operating system uses the *Context* register to address the current user process page map, which resides in the kernel-mapped segment *kseg2*. This register is included solely for use of the operating system.

For all addressing exceptions (except bus errors), this register holds the Virtual Page Number (VPN) from the most recent virtual address for which the translation was invalid. Figure 6–1 shows the format of the *Context* register.

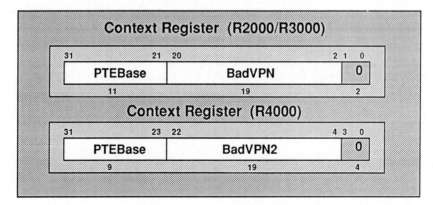

Figure 6–1. Context Register Format

Bit descriptions of the *Context* register are:

- The BadVPN field is not writable. It contains the VPN of the most recently translated virtual address that did not have a valid translation.

- The PTEBase is a read/write field. It indicates the base address of the PTE table of the current user address space.

For R2000 and R3000 processors, the 19-bit BadVPN field contains bits 30..12 (user-segment virtual page number) of the *BadVAddr* register. Bit 31 is excluded because the User TLB (UTLB) miss handler is only invoked on user-segment references.

For R4000 processors, the 19-bit *BadVPN2* field contains bits 31..13 of the virtual address that caused the TLB miss; bit 12 is excluded because a single TLB entry maps to an even-odd page pair. This format can be used directly as an address in a table of pairs of 8-byte PTEs, for a 4-Kbyte page size. For other page and PTE sizes, shifting and masking this value produces an appropriate address.

Error Register (7)

The *Error* register is used only in the R6000, as a control/status register for parity. Figure 6–2 shows the format of the *Error* register.

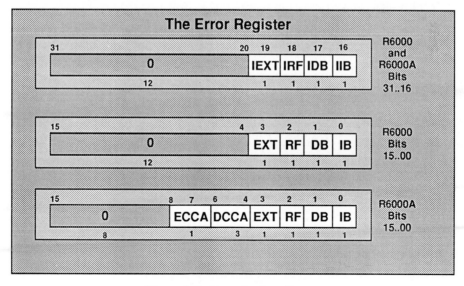

Figure 6–2. Error Register Format

Bit descriptions of the *Error* register are:

- *IEXT* causes the CPU to ignore parity errors that are detected off-chip and re-ported to the CPU by the External Parity Error signal. These include both tag parity errors and external coprocessor parity errors. *Error* register bits are set to reflect the error but no exception will be generated.

- *IRF* causes the CPU to ignore parity errors that are detected from the register file. These errors are not propagated outside the chip because parity is regenerated before it is sent out over the data bus. *Error* register bits are set to reflect the error but no exception is generated.

- *IDB* causes the CPU to ignore parity errors that are detected from the data bus. This covers loads and MFCz operations. *Error* register bits are set to reflect the error but no exception is generated.

- *IIB* causes the CPU to ignore parity errors that are detected from the I-cache bus. *Error* register bits are set to reflect the error but no exception is generated.

- *ECCA* is set to enable the TLB CCA field; if cleared, the default Cache Coherency Algorithm (CCA) is used (see Chapter 4). This bit is cleared at reset.

- *DCCA* is the default CCA for unmapped space, and is used as the CCA when the *ECCA* bit is cleared. This field is initialized to 3 at reset (see Chapter 4 for CCA description); DCCA values of 0, 1, or 2 are undefined.

- *EXT* is set when an external parity error (external parity error chip input) is detected. It is reset by writing a 1 to this bit position.

- *RF* is set when a CPU register file parity error is detected. It is reset by writing a 1 to this bit position.

- *DB* is set when a parity error is detected on the data bus during a load or an MFCz. It is reset by writing a 1 to this bit position.

- *IB* is set when a parity error is detected on the I-cache bus. It is reset by writing a 1 to this bit position.

BadVAddr Register (8)

The *Bad Virtual Address* register is a read-only register that displays the most recently translated virtual address that failed to have a valid translation. Figure 6–3 shows the format of the *Bad Virtual Address* register.

Note: The *Bad Virtual Address* register does not save any information for bus errors. because they are not addressing errors.

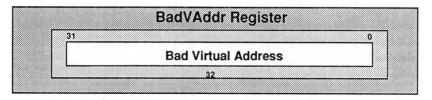

Figure 6–3. BadVAddr Register Format

Compare Register (11)

The *Compare* register, which is available only on the R4000, implements a timer service (also see the *Count* register) which maintains a stable value and does not change on its own. When the value of the *Count* register equals the value of the *Compare* register, interrupt bit IP_7 in the *Cause* register is set. This causes an interrupt to be taken on the next execution cycle in which the interrupt is enabled. Writing a value to the *Compare* register, as a side effect, clears the timer interrupt.

For diagnostic purposes, the *Compare* register is read/write. In normal use however, the *Compare* register is only written. Figure 6–4 shows the format of the *Compare* register.

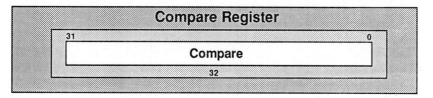

Figure 6–4. Compare Register Format

Status Register (12)

The *Status* register (SR) is a read/write register that contains Kernel and User mode, interrupt enable, and the diagnostic states of the processor. The following list describes *Status* register fields that are used in all R-Series processors; format of the register is shown in Figures 6–5 and 6–6.

- The Interrupt Mask (IM) field is an 8-bit field that controls the enabling of eight interrupt conditions. An interrupt is taken if interrupts are enabled, and the corresponding bits are set in both the Interrupt Mask field of the *Status* register and the Interrupt Pending field of the *Cause* register. The actual width of this register is implementation-dependent; for more information, refer to the Interrupt Pending (IP) field of the *Cause* register.

- The Coprocessor Usability (CU) field is a 4-bit field that controls the usability of four possible coprocessors. Regardless of the CU_0 bit setting, CP0 is *always* considered usable in Kernel mode.

- The Diagnostic Status (*DS*) field is an implementation-dependent 9-bit field used for self-testing, and checking the cache and virtual memory system.

On some processors (R3000A, R4000, and R6000), the Reverse Endian *(RE)* bit, bit 25, is used to reverse the endianness of the machine in User mode. R-Series processors are configured as either Little-endian or Big-endian at system reset. This selection is used in Kernel, Supervisor, and User modes when the *RE* bit is 0; setting this bit to 1 inverts the selection in User mode.

Status Register Format

Figures 6–5 and 6–6 show the formats of the *Status* register. Additional information on the Diagnostic Status (DS) field follows the description of the specific implementations.

The Status Register (R2000, R3000, R6000)												

31 28	27 26	25 24		16 15		8 7	6	5	4	3	2	1 0
CU (Cu3...Cu0)	0	RE	DS	IM		0	KUo	IEo	KUp	IEp	KUc	IEc
4	2	1	9	8		2	1	1	1	1	1	1

CU Controls the usability of each of the four coprocessor unit numbers (1 –> usable; 0 –> unusable). CP0 is always usable when in Kernel mode, regardless of the setting of the CU_0 bit.

RE Reverse Endian in User mode (R3000A, R6000 only).

DS An implementation-dependent diagnostic Status field.

IM Interrupt Mask: controls the enabling of each of the external, internal, coprocessor and software interrupts (0 –> disabled; 1–>enabled). Bits 15..13 are unused on R6000 processors. See description of *Cause* register for further information.

KUo Old Kernel/User mode (0 –> kernel; 1 –> user)

IEo Old Interrupt Enable (0 –> disable; 1 –> enable)

KUp Previous Kernel/User mode (0 –> kernel; 1 –> user)

IEp Previous Interrupt Enable (0 –> disable; 1 –> enable)

KUc Current Kernel/User mode (0 –> kernel; 1 –> user)

IEc Current Interrupt Enable (0 –> disable; 1 –> enable)

0 Reserved for future use: 0 on read; should be 0 on write

Figure 6–5. The Status Register, R2000, R3000, R6000 Format

The Status Register (R4000)

31	28	27	26	25	24		16	15		8	7		5	4	3	2	1	0
CU (Cu3...Cu0)		RP	FR	RE		DS			IM			0			KSU	ERL	EXL	IE
4		1	1	1		9			8			3			2	1	1	1

CU   Controls the usability of each of the four coprocessor unit numbers (1 –> usable; 0 –> unusable). CP0 is always usable when in Kernel mode, regardless of the setting of the CU_0 bit.

RP   Enables reduced-power operation by reducing the clock frequency (0 –> full speed; 1 –> reduced clock). The clock divisor is programmable at boot time.

FR   Enables additional floating-point registers (0 –> 16 registers, 1 –> 32 registers).

RE   Reverse Endian in User mode.

DS   Implementation-dependent diagnostic Status field.

IM   Interrupt Mask: controls the enabling of each of the external, internal, coprocessor and software interrupts (0 –> disabled; 1 –> enabled). See description of *Cause* register for further information.

KSU   Mode (10 –> User, 01 –> Supervisor, 00 –> Kernel)

ERL   Error Level (0 –> normal, 1–> error)

EXL   Exception Level (0 –> normal, 1–> exception)

IE   Interrupt Enable (0 –> disable; 1 –> enable)

0   Reserved for future use: 0 on read; should be 0 on write

Figure 6–6. The Status Register, R4000 Format

R2000, R3000 and R6000 Implementations

For the R2000, R3000, and R6000 processors, the *Status* register contains a three-level stack (current, previous, and old) of the Kernel/User mode bit (*KU*) and the Interrupt Enable (*IE*) bit. The stack is pushed when each exception is taken, and popped by the Restore From Exception (RFE) instruction. These bits can also be directly read or written.

- *KUo/KUp/KUc* (Kernel/User mode: Old/Previous/Current). These three bits constitute a three-level stack showing the old/previous/current mode (0 means Kernel; 1 means User).

- *IEo/IEp/IEc* (Interrupt Enable: Old/Previous/Current). These three bits constitute a three-level stack showing the old/previous/current interrupt enable settings (0 means disable; 1 means enable).

Only one of the CU_1, CU_2, or CU_3 bits can be set to 1 at any time; there is only one *CpCond* input pin (coprocessor condition) and one *CpBusy* input. Coprocessor instructions can be executed only if the corresponding *CU* bit is on.

For the R2000, R3000, and R6000 processors, the contents of the *Status* register are undefined at reset, except for the following bits:

- *TS*, *SWc*, *KUc*, and *IEc* bits are cleared to 0

- *BEV* bit is set to 1.

R4000 Implementation

In the R4000 the three-level stack of *KU* and *IE* is replaced by a base mode, base interrupt enable, and two modifier bits: *EXL* and *ERL*. This allows support for Supervisor mode as well as rapid TLB refill exceptions for the kernel address space.

Interrupt Enable. Interrupts are enabled when all of the following field conditions are true:

- *IE* is set to 1

- *EXL* is cleared to 0

- *ERL* is cleared to 0

At this point the individual cause of the interrupt enables control.

Processor Modes. The following R4000 *Status* register bit settings are required for User, Kernel, and Supervisor modes.

- The processor is in User mode when *KSU* is set to 10, *EXL* is cleared to 0, and *ERL* is cleared to 0.

- The processor is in Supervisor mode when *KSU* is set to 01, *EXL* is cleared to 0, and *ERL* is cleared to 0.

- The processor is in Kernel mode when *KSU* is cleared to 00, *EXL* is set to 1, or *ERL* is set to 1.

Kernel Address Space Accesses. Access to the Kernel address space is allowed when one of the following field conditions is true:

- *KSU* is cleared to 00

- *EXL* is set to 1

- *ERL* is set to 1

Supervisor Address Space Accesses. Access to the Supervisor address space is allowed when one of the following field conditions is true:

- *KSU* is not equal to 10 (not in User mode)

- *EXL* is set to 1

- *ERL* is set to 1

User Address Space Accesses. Access to User address space is always allowed.

Reset. For R4000 processors, the contents of the *Status* register are undefined at reset, except for the following bits:

- *TS* is cleared to 0

- *ERL* and *BEV* are set to 1

- *SR* distinguishes between Reset, and Nonmaskable Interrupt (NMI) or Soft Reset.

Diagnostic Status (DS) Field

Because diagnostic facilities depend heavily on the characteristics of the cache, and likewise the virtual memory system depends on the implementation, the layout of the diagnostic status (DS) field is implementation-dependent. Normally it is used for diagnostic code, although in certain cases it is used by the operating system diagnostic facilities (such as reporting parity errors) and, on some machines, for relatively rare operations such as flushing the caches. In normal operation, the *DS* field is set to zero by operating system code.

R2000, R3000 Implementations of DS. For R2000 and R3000 processors, the diagnostic status bits *BEV*, *TS*, *PE*, *CM*, *PZ*, *SwC*, and *IsC* provide complete fault detection capability, but do not provide extensive fault diagnosis. Figure 6–7 shows the format of the DS field for the R2000 and R3000.

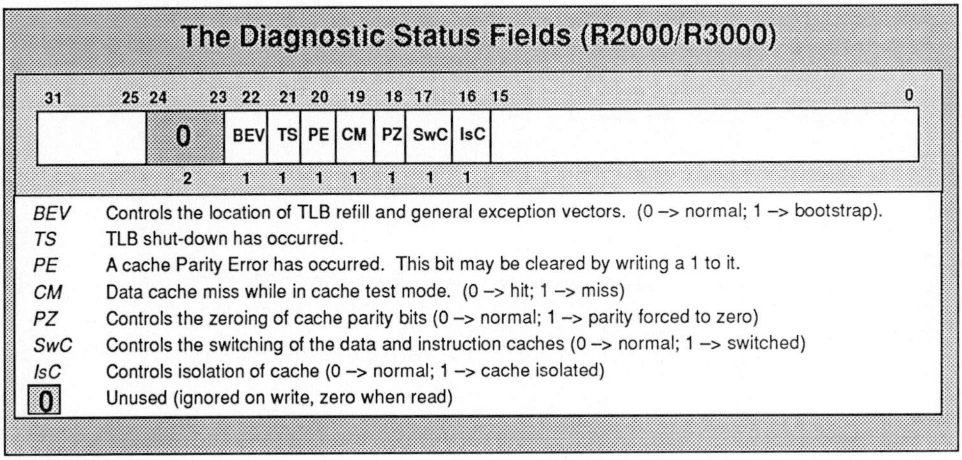

The Diagnostic Status Fields (R2000/R3000)

31	25 24	23 22	21 20	19	18 17	16 15	0
	0	BEV	TS	PE	CM	PZ	SwC	IsC	

| | | 2 | 1 | 1 | 1 | 1 | 1 | 1 | 1 | |

BEV	Controls the location of TLB refill and general exception vectors. (0 –> normal; 1 –> bootstrap).
TS	TLB shut-down has occurred.
PE	A cache Parity Error has occurred. This bit may be cleared by writing a 1 to it.
CM	Data cache miss while in cache test mode. (0 –> hit; 1 –> miss)
PZ	Controls the zeroing of cache parity bits (0 –> normal; 1 –> parity forced to zero)
SwC	Controls the switching of the data and instruction caches (0 –> normal; 1 –> switched)
IsC	Controls isolation of cache (0 –> normal; 1 –> cache isolated)
0	Unused (ignored on write, zero when read)

Figure 6–7. R2000/R3000 Status Register DS Field

R4000 Implementations of DS. Figure 6–8 shows the format of the R4000 diagnostic status (DS) field, along with bit descriptions. All bits in the DS field are read and write, except *TS*.

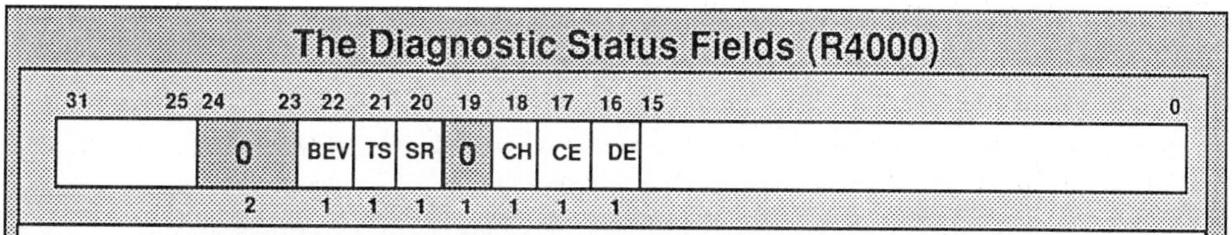

The Diagnostic Status Fields (R4000)

31	25 24	23 22	21 20	19 18	17	16 15	0
	0	BEV TS SR	0	CH CE	DE		
	2	1 1 1	1	1 1	1		

BEV	Controls the location of TLB refill and general exception vectors. (0 –> normal; 1 –> bootstrap)
TS	TLB shutdown has occurred (read-only).
SR	A soft reset has occurred.
CH	"Hit" (tag match and valid state) or "miss" indication for last CACHE Hit Invalidate, Hit Write Back Invalidate, Hit Write Back, Hit Set Virtual, or Create Dirty Exclusive for a secondary cache.
CE	Contents of the *ECC* register are used to set or modify the check bits of the caches when CE –> 1; see the *ECC* register description.
DE	Specifies that cache parity or ECC errors are not to cause exceptions.
0	Reserved for future use: 0 on read; should be 0 on write

Figure 6–8. R4000 Status Register DS Field

R6000 Implementations of DS. Figure 6–9 shows the format of the R6000 diagnostic status (DS) field, along with bit descriptions.

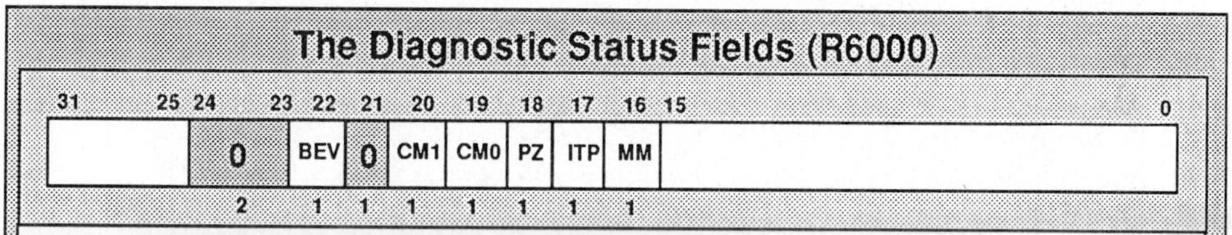

The Diagnostic Status Fields (R6000)

31	25 24	23 22	21 20	19	18	17	16 15	0
	0	BEV 0	CM1 CM0	PZ	ITP	MM		
	2	1 1	1 1	1	1	1		

BEV	controls the location of TLB refill and general exception vectors. (0 –> normal; 1 –> bootstrap).
CM1	Indicates that a cache miss on set 1 of the secondary cache occurred on the last load or store operation.
CM0	Indicates that a cache miss on set 0 of the secondary cache occurred on the last load or store operation.
PZ	Controls the zeroing of cache parity bits (0 –> normal; 1 –> parity forced to zero)
ITP	Inverts tag parity on writes. (0 –> normal; 1 –> inverted parity).
MM	Converts LWL/SWL/LWR/SWR to memory management instructions (0 –> normal; 1 –> memory management)
0	Unused (ignored on write, zero when read)

Figure 6–9. R6000 Status Register DS Field

Status Register Mode Bits and Exception Processing

When an R2000, R3000, or R6000 processor responds to an exception, it saves the *current* Kernel/User mode (*KUc*) and *current* Interrupt Enable mode (*IEc*) bits of the *Status* register in the *previous* mode bits (*KUp* and *IEp*). The *previous* mode bits (*KUp* and *IEp*) are saved in the *old* mode bits (*KUo* and *IEo*). The *current* mode bits (*KUc* and *IEc*) are cleared so the processor can enter Kernel mode and turn off interrupts. This process is shown in Figure 6–10.

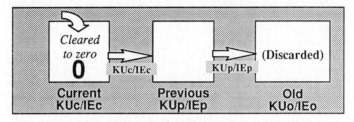

Figure 6–10. Storing the Kernel/User and Interrupt-Enable Mode Bits

This three-level set of *Status* register mode bits lets the CPU respond to two levels of exceptions before software must save the contents of the *Status* register. Figure 6–11 shows how the processor manipulates the *Status* register during exception recognition.

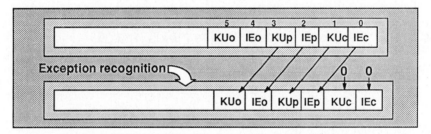

Figure 6–11. The Status Register and Exception Recognition

After an exception handler has completed execution, the CPU must return to the system context that existed prior to the exception (if possible). The Restore From Exception (RFE) instruction provides the mechanism for this return.

The RFE instruction restores control to a process that an exception preempted. When the RFE instruction executes, it restores the *previous* Interrupt Mask (*IEp*) and Kernel/User mode (*KUp*) bits in the *Status* register into the the corresponding *current* status bits (*IEc* and *KUc*). It also restores the *old* status bits (*IEo* and *KUo*) into the corresponding previous status bits (*IEp* and *KUp*). The old status bits (*IEo* and *KUo*) remain unchanged. The actions of the RFE instruction are illustrated in Figure 6–12.

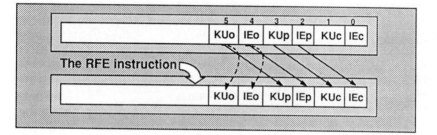

Figure 6–12. Restoring from Exceptions

R4000 exception processing is discussed in the previous subsection, R4000 Implementation, of the section titled, *Status* Register Format.

Cause Register (13)

The *Cause* register is a 32-bit read/write register. Its contents describe the cause of the last exception (for R6000 operations, also see the *Error* register). A 5-bit exception code (*ExcCode*) indicates the cause as listed in Table 6–2. The remaining fields contain detailed information specific to certain exceptions. All bits in the register, with the exception of the *IP(1..0)* bits, are read-only. *IP(1..0)* bits are used for software interrupts. Table 6–2 shows a decoding of the 5-bit Exception Code field.

Table 6–2. The ExcCode Field of Cause Register

The Cause Register ExcCode Field		
Number	Mnemonic	Description
0	Int	Interrupt
1	Mod	TLB modification exception
2	TLBL	TLB exception (load or instruction fetch)
3	TLBS	TLB exception (store)
4	AdEL	Address error exception (load or instruction fetch)
5	AdES	Address error exception (store)
6	IBE	Bus error exception (instruction fetch)
7	DBE	Bus error exception (data reference: load or store)
8	Sys	Syscall exception
9	Bp	Breakpoint exception
10	RI	Reserved instruction exception
11	CpU	Coprocessor Unusable exception
12	Ov	Arithmetic Overflow exception
13	Tr	Trap exception (R4000 and R6000 only)
14	NCD	LDCz/SDCz to uncached address (R6000 only)
14	VCEI	Virtual Coherency Exception Instruction (R4000 only)
15	MC	Machine Check exception (R6000 only)
15	FPE	Floating-Point exception (R4000 only)
16–22	–	Reserved for future use
23	WATCH	Reference to *WatchHi/WatchLo* address (R4000 only)
19–30	–	Reserved for future use
31	VCED	Virtual Coherency Exception Data (R4000 only)

R2000 and R3000 Implementation of the Cause Register

R2000 and R3000 processors have eight interrupts, *IP(7..0)*, which are used as follows:

- *IP(7:2)* map to external interrupts 5..0, and are read-only

- *IP(1..0)* are software interrupts, and can be written into to set or reset software interrupts.

R4000 Implementation of Cause Register

R4000 processors have eight interrupts, *IP(7:0)*, which are used as follows:

- *IP(7..2)*: Reading the *Cause* register returns the inclusive OR of two internal registers for interrupts *IP(6..2)*. One of the internal registers is latched each cycle from input signals, as in the R2000 and R3000 processors; the other register is is read and written by commands on the R4000 system interface port. On reset, *IP(7)* is configured as either a sixth external interrupt, or an internal interrupt that is set when the *Count* register is equal to the *Compare* register.

- *IP(1..0)* are software-only interrupts, and can be written to set or reset software interrupts.

Floating-point exceptions use a separate exception code.

R6000 Implementation of Cause Register

R6000 processors have three external interrupts, *IP(4:2)*, which are used as follows:

- *IP(2)* is used for system bus and interval timer interrupts.

- *IP(3)* is used for the floating-point coprocessor interrupt.

- *IP(4)* is an unused spare.

The *Cause* register format is shown in Figure 6–13; it is designed so that the low order eight bits can be extracted easily and used as a word offset into a table for software interrupt vectoring.

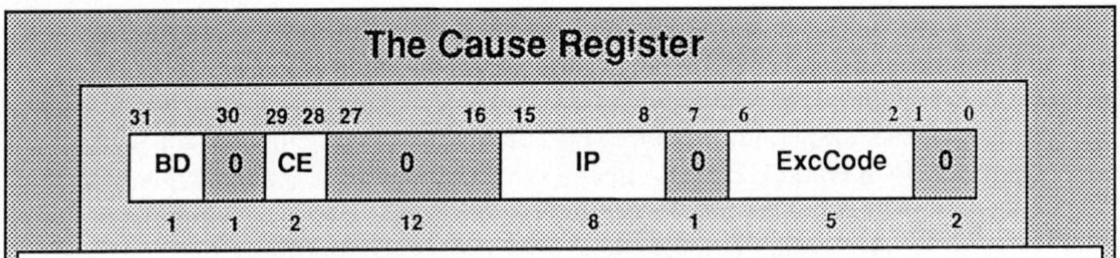

<figure>

The Cause Register

31	30	29 28 27	16 15	8 7 6	2 1 0
BD	0	CE	0	IP	0	ExcCode	0
1	1	2	12	8	1	5	2

BD	The **Branch Delay** (*BD*) bit indicates whether the last exception was taken while executing in a branch delay slot. (0 –> normal; 1 –> delay slot).
CE	The **Coprocessor Error** (*CE*) field indicates the coprocessor unit number referenced when a Coprocessor Unusable exception is taken.
IP	**Interrupt Pending** (*IP*) field indicates which external, internal, coprocessor, and software interrupts are pending. This field reflects the current status, and changes in response to external signals. The number and assignment of the *IP* bits are implementation-dependent.
ExcCode	**Exception Code** field (see Table 6–2)
0	is unused (ignored on write, zero when read)

</figure>

Figure 6–13. Cause Register Format

Exception Program Counter (EPC) Register (14)

The Exception Program Counter, *EPC*, is a 32-bit, read-only register that contains the address where processing resumes after an exception has been serviced.

For synchronous exceptions, the *EPC* register contains either:

- the virtual address of the instruction that was the direct cause of the exception, or

- the virtual address of the immediately preceding branch or jump instruction (when the instruction is in a branch delay slot, and the Branch Delay bit in the *Cause* register is set).

The EPC register is read/write on R4000 processors; on R2000, R3000, and R6000 processors this register is read-only.

The format of the *EPC* register is shown in Figure 6–14.

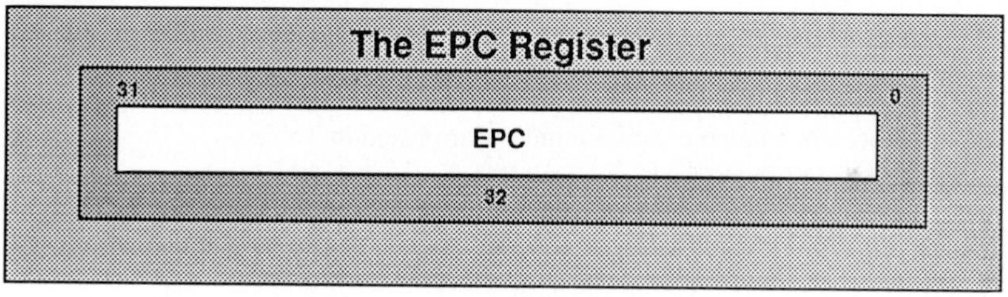

Figure 6–14. EPC Register Format

Processor Revision Identifier (PRId) Register (15)

The Processor Revision Identifier, *PRId*, is a 32-bit, read-only register; it contains information that identifies the implementation and revision level of the CPU and CP0. Figure 6–15 shows the format of the *PRId* register.

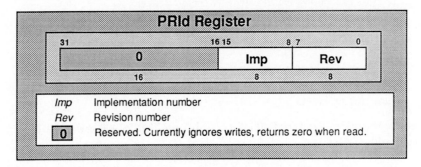

Figure 6–15. Processor Revision Identifier Register Format

The low order byte (bits 7..0) of the *PRId* register is interpreted as a coprocessor unit revision number, and the second byte (bits 15..8) is interpreted as a coprocessor unit implementation number. Coprocessor implementation numbers are listed in Table 6–3. The contents of the high order halfword of the register are not defined.

The revision number is a value of the form $y.x$ where y is a major revision number in bits 7..4 and x is a minor revision number in bits 3..0.

The revision number can distinguish some chip revisions, however MIPS does not guarantee that changes to its chips will necessarily be reflected in the *PRId* register, or that changes to the revision number necessarily reflect real chip changes. For this reason these values are not listed and software should not rely on the revision number in the *PRId* register to characterize the chip.

Table 6–3. Coprocessor Implementation Types

Imp. Number	Description
0x01	MIPS R2000 CPU
0x02	MIPS R3000 CPU
0x03	MIPS R6000 CPU
0x04	MIPS R4000 CPU
0x05	reserved
0x06	MIPS R6000A CPU

Config Register (16)

The *Config* register specifies various configuration options selected on R4000 processors. Some configuration options, as defined by *Config* bits 31..6, are set by the hardware during reset, and are included in this register as read-only status for software. Other configuration options are read/write (defined by *Config* bits 5..0) and controlled by software; on reset these fields are undefined.

The *Config* register should be initialized by software before caches are used. The caches should be completely written back to memory before changing block sizes, and reinitialized after any change is made. Figure 6–16 shows the format of the *Config* register and Table 6–4 lists the field and bit definitions for the *Config* Register.

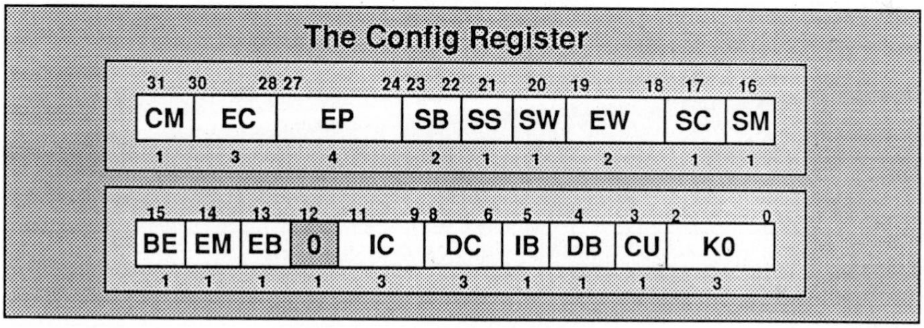

The Config Register

31	30	28 27		24 23	22	21	20	19		18	17	16
CM	EC	EP		SB	SS	SW	EW			SC	SM
1	3	4		2	1	1	2			1	1

15	14	13	12	11	9 8		6	5	4	3	2		0
BE	EM	EB	0	IC		DC		IB	DB	CU	K0		
1	1	1	1	3		3		1	1	1	3		

Figure 6–16. Config Register Format

Table 6–4. Config Register Field and Bit Definitions

Field/Bit Name	Description
CM	Master-Checker Mode (if set, then Master-Checker Mode is enabled) This bit is automatically cleared on a Soft Reset.
EC	System clock ratio: 0 –> processor clock frequency divided by 2 1 –> processor clock frequency divided by 3 2 –> processor clock frequency divided by 4
EP	Transmit data pattern (pattern for write-back data): 0 –> D 1 –> DDx 2 –> DDxx 3 –> DxDx 4 –> DDxxx 5 –> DDxxxx 6 –> DxxDxx 7 –> DDxxxxx 8 –> DxxxDxxx
SB	Secondary Cache block size: 0 –> 4 words 1 –> 8 words 2 –> 16 words 3 –> 32 words
SS	Split Secondary Cache Mode (0 –> instruction and data mixed in secondary cache; 1 –> instruction and data separated by $SCAddr_{17}$)
SW	Secondary cache port width (0 –> 128-bit data path to S-cache; 1 –> 64-bit)
EW	System Port width (0 –> 64-bit; 1 –> 32-bit)
SC	Secondary cache present (if cleared, S-cache present, else no secondary cache)
SM	Dirty Shared coherency state; if set, then Dirty Shared state is disabled, else enabled
BE	BigEndianMem (if set, then kernel and memory are Big Endian, else Little Endian)
EM	ECC mode enable (1 –> ECC mode enabled; 0 –> parity mode enabled)
EB	Block ordering (if set, then sequential, else sub-block)
0	Reserved
IC	ICache Size (ICache size = 2^{12+IC} bytes
DC	DCache Size (DCache size = 2^{12+DC} bytes)
IB	Primary ICache block size (if set, then = 32 bytes, else 16 bytes)
DB	Primary DCache line size (if set, then = 32 bytes, else 16 bytes)
CU	Update on Store Conditional (0 –> Store Conditional uses coherency algorithm specified by TLB; 1 –> SC uses cacheable coherent update on write)
K0	*kseg0* coherency algorithm

Load Linked Address (LLAddr) Register (17)

The Load Linked Address, *LLAddr*, register is an R4000 read/write coprocessor register; it contains the physical address read by the most recent Load Linked instruction. This register is used only for R4000 diagnostic purposes, and serves no function during normal operation. Figure 6–17 shows the format of the *LLAddr* register; *PAddr* represents bits 35..4 of the R4000 physical address.

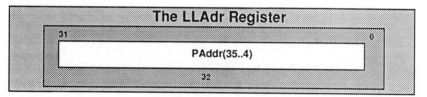

Figure 6–17. LLAdr Register Format

WatchLo (18) and WatchHi (19) Registers

R4000 processors provide a debugging feature to detect references to a selected physical address; load or store operations to the location specified by the R4000 *WatchLo* and *WatchHi* registers cause a Watch exception (described later in this chapter). Figure 6–18 shows the format of the *WatchLo* and *WatchHi* registers.

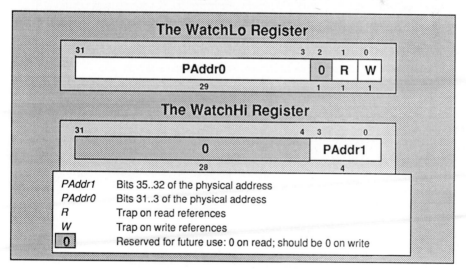

Figure 6–18. WatchLo and WatchHi Register Formats

ECC Register (26)

The *ECC* (Error Correction Code) register is an 8-bit read/write register that is only present on R4000 processors; it reads and writes either secondary-cache data ECC bits or primary-cache data parity bits, for cache initialization, cache diagnostics, or cache error handling. (Tag ECC and parity are loaded from and stored to the *TagLo* register.)

The *ECC* register is loaded by the CACHE operation Index Load Tag. It is:

- written into the primary data cache on store instructions (instead of the computed parity) when the *CE* bit of the *Status* register is set

- substituted for the computed instruction parity for the CACHE operation Fill

- XORed into the computed ECC for the secondary cache for certain primary data cache CACHE operations: Index Write Back Invalidate, Hit Write Back, and Hit Write Back Invalidate.

Figure 6–19 shows the format of the *ECC* register.

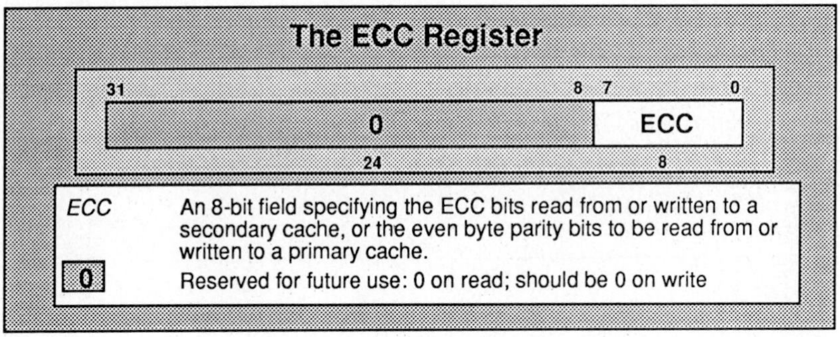

Figure 6–19. ECC Register Format

CacheError Register (27)

The R4000 *CacheErr* register is a 32-bit read-only register which handles ECC errors in the secondary cache and parity errors in the primary cache. Parity errors cannot be corrected. All single- and double-bit ECC errors in the secondary cache tag and data are detected by the R4000 and single-bit errors in the tag are automatically corrected by the R4000. Single-bit ECC errors in the secondary cache data are not automatically corrected.

The *CacheErr* register provides cache index and status bits which indicate the source and nature of the error; it is loaded when a Cache Error exception is taken. Figure 6–20 shows the format of the *CacheErr* register.

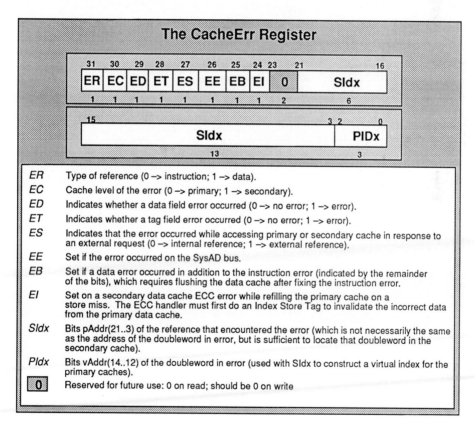

Figure 6–20. CacheErr Register Format

TagLo (28) & TagHi (29) Registers

The R4000 *TagLo* and *TagHi* registers are 32-bit read/write registers that hold either the primary cache tag and parity, or the secondary cache tag and ECC during cache initialization, cache diagnostics, or cache error handling. The *Tag* registers are written by the CACHE and MTC0 instructions.

The *P* and *ECC* fields of these registers are ignored on Index Store Tag operations. Parity and ECC are computed by the store operation.

Figure 6–21 shows the format of these registers for primary cache operations.

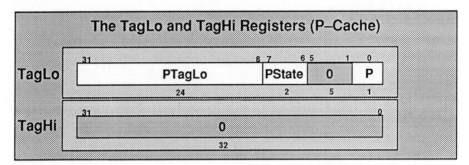

Figure 6–21. TagLo and TagHi Register (P-Cache) Formats

Figure 6–22 shows the format of these registers for secondary cache operations.

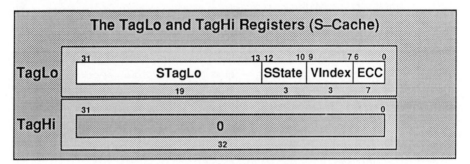

Figure 6–22. TagLo and TagHi Register (S-Cache) Formats

Bit definitions of the *TagLo* and *TagHi* registers are given in Table 6–5.

Table 6–5. The ExcCode Field of Cause Register

Bit Name	Description
PTagLo	A 24-bit field specifying the physical address bits 35..12.
PState	A 2-bit field specifying the primary cache state.
P	A 1-bit field specifying the primary tag even parity bit.
STagLo	A 19-bit field specifying the physical address bits 35..17.
SState	A 3-bit field specifying the secondary cache state.
VIndex	A 3-bit field specifying the virtual index of the associated primary cache line, vAddr(14..12).
ECC	ECC for the STag, SState, and VIndex fields.
0	Reserved for future use: 0 on read; should be 0 on write

ErrorEPC Register (30)

The R4000 *ErrorEPC* register is similar to the *EPC* register, but is used on ECC and parity error exceptions. It is also used to store the PC on Reset, Soft Reset, and NMI exceptions. The read/write *EPC* register contains the virtual address at which instruction processing can resume after servicing an error. The address may be either:

- the virtual address of the instruction that caused the exception

- the virtual address of the immediately preceding branch or jump instruction when that address is in a branch delay slot.

There is no branch delay slot indication for the *ErrorEPC* register. Figure 6–23 shows the format of the *ErrorEPC* register.

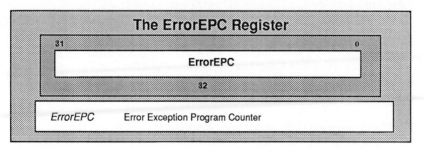

Figure 6–23. ErrorEPC Register Format

Exception Description Details

This section describes each of the R-Series exceptions — its cause, handling, and servicing.

Exception Handling

The exception handling system provides efficient management of relatively infrequent events such as translation misses, arithmetic overflow, I/O interrupts, and system calls.

MIPS architecture defines a certain amount of additional state which is saved in coprocessor registers to analyze the cause of the exception, service the event that caused the exception, and resume the original flow of execution, when applicable.

Exception Operation

To handle an exception, the processor forces execution of a handler, at a fixed address in Kernel mode, with interrupts disabled. To resume normal operation, the Program Counter (PC), operating mode, and interrupt enable must be restored; thus it is *this* context that must be saved when an exception is taken.

When an exception occurs, the *EPC* register is loaded with the restart location at which execution can resume after servicing the exception. The *EPC* register contains the address of the instruction that caused the exception; or, if the instruction was executing in a branch delay slot, the the *EPC* register contains the address of the instruction immediately preceding.

R2000, R3000 and R6000 Implementations

To save and restore the operating mode and interrupt enable, the R2000, R3000, and R6000 processors use a three-level stack for the *KU* and *IE* bits. The *KUc* and *IEc* bits always specify whether the machine is executing in Kernel or User mode, and whether interrupts are enabled or disabled. In the following description, refer to Figures NO TAG and NO TAG.

When an exception (other than Reset) is taken, the values of *KUp*, *IEp*, *KUc*, and *IEc* are saved in *KUo*, *IEo*, *KUp*, and *IEp* respectively. *KUc* and *IEc* are cleared, and the machine begins operating in Kernel mode with interrupts disabled.

On return from exception (RFE instruction), the *KUc*, *IEc*, *KUp*, and *IEp* bits are restored from *KUp*, *IEp*, *KUo*, and *IEo* respectively. The *KUo* and *IEo* bits allow an exception to be taken in a first level exception handler.

This additional level of exception handling is for use in the TLB refill handler; it is not appropriate for nested interrupts, which can be implemented by software to save and restore the *Status* register, *EPC*, and other context on a stack. Figures 6–1, 6–2, and 6–3 illustrate exception handling operations for the R2000, R3000 and R6000 processors.

Figure 6–1 illustrates reset in the R2000 and R3000.

```
T:    undefined
      Random ← 63
      SR ← SR₃₁..₂₃ || 1 || 0 || SR₂₀..₁₈ || 0 || SR₁₆..₂ || 0 || 0
      PC ← 0xbfc0 0000
```

Figure 6–1. R2000 and R3000 Reset

Figure 6–2 illustrates R6000 reset.

```
T:    undefined
      SR ← SR₃₁..₂₃ || 1 || 0 || SR₂₀..₁₈ || 0 || SR₁₆..₂ || 0 || 0
      PC ← 0xbfc0 0000
```

Figure 6–2. R6000 Reset

Figure 6–3 illustrates R2000, R3000, and R6000 exceptions excluding reset.

```
T:    Cause ← BD || 0 || CE || 0¹² || Cause₁₅..₈ || 0 || ExcCode || 0²
      EPC ← PC
      SR ← SR₃₁..₆ || SR₃..₀ || 0²
      if SR₂₂ = 1 then
          PC ← 0xbfc0 0100 + vector
      else
          PC ← 0x8000 0000 + vector
      endif
```

Figure 6–3. R2000, R3000, and R6000 Exceptions (Except Reset)

R4000 Implementation

R4000 processors use a different mechanism for saving and restoring operating mode and interrupt status, to support Supervisor mode and fast TLB refill for all address spaces.

The three sets of *KU* and *IE* bits described under the R2000, R3000, and R6000 implementations are replaced by:

- a single interrupt enable bit (*IE*)

- a base operating mode (User, Supervisor, Kernel)

- an exception level (normal, exception)

- an error level (normal, error).

Interrupts are enabled by setting the *IE* bit to 1 and both levels (exception and error) to *normal*.

The operating mode (*User* or *Supervisor*) is specified by the state of the base mode when the exception level is *normal*; operating mode is Kernel when exception level is *exception*. Exceptions set the exception level to *exception*; the exception handler typically resets to *normal* after saving the appropriate state, and then sets back to *exception* while restoring that state and restarting. Returning from an exception (see the ERET instruction in Appendix A) resets the exception level to *normal*.

Figure 6–4 shows the R4000 reset exception.

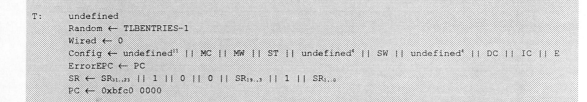

```
T:      undefined
        Random ← TLBENTRIES-1
        Wired ← 0
        Config ← undefined¹¹ || MC || MW || ST || undefined⁴ || SW || undefined⁴ || DC || IC || E
        ErrorEPC ← PC
        SR ← SR₃₁..₂₃ || 1 || 0 || 0 || SR₁₉..₃ || 1 || SR₁..₀
        PC ← 0xbfc0 0000
```

Figure 6–4. R4000 Reset Exception

Figure 6–5 shows the R4000 Soft Reset and NMI exception.

```
T:    ErrorEPC ← PC
      SR ← SR31..23 || 1 || 0 || 1 || SR19..3 || 1 || SR1..0
      PC ← 0xbfc0 0000
```

Figure 6–5. R4000 Soft Reset and NMI Exception

Figure 6–6 shows the R4000 exceptions except Reset, Soft Reset, NMI, and Cache Error.

```
T:    Cause ← BD || 0 || CE || 0^12 || Cause15..8 || 0 || ExcCode || 0^2
      if SR1 = 0 then
          EPC ← PC
      endif
      SR ← SR31..2 || 1 || SR0
      if SR22 = 1 then
          PC ← 0xbfc0 0200 + vector
      else
          PC ← 0x8000 0000 + vector
      endif
```

Figure 6–6. R4000 Exceptions (Except Reset, Soft Reset, NMI, and Cache Error)

Figure 6–7 shows the R4000 Cache Error exception.

```
T:    ErrorEPC ← PC
      CacheErr ← ER || EC || ED || ET || ES || EE || EB || EI || 0^4 || SIdx || PIdx
      SR ← SR31..3 || 1 ||SR1..0
      if SR22 = 1 then
          PC ← 0xbfc0 0200 + 0x100
      else
          PC ← 0xa000 0000 + 0x100
      endif
```

Figure 6–7. R4000 Cache Error Exception

Exception Vector Locations

The Reset, Soft Reset, and NMI exceptions are always vectored to location 0xbfc0 0000. Addresses for other exceptions are a combination of a *vector offset* and a *base address*, determined by the *BEV* bit of the *Status* register. Table 6–1 shows the Vector Base addresses, and Table 6–2 shows the Vector Offset to these addresses.

Table 6–1. Exception Vector Base Addresses

BEV	R2000, R3000, and R6000 Vector Base	R4000 Vector Base
0	0x8000 0000	0x8000 0000
1	0xbfc0 0100	0xbfc0 0200

The vector base for the R4000 Cache Error exception is in *kseg1* (0xa000 0000) instead of *kseg0* (0x8000 0000) when *BEV* is 0. Vector base for the R4000 Cache Error exception is 0xbfc0 0200 when *BEV* is set to a 1.

Table 6–2. Exception Vector Offset Addresses

Exception	R2000, R3000, and R6000 Vector Offset	R4000 Vector Offset
TLB refill, EXL = 0	0x000	0x000
Cache Error	—	0x100
Others	0x080	0x180

Priority of Exceptions

While more than one exception can occur for a single instruction, only one exception is reported, with priority given in the order shown in Table 6–3:

Table 6–3. Exception Priority Order

Reset

Soft Reset (R4000 only)

NMI (R4000 only)

Machine Check (R6000 only)

Address error — Instruction fetch

TLB refill — Instruction fetch

TLB invalid — Instruction fetch

Cache error — Instruction fetch (R4000 only)

Virtual Coherency — Instruction fetch (R4000 only)

Bus error — Instruction fetch

Integer overflow, Trap, System call, Breakpoint,

   Reserved Instruction, Coprocessor Unusable,

   or Floating-Point Exception (R4000 only)

Address error — Data access

TLB refill — Data access

TLB invalid — Data access

TLB modified — Data write

Cache error — Data access (R4000 only)

Watch (R4000 only)

Virtual Coherency — Data access (R4000 only)

Uncached LDC1/SDC1 (R6000 only)

Bus error — Data access

Interrupt

Reset Exception

Cause. The Reset exception occurs when the CPU RESET signal is asserted and then deasserted. This exception is not maskable.

Handling. The CPU provides a special interrupt vector (0xbfc0 0000) for this exception. The Reset vector resides in CPU unmapped and uncached address space; therefore the hardware need not initialize the TLB or the cache to handle this exception. The processor can fetch and execute instructions while the caches and virtual memory are in an undefined state.

The contents of all registers in the CPU are undefined when this exception occurs except for the following:

- For R2000, R3000, and R6000 processors, the *Status* register is undefined, except for *TS*, *SWc*, *KUc*, and *IEc*, which are 0, and *BEV*, which is 1.

- For R4000 processors, the contents of the *Status* register are undefined, except for *SR* and *TS*, which are 0, and *ERL* and *BEV*, which are 1.

- The *Random* register is initialized to the value of its upper bound (see the *Random* register for more information).

- The *Wired* register is initialized to 0 (R4000 only).

Servicing. The Reset exception is serviced by initializing all processor registers, coprocessor registers, caches, and the memory system; by performing diagnostic tests; and by bootstrapping the operating system.

The Reset exception vector is selected to appear within the uncached, unmapped memory space of the machine so that instructions can be fetched and executed while the cache and virtual memory system are still in an undefined state.

Soft Reset Exception

The Soft Reset exception is implemented on R4000 processors only.

Cause. The Soft Reset exception occurs in response to the Soft Reset input signal, and execution begins at the Reset vector when Soft Reset is deasserted. This exception is not maskable.

Handling. The Reset exception vector (0xbfc0 0000) is used for this exception, located within unmapped and uncached address space so that the cache and TLB need not be initialized to handle this exception. The *SR* bit of the *Status* register is set to distinguish this exception from a Reset exception.

The primary purpose of the Soft Reset exception is to reinitialize the processor after a fatal error such as a Master/Checker mismatch. Unlike an NMI, all cache and bus state machines are reset by this exception; like Reset, it can be used on the processor in any state. The caches, TLB, and normal exception vectors need not be properly initialized.

The contents of all registers are preserved when this exception occurs, except for the *ErrorEPC* register, which contains the restart PC, and the *ERL* bit of the *Status* register, which is set to 1. Because the Soft Reset can abort cache and bus operations, cache and memory state is undefined when this exception occurs.

Servicing. The Soft Reset exception is serviced by saving the current processor state for diagnostic purposes, and reinitializing for the Reset exception.

NonMaskable Interrupt (NMI) Exception

The NMI exception is implemented on R4000 processors only.

Cause. The NonMaskable Interrupt (NMI) exception occurs in response to the falling edge of the NMI pin. As the name describes, this exception is not maskable; it occurs regardless of the settings of the *EXL*, *ERL*, and the *IE Status* register bits.

Handling. The Reset exception vector (0xbfc0 0000) is also used for this exception. This vector is located within unmapped and uncached address space so that the cache and TLB need not be initialized to handle an NMI interrupt. The *SR* bit of the *Status* register is set to differentiate this exception from a Reset exception.

Because an NMI could occur in the midst of another exception, in general it is not possible to continue program execution after servicing an NMI.

Unlike Reset and Soft Reset, but like other exceptions, NMI is taken only at instruction boundaries. The state of the caches and memory system are preserved by this exception.

The contents of all registers are preserved when this exception occurs, except for:

- the *ErrorEPC* register, which contains the restart PC
- the *ERL* bit of the *Status* register, which is set to 1
- the *SR* bit of the *Status* register, which is set to 1.

Servicing. The NMI exception is serviced by saving the current processor state for diagnostic purposes, and reinitializing for the Reset exception.

Machine Check Exception

The Machine Check (MC) exception is implemented on R6000 processors only.

Cause. The MC exception occurs when a hardware failure occurs, such as a cache parity error, which cannot be completely and transparently recovered from; that is, it requires software intervention, recovery, or reporting.

This exception is not maskable.

Handling. The common interrupt vector is used for this exception, and the *MC* code in the *Cause* register is set.

The contents of implementation-dependent diagnostic status bits in the *Status* and *Error* registers indicate the precise cause of the exception; however, it is possible that more than one of these bits are pending at the same time.

Servicing. The MC condition is cleared by correcting the condition that caused the MC exception to be asserted. The manner in which this correction is accomplished is dependent upon the individual details of system implementation.

Address Error Exception

Cause. The Address Error exception occurs when an attempt is made to:

- load, fetch, or store a word that is not aligned on a word boundary

- load or store a halfword that is not aligned on a halfword boundary

- load or store a doubleword that is not aligned on a doubleword boundary

- reference a kernel address space from User or Supervisor mode

- reference a Supervisor address space from User mode.

This exception is not maskable.

Handling. The common exception vector is used for this exception. The *AdEL* or *AdES* code in the *Cause* register is set, indicating whether the instruction — as shown by the *EPC* register and *BD* bit in the *Cause* register — caused the exception with an instruction reference, load operation, or store operation.

When this exception occurs, the *BadVAddr* register retains the virtual address that was not properly aligned or which referenced protected address space. The contents of the VPN field of the *Context* and *EntryHi* registers are undefined, as are the contents of the *EntryLo* register.

The *EPC* register points at the instruction that caused the exception, unless this instruction is in a branch delay slot. If in a branch delay slot, the *EPC* register points at the preceding branch instruction, and the *BD* bit of the *Cause* register is set as indication.

Servicing. The process executing at the time is handed a UNIX SIGSEGV (segmentation violation) signal. This error is usually fatal to the process incurring the exception.

TLB Exceptions

There are three different types of TLB exceptions than can occur:

- **TLB Refill** occurs when there is no TLB entry to match a reference to a mapped address space.

- **TLB Invalid** occurs when a virtual address reference matches a TLB entry that is marked invalid.

- **TLB Modified** occurs when a store operation virtual address reference to memory matches a TLB entry which is marked valid but is not dirty/writable.

TLB Refill Exception

Cause. The TLB refill exception occurs when there is no TLB entry to match a reference to a mapped address space. This exception is not maskable.

Handling. A special exception vector is provided for this exception. For R4000 processors, all references use this vector when the *EXL* bit is set to 0 in the *Status* register. For other processor implementations, only references to user address space (from either Kernel or User mode) use this vector; references to the kernel address space use the common exception vector.

The *TLBL* or *TLBS* code in the *Cause* register is set. This code indicates whether the instruction — as shown by the *EPC* register and the *BD* bit in the *Cause* register — caused the miss by an instruction reference, load operation, or store operation.

When this exception occurs, the *BadVAddr*, *Context*, and *EntryHi* registers hold the virtual address that failed address translation. The *EntryHi* register also contains the ASID from which the translation fault occurred. The *Random* register normally contains a valid location in which to place the replacement TLB entry. The contents of the *EntryLo* register are undefined.

The *EPC* register points at the instruction that caused the exception — unless this instruction is in a branch delay slot, in which case the *EPC* points at the preceding branch instruction and the *BD* bit of the *Cause* register is set.

Servicing. To service this exception, the contents of the *Context* register are used as a virtual address to fetch a memory word containing the physical page frame and access control bits. The memory word is placed into the *EntryLo* register (or E*ntryLo0*/*EntryLo1* on the R4000), and the *EntryHi* and *EntryLo* registers are written into the TLB.

It is possible that the virtual address used to obtain the physical address and access control information is on a page that is not resident in the TLB. This is handled by allowing a TLB refill exception in the TLB refill handler. This second exception goes instead to the common exception vector because it is a reference to the kernel address space on R2000, R3000, and R6000 processors, and because the *EXL* bit of the *Status* register is set for R4000 processors.

TLB Invalid Exception

Cause. The TLB invalid exception occurs when a virtual address reference matches a TLB entry that is marked invalid. This exception is not maskable.

Handling. The common exception vector is used for this exception. The *TLBL* or *TLBS* code in the *Cause* register is set. This code indicates whether the instruction — as shown by the *EPC* register, and *BD* bit in the *Cause* register — caused the miss by an instruction reference, load operation, or store operation.

When this exception occurs, the *BadVAddr*, *Context*, and *EntryHi* registers contain the virtual address that failed address translation. The *EntryHi* register also contains the ASID from which the translation fault occurred. The *Random* register normally contains a valid location in which to put the replacement TLB entry. The contents of the *EntryLo* register are undefined.

The *EPC* register points at the instruction that caused the exception — unless this instruction is in a branch delay slot, in which case the *EPC* points at the preceding branch instruction and the *BD* bit of the *Cause* register is set.

Servicing. The valid bit of a TLB entry is typically cleared when:

- a virtual address does not exist

- the virtual address exists, but is not in main memory (a page fault)

- a trap is desired on any reference to the page (for example, to maintain a reference bit).

After servicing the cause of this exception, the TLB entry is located with TLBP (TLB Probe), and replaced by an entry with its valid bit set.

TLB Modified Exception

Cause. The TLB modified exception occurs when a store operation virtual address reference to memory matches a TLB entry which is marked valid but is not dirty/writable. This exception is not maskable.

Handling. The common exception vector is used for this exception, and the *Mod* code in the *Cause* register is set.

When this exception occurs, the *BadVAddr*, *Context*, and *EntryHi* registers contain the virtual address that failed address translation. The *EntryHi* register also contains the ASID from which the translation fault occurred. The contents of the *EntryLo* register are undefined.

The *EPC* register points at the instruction that caused the exception — unless this instruction is in a branch delay slot, in which case the *EPC* points at the preceding branch instruction and the *BD* bit of the *Cause* register is set.

Servicing. The kernel uses the the failing virtual address or virtual page number to identify the corresponding access control information. The page identified may or may not permit write accesses; if writes are not permitted, a *Write Protection Violation* has occurred.

If write accesses are permitted, the page frame is marked dirty/writable by the kernel in its own data structures. The TLBP instruction is used to place the index (of the TLB entry that must be altered) into the *Index* register. The *EntryLo* register is loaded with a word containing the physical page frame and access control bits (with the *D* bit set), and the *EntryHi* and *EntryLo* registers are written into the TLB.

Cache Error Exception

The Cache Error exception is implemented on R4000 processors only.

Cause. The Cache Error exception occurs when either a secondary cache ECC error or primary cache parity error is detected. This exception is not maskable (however error detection can be disabled by the *DE* bit of the *Status* register).

Handling. The processor sets the *ERL* bit in the *Status* register, saves the exception restart address in *ErrorEPC* register, and then transfers to a special vector in uncached space: 0xa000 0100 if the *BEV* bit is 0, otherwise 0xbfc0 0300.

No other registers are changed.

Servicing. All errors should be logged.

Single-bit ECC errors in the secondary cache can be corrected, using the CACHE instruction, and execution resumed through ERET.

Cache parity errors and non-single-bit ECC errors in unmodified cache blocks can be corrected by using the CACHE instruction to invalidate the cache block, then overwriting the old data through a cache miss and resuming execution with ERET. Other errors are not correctable, and are likely to be fatal to the current process.

Virtual Coherency Exception

The Virtual Coherency exception is implemented on R4000 processors only.

Cause. The Virtual Coherency exception occurs when a primary cache miss hits in the secondary cache, but $vAddr_{CACHEBITS-1..12}$ were not equal to the corresponding bits of the PIdx field of the secondary cache tag, and the cache algorithm for the page (from the C field in the TLB) specifies that the page is cached. This exception is not maskable.

Handling. The common exception vector is used for this exception. The *VCEI* or *VCED* code in the *Cause* register is set for instruction and data cache misses respectively. The *BadVAddr* register holds the virtual address that caused the exception.

Servicing. The CACHE instruction can determine the old virtual index, remove the data from the primary caches at the old virtual index, and write the PIdx field of the secondary cache with the new virtual index. At this point, the program can be continued.

Software can avoid the cost of this trap by using consistent virtual primary cache indexes to access the same physical data.

Bus Error Exception

Cause. The Bus Error exception occurs when signaled by board-level circuitry for events such as bus time-out, backplane bus parity errors, and invalid physical memory addresses or access types. This exception is not maskable.

Bus Error occurs only when a cache miss refill, uncached reference, or unbuffered write occurs synchronously; a Bus Error resulting from a buffered write transaction must be reported using the general interrupt mechanism.

Handling. The common interrupt vector is used for a Bus Error exception. The *IBE* or *DBE* code in the *Cause* register is set, signifying whether the instruction — as indicated by the *EPC* register and *BD* bit in the *Cause* register — caused the exception by an instruction reference, load operation, or store operation.

The *EPC* register points at the instruction that caused the exception — unless it is in a branch delay slot, in which case the *EPC* points at the preceding branch instruction and the *BD* bit of the *Cause* register is set.

Servicing. The physical address at which the fault occurred can be computed from information available in the system control coprocessor registers.

- If the *IBE* code in the *Cause* register is set (indicating an instruction fetch reference), the virtual address is contained in the *EPC* register.

- If the *DBE* code is set (indicating a load or store reference), the instruction which caused the exception is located at the virtual address contained in the *EPC* register (or four plus the contents of the *EPC* register if the *BD* bit of the *Cause* register is set).

The virtual address of the load or store reference can then be obtained by interpreting the instruction. The physical address can be obtained by using the TLBP instruction and reading the *EntryLo* register to compute the physical page number.

The process executing at the time of this exception is handed a UNIX SIGBUS (bus error) signal, which is usually fatal.

Integer Overflow Exception

Cause. The Integer Overflow exception occurs when an ADD, ADDI, or SUB instruction results in 2's-complement overflow. This exception is not maskable.

Handling. The common exception vector is used for this exception. The *OV* code in the *Cause* register is set.

The *EPC* register points at the instruction that caused the exception — unless the instruction is in a branch delay slot, in which case the *EPC* points at the preceding branch instruction and the *BD* bit of the *Cause* register is set.

Servicing. The process executing at the time of the exception is handed a UNIX SIGFPE/ FPE_INTOVF_TRAP (floating-point exception/integer overflow) signal. This error is usually fatal to the current process.

Trap Exception

The Trap exception is implemented on R4000 and R6000 processors only.

Cause. The Trap exception occurs when a TGE, TGEU, TLT, TLTU, TEQ, TNE, TGEI, TGEUI, TLTI, TLTUI, TEQI, or TNEI instruction results in a true condition. This exception is not maskable.

Handling. The common exception vector is used for this exception, and the *Tr* code in the *Cause* register is set.

The *EPC* register points at the instruction causing the exception — unless the instruction is in a branch delay slot, in which case the *EPC* points at the preceding branch instruction and the *BD* bit of the *Cause* register is set.

This exception does not occur on R2000 and R3000 processors, since the instructions that cause this exception are not valid.

Servicing. The process executing at the time of a Trap exception is handed a UNIX SIGFPE/FPE_INTOVF_TRAP (floating-point exception/integer overflow) signal. This error is usually fatal.

System Call Exception

Cause. The System Call exception occurs on an attempt to execute the SYSCALL instruction. This exception is not maskable.

Handling. The common exception vector is used for this exception. The *Sys* code in the *Cause* register is set.

The *EPC* register points at the SYSCALL instruction — unless it is in a branch delay slot, in which case the *EPC* points at the preceding branch instruction.

If the SYSCALL instruction is in a branch delay slot, the *BD* bit of the *Status* register is set; otherwise this bit is cleared.

Servicing. When this exception occurs, control is transferred to the applicable system routine. To resume execution, the *EPC* register must be altered so that the SYSCALL instruction is not reexecuted; this is accomplished by adding a value of four to the *EPC* register before returning. If a SYSCALL instruction is in a branch delay slot, a more complicated algorithm is required.

Breakpoint Exception

Cause. The Breakpoint exception occurs when an attempt is made to execute the BREAK instruction. This exception is not maskable.

Handling. The common exception vector is used for this exception, and the *BP* code in the *Cause* register is set.

The *EPC* register points at the BREAK instruction — unless it is in a branch delay slot, in which case the *EPC* points at the preceding branch instruction.

If the BREAK instruction is in a branch delay slot, the *BD* bit of the *Status* register is set, otherwise the bit is cleared.

Servicing. When the Breakpoint exception occurs, control is transferred to the applicable system routine. Additional distinctions can be made from the unused bits of the BREAK instruction (bits 25..6), and from loading the contents of the instruction at which the *EPC* register points. (A value of four must be added to the contents of the *EPC* register to locate the instruction if it resides in a branch delay slot.)

To resume execution, the *EPC* register must be altered so that the BREAK instruction is not reexecuted; this is accomplished by adding the value of four to the *EPC* register before returning. If a BREAK instruction is in a branch delay slot, interpretation of the branch instruction is required to resume execution.

Reserved Instruction Exception

Cause. The Reserved Instruction exception occurs when an attempt is made to execute an instruction whose major opcode (bits 31..26) is undefined, or a SPECIAL instruction whose minor opcode (bits 5..0) is undefined. On R6000 and R4000 processors, this exception also occurs on REGIMM instructions whose minor opcode (bits 20..16) is undefined. This exception is not maskable.

Handling. The common exception vector is used for this exception, and the *RI* code in the *Cause* register is set.

The *EPC* register points at the reserved instruction — unless it is in a branch delay slot, in which case the *EPC* points at the preceding branch instruction.

Servicing. In current systems, no instructions in the MIPS ISA are interpreted. The process executing at the time of this exception is handed a UNIX SIGILL/ ILL_RESOP_FAULT (illegal instruction/reserved operand fault) signal. This error is usually fatal.

Coprocessor Unusable Exception

Cause. The Coprocessor Unusable exception occurs when an attempt is made to execute a coprocessor instruction for either:

- a corresponding coprocessor unit that has not been marked usable, or

- CP0 instructions, when the unit has not been marked usable and the process is executing in User mode.

This exception is not maskable.

Handling. The common exception vector is used for this exception, and the *CpU* code in the *Cause* register is set.

The contents of the Coprocessor Usage Error field of the coprocessor *Control* register indicate which coprocessor of the four was referenced.

The *EPC* register points at the unusable coprocessor instruction — unless it is in a branch delay slot, in which case the *EPC* points at the preceding branch instruction.

Servicing. The coprocessor unit to which an attempted reference was made is identified by the Coprocessor Usage Error field. Results are one of the following:

- If the process is entitled to access, the coprocessor is marked usable and the corresponding user state is restored to the coprocessor.

- If the process is entitled to access the coprocessor, but the coprocessor does not exist, or has failed, interpretation of the coprocessor instruction is possible.

- If the *BD* bit is set in the *Cause* register, the branch instruction must be interpreted; then the coprocessor instruction can be emulated and execution resumed with the *EPC* register advanced past the coprocessor instruction.

- If the process is not entitled to access the coprocessor, the process executing at the time is handed a UNIX SIGILL/ILL_PRIVIN_FAULT (illegal instruction/privileged instruction fault) signal. This error is usually fatal.

Floating-Point Exception

Cause. The Floating-Point exception is used only by the R4000 floating-point coprocessor; other implementations use one of the hardware interrupts for this exception. The Floating-Point exception is not maskable.

Handling. The common exception vector is used for this exception, and the *FPE* code in the *Cause* register is set.

The contents of the *Floating-Point Control Status* register indicate the cause of this exception.

Servicing. This exception is cleared by clearing the appropriate bit in the *Floating-Point Control Status* register. For an unimplemented instruction exception, the kernel should emulate the instruction; for other exceptions, the kernel should pass the exception to the user program which caused the exception.

Watch Exception

The Watch exception is implemented on R4000 processors only.

Cause. The Watch exception occurs when a load or store instruction references the physical address specified in the *WatchLo/WatchHi* system control coprocessor registers. The *WatchLo* register specifies whether a load or store initiated this exception.

The CACHE instruction never causes a Watch exception.

The Watch exception is postponed while the *EXL* bit is set in the *Status* register, and Watch is only maskable by setting *EXL* in the *Status* register.

Handling. The common exception vector is used for this exception, and the *Watch* code in the *Cause* register is set.

Servicing. The Watch exception is a debugging aid; typically the exception handler transfers control to a debugger, allowing the user to examine the situation. To continue, the Watch exception must be disabled to execute the faulting instruction, and then the Watch exception must be reenabled. The faulting instruction can be executed either by interpretation or by setting breakpoints.

Uncached LDCz/SDCz Exception

The Uncached LDCz/SDCz exception is implemented on R6000 processors only.

Cause. The Uncached LDCz/SDCz exception occurs when a doubleword access is made to an uncached address. This exception is not maskable.

Handling. The common exception vector is used for this exception, and the *NCD* code in the *Cause* register is set.

Servicing. The exception handler emulates a doubleword access and resumes execution.

Interrupt Exception

Cause. The Interrupt exception occurs when one of the eight interrupt conditions is asserted. The significance of these interrupts is dependent upon the specific processor implementation.

Each of the eight interrupts can be masked by clearing the corresponding bit in the *Int-Mask* field of the *Status* register, and all of the eight interrupts can be masked at once by clearing the *IEc* bit of the *Status* register.

Handling. The common exception vector is used for this exception, and the *Int* code in the *Cause* register is set.

The IP field of the *Cause* register indicates the current interrupt requests. It is possible that more than one of the bits will be simultaneously set — or even *no* bits may be set — if an interrupt is asserted and then deasserted before this register is read.

Servicing. If the interrupt is caused by one of the two software-generated exceptions (SW_1 or SW_0), the interrupt condition is cleared by setting the corresponding *Cause* register bit to 0.

If the interrupt is hardware-generated, the interrupt condition is cleared by correcting the condition causing the interrupt pin to be asserted. The manner in which this is accomplished is implementation-dependent.

7
FPU Overview

The MIPS Floating-Point Unit (FPU) operates as a coprocessor for the CPU and extends the CPU instruction set to perform arithmetic operations on values in floating-point representations. The FPU, with associated system software, fully conforms to the requirements of ANSI/IEEE Standard 754–1985, "IEEE Standard for Binary Floating-Point Arithmetic." In addition, the MIPS architecture fully supports the recommendations of the standard. Figure 7–1 illustrates the functional organization of the FPU.

Note: FPA and FPU are used interchangeably to refer to the same device.

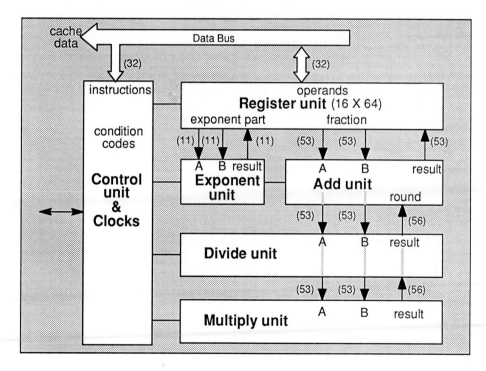

Figure 7–1. FPU Functional Block Diagram

FPU Features

- **Full 64-bit operation.** The FPU contains 16 64-bit registers that hold single precision or double precision values. The FPU also includes a 32-bit *Status/Control* register that provides access to all IEEE-Standard exception handling capabilities.

- **Load/Store Instruction Set.** Like the CPU, the FPU uses a load/store-oriented instruction set, with single-cycle load and store operations. Floating-point operations are started in a single cycle and their execution is overlapped with other fixed-point or floating-point operations.

- **Tightly coupled Coprocessor Interface.** The FPU connects to the CPU to form a tightly coupled unit with a seamless integration of floating-point and fixed-point instruction sets. Since each unit receives and executes instructions in parallel, some floating-point instructions can execute at the same single-cycle per instruction rate as fixed-point-instructions.

FPU Programming Model

This section describes the organization of data in registers and in memory, and the set of general registers available. This section also gives a summary description of the FPU registers.

As shown in Figure 7–2, The FPU provides three types of registers:

- *Floating-Point General Purpose* Registers (*FGRs*)
- *Floating-Point* Registers (*FPRs*)
- *Floating-Point Control* Registers (*FCRs*)

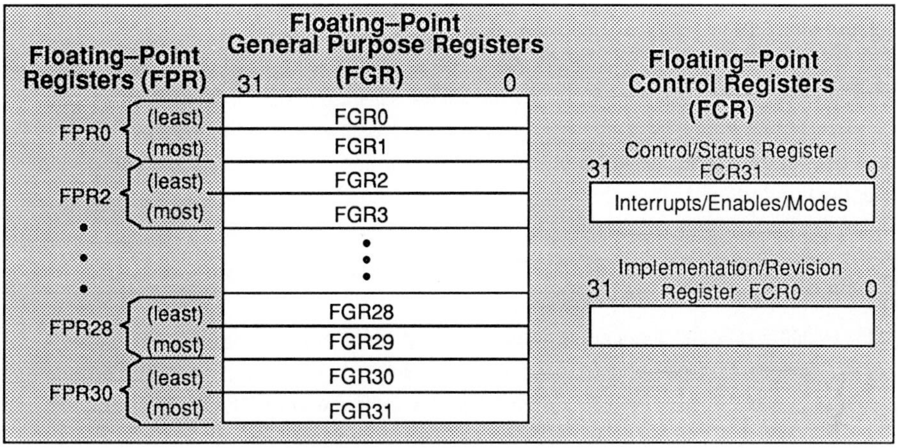

Figure 7–2. FPU Registers

Floating-Point General Purpose registers *(FGRs)* are directly addressable, physical registers. The FPU provides 32 *FGRs*, each of which is 32-bits wide.

Floating-Point registers *(FPRs)* are logical registers that store data values during floating-point operations. Each of the 16 *FPRs* is 64 bits wide and is formed by concatenating two adjacent *FGRs*. Depending on the requirements of an operation, *FPRs* hold either single or double precision floating-point values.

Floating-Point Control registers *(FCRs)* provide rounding mode control, exception handling, and state saving. The *FCRs* include the *Control/Status* register and the *Implementation/Revision* register.

Floating-Point General Purpose Registers (FGRs)

The 32 *FGRs* on the FPU are directly addressable 32–bit registers used in floating-point operations and individually accessible through move, load, and store instructions. Tables 7–1 and 7–2 list the *FGRs*, as arranged from the viewpoint of the processor and coprocessor respectively.

Implementation Note:

In the R4000 and R6000, there are two views of the 32 coprocessor general purpose registers.
- From the standpoint of the central processor, which has no intrinsic representation of coprocessor registers, the *FGRs* are simply 32 single-word (32-bit) registers accessed over an external 32-bit bus.
- From the standpoint of the floating-point processor, collections of single-word registers form floating-point registers, on which floating-point operations are performed.

Regardless of the MIPS processor byte ordering, the coprocessor general purpose registers appear as shown in Table 7–1 (from the viewpoint of the MIPS processor).

Table 7–1. Floating-Point General Purpose Register Layout--Processor Viewpoint

FGR Number	Usage	FGR Number	Usage
FGR0	FPR 0 (least)	FGR16	FPR 16 (least)
FGR1	FPR 0 (less)	FGR17	FPR 16 (less)
FGR2	FPR 0 (more) or 2 (least)	FGR18	FPR 16 (more) or 18 (least)
FGR3	FPR 0 (most) or 2 (less)	FGR19	FPR 16 (most) or 18 (less)
FGR4	FPR 4 (least)	FGR20	FPR 20 (least)
FGR5	FPR 4 (less)	FGR21	FPR 20 (less)
FGR6	FPR 4 (more) or 6 (least)	FGR22	FPR 20 (more) or 22 (least)
FGR7	FPR 4 (most) or 6 (less)	FGR23	FPR 20 (most) or 22 (less)
FGR8	FPR 8 (least)	FGR24	FPR 24 (least)
FGR9	FPR 8 (less)	FGR25	FPR 24 (less)
FGR10	FPR 8 (more) or 10 (least)	FGR26	FPR 24 (more) or 26 (least)
FGR11	FPR 8 (most) or 10 (less)	FGR27	FPR 24 (most) or 26 (less)
FGR12	FPR 12 (least)	FGR28	FPR 28 (least)
FGR13	FPR 12 (less)	FGR29	FPR 28 (less)
FGR14	FPR 12 (more) or 14 (least)	FGR30	FPR 28 (more) or 30 (least)
FGR15	FPR 12 (most) or 14 (less)	FGR31	FPR 28 (most) or 30 (less)

Regardless of the MIPS processor byte ordering, the coprocessor general purpose registers are assembled within the FPU as shown in Table 7–2.

Table 7–2. Floating-Point General Purpose Register Layout—Coprocessor Viewpoint

FPR Number	FGR Registers Referenced			
	(Most)	(More)	(Less)	(Least)
FPR0	FGR[3]	FGR[2]	FGR[1]	FGR[0]
FPR2			FGR[3]	FGR[2]
FPR4	FGR[7]	FGR[6]	FGR[5]	FGR[4]
FPR6			FGR[7]	FGR[6]
FPR8	FGR[11]	FGR[10]	FGR[9]	FGR[8]
FPR10			FGR[11]	FGR[10]
FPR12	FGR[15]	FGR[14]	FGR[13]	FGR[12]
FPR14			FGR[15]	FGR[14]
FPR16	FGR[19]	FGR[18]	FGR[17]	FGR[16]
FPR18			FGR[19]	FGR[18]
FPR20	FGR[23]	FGR[22]	FGR[21]	FGR[20]
FPR22			FGR[23]	FGR[22]
FPR24	FGR[27]	FGR[26]	FGR[25]	FGR[24]
FPR26			FGR[27]	FGR[26]
FPR28	FGR[31]	FGR[30]	FGR[29]	FGR[28]
FPR30			FGR[31]	FGR[30]

Coprocessor general purpose registers are read and written by instructions executing in either Kernel or User mode.

Floating-Point Registers

The FPU provides 16 *Floating-Point* registers (*FPRs*). These logical 64-bit registers hold floating-point values during floating-point operations and are physically formed from the *General Purpose* registers (*FGRs*).

The *FPRs* hold values in either single or double precision floating-point format. Only even numbers are used to address *FPRs*: odd *FPR* register numbers are invalid. During single precision floating-point operations, only the even-numbered (least, as shown in Table 7–1) general registers are used, and during double precision floating-point operations, the general registers are accessed in double pairs. Thus, in a double precision operation, selecting *Floating-Point Register 0* (*FPR0*) addresses adjacent *Floating-Point General Purpose* registers *FGR0* and *FGR1*.

Floating-Point Control Registers

MIPS coprocessors can have as many as 32 control registers. FPU coprocessors implement the following *Floating-Point Control* registers (*FCRs*), which can be accessed only by move operations. The registers are described below:

- The *Control/Status* register *(FCR31)* controls and monitors exceptions, holds the result of compare operations, and establishes rounding modes.

- The *Implementation/Revision* register *(FCR0)* holds revision information about the FPU.

Table 7–3 lists the assignments of the *FCRs*.

Table 7–3. Floating-Point Control Register Assignments

FCR Number	Use
FCR0	Coprocessor implementation and revision register
FCR1–30	Reserved
FCR31	Rounding mode, cause, trap enables, and flags

Control/Status Register FCR31 (Read and Write)

The *Control/Status* register, *FCR31*, contains control and status data and can be accessed by instructions in either Kernel or User mode. It controls the arithmetic rounding mode and the enabling of User-mode traps. It also identifies exceptions that occurred in the most recently executed instruction, and any exceptions that may have occurred without being trapped. Figure 7–3 shows the bit assignments of *FCR31*.

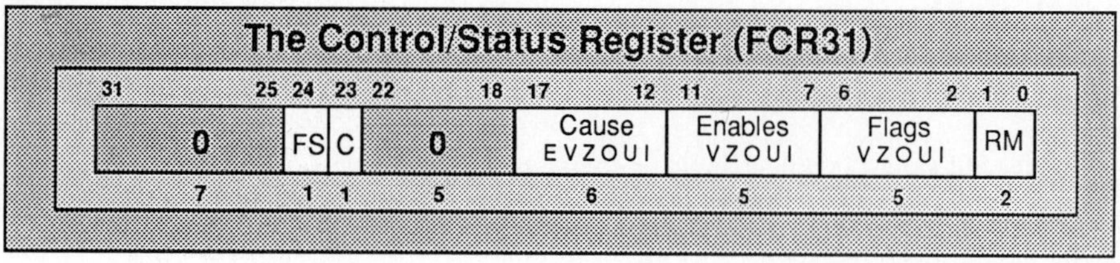

Figure 7–3. FP Control/Status Register Bit Assignments

When the *Control/Status* register is read using a Move Control From Coprocessor 1 (CFC1) instruction, all unfinished instructions in the pipeline are completed before the contents of the register are moved to the main processor. If a floating-point exception occurs as the pipeline empties, the exception is taken and the CFC1 instruction can be reexecuted after the exception is serviced.

The bits in the *Control/Status* register can be set or cleared by writing to the register using a Move Control To Coprocessor 1 (CTC1) instruction. This register must only be written to when the FPU is not actively executing floating-point operations: this can be ensured by first reading the contents of the register to empty the pipeline.

IEEE Standard 754. IEEE Standard 754 specifies that floating-point operations detect certain exceptional cases, raise flags, and optionally invoke an exception handler when an exception occurs. These features are implemented in the MIPS architecture with the Cause, Enable, and Flag fields of the *Control/Status* register. These flag bits implement IEEE 754 exception status flags, and the cause and enable bits implement exception handling.

Control/Status Register FS Bit. Bit 24 of the *Control/Status* register is the *FS* bit. The *FS* bit is implemented on R4000 processors only and when the bit is set, denormalized results are flushed to zero instead of causing an unimplemented operation exception.

Control/Status Register Condition Bit. Bit 23 of the *Control/Status* register is the *Condition* bit. When a floating-point Compare operation takes place, the result is stored at bit 23 in order that the state of the condition line can be saved or restored. The *C* bit is set to 1 if the condition is true; the bit is cleared to 0 if the condition is false. Bit 23 is affected only by compare and Move Control To FPU instructions.

Control/Status Register Cause, Flag, and Enable Bits. Figure 7–4 illustrates the Cause, Flag, and Enable bit assignments in the *Control/Status* register.

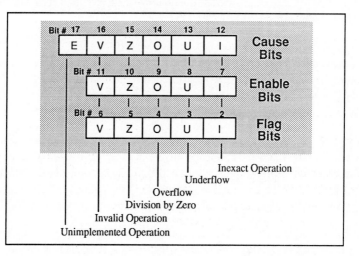

Figure 7–4. Control/Status Register Cause/Flag/Enable Bits

Bits 17:12 in the *Control/Status* register contains Cause bits, as shown in Figure 7–4, which reflect the results of the most recently executed instruction. The Cause bits are a logical extension of the CP0 *Cause* register; they identify the exceptions raised by the last floating-point operation and raise an interrupt or exception if the corresponding enable bit is set.

The Cause bits are written by each floating-point operation (but not by load, store, or move operations). Unimplemented Operation (*U*) is set to 1 if software emulation is required, otherwise it remains 0. The other bits are set to 0 or 1 to indicate the occurrence or non-occurrence (respectively) of an IEEE 754 exception.

A floating-point interrupt or exception is generated any time a Cause bit and the corresponding Enable bit are both set. A floating-point operation that sets an enabled Cause bit forces an immediate interrupt or exception, as does setting both Cause and Enable bits with CTC1.

Implementation Note:

The R2000, R3000, and R6000 processors use external interrupts to cause a trap, whereas the R4000 processor uses an exception. R4000 floating-point exceptions cannot be disabled.

There is no enable for Unimplemented Operation (U). Setting Unimplemented Operation always generates a floating-point interrupt or exception.

When a floating-point interrupt or exception is taken, no results are stored, and the only state affected are the Cause and Flag bits. Exceptions caused by an immediately previous floating-point operation can be determined by reading the Cause field.

Before returning from a floating-point interrupt, exception, or doing a CTC1, software must first clear the enabled Cause bits to prevent a repeat of the interrupt. Thus User-mode programs can never observe enabled Cause bits set; if this information is required in a User-mode handler, it must be passed somewhere other than the *Status* register.

The appropriate Flag bits are set by the operation when a User-mode exception handler is invoked. This is not implemented in hardware; floating-point exception software is responsible for setting these bits before invoking a user handler.

For a floating-point operation that sets only unenabled Cause bits, no interrupt occurs and the default result defined by IEEE 754 is stored. In this case, the exceptions that were caused by the immediately previous floating-point operation can be determined by reading the Cause field.

Table 7–4 lists the meanings of each bit in the Cause field. If more than one exception occurs on a single instruction, each appropriate bit will be set.

Table 7–4. Cause Field Bit Definitions

Cause Field Bit	Description
E	Unimplemented operation
V	Invalid operation
Z	Division by zero
I	Inexact exception
O	Overflow exception
U	Underflow exception

The Flag bits are cumulative and indicate that an exception was raised on some operation since they were explicitly reset. Flag bits are set to 1 if an IEEE 754 exception is raised, and remain unchanged otherwise. The Flag bits are never cleared as a side effect of floating-point operations, but can be set or cleared by writing a new value into the *Status* register, using a Move To Coprocessor Control instruction.

Control/Status Register Rounding Mode Control Bits. Bits 1 and 0 in the *Control/Status* register comprise the Rounding Mode (RM) field. These bits specify the rounding mode that the FPU uses for all floating-point operations as shown in Table 7–5.

Table 7–5. Rounding Mode Bit Decoding

Rounding Mode	Mnemonic	Description
0	RN	Round result to nearest representable value; round to value with least significant bit zero when the two nearest representable values are equally near.
1	RZ	Round toward zero: round to value closest to and not greater in magnitude than the infinitely precise result.
2	RP	Round toward +∞: round to value closest to and not less than the infinitely precise result.
3	RM	Round toward − ∞: round to value closest to and not greater than the infinitely precise result.

Implementation and Revision Register FCR0 (Read Only)

The FPU control register zero (*FCR0*) contains values that define the implementation and revision number of the FPU. This information can be used to determine the coprocessor revision and performance level, and can also used by diagnostic software.

The low-order two bytes of the *Implementation and Revision* register, *FCR0*, are defined as shown in Figure 7–5.

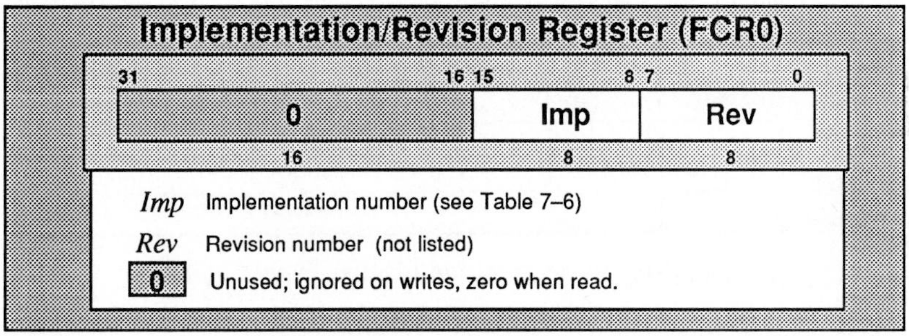

Figure 7–5. Implementation/Revision Register

Bits 15 through 8 identify the implementation number, as shown in Table 7–6, and bits 7 through 0 identify the revision number. The revision number is a value of the form $y.x$ where y is a major revision number held in bits 7..4, and x is a minor revision number held in bits 3..0. The revision number can distinguish some chip revisions, however MIPS does not guarantee that changes to its chips are necessarily reflected by the revision number, or that changes to the revision number necessarily reflect real chip changes. For this reason revision number values are not listed in Table 7–6, and software should not rely on the revision number to characterize the chip.

Table 7–6. FCR0 Coprocessor Implementation Types

Imp. Number	Description
0x00	software
0x01	reserved
0x02	MIPS R2010 FPU
0x03	MIPS R3010 FPU
0x04	MIPS R6010 FPU
0x05	MIPS R4000 FPU

Floating-Point Formats

The FPUs perform both 32-bit (single precision) and 64-bit (double precision) IEEE standard floating-point operations.

R2010/R3010 Operations

The R2010 and R3010 implement single and double precision operations; the 32-bit single precision format has a 24-bit signed-magnitude fraction field (f+s) and an 8-bit exponent (e), as shown in Figure 7–6.

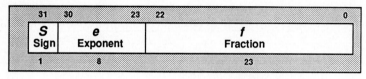

31	30	23	22	0
S Sign	*e* Exponent		*f* Fraction	
1	8		23	

Figure 7–6. Single Precision Floating-Point Format

The 64-bit double precision format has a 53-bit signed-magnitude fraction field (f+s) and an 11-bit exponent, as shown in Figure 7–7.

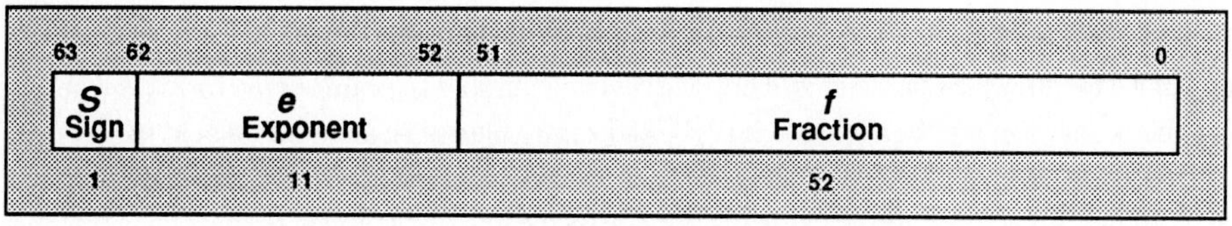

63	52	52	51	0
S Sign	*e* Exponent		*f* Fraction	
1	11		52	

Figure 7–7. Double Precision Floating-Point Format

R4000 and R6010 Operations

The R4000 and R6000 implementations use the same single and double precision formats described in Figures 7–6 and 7–7.

Numbers in these floating-point formats are composed of three fields:

- 1-bit sign: s
- biased exponent: $e = E + bias$
- fraction: $f = .b_1b_2...b_{P-1}$

The range of the unbiased exponent E includes every integer between two values E_{min} and E_{max} inclusive, and also two other reserved values: $E_{min} - 1$ to encode ± 0 and denormalized numbers, and $E_{max} + 1$ to encode $\pm\infty$ and NaNs (Not a Number). For single and double precision formats, each representable nonzero numerical value has just one encoding.

For single and double precision formats, the value of a number, v, is determined by the equations shown in Table 7–7.

Table 7–7. Equations for Calculating Values in Single-
and Double Precision Floating-Point Format

(1)	if $E = E_{max}+1$ and $f \neq 0$, then v is NaN, regardless of s.
(2)	if $E = E_{max}+1$ and $f = 0$, then $v = (-1)^s \infty$.
(3)	if $E_{min} \leq E \leq E_{max}$, then $v = (-1)^s 2^E(1.f)$
(4)	if $E = E_{min}-1$ and $f \neq 0$, then $v = (-1)^s 2^{E_{min}}(0.f)$.
(5)	if $E = E_{min}-1$ and $f = 0$, then $v = (-1)^s 0$.

For all floating-point formats, if v is NaN, the most significant bit of f determines whether the value is a signaling or quiet NaN. v is a signaling NaN if the most significant bit of f is set; otherwise v is a quiet NaN. Table 7–8 defines the values for the format parameters.

Table 7–8. *Floating-Point Format Parameter Values*

Parameter	Format	
	Single	Double
f	24	53
E_{max}	+127	+1023
E_{min}	−126	−1022
exponent *bias*	+127	+1023
exponent width in bits	8	11
integer bit	hidden	hidden
fraction width in bits	24	53
format width in bits	32	64

Minimum and maximum floating-point values are given in Table 7–9.

Table 7–9. *Minimum and Maximum Floating-Point Values*

Float Minimum	1.40129846e−45
Float Minimum Norm.	1.17549435e−38
Float Maximum	3.40282347e+38
Double Minimum	4.9406564584124654e−324
Double Minimum Norm	2.2250738585072014e−308
Double Maximum	1.7976931348623157e+308

Binary Fixed-Point Format

Binary fixed-point values are held in 2's-complementary format. Unsigned fixed-point values are not directly provided by the floating-point instruction set. Binary fixed-point format is shown in Figure 7–8.

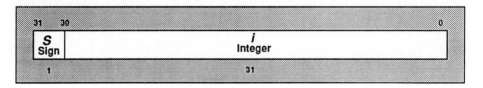

Figure 7–8. *Binary Fixed-Point Format*

Number Definitions

This section contains the definition of the following number types specified in the IEEE 754 standard:

- normalized numbers
- denormalized numbers
- infinity
- zero

For more information, refer to the *ANSI/IEEE Std 754–1985 IEEE Standard for Binary Floating-Point Arithmetic*.

Normalized Numbers

Most floating-point calculations are performed on normalized numbers. For single precision operations, normalized numbers have a biased exponent that ranges from 1 to 254 (–126 to +127 unbiased) and a normalized fraction field, meaning that the leftmost, or hidden, bit is one. In decimal notation, this allows representation of a range of positive and negative numbers from approximately 10^{38} to 10^{-38}, with accuracy to seven decimal places.

Denormalized Numbers

Denormalized numbers have a zero exponent and a denormalized (hidden bit equal to zero) non-zero fraction field.

Infinity

Infinity has an exponent of all ones and a fraction field equal to zero. Both positive and negative infinity are supported.

Zero

Zero has an exponent of zero, a hidden bit equal to zero, and a value of zero in the fraction field. Both +0 and –0 are supported.

Coprocessor Operation

The FPU continually monitors the CPU instruction stream. If an instruction does not apply to the coprocessor, it is ignored; if an instruction does apply to the coprocessor, the FPU executes that instruction and transfers necessary result and exception data synchronously to the main processor.

The FPU performs three types of operations:

- loads and stores
- moves
- two- and three-register floating-point operations.

Load, Store, and Move Operations

Load, store, and move operations move data between memory or the CPU registers, and the FPU registers. These operations perform no format conversions and cause no floating-point exceptions.

Load, store, and move operations reference a single 32-bit word (on the R2000, R3000, R4000, and R6000) and 64-bit doubleword (on the R4000 and R6000) of either the *Floating-Point General Purpose* registers (*FGRs*) or the *Floating-Point Control* registers (*FCRs*).

Floating-Point Operations

The FPU supports the following floating-point operations:

- add
- subtract
- multiply
- divide
- square root (R4000/R6000 only)
- move
- floor

- absolute value
- negate
- compare
- truncate
- round
- ceiling
- convert

In addition, the FPU supports conversions between floating-point formats and fixed-point formats. Refer to Chapter 8 for a complete description of all the FPU instructions.

Exceptions

The FPU supports all five IEEE standard exceptions:

- Invalid Operation
- Inexact Operation
- Division by Zero
- Overflow
- Underflow

The FPU also supports the optional, Unimplemented Operation exception that allows unimplemented instructions to trap to software emulation routines. For more information on FPU exceptions, refer to Chapter 9.

Instruction Set Overview

All FPU instructions are 32 bits long, aligned on a word boundary, and can be divided into the following groups:

- Load, store, and move instructions move data between memory, the main processor, and the *FPU General Purpose* registers.

- Computational instructions perform arithmetic operations on floating-point values in the FPU registers.

- Conversion instructions perform conversion operations between the various data formats.

- Compare instructions perform comparisons of the contents of registers and set a condition bit based on the results.

Table 7–10 lists the instruction set of the FPU. A more detailed summary is contained in Chapter 8 and a complete description of each instruction is provided in Appendix B.

Table 7–10. FPU Instruction Summary

OP	Description	OP	Description
	Load/Store/Move Instructions		**Computational Instructions**
LWC1	Load Word to FPU	ADD.fmt	Floating–point Add
SWC1	Store Word from FPU	SUB.fmt	Floating–point Subtract
LDC1	Load Doubleword to FPU*	MUL.fmt	Floating–point Multiply
SDC1	Store Doubleword From FPU*	DIV.fmt	Floating–point Divide
MTC1	Move word To FPU	SQRT.fmt	Floating–point Square Root*
MFC1	Move word From FPU	ABS.fmt	Floating–point Absolute value
CTC1	Move Control word To FPU	MOV.fmt	Floating–point Move
CFC1	Move Control word From FPU	NEG.fmt	Floating–point Negate
			Compare Instructions
	Conversion Instructions	C.cond.fmt	Floating–point Compare
CVT.S.fmt	Floating–point Convert to Single FP		
CVT.D.fmt	Floating–point Convert to Double FP		
CVT.W.fmt	Floating–point Convert to Single Fixed Point		**Branch on FP Condition**
ROUND.w.fmt	Floating–point Round*	BC1T	FP Branch if True
TRUNC.w.fmt	Floating–point Truncate*	BC1F	FP Branch if False
CEIL.w.fmt	Floating–point Ceiling*	BC1TL	FP Branch if True Likely*
FLOOR.w.fmt	Floating–point Floor*	BC1FL	FP Branch if False Likely*
	*R4000/R6000 only		

8

FPU Instruction Set Summary
& Instruction Pipeline

This chapter provides a summary of the FPU instruction set including a detailed discussion of the FPU instruction pipeline, which permits the overlapping of instructions to increase the effective instruction execution rate.

Note: FPA and FPU are used interchangeably to refer to the same device.

Instruction Set Summary

The floating-point instructions supported by the FPU are implemented using the coprocessor unit 1 (COP1) operation instructions of the CPU instruction set. The basic operations the FPU performs are:

- load and store operations from/to the FPU registers
- moves between FPU and CPU registers
- computational operations including floating-point add, subtract, multiply, divide, and convert instructions
- floating-point comparisons

The Branch On Coprocessor 1 condition (BC1T/BC1F) operations are also COP1 operations and are described in this chapter. However, these instructions are implemented entirely by the CPU, using the CpCond input from the FPU.

Load, Store, and Move Instructions

All movement of data between the FPU and memory is accomplished by:

- Load Word To Coprocessor 1 (LWC1) and Store Word To Coprocessor 1 (SWC1) instructions, which reference a single 32-bit word of the FPU general registers

- Load Doubleword (LDC1) and Store Doubleword (SDC1) instructions, which are used only in R4000 and R6000 processors.

These load and store operations are unformatted; no format conversions are performed and therefore no floating-point exceptions occur due to these operations.

Data can also be moved directly between the FPU and the CPU by Move To Coprocessor 1 (MTC1) and Move From Coprocessor 1 (MFC1) instructions. Like the floating-point load and store operations, these operations perform no format conversions and never cause floating-point exceptions.

In R2000 and R3000 processors, load and move-to operations have a delay of one instruction. That is, the data being loaded from memory or the CPU into an FPU register is not available to the instruction immediately following the load instruction: the data is available to the second instruction after the load instruction. (Refer to Table 8–6, and the sections at the end of this chapter for a detailed discussion of load instruction latency.)

In R4000 and R6000 processors, the instruction immediately following a load can use the contents of the loaded register. In such cases the hardware interlocks, requiring additional real cycles, so scheduling load delay slots is desirable, though not required for functional code.

All coprocessor loads and stores reference the following aligned data items:

- For word loads and stores, the access type is always WORD, and the low order two bits of the address must always be zero.

- For doubleword loads and stores, the access type is always DOUBLEWORD, and the low order three bits of the address must always be zero.

Regardless of byte-numbering order (endianness), the address specifies the byte that has the smallest byte address in the addressed field. For a Big-endian system, it is the leftmost byte; for a Little-endian system, it is the rightmost byte.

Table 8–1 summarizes the load, store, and move instructions.

Table 8–1. FPU Load, Store and Move Instruction Summary

Instruction	Format and Description
Load Word to FPA (coprocessor 1)	*LWC1 ft,offset(base)* `op base ft offset` Sign-extend 16-bit *offset* and add to contents of CPU register *base* to form address. Load contents of addressed word into FPU general register *ft*.
Store Word from FPA (coprocessor 1)	*SWC1 ft,offset(base)* Sign-extend 16-bit *offset* and add to contents of CPU register *base* to form address. Store the contents of FPU general register *ft* at addressed location.
Load Double-word to FPA (coprocessor 1)	*LDC1 ft,offset(base)* **R4000 and R6000 only** Sign-extend 16-bit *offset* and add to contents of CPU register *base* to form address. Load contents of addressed doubleword into FPU general registers *ft* and *ft+1*.
Store Double-word from FPA (coprocessor 1)	*SDC1 ft,offset(base)* **R4000 and R6000 only** Sign-extend 16-bit *offset* and add to contents of CPU register *base* to form address. Store the 64-bit contents of FPU general registers *ft* and *ft+1* at addressed location.
Move Word to FPA (coprocessor 1)	*MTC1 rt,fs* `COP1 sub rt fs 0` Move contents of CPU register *rt* into FPU general register *fs*.
Move Word from FPA (coprocessor 1)	*MFC1 rt,fs* Move contents of FPU general register *fs* into CPU register *rt*.
Move Control Word to FPA (coprocessor 1)	*CTC1 rt,fs* Move contents of CPU register *rt* into FPU control register *fs*.
Move Control Word from FPA (coprocessor 1)	*CFC1 rt,fs* Move contents of FPU control register *fs* into CPU register *rt*.

Floating-Point Computational Instructions

Computational instructions perform arithmetic operations on floating-point values in registers. There are four categories of computational instructions, as shown in Table 8–2.

- **3 -Operand Register-Type** instructions, which perform floating-point addition, subtraction, multiplication, division, and square root (*SQRT* is R4000 and R6000 only) operations.

- **2-Operand Register-Type** instructions, which perform floating-point absolute value, move, and negate operations.

- **Convert** instructions, which perform conversions between the various data formats.

- **Compare** instructions, which perform comparisons of the contents of two registers and set or clear a condition signal based on the result of the comparison.

Table 8–2. *FPU Computational Instruction Summary*

Instruction	Format and Description COP1 | fmt | ft | fs | fd | function
Floating–Point Add	ADD.*fmt* fd,fs,ft Interpret the contents of FPU registers *fs* and *ft* in the specified format (*fmt*) and add arithmetically. Place the rounded result in FPU register *fd*.
Floating–Point Subtract	SUB.*fmt* fd,fs,ft Interpret the contents of FPU registers *fs* and *ft* in the specified format (*fmt*) and arithmetically subtract. Place the rounded result in FPU register *fd*.
Floating–Point Multiply	MUL.*fmt* fd,fs,ft Interpret the contents of FPU registers *fs* and *ft* in the specified format (*fmt*) and arithmetically multiply. Place the rounded result in FPU register *fd*.
Floating–Point Divide	DIV.*fmt* fd,fs,ft Interpret the contents of FPU registers *fs* and *ft* in the specified format (*fmt*) and arithmetically divide *fs* by *ft*. Place the rounded result in FPU register *fd*.
Floating–Point Absolute Value	ABS.*fmt* fd,fs Interpret the contents of FPU register *fs* in the specified format (*fmt*) and take arithmetic absolute value. Place the result in FPU register *fd*.
Floating–Point Move	MOV.*fmt* fd,fs Interpret the contents of FPU register *fs* in the specified format (*fmt*) and copy into FPU register *fd*.
Floating–Point Negate	NEG.*fmt* fd,fs Interpret the contents of FPU register *fs* in the specified format (*fmt*) and take arithmetic negation. Place the result in FPU register *fd*.
Floating–Point Convert to Single FP Format	CVT.S.*fmt* fd,fs Interpret the contents of FPU register *fs* in the specified format (*fmt*) and arithmetically convert to single binary floating-point format. Place the rounded result in FPU register *fd*.
Floating–Point Convert to Double FP Format	CVT.D.*fmt* fd,fs Interpret the contents of FPU register *fs* in the specified format (*fmt*) and arithmetically convert to the double binary floating-point format. Place the rounded result in FPU register *fd*.
Floating–Point Convert to Single Fixed–Point Format	CVT.W.*fmt* fd,fs Interpret the contents of FPU register *fs* in the specified format (*fmt*) and arithmetically convert to the single fixed-point format. Place the result in FPU register *fd*.
Floating–Point Compare	C.*cond*.*fmt* fs,ft Interpret the contents of FPU registers *fs* and *ft* in the specified format (*fmt*) and compare arithmetically. The result is determined by the comparison and the specified condition (*cond*). After a 1-instruction delay, the condition is available for testing by the CPU with the Branch on Floating-Point Coprocessor Condition (*BC1T*, *BC1F*) instructions.
Floating–Point Square root	SQRT.*fmt* fd,fs **R4000 and R6000 only** Interpret the contents of FPU register *fs* in the specified format (*fmt*) and take the positive arithmetic square root. Result is rounded then placed in the FPU register *fd*.

Table 8–2. *FPU Computational Instruction Summary (cont.)*

Instruction	Format and Description	COP1	fmt	ft	fs	fd	function
Floating–point Round	*ROUND.W.fmt* fd,fs **R4000 and R6000 only** Interpret the contents of FPU register *fs* in the specified format (*fmt*) and arithmetically convert to the single fixed-point format. Place the result in FPU register *fd*.
Floating–point Truncate	*TRUNC.W.fmt* fd,fs **R4000 and R6000 only** Interpret the contents of FPU register *fs* in the specified format (*fmt*) and arithmetically convert to the single fixed-point format. Place the result in FPU register *fd*.
Floating–point Ceiling	*CEIL.W.fmt* fd,fs **R4000 and R6000 only** Interpret the contents of FPU register *fs* in the specified format (*fmt*) and arithmetically convert to the single fixed-point format. Place the result in FPU register *fd*.
Floating–point Floor	*FLOOR.W.fmt* fd,fs **R4000 and R6000 only** Interpret the contents of FPU register *fs* in the specified format (*fmt*) and arithmetically convert to the single fixed-point format. Place the result in FPU register *fd*.

In the instruction formats shown in Table 8–2 , the *fmt* term appended to the instruction op-code is the data format specifier: *s* specifies single precision binary floating-point, *d* specifies double precision binary floating-point, and *w* specifies binary fixed-point.

For example, an ADD.d specifies that the operands for the addition operation are double precision binary floating-point values.

Note: When *fmt* is single precision or binary fixed-point, the odd register of the destination is undefined.

Floating-Point Relational Operations

The floating-point Compare (C.fmt.cond) instructions interpret the contents of two FPU registers (*fs, ft*) in the specified format (*fmt*) and arithmetically compares them. A result is determined based on the comparison and conditions (*cond*) specified in the instruction. Table 8–3 lists the conditions that can be specified for the Compare instruction and Table 8–4 summarizes the floating-point relational operations that are performed.

Table 8–3. Relational Mnemonic Definitions

Mnemonic	Definition	Mnemonic	Definition
F	False	T	True
UN	Unordered	OR	Ordered
EQ	Equal	NEQ	Not Equal
UEQ	Unordered or Equal	OLG	Ordered or Less than or Greater than
OLT	Ordered Less Than	UGE	Unordered or Greater than or Equal
ULT	Unordered or Less Than	OGE	Ordered Greater Than
OLE	Ordered Less than or Equal	UGT	Unordered or Greater Than
ULE	Unordered or Less than or Equal	OGT	Ordered Greater Than
SF	Signaling False	ST	Signaling True
NGLE	Not Greater than or Less than or Equal	GLE	Greater than, or Less than or Equal
SEQ	Signaling Equal	SNE	Signaling Not Equal
NGL	Not Greater than or Less than	GL	Greater Than or Less Than
LT	Less Than	NLT	Not Less Than
NGE	Not Greater than or Equal	GE	Greater Than or Equal
LE	Less than or Equal	NLE	Not Less Than or Equal
NGT	Not Greater Than	GT	Greater Than

Table 8–4 is derived from the IEEE floating-point standard and describes the 26 predicates named in the standard. This table includes six additional predicates (for a total of 32) to round out the set of possible predicates based on the conditions tested by a comparison. Four mutually exclusive relations are possible: less than, equal, greater than, and unordered. Invalid Operation exceptions occur only when comparisons include the *less than* (<) or *greater than* (>) characters but not the *unordered* (?) character in the ad hoc form of the predicate.

Table 8–4. Floating-Point Relational Operators

Predicates			Relations				Invalid operation exception if unordered
Mnemonic	ad hoc	FORTRAN	Greater than	Less than	Equal	Unordered	
F	false		F	F	F	F	No
UN	?		F	F	F	T	No
EQ	=	.EQ.	F	F	T	F	No
UEQ	?=	.UE.	F	F	T	T	No
OLT	NOT(?>=)	.NOT..UG.	F	T	F	F	No
ULT	?<	.UL.	F	T	F	T	No
OLE	NOT(?>)	.NOT..UG.	F	T	T	F	No
ULE	?<=	.ULE.	F	T	T	T	No
OGT	NOT(?<=)	.NOT..ULE.	T	F	F	F	No
UGT	?>	.UGT.	T	F	F	T	No
OGE	NOT(?<)	.NOT..UL.	T	F	T	F	No
UGE	?>=	.UGE.	T	F	T	T	No
OGL	NOT(?=)		T	T	F	F	No
NEQ	NOT(=)	.NE.	T	T	F	T	No
OR	NOT(?)		T	T	T	F	No
T	true		T	T	T	T	No
SF			F	F	F	F	Yes
NGLE	NOT(<=>)	.NOT..LEG	F	F	F	T	Yes
SEQ			F	F	T	F	Yes
NGL	NOT(<>)	.NOT..LG.	F	F	T	T	Yes
LT	<	.LT.	F	T	F	F	Yes
NGE	NOT(>=)	.NOT..GE.	F	T	F	T	Yes
LE	<=	.LE.	F	T	T	F	Yes
NGT	NOT(>)	.NOT..GT.	F	T	T	T	Yes
GT	>	.GT.	T	F	F	F	Yes
NLE	NOT(<=)	.NOT..LE.	T	F	F	T	Yes
GE	>=	.GE.	T	F	T	F	Yes
NLT	NOT(<)	.NOT..LT.	T	F	T	T	Yes
GL	<>	.LG.	T	T	F	F	Yes
SNE			T	T	F	T	Yes
GLE	<=>	.LEG.	T	T	T	F	Yes
ST			T	T	T	T	Yes

Branch on FPU Condition Instructions

Table 8–5 summarizes the four Branch on FPU (coprocessor unit 1) condition instructions that can be used to test the result of the FPU Compare (C.cond) instructions. In this table, *delay slot* refers to the instruction immediately following the branch instruction. Refer to Chapter 1 for a discussion of the branch delay slot.

Table 8–5. Branch on FPU Condition Instructions.

Instruction	Format and Description	COP1 BC br offset
Branch on FPA True	*BC1T* Compute a branch target address by adding the address of the instruction in the delay slot and the 16-bit *offset* (shifted left two bits and sign extended to 32 bits). Branch to the target address (with a delay of one instruction) if the FPU condition line is true.	
Branch on FPA False	*BC1F* Compute a branch target address by adding the address of the instruction in the delay slot and the 16-bit *offset* (shifted left two bits and sign extended to 32 bits). Branch to the target address (with a delay of one instruction) if the FPU condition line is false.	
Branch on FPA True Likely	*BC1TL* **R4000 and R6000 only** Compute a branch target address by adding the address of the instruction in the delay slot and the 16-bit *offset* (shifted left two bits and sign extended to 32 bits). Branch to the target address (with a delay of one instruction) if the FPU condition line is true. If conditional branch is not taken, the instruction in the branch delay slot is nullified.	
Branch on FPA False Likely	*BC1FL* **R4000 and R6000 only** Compute a branch target address by adding the address of the instruction in the delay slot and the 16-bit *offset* (shifted left two bits and sign extended to 32 bits). Branch to the target address (with a delay of one instruction) if the FPU condition line is false. If conditional branch is not taken, the instruction in the branch delay slot is nullified.	

FPU Instruction Pipeline

The FPU provides an instruction pipeline that parallels the CPU instruction pipeline. This section describes R-Series implementations of the FPU instruction pipeline.

R2000/R3000 Implementation

The six pipeline stages (also termed "pipe stages") of the R2010/R3010 FPU instruction pipeline are shown in Figure 8–1. Each stage has two phases, φ1 and φ2

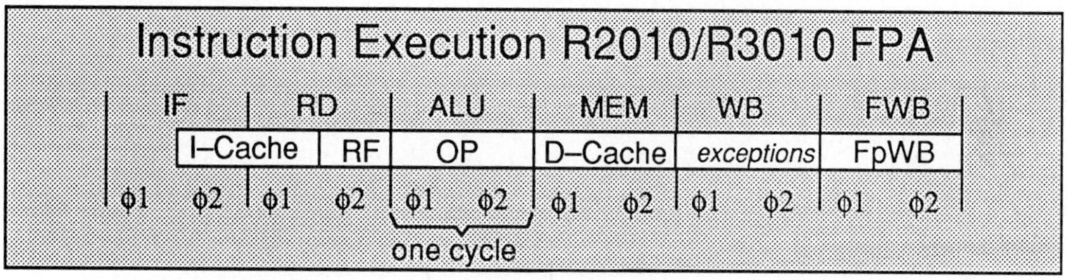

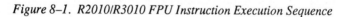

Instruction Execution R2010/R3010 FPA

IF		RD		ALU		MEM		WB		FWB	
I–Cache		RF	OP		D–Cache		exceptions		FpWB		
φ1	φ2	φ1	φ2	φ1	φ2	φ1	φ2	φ1	φ2	φ1	φ2

one cycle

Figure 8–1. R2010/R3010 FPU Instruction Execution Sequence

IF—Instruction Fetch. The CPU calculates the instruction address required to read an instruction from the I-cache. The instruction address is generated and output during phase 2 (φ2) of this pipe stage. No action is required of the FPU during this pipe stage since the main processor is responsible for address generation. The instruction is not actually read into the processor until the beginning (phase 1) of the RD pipe stage.

RD—Read. The instruction is present on the data bus during phase 1 of this pipe stage; the FPU decodes the data on the bus to determine if it is an instruction for the FPU. The FPU reads any required operands from its registers (RF = Register Fetch) while decoding the instruction.

ALU—Arithmetic/Logic Unit operation. If it is an FPU instruction, execution commences during this pipe stage. If the instruction causes an exception, the FPU notifies the CPU. If the FPU requires additional time to complete this instruction, it initiates a stall during this pipe stage.

MEM—Memory. If this is a coprocessor load or store instruction, the FPU presents or captures the data during phase 2 of this pipe stage. If an interrupt is taken by the main processor, it notifies the FPU during phase 2 of this pipe stage.

WB—Write Back. If the instruction currently in this pipe stage caused an exception, the main processor notifies the FPU. Thus, the FPU uses this pipe stage to deal solely with exceptions.

FWB—Floating-Point Write Back. The FPU uses this stage to write back ALU results to its register file. This stage is equivalent to the WB stage in the main processor.

R4000 Implementation

The R4000 FPU is resident on the CPU. It shares the same 8-stage pipeline architecture with the CPU, as described in Chapter 2.

R6010 Implementation

The R6010 has the same pipeline as the main processor except for an additional FPWriteBack stage (labelled WE in Figure 8–2) to accommodate the Load Doubleword to FPU (LDC1) instruction.

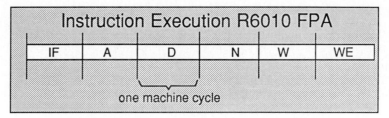

Figure 8–2. R6000 FPU Instruction Execution Sequence

Instruction Execution

Figure 8–3 illustrates how the six instructions overlap in the FPU pipeline. In this figure, the R2000/R3000 FPU pipeline is an example; the R4000 and R6000 FPUs operate on the same principle.

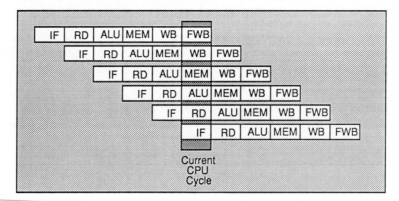

Figure 8–3. R2000/R3000 FPU Instruction Pipeline

Figure 8–3 assumes that each instruction can be completed in a single cycle. Most FPU instructions, however, require more than one cycle to execute. Therefore, the FPU must stall the pipeline if an instruction execution cannot proceed because of register or resource conflicts. Figure 8–4 illustrates the effect of a three-cycle stall on the FPU pipeline.

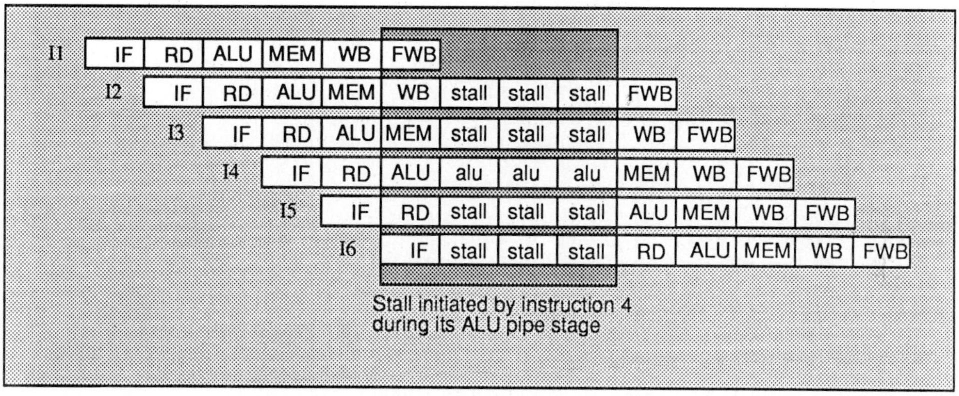

I1	IF	RD	ALU	MEM	WB	FWB							
I2		IF	RD	ALU	MEM	WB	stall	stall	stall	FWB			
I3			IF	RD	ALU	MEM	stall	stall	stall	WB	FWB		
I4				IF	RD	ALU	alu	alu	alu	MEM	WB	FWB	
I5					IF	RD	stall	stall	stall	ALU	MEM	WB	FWB
I6						IF	stall	stall	stall	RD	ALU	MEM	WB	FWB

Stall initiated by instruction 4
during its ALU pipe stage

Figure 8–4. R2000/R3000 FPU Pipeline Stall

To mitigate the performance impact that would result from stalling the instruction pipeline, the FPU allows instructions to overlap so that instruction execution can proceed as long as there are no resource conflicts, data dependencies, or exception conditions. The following sections describe and illustrate the timing and overlapping of FPU instructions.

Instruction Execution Times

Unlike the CPU, which executes almost all instructions in a single cycle, the time required to execute FPU instructions operates within a larger range.

Table 8–6 gives the minimum latency, in processor pipeline cycles, of each floating-point operation for the currently implemented configurations. These latency calculations assume the result of the operation is immediately used in a succeeding operation.

Table 8–6. Floating-Point Operation Latencies

Operation	Pipeline cycles								
	R2010, R3010			R4000			R6010		
fmt	S	D	W	S	D	W	S	D	W
ADD.fmt	2	2	(c)	4	4	(c)	3	3–4(e)	(c)
SUB.fmt	2	2	(c)	4	4	(c)	3	3–4(e)	(c)
MUL.fmt	4	5	(c)	7	8	(c)	4(f)	6(f)	(c)
DIV.fmt	12	19	(c)	23	36	(c)	14(f)	24(f)	(c)
SQRT.fmt	(d)	(d)	(c)	54	112	(c)	23(f)	42(f)	(c)
ABS.fmt	1	1	(c)	2	2	(c)	2	2	(c)
MOV.fmt	1	1	(c)	1	1	(c)	2	2	(c)
NEG.fmt	1	1	(c)	2	2	(c)	2	2	(c)
ROUND.W.fmt	(d)	(d)	(c)	4	4	(c)	3	3–4(e)	(c)
TRUNC.W.fmt	(d)	(d)	(c)	4	4	(c)	3	3–4(e)	(c)
CEIL.W.fmt	(d)	(d)	(c)	4	4	(c)	3	3–4(e)	(c)
FLOOR.W.fmt	(d)	(d)	(c)	4	4	(c)	3	3–4(e)	(c)
CVT.S.fmt	(c)	2	3	(c)	4	6	(c)	3–4(e)	3
CVT.D.fmt	1	(c)	3	2	(c)	5	3	(c)	3
CVT.W.fmt	2	2	(c)	4	4	(c)	3	3–4(e)	(c)
C.fmt.cond	2(a)	2(a)	(c)	3(a)	3(a)	(c)	2(a)	2(a)	(c)
BC1T		1			1			1	
BC1F		1			1			1	
BC1TL		(g)			1			1	
BC1FL		(g)			1			1	
LWC1		2(a)			3			2–3(b)	
SWC1		1			1			1–2(b)	
LDC1		(a)(d)			3			2–3(b)	
SDC1		(d)			1			2	
MTC1		2(a)			3(a)			2(a)	
MFC1		2			3			2	
CTC1		2(a)			3(a)			6(a)	
CFC1		2			3			2	

Key for Table 8–6:

(a) Software *must* schedule operations to avoid reading the floating-point register that is the target of a floating-point load or move to floating-point unit instruction less than two instructions later, and must schedule a floating-point branch instruction two or more instructions after a floating-point compare instruction.

(b) Use the smaller figure for most operations, unless the next instruction is a store: SWC1, SDC1, SW, SWL, SWR, SH, SHU, SB, SBU; or move-to-or-from coprocessor: MTCz, CTCz, MFCz, CFCz.

(c) These operations are illegal.

(d) These operations are only provided through software interpretation.

(e) Operation latency depends on the preceding instructions and the operation that produced the operands of this instruction.

(f)   If the R6010 is programmed to use the 60 MHz latencies for the B3110 chip, the latencies are: MUL.S=4; MUL.D=5; DIV.S=12; DIV.D=20; SQRT.S=20; SQRT.D=36.

(g)   These operations are not available on R2000 or R3000.

Scheduling FPU Instructions

The floating-point architecture permits pipelining of operations and overlapping of floating-point operations with floating-point load, store, and move with other processor operations. Current implementations use these features to varying degrees.

R2010/R3010 Implementation

The R2010 and R3010 floating-point chips permit loads to execute concurrently if they do not modify a pending floating-point op *Result* register, and stores to execute concurrently if they do not use a pending floating-point op *Result* register. Fixed-point operations can also execute concurrently with floating-point operations.

R6010 Implementation

The R6010 floating-point controller provides precise floating-point operations, in the form of the R2010, R3010, and R4000 designs. Loads, stores, and fixed-point operations execute concurrently with floating-point operations. Multiplies, divides, and square roots execute in one floating-point unit, and the other operations execute in another (with some restrictions, see Appendix F). Operations in the same unit cannot overlap, but operations in different units can. In some instances, the R6010 lacks bypassing so the latency of most operations is one cycle longer than the computation time of the floating-point unit.

R4000 Implementation

The R4000 implements the floating-point unit directly on-chip. Both the CPU and floating-point unit use more pipelining than other MIPS processors; thus, the latency of R4000 operations are longer when measured in cycles, but are comparable or significantly faster when measured in absolute time. The longer cycle counts do make it profitable to partially pipeline some of the floating-point units.

The R4000 floating-point coprocessor implements three separate operation (op) units: multiply, divide, and an adder for remaining operations.

Multiplies and divides can overlap with adder operations, however they use the adder on their final cycles, which imposes some limitations.

The multiply unit can begin a new double precision multiply every four cycles, and a new single precision multiply every three cycles. The adder generally begins a new operation one cycle before the previous cycle completes; therefore, a floating-point add or subtract can start every three cycles.

The R4000 floating-point coprocessor pipeline is fully bypassed.

FPU Pipeline Overlapping

This section describes pipelining and overlapping as it applies to MIPS R-Series processors.

R2010/R3010 FPUs

Figure 8–5 illustrates the overlapping of several FPU (and non-FPU) instructions. In this figure, the first instruction (DIV.S) requires a total of 12 cycles for execution but only the first cycle and last three cycles preclude the simultaneous execution of other FPU instructions. Similarly, the second instruction (MUL.S) has two cycles in the middle of its total of four required cycles that can be used to advance the execution of the third (ADD.S) and fourth (SWC1) instructions shown in the figure.

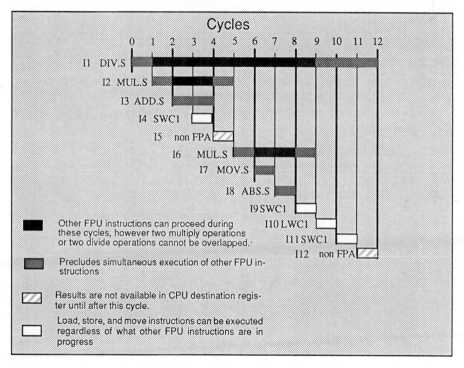

Figure 8–5. Overlapping FPU Instructions

Although processing of a single instruction consists of six pipe stages, the FPU does not require that an instruction actually be completed within six cycles to avoid stalling the instruction pipeline. If a subsequent instruction does not require FPU resources being used by a preceding instruction and has no data dependencies on preceding uncompleted instructions, then execution continues.

Figure 8–6 illustrates the progression of the R2000/R3000 FPU instruction pipeline with some overlapped FPU instructions. The first instruction (DIV.S) in this figure requires eight additional cycles beyond its FWB pipe stage before it completes. The pipeline need not be stalled however, because FPU instructions are overlapped in a way that avoids resource conflicts.

Figure 8–6 also assumes there are no data dependencies that would stall the pipeline. For example, if any instruction before I13 required the results of the DIV.S (I1) instruction, the pipeline would be stalled until those results were made available.

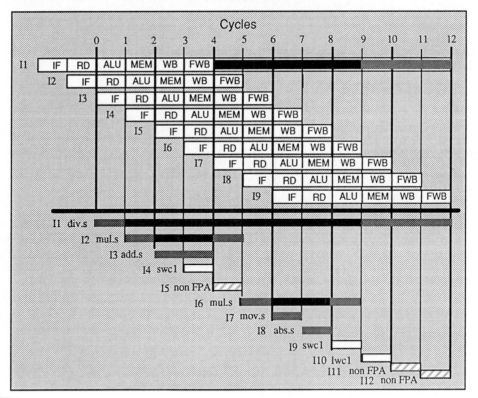

Figure 8–6. Overlapped Instructions in the R2000/R3000 FPU Pipeline

R4000 FPU

The R4000 on-chip FPU has three operational (op) units: adder, divider, and multiplier. Each op unit is controlled by an FPU resource scheduler, which issues instructions under certain constraints, as described in the following section.

Table 8–7 lists the pipe stages used in the op units (although not all stages are used by each unit).

Table 8–7. R4000 FPU Operational Unit Pipe Stages

Stage	Description
A	FPU Adder Mantissa Add stage
E	FPU Adder Exception Test stage
EX	CPU EX stage
M	FPU Multiplier 1st stage
N	FPU Multiplier 2nd stage
R	FPU Adder Result Round stage
S	FPU Adder Operand Shift stage
U	FPU Unpack stage

Instruction Scheduling Constraints

The FPU resource scheduler is kept from issuing instructions to FPU operation units (adder, mulitplier, and divider) by the limitations in their micro-architectures listed below. If any of the following constraints are violated, the operation unit assumes the outstanding instruction in its pipe is discarded, and then continues operation on the most recently issued instruction.

1. FPU Divider. Handles only one non-overlapped divide instruction in its pipe at any one time.

2. FPU Multiplier. Allows up to two pipelined MUL.[S,D] instructions to be processed as long as the following constraints are met: two idle cycles are required after MUL.S (shown in Figure 8–7), and three idle cycles are required after MUL.D (shown in Figure 8–8). These figures are not meant to imply that back-to-back multiplies are allowed. Rather, as shown in Figure 8–7, I2 and I3 are illegal and I5, I6, I7, and I8 are successive stages of I4, referenced to I1. Figure 8–8 is similar, in that I6, I7, and I8 are successive stages of I5.

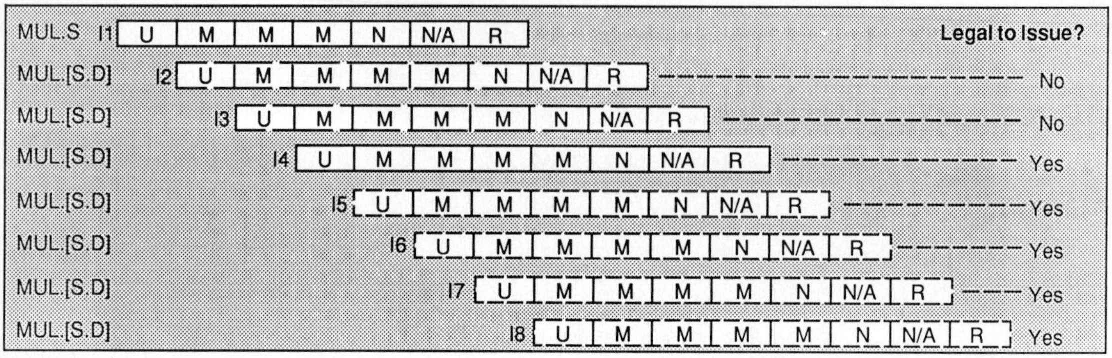

MUL.S I1	U	M	M	M	N	N/A	R			Legal to Issue?
MUL.[S.D] I2	U	M	M	M	M	N	N/A	R	————————	No
MUL.[S.D] I3	U	M	M	M	M	N	N/A	R	————————	No
MUL.[S.D] I4	U	M	M	M	M	N	N/A	R	————————	Yes
MUL.[S.D] I5	U	M	M	M	M	N	N/A	R	————————	Yes
MUL.[S.D] I6	U	M	M	M	M	N	N/A	R	————————	Yes
MUL.[S.D] I7	U	M	M	M	M	N	N/A	R	————	Yes
MUL.[S.D] I8	U	M	M	M	M	N	N/A	R		Yes

Figure 8–7. MUL.S Instruction Scheduling in R4000 FPU Multiplier

MUL.D I1	U	M	M	M	M	N	N/A	R		Legal to Issue?
MUL.[S.D] I2	U	M	M	M	M	N	N/A	R	————————————	No
MUL.[S.D] I3	U	M	M	M	M	N	N/A	R	————————————	No
MUL.[S.D] I4	U	M	M	M	M	N	N/A	R	———————————	No
MUL.[S.D] I5	U	M	M	M	M	N	N/A	R	—————————	Yes
MUL.[S.D] I6	U	M	M	M	M	N	N/A	R	———————	Yes
MUL.[S.D] I7	U	M	M	M	M	N	N/A	R	———	Yes
MUL.[S.D] I8	U	M	M	M	M	N	N/A	R		Yes

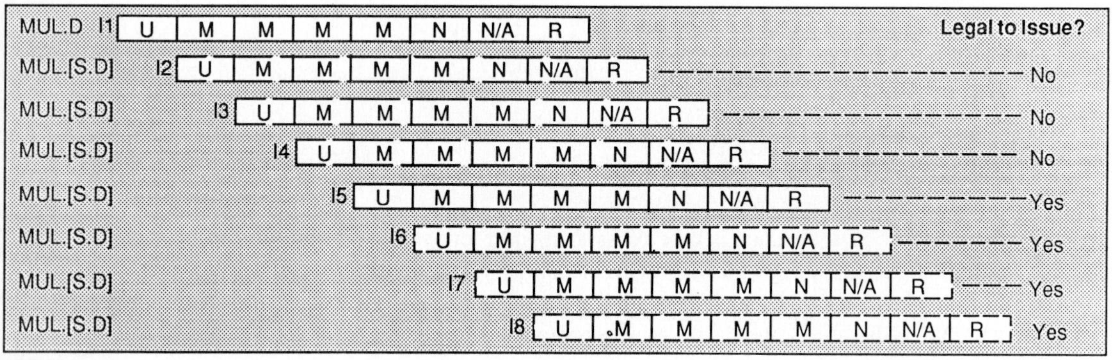

Figure 8–8. MUL.D Instruction Scheduling in R4000 FPU Multiplier

3. FPU Adder. The following constraints must be met in the FPU adder op unit:

- The adder op unit allows one clock cycle overlap between each newly-issued instruction and the instruction being completed (as shown in Figure 8–9).

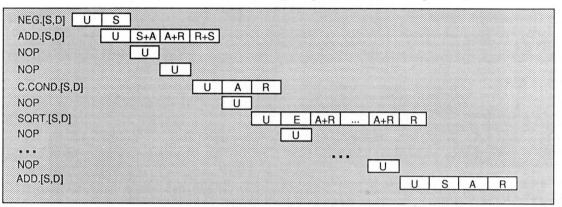

Figure 8–9. Instruction Cycle Overlap in R4000 FPU Adder

- The adder allows the cleanup stages (A, R) of a multiply instruction to be pipelined with the execution of ADD.[S,D], SUB.[S,D] or C.COND.[S,D], as long as no two instructions attempt to simultaneously use the same A and R pipe stages. For instance, Figure 8–10 shows a resource conflict between the mantissa add (A, stage 7) of instructions 1, 5, and 6. This figure also shows the resource conflict between result round (R) stage 8 of instructions 1, 5, and 6. The multiply cleanup cycles (A, R) can neither overlap nor pipeline with any other instruction currently in the adder's pipe. These constraints are shown in Figures 8–11, 8–12, and 8–13.

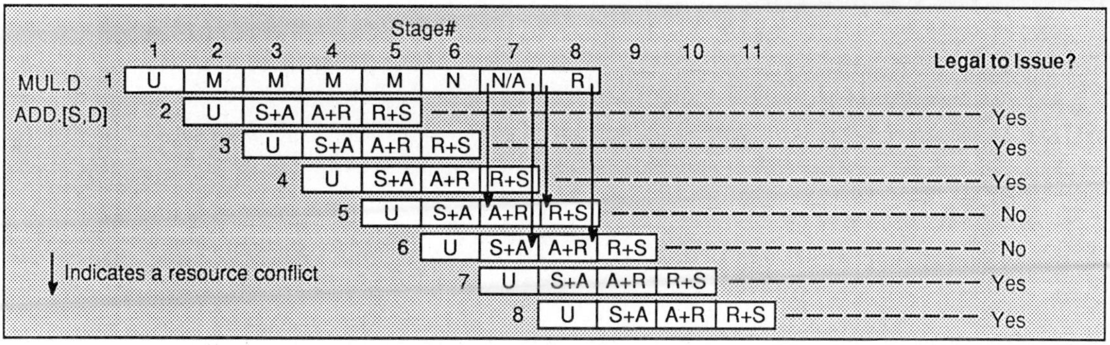

Figure 8–10. MUL.D and ADD.[S,D] Cycle Conflict in R4000 FPU Adder

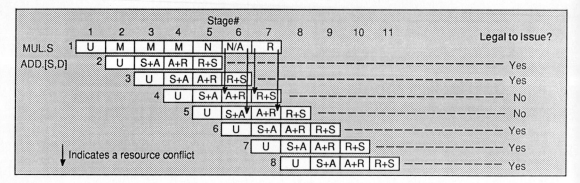

Figure 8–11. MUL.S and ADD.[S,D] Cycle Conflict in R4000 FPU Adder

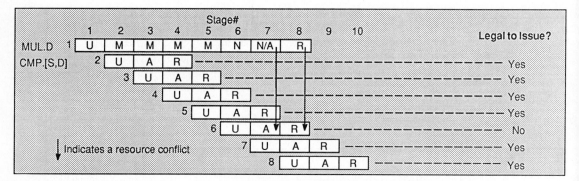

Figure 8–12. MUL.D and CMP.[S,D] Cleanup Cycle Conflict in R4000 FPU Adder

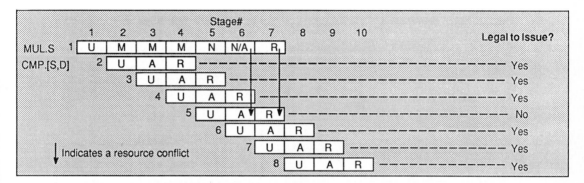

Figure 8–13. MUL.S and CMP.[S,D] Cleanup Cycle Conflict in R4000 FPU Adder

- The adder does not allow the preparation (U stage) and cleanup cycles (N, A, R) of a divide instruction to be pipelined with any other instruction, however the adder does allow the last cycle of preparation or cleanup to be overlapped one clock by the following instructions's U stage (the CPU EX cycle) as shown in Figure 8–14.

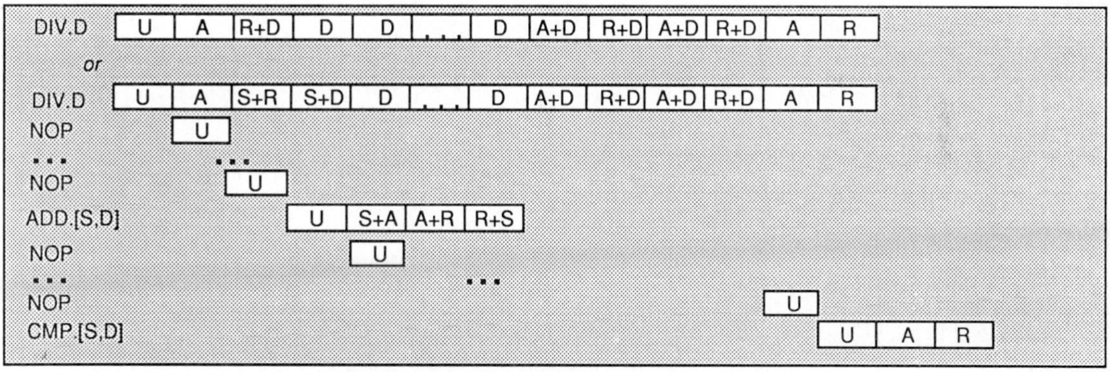

DIV.D	U	A	R+D	D	D	...	D	A+D	R+D	A+D	R+D	A	R

or

DIV.D   U A S+R S+D D ... D A+D R+D A+D R+D A R
NOP   U
...
NOP   U
ADD.[S,D]   U S+A A+R R+S
NOP   U
...
NOP   U
CMP.[S,D]   U A R

Figure 8–14. R4000 Adder Prep and Cleanup Cycle Overlap

Instruction Latency, Repeat Rate and Pipeline Stage Sequences

Table 8–8 shows the latency and repeat rate between instructions, together with the sequence of pipeline stages for each instruction. For instance, the latency of the ADD.[S,D] is 4, which means it takes four processor cycles to complete. The Repeat Rate column indicates how soon an instruction can be repeated; for instance, an ADD.[S,D] can repeated after the conclusion of the third pipeline stage.

Table 8–8. Latency, Repeat Rate, and Pipe Stages of R4000 FPU Instructions

Instruction Type	Latency	Repeat Rate	Pipeline Stage Sequence
MOV.[S,D]	1	1	EX
ADD.[S,D]	4	3	U –> S+A –> A+R –> R+S
SUB.[S,D]	4	3	U –> S+A –> A+R –> R+S
C.COND.[S,D]	3	2	U –> A –> R
NEG.[S,D]	2	1	U –> S
ABS.[S,D]	2	1	U –> S
CVT.S.W	6	5	U –> A –> R –> S –> A –> R
CVT.D.W	5	4	U –> S –> A –> R –> S
CVT.S.L	7	6	U –> A –> R –> S –> S –> A –> R
CVT.D.L	4	3	U –> A –> R –> S
CVT.D.S	2	1	U –> S
CVT.S.D	4	3	U –> S –> A –> R
CVT.W.[S,D] *or* ROUND.W.[S,D] *or* TRUNC.W.[S,D] *or* CEIL.W.[S,D] *or* FLOOR.W.[S,D]	4	3	U –> S –> A –> R
MUL.S	7	3	U –> E/M –> M –> M –> N –> N/A –> R
MUL.D	8	4	U –> E/M –> M –> M –> M –> N –> N/A –> R
DIV.S	23	22	U –> S+A –> S+R –> S –> D...D –> D/A –> D/R –> D/A –> D/R–>A–>R
DIV.D	36	35	U –> A –> R –> D...D –> D/A –> D/R –> D/A –>D/R –> A –> R
SQRT.S	2–54	2–53	U –> E –> A+R –>......–> A+R –> A –> R
SQRT.D	2–112	2–111	U –> E –> A+R –>......–> A+R –> A –> R

Resource Scheduling Rules

The R4000 FPU Resource Scheduler issues instructions while adhering to the rules described below. These scheduling rules optimize op unit executions; if the following rules are not followed the hardware interlocks to guarantee correct operation.

Div.[S,D] can start only when all of the following conditions are met in the RF stage.

- The divider is idle.
- The adder is idle; otherwise it must be in its second-to-last execution cycle.
- The multiplier is idle; otherwise, it must be in its first execution cycle.

Idle means an operation unit — adder, multiplier, or divider — is either not processing any instruction, or is currently at its last execution cycle completing an instruction.

Mul.[S,D] can start only when all of the following conditions are met in the RF stage.

- The multiplier is idle; otherwise it must either be:
  - within the third execution cycle (EX+2) if the most recent instruction in multiplier's pipe is MUL.S, or
  - within the fourth execution cycle (EX+3) if the most recent instruction in multiplier's pipe is MUL.D.
- The adder is idle; otherwise it must not be:
  - processing the first execution cycle (EX) of a conversion from long integer to short floating-point, CVT.S.L
  - within the first three preparation cycles (EX..EX+2) of a DIV.S
  - in the second preparation cycle (EX+1) of a DIV.D
  - processing a square root instruction.
- The divider is idle; otherwise it must not be:
  - executing within the last fifteen cycles of a DIV.[S,D]
  - in the second execution cycle (EX+1) of a DIV.D
  - in the first three execution cycles (EX..EX+2) of a DIV.S.

SQRT.[S,D] can start when all of the following conditions are met in the RF stage.

- The adder is idle; otherwise it must be in its second-to-last execution cycle.
- The multiplier must be idle.
- The divider must be idle.

CVT.fmt instructions can only start when all of the following conditions are met in the RF stage.

- The adder is idle; otherwise it must be in its second-to-last execution cycle.
- The multiplier is idle; otherwise the required state of the multiplier is dependent on the type of conversion instruction bring executed, as described below.
  - If the instruction is an CVT.S.L, CVT.S.W or CVT.D.W, the multiplier must be idle.
  - If the instruction is an CVT.D.L, CVT.S.D, CVT.W.[S,D], CEIL.W.[S,D], FLOOR.W.[S,D], ROUND.W.[S,D], or TRUNC.W.[S,D], the multiplier must not be executing beyond the first cycle (EX) of a MUL.S or the second cycle (EX+1) of a MUL.D. If two multiply instructions have already been initiated in the multiplier, none of these convert instructions are allowed to start.
  - If the instruction is an CVT.D.S, the multiplier must not be executing the second-to-last execution cycle of either the first or second MUL.[S,D] in the multiplier pipe.
- The divider is idle; otherwise it must not be executing the first three (EX..EX+2) nor the last fifteen cycles of a DIV.[S,D].

ADD.[S,D] or **SUB.[S,D]** can start only when all of the following conditions are met in the RF stage.

- The adder is idle; otherwise it must be in its second-to-last execution cycle.
- The multiplier is idle; otherwise, among two possible MUL.[S,D] instructions, it must not be executing within either the fourth or fifth execution cycle from the last.
- The divider is idle; otherwise it must not be executing within the first three (EX..EX+2) nor the last fifteen cycles of a DIV.[S,D].

NEG.[S,D] or **ABS.[S,D]** can start only when all of the following conditions are met in the RF stage.

- The adder is idle; otherwise it must be in its second-to-last execution cycle.
- The multiplier is idle; otherwise it must not be executing the second-to-last execution cycle.
- The divider is idle; otherwise it must not be executing the first three (EX..EX+2) nor the last fifteen cycles of a DIV.[S,D].

C.COND.[S,D] can start only when all of the following conditions are met in the RF stage.

- The adder is idle; otherwise it must be in its second-to-last execution cycle.
- The multiplier is idle; otherwise it must not be executing the fourth cycle from the last.
- The divider is idle; otherwise it must not be executing the first three (EX..EX+2) nor the last fifteen cycles of a DIV.[S,D].

R6010 FPU

This section describes the latencies of R6010 FPU instructions. The following constraints must be observed, with regard to dependencies and stalls:

- CTC1 is dependent upon all FPU multiplier operations, and therefore stalls until all active floating-point multiplier operations complete. This is required to ensure proper ordering of writes to the FPU *Control/Status* register.

- CFC1 is dependent upon all other instructions, and CFC1 stalls until all active instructions complete. This is required to ensure that the correct value is retrieved from the FPU *Control/Status* register.

- In some cases stalls can cause the code to take a greater number of cycles than would otherwise be expected. The penalties incurred are listed in Table 8–9.

Table 8–9. Stall Penalties for R6010 FPU Instructions

Situation Causing the Stall	Stall Penalty Incurred
Any non-double load followed by any store operation*	1
LDC1 followed by any store operation*	2
Any store operation* followed by any other store operation* (except MTC1/CTC1 followed by MTC1/CTC1 or MFC1/CFC1 followed by CFC1/MFC1)	1
SDC1 followed by MTC1/CTC1 or any non-FPU store	2

*Store operations include MTC1, CTC1, MFC1, and CFC1

- Multiple operations to the multiplier (MUL, DIV, SQRT) can interfere with one another because of data bus conflicts. When this conflict occurs, the operation attempting to return its result is given data bus priority, which can cause the operation sending its operands to stall for one (single precision op) or two (double precision op) cycles.

Table 8–10 lists the latencies of R6010 FPU instructions.

Table 8–10. Latency of R6010 FPU Instructions

Operation Format	Clock Cycles S	D	W	Operation Format	S	Clock Cycles D	W	
ADD.fmt	3	3–4(a)	x	SUB.fmt	3	3–4(a)	x	
MUL.fmt(β)	4	6	x	DIV.fmt(b)	14	24	x	
SQRT.fmt(β)	23	42	x	ABS.fmt	2	2	x	
MOV.fmt	2	2	x	NEG.fmt	2	2	x	
ROUND.W.fmt	3	3–4(a)	x	TRUNC.W.fmt	3	3–4(a)	x	
CEIL.fmt	3	3–4(a)	x	FLOOR.W.fmt	3	3–4(a)	x	
CVT.S.fmt	x	3–4(a)	3	CVT.D.fmt	3	x	3	
CVT.W.fmt	3	3–4(a)	x					
C.fmt.cond	2(c)	2(c)	x					
BC1T		1		BC1F		1		
BC1TL		1		BC1FL		1		
LWC1		2		SWC1		1		
LDC1		2		SDC1		2		
MTC1		2		MFC1		2		
CTC1		5(d)		CFC1		2		

Key to Table 8–10

(a)   The larger latency should be used for COP1.d in the following sequences:

```
LDC1, MUL.d, DIV.d, or SQRT.d
        •
        •
        •
COP1.d                              (dependent on above, and at
                                    minimum spacing or less
                                    from above)

SDC1, MUL.d, DIV.d, or SQRT.d
COP1.d
```

(b)   If the FPU is revision 3.0 or greater, the latencies are: MUL.s, 4; MUL.d, 5; DIV.s, 12; DIV.d, 20; SQRT.s, 20; SQRT.d, 36.

(c)   Software must schedule a dependent floating-point branch 2 or more instructions after a floating-point compare.

(d)   CTC1 instructions require that that no new floating-point operations be started until the instruction completely exits the pipeline. This is required to ensure that the FPU *Control/Status* register has the correct value (rounding mode, etc.) before the instruction is started.

9
Floating-Point Exceptions

This chapter describes how the FPU handles floating-point exceptions. A floating-point exception occurs whenever the FPU cannot handle the operands or results of a floating-point operation in the normal way. The FPU responds either by generating an interrupt to initiate a software trap or by setting a status flag.

The *Control/Status* register described in Chapter 6 contains an enable bit for each exception type, which determines whether an exception will cause the FPU to initiate a trap or set a status flag. If a trap is taken, the FPU remains in the state found at the beginning of the operation, and a software exception handling routine is executed. If no trap is taken, an appropriate value is written into the FPU destination register and execution continues.

The FPU supports the five IEEE Standard 754 exceptions:

- Inexact (I)
- Overflow (O)
- Underflow (U)
- Divide by Zero (Z)
- Invalid Operation (V)

with Cause bits, enables, and Flag bits (status flags).

The FPU adds a sixth exception type, unimplemented operation (E), to be used when the FPU cannot implement the standard MIPS floating-point architecture, including cases where the FPU cannot determine the correct exception behavior. This exception indicates that a software implementation must be used. The unimplemented operation exception has no enable or Flag bit; whenever this exception occurs, an unimplemented exception trap is taken (if the FPU interrupt input to the CPU is enabled).

Figure 9–1 illustrates the *Control/Status* register bits used to support exceptions.

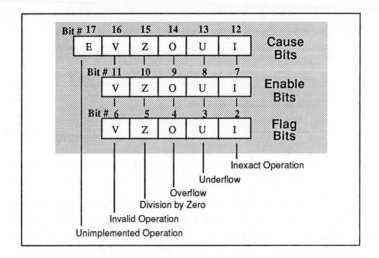

Figure 9–1. Control/Status Register Exception/Flag/TrapEnable Bits

Each of the five IEEE standard exceptions (V, Z, O, U, I) is associated with a trap under user control, which is enabled by setting one of the five Enable bits. When an exception occurs, both the corresponding Cause and Flag bits are set. If the corresponding Enable bit is set, the FPU generates an interrupt to the CPU and the subsequent exception processing allows a trap to be taken.

Exception Trap Processing

When a floating-point exception trap is taken, the *Cause* register indicates that the floating-point coprocessor is the cause of the exception trap. For R4000 processors, the FPE code is used; for other systems, a dedicated external interrupt code is typically used. The Cause bits of the floating-point *Control/Status* register indicate the reason for the floating-point exception; these bits are in effect an extension of the system coprocessor *Cause* register.

Precise Exception Handling

Floating-point operations require greater latency than most other operations performed by the MIPS R-Series processors. To make the processor report floating-point exception traps precisely (making the address available of the instruction that caused the exception), the trap must be reported within the relatively short time permitted by the processor.

Normally, this reporting time is much shorter than the time required to perform the operation. If the execution pipeline is permitted to continue while the operation is performed, the processor would continue beyond the point at which the trap can be precisely reported. A simple solution for making precise floating-point exceptions is to stall the processor until the operation is complete and all exceptions can be determined. However this removes all opportunities for pipelining and overlapping of floating-point loads, stores, and operations, as well as CPU operations. As such, this simple solution would have a significant performance impact.

On the other hand, an operation can be determined *not* to be the cause of an exception, either by examining the operands or by performing simple operations that complete in time to interlock the processor and later report a precise exception trap. This is accomplished by performing simple checks on a subset of the bits of floating-point operands, ensuring the dynamic frequency of such interlocks is low. For example, in a single precision ADD, if the biased exponent field of both operands is less than 192, floating-point overflow does not occur. It is important to note that this is a sufficient but not necessary condition to ensure floating-point overflow does not occur; the sum of two values whose exponent fields are greater than 192 may or may not actually lead to an overflow. The key idea is to make these simple operations pessimistic — that they correctly predict all cases in which the operation causes an exception trap, although they may over-predict a trap when none actually occurs.

For all exception traps (except the Inexact exception trap), these pessimistic predictions are fairly easy to produce. For an Inexact exception trap, it is assumed that the trap is predicted whenever it is enabled. The efficiency of this technique depends on how often the prediction is pessimistic.

Finally, assuming that the floating-point coprocessor is implemented with precise exception handling, the CPU *EPC* register will contain the address of the instruction that caused the exception. Using this register, the operation and operands of the instruction can be retrieved from memory.

Imprecise Exception Handling

Because of the benefits of using the pessimistic technique in precise exception handling, imprecise exceptions are not recommended as an implementation strategy. They are, however, permitted by the architecture. Imprecise exceptions reduce the ability of software to debug code containing floating-point coprocessor operations, and may increase overhead in handling exception traps.

Only one exception trap can be reported from an instruction sequence; the single exception register requires all operation pipelining be eliminated when any exception is possible. This permits implementations to reduce pipeline control complexity — at the expense, however, of reduced performance when result exceptions *do* occur. Underflow, overflow, and inexact exceptions must be predicted when the traps are enabled. Denormalized results must either be handled in hardware or predicted, because pipelined instructions can each produce an exceptional result. The mechanism for performing this determination is similar to that of the precise exception case, except that the pipeline can advance past the instruction while the determination is made, as long as no additional floating-point instructions are permitted to execute.

A less aggressively pipelined machine can perform only one floating-point operation at any time, but permits load and store operations to execute concurrently. This requires an interlock against any further use of the single result register specified in the executing operation or any modification of the source registers while exception traps are pending. If all such traps are disabled and default dispositions assigned to the destination when exceptions occur, the source register conflicts can be ignored by the hardware.

When floating-point exception traps are imprecise, the processor *EPC* register does not contain the address of the instruction that caused the exception. Normally, the *EPC* register contains an address that is a successor (by one or more instructions) to the exception-causing instruction. In this case, the EIR contains the instruction that caused the exception. This arrangement permits the execution of floating-point operations in the coprocessor to occur in parallel with the execution of fixed-point CPU operations and, in some implementations, in parallel with certain floating-point load and store instructions.

Flags

For each IEEE exception, a Flag bit is provided. This Flag bit is set on any occurrence of its corresponding exception condition, with no corresponding exception trap signaled. The Flag bit is reset by writing a new value into the *Status* register; flags can be saved and restored individually, or as a group, by software.

When no exception trap is signaled, a default action is taken by the floating-point coprocessor, which provides a substitute value for the exception-causing result of the floating-point operation. The particular default action taken depends upon the type of exception, and in the case of the Overflow exception, the current rounding mode. Table 9–1 lists the default action taken by the FPU for each of the IEEE exceptions.

Table 9–1. Default FPU Exception Actions

Field	Description	Rounding mode	Default action
V	Invalid operation		Supply a quiet Not a Number (NaN)
Z	Division by zero		Supply a properly signed ∞
O	Overflow exception	RN	Modify overflow values to ∞ with the sign of the intermediate result
		RZ	Modify overflow values to the format's largest finite number with the sign of the intermediate result
		RP	Modify negative overflows to the format's most negative finite number; modify positive overflows to + ∞
		RM	Modify positive overflows to the format's largest finite number; modify negative overflows to – ∞
U	Underflow exception		Supply a rounded result
I	Inexact exception		Supply a rounded result

The FPU detects internally the eight conditions that can cause exceptions. When the FPU encounters one of these unusual situations, it causes either an IEEE exception or an Unimplemented Operation exception (E). Table 9–2 lists the exception-causing situations and contrasts the behavior of the FPU with the requirements of the IEEE standard.

Table 9–2. FPU Exception-Causing Conditions

FPA Internal result	IEEE Stndrd	Trap Enab.	Trap Disab.	Note
Inexact result	I	I	I	Loss of Accuracy
Exponent overflow	O I*	O I	O I	Normalized exponent > Emax
Divide by zero	Z	Z	Z	Zero is (exponent = Emin–1, mantissa = 0)
Overflow on convert	V	V	E	Source out of integer range
Signaling NaN source	V	V	E	Quiet NaN source produces quiet NaN result
Invalid operation	V	V	E	0/0, etc.
Exponent underflow	U	E	E	Normalized exponent < Emin
Denormalized source	none	E	E	Exponent = E–1 and mantissa <> 0

* Standard specifies inexact exception on overflow only if overflow trap is disabled.

The following sections describe the conditions that cause the FPU to generate each of its exceptions and details the FPU response to each exception-causing situation.

Inexact Exception (I)

The FPU generates the Inexact exception if the rounded result of an operation is not exact or if it overflows.

Note: The FPU usually examines the operands of floating-point operations before execution actually begins to determine (based on the exponent values of the operands) if the operation can *possibly* cause an exception. If there is a possibility of an instruction causing an exception trap, then the FPU uses a coprocessor stall mechanism to execute the instruction. It is impossible, however, for the FPU to predetermine if an instruction will produce an inexact result. Therefore, if Inexact exception traps are enabled, the FPU uses the coprocessor stall mechanism to execute all floating-point operations that require more than one cycle. Since this mode of execution can impact performance, Inexact exception traps should be enabled only when necessary.

Trap Enabled Results: If Inexact exception traps are enabled, the result register is not modified and the source registers are preserved.

Trap Disabled Results: The rounded or overflowed result is delivered to the destination register if no other software trap occurs.

Overflow Exception (O)

The Overflow exception is signaled when the magnitude of the rounded floating-point result, if the exponent range were to be unbounded, is larger than the destination format's largest finite number. (This exception also sets the Inexact exception and Flag bits.)

Trap Enabled Results: The result register is not modified, and the source registers are preserved.

Trap Disabled Results: The result, when no trap occurs, is determined by the rounding mode and the sign of the intermediate result (as listed in Table 9–1).

Division-by-Zero Exception (Z)

The Division-by-Zero exception is signaled on an implemented divide operation if the divisor is zero and the dividend is a finite non-zero number. Software can simulate this exception for other operations that produce a signed infinity, such as $\ln(0)$, $\sec(\pi/2)$, $\csc(0)$, or 0^{-1}.

Trap Enabled Results: The result register is not modified, and the source registers are preserved.

Trap Disabled Results: The result, when no trap occurs, is a correctly signed infinity.

Invalid Operation Exception (V)

The Invalid Operation exception is signaled if one or both of the operands are invalid for an implemented operation. The MIPS ISA defines the result, when the exception occurs without a trap, as a quiet Not a Number (NaN). The invalid operations are:

- Addition or subtraction: magnitude subtraction of infinities, such as: $(+\infty) + (-\infty)$ or $(-\infty) - (-\infty)$
- Multiplication: 0 times ∞, with any signs.
- Division: 0/0, or ∞/∞, with any signs.
- Conversion of a floating-point number to a fixed-point format when an overflow, or operand value of infinity or NaN, precludes a faithful representation in that format.
- Comparison of predicates involving < or > without ?, when the operands are unordered.
- Any arithmetic operation on a signaling NaN. A move (MOV) operation is not considered to be an arithmetic operation, but absolute value (ABS) and negate (NEG) are considered to be arithmetic operations and will cause this exception if one or both operands is a signaling NaN.
- Square root: $\sqrt{x}$, where x is less than zero.

Software can simulate the Invalid Operation exception for other operations that are invalid for the given source operands. Examples of these operations include IEEE 754-specified functions implemented in software, such as Remainder: x REM y, where y is zero or x is infinite; conversion of a floating-point number to a decimal format whose value causes an overflow, or is infinity or NaN; and transcendental functions, such as ln (–5) or cos^{-1}(3). Refer to Appendix B for examples or for routines to handle these cases.

Trap Enabled Results: The original operand values are undisturbed.

Trap Disabled Results: The FPU always signals an Unimplemented exception because it does not create the NaN that the IEEE standard specifies should be returned under these circumstances.

Underflow Exception (U)

Two related events contribute to the Underflow exception:

- the creation of a tiny non-zero result between $\pm2^{Emin}$ which can cause some later exception because it is so tiny;
- the extraordinary loss of accuracy during the approximation of such tiny numbers by denormalized numbers.

IEEE Standard 754 permits a choice in the manner in which these events are detected but requires they be detected the same way for all operations.

The IEEE standard specifies that *tininess* may be detected either:

- after rounding (when a nonzero result, computed as though the exponent range were unbounded, would lie strictly between $\pm2^{Emin)}$, or
- before rounding (when a nonzero result, computed as though the exponent range and the precision were unbounded, would lie strictly between $\pm2^{Emin}$).

The MIPS architecture requires that tininess be detected after rounding.

Loss of accuracy can be detected as either:

- Denormalization loss (when the delivered result differs from what would have been computed if the exponent range were unbounded), or
- Inexact result (when the delivered result differs from what would have been computed if the exponent range and precision were both unbounded).

The MIPS architecture requires that loss of accuracy be detected as inexact result.

The R2000/R3000 processors do not generate the Underflow exception directly; it is implemented in software.

Trap Enabled Results: When an underflow trap is enabled, underflow is signaled when tininess is detected regardless of loss of accuracy. If underflow traps are enabled, the result register is not modified, and the source registers are preserved.

Trap Disabled Results: When an underflow trap is not enabled, underflow is signaled (using the underflow flag) only when both tininess and loss of accuracy have been detected. The delivered result might be zero, denormalized, or $\pm2^{Emin}$

Unimplemented Instruction Exception (E)

Any attempt to execute an instruction with an operation code or format code that has been reserved for future definition sets the *Unimplemented* cause bit, and traps. The operand and destination registers remain undisturbed and the instruction is emulated in software. Any of the IEEE 754 exceptions can arise from the emulated operation, and these exceptions in turn are simulated.

The Unimplemented Instruction exception can also be signaled when unusual operands or result conditions are detected that the implemented hardware cannot properly handle. These include:

- Denormalized operand
- Not a Number operand
- Invalid operation with trap disabled   (R2000, R3000, and R6000 only)
- Denormalized result
- Underflow
- SQRT (R2000 and R3000 only)
- Reserved opcodes
- Unimplemented formats
- Operations which are invalid for their format (for instance, CVT.S.S)

Note: Denormalized and NaN operands are only trapped if the instruction is a convert or computational operation. Moves do not trap if their operands are either denormalized or NaNs.

The use of this exception for such conditions is optional; most of these conditions are newly developed and are not expected to be widely used in early implementations. Loopholes are provided in the architecture so that these conditions can be implemented with assistance provided by software, maintaining full compatibility with the IEEE standard.

Trap Enabled Results: The original operand values are undisturbed.

Trap Disabled Results: This trap cannot not be disabled.

Saving and Restoring State

In R2000 and R3000 implementations, 32 single-word coprocessor load or store operations save or restore the coprocessor floating-point register state in memory. In an R4000 or R6000 implementation, 16 doubleword coprocessor load or store operations are required. The remaining control and status information can be saved or restored through Move To/From Coprocessor Control Register instructions, and saving and restoring the processor registers. Normally, the *Control/Status* register is saved first and restored last.

When coprocessor *Control* register (*R31*) is read, and the coprocessor is executing one or more floating-point instruction, the instruction(s) in progress are either completed or reported as exceptions. The architecture requires no more than one of these pending instructions can cause an exception. If one of the pending instructions cannot be completed, the instruction is placed in the *Exception* register, if present, and information indicating the type of exception is placed in the *Control/Status* register. State information in the status word indicates that exceptions are pending when state is restored.

Writing a zero value to the Cause field of *Control* register *31* clears all pending exceptions, permitting normal processing to be restarted after the floating-point register state is restored.

The Cause field of the *Control/Status* register holds the results of only one instruction; the FPU examines source operands before an operation is initiated to determine if the instruction can possibly cause an exception. If an exception is possible, the FPU executes the instruction in stall mode to ensure that no more than one instruction (that might cause an exception) is executed at a time.

Trap Handlers for IEEE Standard Exceptions

The IEEE Standard 754 strongly recommends that users be allowed to specify a trap handler for any of the five standard exceptions, which can compute or specify a substitute result be placed in the destination register of the operation.

By retrieving an instruction using the processor *EPC* register, the trap handler determines:

- the exceptions occurring during the operation
- the operation being performed
- the destination format

On Overflow or Underflow exceptions (except for conversions), and on Inexact exceptions, the trap handler gains access to the correctly rounded result by examining the source registers and simulating the operation in software.

On Overflow or Underflow exceptions encountered on floating-point conversions, and on Invalid Operation and Divide-by-Zero exceptions, the trap handler gains access to the operand values by examining the source registers of the instruction.

The IEEE Standard 754 recommends that, if enabled, the overflow and underflow traps take precedence over a separate inexact trap. This prioritization is accomplished in software; hardware sets the bits for both the Inexact exception and the Overflow or Underflow exception.

A
CPU Instruction Set Details

This appendix provides a detailed description of the operation of each R-Series processor instruction. The instructions are listed in alphabetical order.

Refer to Appendix B for a detailed description of the FPU instructions.

The exceptions that may occur due to the execution of each instruction are listed after the description of each instruction. The description of the immediate causes and manner of handling exceptions is omitted from the instruction descriptions in this chapter. Refer to Chapter 6 for detailed descriptions of exceptions and handling.

Figures at the end of this appendix lists the bit encoding for the constant fields of each instruction, and the bit encoding for each individual instruction is included with that instruction.

Instruction Classes

CPU instructions are divided into the following classes:

- **Load/Store** instructions move data between memory and general registers. They are all I-type instructions, since the only addressing mode supported is *base register + 16-bit immediate offset*.

- **Computational** instructions perform arithmetic, logical and shift operations on values in registers. They occur in both R-type (both operands are registers) and I-type (one operand is a 16-bit immediate) formats.

- **Jump** and **Branch** instructions change the control flow of a program. Jumps are always to absolute 26-bit word addresses (J-type format), or 32-bit register addresses (R-type, for returns and dispatches). Branches have 16-bit offsets relative to the program counter (I-type). **Jump and Link** instructions save a return address in Register 31.

- **Coprocessor** instructions perform operations in the coprocessors. Coprocessor loads and stores are I-type. Coprocessor computational instructions have coprocessor-dependent formats (see the FPU instructions). Coprocessor zero (CP0) instructions manipulate the memory management and exception handling facilities of the processor.

- **Special** instructions perform a variety of tasks, including movement of data between special and general registers, trap, and breakpoint. They are always R-type.

Instruction Formats

Every CPU instruction consists of a single word (32 bits) aligned on a word boundary and the major instruction formats are shown in Figure A–1.

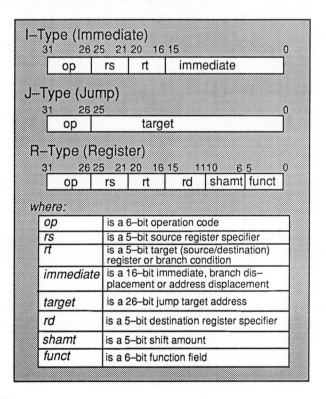

Figure A–1. CPU Instruction Formats

Instruction Notation Conventions

In this appendix, all variable subfields in an instruction format (such as *rs, rt, immediate*, etc.) are shown in lower-case names.

For the sake of clarity, we sometimes use an alias for a variable subfield in the formats of specific instructions. For example, we use *rs = base* in the format for load and store instructions. Such an alias is always lower case, since it refers to a variable subfield.

Figures with the actual bit encoding for all the mnemonics are located at the end of this Appendix, and the bit encoding also accompanies each instruction.

In the instruction descriptions that follow, the *Operation* section describes the operation performed by each instruction using a high-level language notation. Special symbols used in the notation are described in Table A–1.

Table A–1. CPU Instruction Operation Notations

Symbol	Meaning
$\leftarrow$	Assignment
$\parallel$	Bit string concatenation
x^y	Replication of bit value x into a y-bit string. Note that x is always a single-bit value.
$x_{y..z}$	Selection of bits y through z of bit string x. Little-endian bit notation is always used. If y is less than z, this expression is an empty (zero length) bit string.
$+$	Two's complement or floating point addition
$-$	Two's complement or floating point subtraction
$*$	Two's complement or floating point multiplication
div	Two's complement integer division
mod	Two's complement modulo
$/$	Floating point division
$<$	Two's complement less than comparison
and	Bitwise logic AND
or	Bitwise logic OR
xor	Bitwise logic XOR
nor	Bitwise logic NOR
GPR[x]	General Register x. The content of GPR[0] is always zero. Attempts to alter the content of GPR[0] have no effect.
CPR[z,x]	Coprocessor unit z, general register x
CCR[z,x]	Coprocessor unit z, control register x
COC[z]	Coprocessor unit z condition signal.
BigEndianMem	Big-endian mode as configured at reset (0 –> Little, 1 –> Big). Specifies the endianess of the memory interface (see LoadMemory and StoreMemory), and the endianess of Kernel and Supervisor mode execution.
ReverseEndian	Signal to reverse the endianess of load and store instructions. This feature is available in User mode only, and is effected by setting the *RE* bit of the *Status* register. Thus ReverseEndian may be computed as (SR$_{25}$ and User mode). R3000A, R4000 and R6000 only.
BigEndianCPU	The endianess for load and store instructions (0 –> Little, 1 –>Big). In User mode, this endianess may be reversed by setting SR$_{25}$. Thus BigEndianCPU may be computed as BigEndianMem XOR ReverseEndian.
LLbit	Bit of state to specify synchronization instructions. Set by LL, cleared by RFE, ERET and Invalidate, and read by SC. (R4000/R6000 only)
T+i:	Indicates the time steps between operations. Each of the statements within a time step are defined to be executed in sequential order (as modified by conditional and loop constructs). Operations which are marked T+i: are executed at instruction cycle i relative to the start of execution of the instruction. Thus, an instruction which starts at time j executes operations marked T+i: at time $i + j$. The interpretation of the order of execution between two instructions of two operations which execute at the same time should be pessimistic; the order is not defined.

Instruction Notation Examples

The following examples illustrate the application of some of the instruction notation conventions:

Example #1:

$$\text{GPR[rt]} \leftarrow \text{immediate} \| 0^{16}$$

Sixteen zero bits are concatenated with an immediate value (typically 16 bits), and the 32–bit string (with the lower 16 bits set to zero) is assigned to General Purpose Register *rt.*

Example #2:

$$(\text{immediate}_{15})^{16} \| \text{immediate}_{15..0}$$

Bit 15 (the sign bit) of an immediate value is extended for 16 bit positions, and the result is concatenated with bits 15 through 0 of the immediate value to form a 32–bit sign extended value.

Load and Store Instructions

In the R2000/R3000 implementation of the ISA, all loads are implemented with a delay of one instruction. That is, the instruction immediately following a load cannot use the contents of the register which will be loaded with the data being fetched from storage. An exception is the target register for the Load Word Left and Load Word Right instructions, which may be specified as the same register used as the destination of a load instruction that immediately precedes it.

In the R4000/R6000 implementation, the instruction immediately following a load may use the contents of the register loaded. In such cases, the hardware interlocks, requiring additional real cycles, so scheduling load delay slots is still desirable — although not required for functional code.

Two special instructions are provided in the R4000/R6000 implementation of the ISA, Load Linked and Store Conditional. These instructions are used in carefully coded sequences to provide one of several synchronization primitives, including test-and-set, bit-level locks, semaphores, and sequencers/event counts.

In the load/store operation descriptions, the functions listed in Table A–2 are used to summarize the handling of virtual addresses and physical memory.

Table A–2. Load/Store Common Functions

Function	Meaning
AddressTranslation	Uses the TLB to find the physical address given the virtual address. The function fails and an exception is taken if the page containing the virtual address is not present in the TLB.
LoadMemory	Uses the cache and main memory to find the contents of the word containing the specified physical address. The low order two bits of the address and the access type field indicates which of each of the four bytes within the data word need to be returned. If the cache is enabled for this access, the entire word is returned and loaded into the cache.
StoreMemory	Uses the cache, write buffer and main memory to store the word or part of word specified as data in the word containing the specified physical address. The low order two bits of the address and the access type field indicates which of each of the four bytes within the data word should be stored.

The access type field indicates the size of the data item to be loaded or stored as shown in Table A–3. Regardless of access type or byte-numbering order (endianness), the address specifies the byte which has the smallest byte address of the bytes in the addressed field. For a Big-endian machine, this is the leftmost byte and contains the sign for a 2's-complement number; for a Little-endian machine, this is the rightmost byte and contains the lowest precision byte.

Table A–3. Access Type Specifications for Loads/Stores

Access type Mnemonic	Value	Meaning
DOUBLEWORD	7	doubleword (64 bits)
SEPTIBYTE	6	seven bytes (56 bits)
SEXTIBYTE	5	six bytes (48 bits)
QUINTIBYTE	4	five bytes (40 bits)
WORD	3	word (32 bits)
TRIPLEBYTE	2	triple-byte (24 bits)
HALFWORD	1	halfword (16 bits)
BYTE	0	byte (8 bits)

The bytes within the addressed doubleword which are used can be determined directly from the access type and the three low order bits of the address, as shown in Chapter 3.

Jump and Branch Instructions

All jump and branch instructions are implemented with a delay of exactly one instruction. That is, the instruction immediately following a jump or branch (i.e., occupying the delay slot) is always executed while the target instruction is being fetched from storage. It is not valid for a delay slot to be occupied itself by a jump or branch instruction; however, this error is not detected, and the results of such an operation are undefined.

If an exception or interrupt prevents the completion of a legal instruction during a delay slot, the hardware sets the *EPC* register to point at the jump or branch instruction which precedes it. When the code is restarted, both the jump or branch instructions and the instruction in the delay slot are reexecuted.

Because jump and branch instructions may be restarted after exceptions or interrupts, they must be restartable. Therefore, when a jump or branch instruction stores a return link value, register 31 (the register in which the link is stored) may not be used as a source register.

Since instructions must be word-aligned, a Jump Register or Jump and Link Register instruction must use a register whose two low order bits are zero. If these low order bits are not zero, an address exception will occur when the jump target instruction is subsequently fetched.

Coprocessor Instructions

The MIPS architecture provides four coprocessor units, or classes. Coprocessors are alternate execution units, which have separate register files from the CPU. R-Series coprocessors have 2 register spaces, each with 32 32-bit registers. The first space, *coprocessor general* registers, may be directly loaded from memory and stored into memory, and their contents may be transferred between the coprocessor and processor. The second, *coprocessor control* registers, may only have their contents transferred directly between the coprocessor and processor. Coprocessor instructions may alter registers in either space.

Normally, by convention, *Coprocessor Control Register 0* is interpreted as a *Coprocessor Implementation And Revision* register. However, the system control coprocessor (CP0) uses *Coprocessor General Register 15* for the processor/coprocessor revision register. The register's low order byte (bits 7..0) is interpreted as a coprocessor unit revision number. The second byte (bits 15..8) is interpreted as a coprocessor unit implementation descriptor. The revision number is a value of the form $y.x$ where y is a major revision number in bits 7..4 and x is a minor revision number in bits 3..0.

The contents of the high order halfword of the register are not defined (currently read as 0 and should be 0 when written).

System Control Coprocessor (CP0) Instructions

There are some special limitations imposed on operations involving CP0 that is incorporated within the CPU. Although load and store instructions to transfer data to and from coprocessors and move control to/from coprocessor instructions are generally permitted by the MIPS architecture, CP0 is given a somewhat protected status since it has responsibility for exception handling and memory management. Therefore, the move to/from coprocessor instructions are the only valid mechanism for reading from and writing to the CP0 registers.

Several coprocessor operation instructions are defined for CP0 to directly read, write, and probe TLB entries and to modify the operating modes in preparation for returning to User mode or interrupt-enabled states.

ADD   **ADD**

31 26	25 21	20 16	15 11	10 6	5 0
SPECIAL 000000	rs	rt	rd	0 00000	ADD 100000
6	5	5	5	5	6

Format:

ADD rd,rs,rt

Description:

The contents of general register *rs* and the contents of general register *rt* are added to form a 32-bit result. The result is placed into general register *rd*.

An overflow exception occurs if the two highest order carry-out bits differ (2's-complement overflow).   The destination register *rd* is not modified when an integer overflow exception occurs.

Operation:

> T: GPR[rd] ←GPR[rs] + GPR[rt]

Exceptions:

Overflow exception

ADDI

Add Immediate

31 26	25 21	20 16	15 0
ADDI 001000	rs	rt	immediate
6	5	5	16

Format:

ADDI rt,rs,immediate

Description:

The 16-bit *immediate* is sign-extended and added to the contents of general register *rs* to form a 32-bit result. The result is placed into general register *rt*.

An overflow exception occurs if the two highest order carry-out bits differ (2's-complement overflow). The destination register *rt* is not modified when an integer overflow exception occurs.

Operation:

$$T: \quad GPR[rt] \leftarrow GPR[rs] + (immediate_{15})^{16} \,||\, immediate_{15..0}$$

Exceptions:

Overflow exception

Add Immediate Unsigned

ADDIU

31 26	25 21	20 16	15 0
ADDIU 001001	rs	rt	immediate
6	5	5	16

Format:

ADDIU rt,rs,immediate

Description:

The 16-bit *immediate* is sign-extended and added to the contents of general register *rs* to form a 32-bit result. The result is placed into general register *rt*. No integer overflow exception occurs under any circumstances.

The only difference between this instruction and the ADDI instruction is that ADDIU never causes an overflow exception.

Operation:

$$T: \quad GPR[rt] \leftarrow GPR[rs] + (immediate_{15})^{16} \parallel immediate_{15..0}$$

Exceptions:

None.

ADDU

ADD Unsigned

31 26	25 21	20 16	15 11	10 6	5 0
SPECIAL 000000	rs	rt	rd	0 00000	ADDU 100001
6	5	5	5	5	6

Format:

ADDU rd,rs,rt

Description:

The contents of general register *rs* and the contents of general register *rt* are added to form a 32-bit result. The result is placed into general register *rd*.

No overflow exception occurs under any circumstances.

The only difference between this instruction and the ADD instruction is that ADDU never causes an overflow exception.

Operation:

```
T:    GPR[rd] ← GPR[rs] + GPR[rt]
```

Exceptions:

None.

And **AND**

31 26	25 21	20 16	15 11	10 6	5 0
SPECIAL 000000	rs	rt	rd	0 00000	AND 100100
6	5	5	5	5	6

Format:

AND rd,rs,rt

Description:

The contents of general register *rs* are combined with the contents of general register *rt* in a bit-wise logical AND operation. The result is placed into general register *rd*.

Operation:

T: GPR[rd] ← GPR[rs] *and* GPR[rt]

Exceptions:

None.

ANDI

And Immediate

ANDI 001100	rs	rt	immediate
6	5	5	16

31   26 25   21 20   16 15   0

Format:

ANDI rt,rs,immediate

Description:

The 16-bit *immediate* is zero-extended and combined with the contents of general register *rs* in a bit-wise logical AND operation. The result is placed into general register *rt*.

Operation:

T: GPR[rt] $\leftarrow$ 0^{16} || (immediate *and* GPR[rs]$_{15..0}$)

Exceptions:

None.

Branch On Coprocessor z False | BCzF

31 26	25 21	20 16	15 0
COPz 0100xx*	BC 01000	BCF 00000	offset
6	5	5	16

Format:

BCzF offset

Description:

A branch target address is computed from the sum of the address of the instruction in the delay slot and the 16-bit *offset*, shifted left two bits and sign-extended to 32 bits. If coprocessor *z*'s condition signal (CpCond), as sampled during the previous instruction, is false, then the program branches to the target address with a delay of one instruction.

Because the condition line is sampled during the previous instruction, there must be at least one instruction between this instruction and a coprocessor instruction that changes the condition line.

Operation:

T−1: condition ← *not* COC[z]
T: target ← (offset$_{15}$)^{14} || offset || 0^2
T+1: if condition then
$\qquad$ PC ← PC + target
$\qquad$ endif

Exceptions:

Coprocessor unusable exception

See the table, "Opcode Bit Encoding" on next page, or "CPU Instruction Opcode Bit Encoding" at the end of Appendix A.

BCzF   **Branch On Coprocessor z False**
                                                        (continued)

Opcode Bit Encoding:

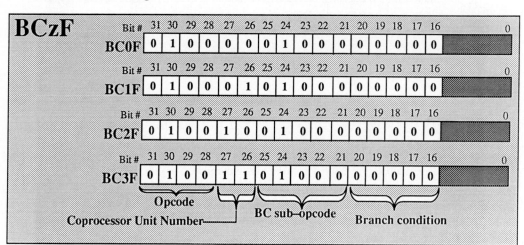

Branch On Coprocessor z False Likely   BCzFL

COPz 0100xx*	BC 01000	BCFL 00010	offset
6	5	5	16

(bit fields: 31   26 25   21 20   16 15   0)

Format:

BCzFL offset

Description:

A branch target address is computed from the sum of the address of the instruction in the delay slot and the 16-bit *offset*, shifted left two bits and sign-extended. If the contents of coprocessor z's condition line, as sampled during the previous instruction, is false, the target address is branched to with a delay of one instruction.

Because the condition line is sampled during the previous instruction, there must be at least one instruction between this instruction and a coprocessor instruction that changes the condition line.

If the conditional branch is *not* taken, the instruction in the branch delay slot is nullified.

This instruction is not valid for R2000/R3000 processors, however it does *not* cause a reserved instruction exception.

*See the table, ''Opcode Bit Encoding'' on next page, or ''CPU Instruction Opcode Bit Encoding'' at the end of Appendix A.

BCzFL   **Branch On Coprocessor z False Likely**
                                                                    (continued)

R4000/R6000 Operation:

> T−1: condition ← *not* COC[z]
> T: target ← (offset$_{15}$)^{14} || offset || 0^2
> T+1: if condition then
>   PC ← PC + target
>   else
>   NullifyCurrentInstruction
>   endif

Exceptions:

Coprocessor unusable exception

Opcode Bit Encoding:

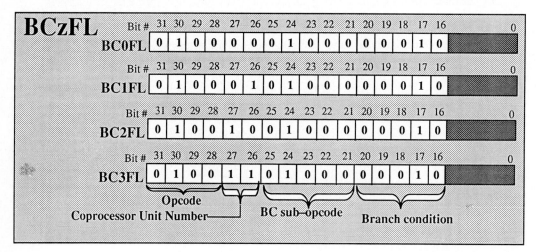

Branch On Coprocessor z True $\qquad$ BCzT

31 26	25 21	20 16	15 0
COPz 0 1 0 0 x x*	BC 0 1 0 0 0	BCT 0 0 0 0 1	offset
6	5	5	16

Format:

BCzT   offset

Description:

A branch target address is computed from the sum of the address of the instruction in the delay slot and the 16-bit *offset*, shifted left two bits and sign-extended to 32 bits. If the coprocessor *z*'s condition signal (CpCond) is true, then the program branches to the target address, with a delay of one instruction.

Because the condition line is sampled during the previous instruction, there must be at least one instruction between this instruction and a coprocessor instruction that changes the condition line.

Operation:

$$
\begin{aligned}
&\text{T-1:} && \text{condition} \leftarrow \text{COC[z]} \\
&\text{T:} && \text{target} \leftarrow (\text{offset}_{15})^{14} \,\|\, \text{offset} \,\|\, 0^2 \\
&\text{T+1:} && \text{if condition then} \\
&&& \qquad \text{PC} \leftarrow \text{PC} + \text{target} \\
&&& \text{endif}
\end{aligned}
$$

Exceptions:

Coprocessor unusable exception

*See the table, "Opcode Bit Encoding" on next page, or "CPU Instruction Op-
code Bit Encoding" at the end of Appendix A.

BCzT **Branch On Coprocessor z True**
(continued)

Opcode Bit Encoding:

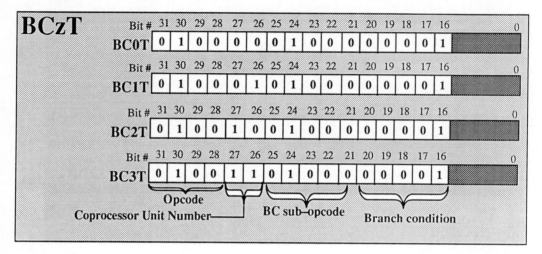

Branch On Coprocessor z True Likely

BCzTL

COPz 0100xx*	BC 01000	BCTL 00011	offset
6	5	5	16

(Bit positions: 31, 26, 25, 21, 20, 16, 15, 0)

Format:

BCzTL   offset

Description:

A branch target address is computed from the sum of the address of the instruction in the delay slot and the 16-bit *offset*, shifted left two bits and sign-extended. If the contents of coprocessor z's condition line, as sampled during the previous instruction, is true, the target address is branched to with a delay of one instruction.

Because the condition line is sampled during the previous instruction, there must be at least one instruction between this instruction and a coprocessor instruction that changes the condition line.

If the conditional branch is *not* taken, the instruction in the branch delay slot is nullified.

This instruction is not valid for R2000/R3000 processors, but does not cause a reserved instruction exception.

*See the table, "Opcode Bit Encoding" on next page, or "CPU Instruction Opcode Bit Encoding" at the end of Appendix A.

BCzTL   Branch On Coprocessor z True Likely
(continued)

R4000/R6000 Operation:

```
T-1:  condition ← COC[z]
T:    target ← (offset₁₅)¹⁴ || offset || 0²
T+1:  if condition then
             PC ← PC + target
      else
             NullifyCurrentInstruction
      endif
```

$$T{-}1: \quad condition \leftarrow COC[z]$$
$$T: \quad target \leftarrow (offset_{15})^{14} \;||\; offset \;||\; 0^2$$
$$T{+}1: \quad \text{if condition then}$$
$$PC \leftarrow PC + target$$
$$\text{else}$$
$$NullifyCurrentInstruction$$
$$\text{endif}$$

Exceptions:

Coprocessor unusable exception

Opcode Bit Encoding:

BCzTL

BC0TL	Bit #	31	30	29	28	27	26	25	24	23	22	21	20	19	18	17	16		0
		0	1	0	0	0	0	0	1	0	0	0	0	0	0	1	1		

BC1TL	Bit #	31	30	29	28	27	26	25	24	23	22	21	20	19	18	17	16		0
		0	1	0	0	0	1	0	1	0	0	0	0	0	0	1	1		

BC2TL	Bit #	31	30	29	28	27	26	25	24	23	22	21	20	19	18	17	16		0
		0	1	0	0	1	0	0	1	0	0	0	0	0	0	1	1		

BC3TL	Bit #	31	30	29	28	27	26	25	24	23	22	21	20	19	18	17	16		0
		0	1	0	0	1	1	0	1	0	0	0	0	0	0	1	1		

Opcode
Coprocessor Unit Number
BC sub–opcode
Branch condition

Branch On Equal

BEQ

BEQ 000100	rs	rt	offset
6	5	5	16

31   26 25   21 20   16 15   0

Format:

BEQ rs,rt,offset

Description:

A branch target address is computed from the sum of the address of the instruction in the delay slot and the 16-bit *offset*, shifted left two bits and sign-extended to 32 bits. The contents of general register *rs* and the contents of general register *rt* are compared. If the two registers are equal, then the program branches to the target address, with a delay of one instruction.

Operation:

> T: target $\leftarrow$ (offset$_{15}$)^{14} || offset || 0^2
>   condition $\leftarrow$ (GPR[rs] = GPR[rt])
> T+1:   if condition then
>   PC $\leftarrow$ PC + target
>   endif

Exceptions:

None.

BEQL

Branch On Equal Likely

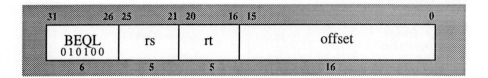

31 26	25 21	20 16	15 0
BEQL 010100	rs	rt	offset
6	5	5	16

Format:

BEQL rs,rt,offset

Description:

A branch target address is computed from the sum of the address of the instruction in the delay slot and the 16-bit offset, shifted left two bits and sign-extended. The contents of general register *rs* and the contents of general register *rt* are compared. If the two registers are equal, the target address is branched to, with a delay of one instruction. If the conditional branch is *not* taken, the instruction in the branch delay slot is nullified.

This instruction is not valid for R2000/R3000 processors.

R4000/R6000 Operation:

```
T:     target ← (offset₁₅)¹⁴ || offset || 0²
       condition ← (GPR[rs] = GPR[rt])
T+1:   if condition then
               PC ← PC + target
       else
               NullifyCurrentInstruction
       endif
```

Exceptions:

Reserved Instruction exception (R2000/R3000 only)

Branch On Greater Than
Or Equal To Zero
BGEZ

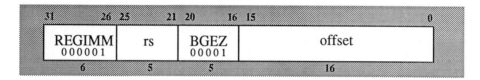

31 26	25 21	20 16	15 0
REGIMM 000001	rs	BGEZ 00001	offset
6	5	5	16

Format:

BGEZ rs,offset

Description:

A branch target address is computed from the sum of the address of the instruction in the delay slot and the 16-bit *offset*, shifted left two bits and sign-extended to 32 bits. If the contents of general register *rs* have the sign bit cleared, then the program branches to the target address, with a delay of one instruction.

Operation:

T:	target $\leftarrow$ (offset$_{15}$)^{14} || offset || 0^2
	condition $\leftarrow$ (GPR[rs]$_{31}$ = 0)
T+1:	if condition then
	PC $\leftarrow$ PC + target
	endif

Exceptions:

None.

BGEZAL

**Branch On Greater Than
Or Equal To Zero And Link**

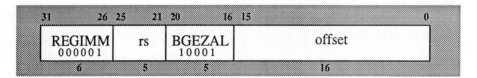

31 26	25 21	20 16	15 0
REGIMM 000001	rs	BGEZAL 10001	offset
6	5	5	16

Format:

BGEZAL rs,offset

Description:

A branch target address is computed from the sum of the address of the instruction in the delay slot and the 16-bit *offset,* shifted left two bits and sign-extended to 32 bits. Unconditionally, the address of the instruction after the delay slot is placed in the link register, *r31*. If the contents of general register *rs* have the sign bit cleared, then the program branches to the target address, with a delay of one instruction.

General register *rs* may not be general register *31*, because such an instruction is not restartable. An attempt to execute this instruction is *not* trapped, however.

Operation:

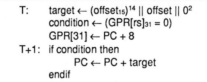

```
T:      target ← (offset₁₅)¹⁴ || offset || 0²
        condition ← (GPR[rs]₃₁ = 0)
        GPR[31] ← PC + 8
T+1:  if condition then
            PC ← PC + target
        endif
```

Exceptions:

None.

Branch On Greater Than Or Equal To Zero And Link Likely   # BGEZALL

31 26	25 21	20 16	15 0
REGIMM 000001	rs	BGEZALL 10011	offset
6	5	5	16

Format:

BGEZALL rs,offset

Description:

A branch target address is computed from the sum of the address of the instruction in the delay slot and the 16-bit *offset,* shifted left two bits and sign-extended. Unconditionally, the address of the instruction after the delay slot is placed in the link register, *r31*. If the contents of general register *rs* have the sign bit cleared, then the program branches to the target address, with a delay of one instruction.

General register *rs* may not be general register *31*, because such an instruction is not restartable. An attempt to execute this instruction is *not* trapped, however. If the conditional branch is *not* taken, the instruction in the branch delay slot is nullified.

This instruction is not valid for R2000/R3000 processors, however it does not cause a reserved instruction exception.

R4000/R6000 Operation:

```
T:     target ← (offset₁₅)¹⁴ || offset || 0²
       condition ← (GPR[rs]₃₁ = 0)
       GPR[31] ← PC + 8
T+1:   if condition then
               PC ← PC + target
       else
               NullifyCurrentInstruction
       endif
```

Exceptions:

None

BGEZL

**Branch On Greater
Than Or Equal To Zero Likely**

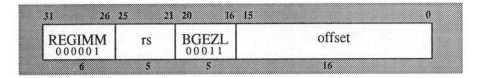

31 26	25 21	20 16	15 0
REGIMM 000001	rs	BGEZL 00011	offset
6	5	5	16

Format:

BGEZL rs,offset

Description:

A branch target address is computed from the sum of the address of the instruction in the delay slot and the 16-bit *offset*, shifted left two bits and sign-extended. If the contents of general register *rs* have the sign bit cleared, then the program branches to the target address, with a delay of one instruction. If the conditional branch is *not* taken, the instruction in the branch delay slot is nullified.

This instruction is not valid for R2000/R3000 processors, however it does not cause a reserved instruction exception.

R4000/R6000 Operation:

```
T:     target ← (offset₁₅)¹⁴ || offset || 0²
       condition ← (GPR[rs]₃₁ = 0)
T+1:   if condition then
              PC ← PC + target
       else
              NullifyCurrentInstruction
       endif
```

$$\text{target} \leftarrow (\text{offset}_{15})^{14} \,\|\, \text{offset} \,\|\, 0^2$$
$$\text{condition} \leftarrow (\text{GPR}[rs]_{31} = 0)$$

Exceptions:

None

Branch On Greater Than Zero

BGTZ

31 26	25 21	20 16	15 0
BGTZ 000111	rs	0 00000	offset
6	5	5	16

Format:

BGTZ rs,offset

Description:

A branch target address is computed from the sum of the address of the instruction in the delay slot and the 16-bit *offset*, shifted left two bits and sign-extended to 32 bits. The contents of general register *rs* are compared to zero. If the contents of general register *rs* have the sign bit cleared and are not equal to zero, then the program branches to the target address, with a delay of one instruction. This instruction is only valid when *rt* = 0.

Operation:

T: target $\leftarrow$ (offset$_{15}$)^{14} || offset || 0^2
         condition $\leftarrow$ (GPR[rs]$_{31}$ = 0) *and* (GPR[rs] $\neq 0^{32}$)
T+1:   if condition then
            PC $\leftarrow$ PC + target
         endif

Exceptions:

None.

BGTZL

**Branch On Greater
Than Zero Likely**

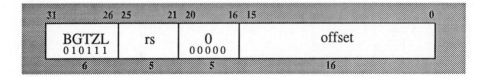

Format:

BGTZL rs,offset

Description:

A branch target address is computed from the sum of the address of the instruction in the delay slot and the 16-bit *offset*, shifted left two bits and sign-extended. The contents of general register *rs* are compared to zero. If the contents of general register *rs* have the sign bit cleared and are not equal to zero, then the program branches to the target address, with a delay of one instruction. This instruction is only valid when *rt* = 0. If the conditional branch is *not* taken, the instruction in the branch delay slot is nullified.

This instruction is not valid for R2000/R3000 processors.

R4000/R6000 Operation:

```
T:      target ← (offset₁₅)¹⁴ || offset || 0²
        condition ← (GPR[rs]₃₁ = 0) and  (GPR[rs] ≠ 0³²)
T+1:    if condition then
                PC ← PC + target
        else
                NullifyCurrentInstruction
        endif
```

Exceptions:

Reserved Instruction exception (R2000/R3000 only).

Branch on Less Than Or Equal To Zero

BLEZ

BLEZ 000110	rs	0 00000	offset
6	5	5	16

31   26 25   21 20   16 15   0

Format:

BLEZ rs,offset

Description:

A branch target address is computed from the sum of the address of the instruction in the delay slot and the 16-bit *offset*, shifted left two bits and sign-extended to 32 bits. The contents of general register *rs* are compared to zero. If the contents of general register *rs* have the sign bit set, or are equal to zero, then the program branches to the target address, with a delay of one instruction. This instruction is only valid when *rt* = 0.

Operation:

$$
\begin{aligned}
&T: &&\text{target} \leftarrow (\text{offset}_{15})^{14} \,\|\, \text{offset} \,\|\, 0^2 \\
& &&\text{condition} \leftarrow (\text{GPR[rs]}_{31} = 1) \ or \ (\text{GPR[rs]} = 0^{32}) \\
&T+1: &&\text{if condition then} \\
& &&\qquad \text{PC} \leftarrow \text{PC} + \text{target} \\
& &&\text{endif}
\end{aligned}
$$

Exceptions:

None.

BLEZL

**Branch on Less Than
Or Equal To Zero Likely**

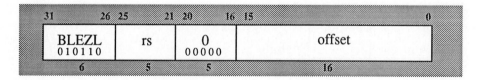

31 26	25 21	20 16	15 0
BLEZL 010110	rs	0 00000	offset
6	5	5	16

Format:

BLEZL rs,offset

Description:

A branch target address is computed from the sum of the address of the instruction in the delay slot and the 16-bit *offset*, shifted left two bits and sign-extended. The contents of general register *rs* is compared to zero. If the contents of general register *rs* have the sign bit set, or are equal to zero, then the program branches to the target address, with a delay of one instruction. This instruction is only valid when $rt = 0$.

If the conditional branch is *not* taken, the instruction in the branch delay slot is nullified.

This instruction is not valid for R2000/R3000 processors.

R4000/R6000 Operation:

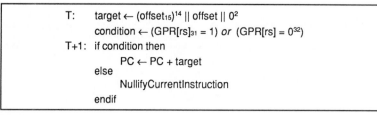

```
T:      target ← (offset₁₅)¹⁴ || offset || 0²
        condition ← (GPR[rs]₃₁ = 1) or (GPR[rs] = 0³²)
T+1:    if condition then
                PC ← PC + target
        else
                NullifyCurrentInstruction
        endif
```

Exceptions:

Reserved Instruction exception (R2000/R3000 only).

Branch On Less Than Zero **BLTZ**

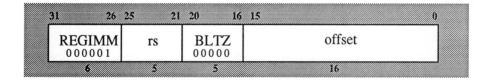

31 26	25 21	20 16	15 0
REGIMM 000001	rs	BLTZ 00000	offset
6	5	5	16

Format:

BLTZ rs,offset

Description:

A branch target address is computed from the sum of the address of the instruction in the delay slot and the 16-bit *offset*, shifted left two bits and sign-extended to 32 bits. If the contents of general register *rs* have the sign bit set, then the program branches to the target address, with a delay of one instruction.

Operation:

$$
\begin{aligned}
&\text{T:} \quad \text{target} \leftarrow (\text{offset}_{15})^{14} \,||\, \text{offset} \,||\, 0^2 \\
&\qquad \text{condition} \leftarrow (\text{GPR[rs]}_{31} = 1) \\
&\text{T+1:} \quad \text{if condition then} \\
&\qquad\qquad PC \leftarrow PC + \text{target} \\
&\qquad \text{endif}
\end{aligned}
$$

Exceptions:

None.

BLTZAL

**Branch On Less
Than Zero And Link**

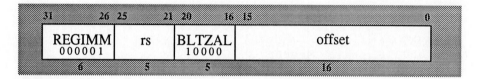

Format:

BLTZAL rs,offset

Description:

A branch target address is computed from the sum of the address of the instruction in the delay slot and the 16-bit *offset,* shifted left two bits and sign-extended to 32 bits. Unconditionally, the address of the instruction after the delay slot is placed in the link register, *r31.* If the contents of general register *rs* have the sign bit set, then the program branches to the target address, with a delay of one instruction.

General register *rs* may not be general register *31*, because such an instruction is not restartable. An attempt to execute this instruction is *not* trapped, however.

Operation:

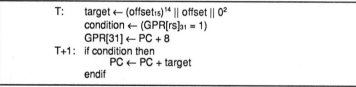

```
T:      target ← (offset₁₅)¹⁴ || offset || 0²
        condition ← (GPR[rs]₃₁ = 1)
        GPR[31] ← PC + 8
T+1:    if condition then
                PC ← PC + target
        endif
```

Exceptions:

None.

Branch On Less
Than Zero And Link Likely

BLTZALL

REGIMM 000001	rs	BLTZALL 10010	offset
6	5	5	16

Format:

BLTZALL rs,offset

Description:

A branch target address is computed from the sum of the address of the instruction in the delay slot and the 16-bit *offset,* shifted left two bits and sign-extended. Unconditionally, the address of the instruction after the delay slot is placed in the link register, *r31*. If the contents of general register *rs* have the sign bit set, then the program branches to the target address, with a delay of one instruction.

General register *rs* may not be general register *31*, because such an instruction is not restartable. An attempt to execute this instruction is *not* trapped, however. If the conditional branch is *not* taken, the instruction in the branch delay slot is nullified.

This instruction is not valid for R2000/R3000 processors, but does not cause a reserved instruction exception.

R4000/R6000 Operation:

```
T:    target ← (offset₁₅)¹⁴ || offset || 0²
      condition ← (GPR[rs]₃₁ = 1)
      GPR[31] ← PC + 8
T+1: if condition then
         PC ← PC + target
      else
         NullifyCurrentInstruction
      endif
```

$$T: \quad target \leftarrow (offset_{15})^{14} \,||\, offset \,||\, 0^2$$
$$condition \leftarrow (GPR[rs]_{31} = 1)$$
$$GPR[31] \leftarrow PC + 8$$
$$T+1: \text{if condition then}$$
$$PC \leftarrow PC + target$$
$$\text{else}$$
$$NullifyCurrentInstruction$$
$$\text{endif}$$

Exceptions:

None

BLTZL

Branch On Less Than Zero Likely

31 26	25 21	20 16	15 0
REGIMM 000001	rs	BLTZL 00010	offset
6	5	5	16

Format:

BLTZ rs,offset

Description:

A branch target address is computed from the sum of the address of the instruction in the delay slot and the 16-bit *offset*, shifted left two bits and sign-extended. If the contents of general register *rs* have the sign bit set, then the program branches to the target address, with a delay of one instruction. If the conditional branch is *not* taken, the instruction in the branch delay slot is nullified.

This instruction is not valid for R2000/R3000 processors, but does not cause a reserved instruction exception..

R4000/R6000 Operation:

```
T:      target ← (offset₁₅)¹⁴ || offset || 0²
        condition ← (GPR[rs]₃₁ = 1)
T+1:    if condition then
                PC ← PC + target
        else
                NullifyCurrentInstruction
        endif
```

Exceptions:

None

Branch On Not Equal

BNE

31 26 25	21 20	16 15	0
BNE 000101	rs	rt	offset
6	5	5	16

Format:

BNE rs,rt,offset

Description:

A branch target address is computed from the sum of the address of the instruction in the delay slot and the 16-bit *offset,* shifted left two bits and sign-extended to 32 bits. The contents of general register *rs* and the contents of general register *rt* are compared. If the two registers are not equal, then the program branches to the target address, with a delay of one instruction.

Operation:

```
T:     target ← (offset₁₅)¹⁴ || offset || 0²
       condition ← (GPR[rs] ≠ GPR[rt])
T+1:   if condition then
           PC ← PC + target
       endif
```

Exceptions:

None.

BNEL

Branch On Not Equal Likely

31 26	25 21	20 16	15 0
BNEL 010101	rs	rt	offset
6	5	5	16

Format:

BNEL rs,rt,offset

Description:

A branch target address is computed from the sum of the address of the instruction in the delay slot and the 16-bit *offset,* shifted left two bits and sign-extended. The contents of general register *rs* and the contents of general register *rt* are compared. If the two registers are not equal, then the program branches to the target address, with a delay of one instruction.

If the conditional branch is *not* taken, the instruction in the branch delay slot is nullified.

This instruction is not valid for R2000/R3000 processors.

R4000/R6000 Operation:

```
T:     target ← (offset15)14 || offset || 02
       condition ← (GPR[rs] ≠ GPR[rt])
T+1:   if condition then
            PC ← PC + target
       else
            NullifyCurrentInstruction
       endif
```

Exceptions:

Reserved Instruction exception (R2000/R3000 only).

Breakpoint # BREAK

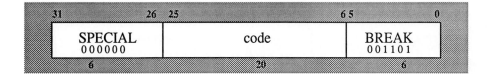

Format:

BREAK

Description:

A breakpoint trap occurs, immediately and unconditionally transferring control to the exception handler.

The code field is available for use as software parameters, but is retrieved by the exception handler only by loading the contents of the memory word containing the instruction.

Operation:

```
        T:    BreakpointException
```

Exceptions:

Breakpoint exception

CACHE

Cache

31	26	25	21	20	16	15	0
CACHE 101111		base		op		offset	
6		5		5		16	

Format:

CACHE op,offset(base)

Description:

The 16-bit *offset* is sign-extended and added to the contents of general register *base* to form a virtual address. The virtual address is translated to a physical address using the TLB, and the 5-bit sub-opcode specifies a cache operation for that address.

This operation is only valid for R4000 processors. If CP0 is not usable (User or Supervisor mode) the CP0 enable bit in the *Status* register is clear, and a coprocessor unusable exception is taken. The operation of this instruction on any operation/cache combination not listed below, or on a secondary cache when none is present, is undefined. The operation of this instruction on uncached addresses is also undefined.

The Index operation uses part of the virtual address to specify a cache block.

For a primary cache of $2^{CACHESIZE}$ bytes with $2^{BLOCKSIZE}$ bytes per tag, vAddr$_{CACHESIZE .. BLOCKSIZE}$ specifies the block. For a secondary cache of $2^{CACHESIZE}$ bytes with $2^{BLOCKSIZE}$ bytes per tag, pAddr$_{CACHESIZE .. BLOCKSIZE}$ specifies the block.

Index Load Tag also uses vAddr$_{BLOCKSIZE .. 3}$ to select the doubleword for reading ECC or parity. When the *CE* bit of the *Status* register is set, Hit WriteBack, Hit WriteBack Invalidate, Index WriteBack Invalidate, and Fill also use vAddr$_{BLOCKSIZE .. 3}$ to select the doubleword that has its ECC or parity modified. This operation is performed unconditionally.

The Hit operation accesses the specified cache as normal data references, and performs the specified operation if the cache block contains valid data with the specified physical address (a hit). If the cache block is invalid or contains a different address (a miss), no operation is performed.

Cache   CACHE
(continued)

Write back from a primary cache goes to the secondary cache (if there is one), otherwise to memory. Write back from a secondary cache always goes to memory. A secondary write back always writes the most recent data — the data comes from the primary data cache, if present, and modified (the *W* bit is set). Otherwise the data comes from the specified secondary cache. The address to be written is specified by the cache tag and not the translated physical address.

TLB Refill and TLB Invalid exceptions can occur on any operation. For Index operations (where the physical address is used to index the cache but need not match the cache tag) unmapped addresses may be used to avoid TLB exceptions. This operation never causes TLB Modified or Virtual Coherency exceptions. Bits 17..16 of the instruction specify the cache as follows:

Code	Name	Cache
0	I	primary instruction
1	D	primary data
2	SI	secondary instruction
3	SD	secondary data (or combined instruction/data)

Bits 20..18 of the instruction specify the operation as follows:

Code	Caches	Name	Operation
0	I, SI	Index Invalidate	Set the cache state of the cache block to Invalid.
0	D	Index WriteBack Invalidate	Examine the cache state and *W* bit of the primary data cache block at the index specified by the virtual address. If the state is not Invalid and the *W* bit is set, then write back the block to the secondary cache (if present) or to memory (if no secondary cache). The address to write is taken from the primary cache tag. When a secondary cache is present, and the *CE* bit of the *Status* register is set, the content of the *ECC* register is XORed into the computed check bits during the write to the secondary cache for the addressed doubleword. Set cache state of primary cache block to Invalid.
0	SD	Index WriteBack Invalidate	Examine the cache state of the secondary data cache block at the index specified by the physical address. If the state is Dirty Exclusive or Dirty Shared, then write back the block to memory and set the cache state to Invalid. The address to write is taken from the secondary cache tag, which is not necessarily the physical address used to index the cache. Like all secondary write-backs, the operation writes any modified data (*W* bit set) from the primary data cache. Unlike Hit Write-back Invalidate the operation does not invalidate or clear the *W* bit in the primary D-cache. In all cases, the secondary cache block state is set to Invalid.
1	all	Index Load Tag	Read the tag for the cache block at the specified index and place it into the *TagLo* and *TagHi* CP0 registers, ignoring ECC and parity errors. Also load the data ECC or parity bits into the *ECC* register.

CACHE

Cache
(continued)

Code	Caches	Name	Operation
2	all	Index Store Tag	Write the tag for the cache block at the specified index from the *TagLo* and *TagHi* CP0 registers.
3	SD	Create Dirty Exclusive	This operation is used to avoid loading data needlessly from memory when writing new contents into an entire cache block. If the cache block is valid but does not contain the specified address (a valid miss) the secondary block is vacated. The data is written back to memory if dirty and all matching blocks in both primary caches are invalidated. As usual during a secondary write-back, if the primary data cache contains modified data (matching blocks with *W* bit set) that modified data is written to memory. If the cache block is valid and does contain the specified physical address (a hit), then the operation cleans up the primary caches to avoid any virtual alias problems: all blocks in both primary caches that match the secondary line are invalidated without write back. Note that the search for matching primary blocks uses the virtual index of the PIdx field of the secondary cache tag (the virtual index to the location last used) and not the virtual index of the virtual address used in the operation (the virtual index to the location now being used). If the secondary tag and address do not match (miss), or the tag and address do match (hit) and the block is in a shared state, send an invalidate for the specified address on the system interface. In all cases, set the cache block tag to the specified physical address, set the cache state to Dirty Exclusive, and set the virtual index field from the virtual address. The *CH* bit in the *Status* register is set or cleared to indicate a hit or miss.
3	D	Create Dirty Exclusive	This operation is used to avoid loading data needlessly from secondary cache or memory when writing new contents into an entire cache block. If the cache block does not contain the specified address, and the block is dirty, write it back to the secondary cache or memory. In all cases, set the cache block tag to the specified physical address, set the cache state to Dirty Exclusive.
4	I, D	Hit Invalidate	If the cache block contains the specified address, mark the cache block invalid.
4	SI, SD	Hit Invalidate	If the cache block contains the specified address, mark the cache block invalid and also invalidate all matching blocks, if present, in the primary caches (the PIdx field of the secondary tag is used to determine the locations in the primaries to search). The *CH* bit in the *Status* register is set or cleared to indicate a hit or miss.
5	D	Hit WriteBack Invalidate	If the cache block contains the specified address, write back the data if it is dirty, and mark the cache block invalid. When a secondary cache is present and the *CE* bit of the *Status* register is set, contents of the *ECC* register is XORed into the computed check bits during the write to the secondary cache for the addressed doubleword.

Cache
(continued)

CACHE

Code	Caches	Name	Operation
5	SD	Hit WriteBack Invalidate	If the cache block contains the specified address, write back the data if it is dirty, and mark the secondary cache block and all matching blocks in both primary caches invalid. As usual with secondary write-backs, modified data in the primary data cache (matching block with the W bit set) is used during the write-back. The PIdx field of the secondary tag is used to determine the locations in the primaries to check for matching primary blocks. The CH bit in the *Status* register is set or cleared to indicate a hit or miss.
5	I	Fill	Fill the primary instruction cache block from secondary or memory. If the CE bit of the *Status* register is set, the contents of the ECC register is used instead of the computed parity bits for addressed doubleword when written to the instruction cache.
6	D	Hit WriteBack	If the cache block contains the specified address, and the W bit is set, write back the data to memory or the secondary cache, and clear the W bit. When a secondary cache is present, and the CE bit of the *Status* register is set, the contents of the ECC register is XORed into the computed check bits during the write to the secondary cache for the addressed doubleword.
6	SD	Hit WriteBack	If the cache block contains the specified address, and the cache state is Dirty Exclusive or Dirty Shared, write back the data to memory, and change the cache state to Clean Exclusive or Shared, respectively. The CH bit in the *Status* register is set or cleared to indicate a hit or miss. The write back looks in the primary data cache for modified data, but does *not* invalidate or clear the W bit in the primary data cache. This state, although perhaps not intuitive, is consistent since the primary block contains data that is at least as current as that in memory or secondary cache. A subsequent write-back of the primary line without further modification would be redundant, but not incorrect.
6	I	Hit WriteBack	If the cache block contains the specified address, write back the data unconditionally. When a secondary cache is present, and the CE bit of the *Status* register is set, the contents of the ECC register is XORed into the computed check bits during the write to the secondary cache for the addressed doubleword.
7	SI, SD	Hit Set Virtual	This operation is used to change the virtual index of secondary cache contents avoiding unnecessary memory operations. If the cache block contains the specified address, invalidate matching blocks in the primary caches at the index formed by concatenating PIdx in the secondary cache tag (not the virtual address of the operation) and $vAddr_{11..4}$, then set the virtual index field of the secondary cache tag from the specified virtual address. Modified data in the primary data cache is not preserved by the operation and should be explicitly written back before this operation. The CH bit in the *Status* register is set or cleared to indicate a hit or miss.

Exceptions:

Coprocessor unusable exception
Reserved instruction exception (non-R4000)

CFCz

Move Control From
Coprocessor

COPz 0100xx*	CF 00010	rt	rd	0 00000
6	5	5	5	11

Bits: 31 26 25 21 20 16 15 11 10 0

Format:

CFCz   rt,rd

Description:

The contents of coprocessor control register *rd* of coprocessor unit *z* are loaded into general register *rt*.

This instruction is not valid for CP0.

Operation:

T:	data ← CCR[z,rd]
T + 1:	GPR[rt] ← data

Exceptions:

Coprocessor unusable exception

*Opcode Bit Encoding:

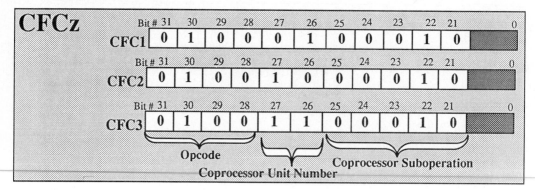

Coprocessor Operation   COPz

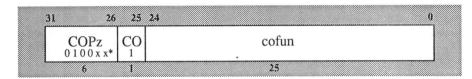

COPz 0 1 0 0 x x*	CO 1	cofun
6	1	25

31   26   25   24   0

Format:

COPz   cofun

Description:

A coprocessor operation is performed. The operation may specify and reference internal coprocessor registers, and may change the state of the coprocessor condition line, but does not modify state within the processor or the cache/memory system. Details of coprocessor operations are contained in Appendix B.

Operation:

> T: CoprocessorOperation (z, cofun)

Exceptions:

Coprocessor unusable exception
Coprocessor interrupt or Floating-Point Exception (R4000 CP1 only)

Opcode Bit Encoding:

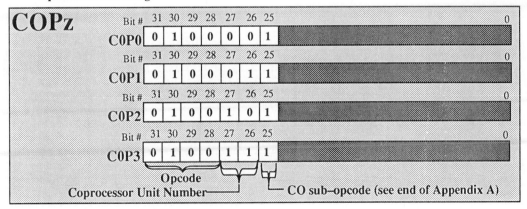

CTCz

**Move Control to
Coprocessor**

31 26	25 21	20 16	15 11	10 0
COPz 0 1 0 0 x x *	CT 0 0 1 1 0	rt	rd	0 000 0000 0000
6	5	5	5	11

Format:

CTCz   rt,rd

Description:

The contents of general register *rt* are loaded into control register *rd* of coprocessor unit *z*.

This instruction is not valid for CP0.

Operation:

```
T:      data ← GPR[rt]
T + 1:  CCR[z,rd] ← data
```

Exceptions:

Coprocessor unusable exception

*Opcode Bit Encoding:

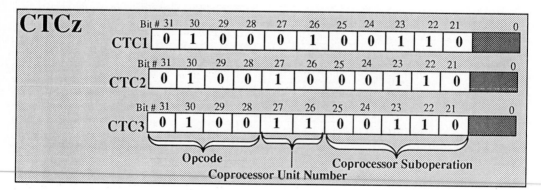

MIPS RISC Architecture

Divide
DIV

SPECIAL 000000	rs	rt	0 00 0000 0000	DIV 011010
6	5	5	10	6

Format:

DIV rs,rt

Description:

The contents of general register *rs* are divided by the contents of general register *rt,* treating both operands as 32-bit 2's-complement values. No overflow exception occurs under any circumstances, and the result of this operation is undefined when the divisor is zero.

This instruction is only valid when *rd* = 0; it is typically followed by additional instructions to check for a zero divisor and for overflow.

When the operation completes, the quotient word of the double result is loaded into special register *LO*, and the remainder word of the double result is loaded into special register *HI*.

If either of the two preceding instructions is MFHI or MFLO, the results of those instructions are undefined. Correct operation requires separating reads of *HI* or *LO* from writes by two or more instructions.

Operation:

```
T–2:  LO  ← undefined
      HI  ← undefined
T–1:  LO  ← undefined
      HI  ← undefined
T:    LO  ← GPR[rs] div GPR[rt]
      HI  ← GPR[rs] mod GPR[rt]
```

Exceptions:

None.

DIVU
Divide Unsigned

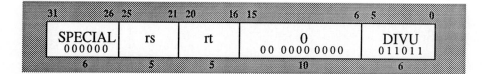

Format:

DIVU rs,rt

Description:

The contents of general register *rs* are divided by the contents of general register *rt*, treating both operands as unsigned values. No integer overflow exception occurs under any circumstances, and the result of this operation is undefined when the divisor is zero.

This instruction is only valid when *rd* = 0; it is typically followed by additional instructions to check for a zero divisor.

When the operation completes, the quotient word of the double result is loaded into special register *LO*, and the remainder word of the double result is loaded into special register *HI*.

If either of the two preceding instructions is MFHI or MFLO, the results of those instructions are undefined. Correct operation requires separating reads of *HI* or *LO* from writes by two or more instructions.

Operation:

```
T-2: LO  ← undefined
     HI  ← undefined
T-1: LO  ← undefined
     HI  ← undefined
T:   LO  ← (0 || GPR[rs]) div (0 || GPR[rt])
     HI  ← (0 || GPR[rs]) mod (0 || GPR[rt])
```

Exceptions:

None.

Exception Return ERET

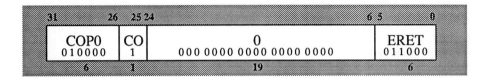

31 26	25 24	6 5 0
COP0 010000	CO 1	0 000 0000 0000 0000 0000	ERET 011000
6	1	19	6

Format:

ERET

Description:

ERET is the R4000 instruction for returning from an interrupt, exception, or error trap. Unlike a branch or jump instruction, ERET does not execute the next instruction.

ERET must not itself be placed in a branch delay slot.

If the processor is servicing an error trap ($SR_2 = 1$), then load the PC from the *ErrorEPC* and clear the *ERL* bit of the *Status* register (SR_2). Otherwise ($SR_2 = 0$), load the PC from the *EPC*, and clear the *EXL* bit of the *Status* register (SR_1).

An ERET executed between a LL and SC also causes the SC to fail.

R4000 Operation:

```
T:   if SR₂ = 1 then
            PC ← ErrorEPC
            SR ← SR₃₁..₃ || 0 || SR₁..₀
     else
            PC ← EPC
            SR ← SR₃₁..₂ || 0 || SR₀
     endif
     LLbit ← 0
```

Exceptions:

Coprocessor unusable exception
Reserved instruction exception (non-R4000)

J

Jump

31 26	25 0
J 0 0 0 0 1 0	target
6	26

Format:

J target

Description:

The 26-bit target address is shifted left two bits and combined with the high order four bits of the address of the delay slot. The program unconditionally jumps to this calculated address with a delay of one instruction.

Operation:

T: temp ← target
T+1: PC ← $PC_{31..28}$ || temp || 0^2

Exceptions:

None.

Jump And Link **JAL**

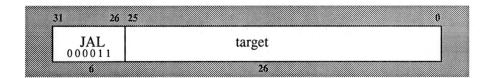

Format:

JAL target

Description:

The 26-bit target address is shifted left two bits and combined with the high order four bits of the address of the delay slot. The program unconditionally jumps to this calculated address with a delay of one instruction. The address of the instruction after the delay slot is placed in the link register, *r31*.

Operation:

```
T:     temp ← target
       GPR[31] ← PC + 8
T+1:   PC ← PC 31..28 || temp || 0²
```

Exceptions:

None.

JALR

Jump And Link Register

31 26	25 21	20 16	15 11	10 6	5 0
SPECIAL 000000	rs	0 00000	rd	0 00000	JALR 001001
6	5	5	5	5	6

Format:

JALR rs
JALR rd, rs

Description:

The program unconditionally jumps to the address contained in general register *rs*, with a delay of one instruction. The address of the instruction after the delay slot is placed in general register *rd*. The default value of *rd*, if omitted in the assembly language instruction, is 31.

Register specifiers *rs* and *rd* may not be equal, because such an instruction does not have the same effect when reexecuted. However, an attempt to execute this instruction is *not* trapped, and the result of executing such an instruction is undefined.

Since instructions must be word-aligned, a *Jump and Link Register* instruction must specify a target register (*rs*) whose two low order bits are zero. If these low order bits are not zero, an address exception will occur when the jump target instruction is subsequently fetched.

Operation:

```
T:    temp ← GPR [rs]
      GPR[rd] ← PC + 8
T+1:  PC ← temp
```

Exceptions:

None.

Jump Register

JR

SPECIAL 000000	rs	0 000 0000 0000 0000	JR 001000
6	5	15	6

Format:

JR rs

Description:

The program unconditionally jumps to the address contained in general register *rs*, with a delay of one instruction. This instruction is only valid when *rd* = 0.

Since instructions must be word-aligned, a *Jump Register* instruction must specify a target register (*rs*) whose two low order bits are zero. If these low order bits are not zero, an address exception will occur when the jump target instruction is subsequently fetched.

Operation:

```
T:     temp ← GPR[rs]
T+1:  PC ← temp
```

Exceptions:

None.

LB

Load Byte

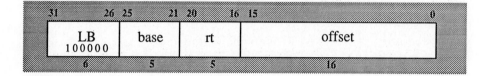

Format:

LB rt,offset(base)

Description:

The 16-bit *offset* is sign-extended and added to the contents of general register *base* to form a virtual address. The contents of the byte at the memory location specified by the effective address are sign-extended and loaded into general register *rt*.

In R2000/R3000 implementations, the contents of general register *rt* are undefined for time T of the instruction immediately following this load instruction.

R2000/R3000 Operation:

```
T:      vAddr ← ((offset₁₅)¹⁶ || offset₁₅..₀) + GPR[base]
        (pAddr, uncached) ← AddressTranslation (vAddr, DATA)
        mem ← LoadMemory (uncached, BYTE, pAddr, vAddr, DATA)
        byte ← vAddr₁..₀ xor BigEndianCPU²
        GPR[rt] ← undefined
T+1:    GPR[rt] ← (mem₇₊₈*byte)²⁴ || mem₇₊₈*byte..₈*byte
```

Load Byte
(continued)

R4000/R6000 Operation:

T: $\quad$ vAddr ← ((offset$_{15}$)^{16} || offset$_{15..0}$) + GPR[base]
$\quad$ (pAddr, uncached) ← AddressTranslation (vAddr, DATA)
$\quad$ pAddr ← pAddr$_{PSIZE-1..2}$ || (pAddr$_{1..0}$ *xor* ReverseEndian^2)
$\quad$ mem ← LoadMemory (uncached, BYTE, pAddr, vAddr, DATA)
$\quad$ byte ← vAddr$_{1..0}$ *xor* BigEndianCPU^2
$\quad$ GPR[rt] ← (mem$_{7+8*byte}$)^{24} || mem$_{7+8*byte..8*byte}$

Exceptions:

TLB refill exception
TLB invalid exception
Bus error exception
Address error exception

LBU Load Byte Unsigned

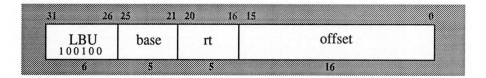

31 26	25 21	20 16	15 0
LBU 100100	base	rt	offset
6	5	5	16

Format:

LBU rt,offset(base)

Description:

The 16-bit *offset* is sign-extended and added to the contents of general register *base* to form a virtual address. The contents of the byte at the memory location specified by the effective address are zero-extended and loaded into general register *rt*. In R2000/R3000 implementations, the contents of general register *rt* are undefined for time T of the instruction immediately following this load instruction.

R2000/R3000 Operation:

```
T:      vAddr ← ((offset₁₅)¹⁶ || offset₁₅..₀) + GPR[base]
        (pAddr, uncached) ← AddressTranslation (vAddr, DATA)
        mem ← LoadMemory (uncached, BYTE, pAddr, vAddr, DATA)
        byte ← vAddr₁..₀ xor BigEndianCPU²
        GPR[rt] ← undefined
T+1:    GPR[rt] ← 0²⁴ || mem₇₊₈*byte..8*byte
```

R4000/R6000 Operation:

```
T:      vAddr ← ((offset₁₅)¹⁶ || offset₁₅..₀) + GPR[base]
        (pAddr, uncached) ← AddressTranslation (vAddr, DATA)
        pAddr ← pAddrPSIZE-1..2 || (pAddr₁..₀ xor ReverseEndian²)
        mem ← LoadMemory (uncached, BYTE, pAddr, vAddr, DATA)
        byte ← vAddr₁..₀ xor BigEndianCPU²
        GPR[rt] ← 0²⁴ || mem₇₊₈*byte..8*byte
```

Exceptions:

TLB refill exception   TLB invalid exception
Bus error exception   Address error exception

Load Doubleword To Coprocessor

LDCz

LDCz 1 1 0 1 x x*	base	rt	offset
6	5	5	16

(bit positions: 31 26 25 21 20 16 15 0)

Format:

LDCz rt,offset(base)

Description:

The 16-bit *offset* is sign-extended and added to the contents of general register *base* to form a virtual address. The processor reads a doubleword from the addressed memory location and makes the data available to coprocessor unit *z*. The manner in which each coprocessor uses the data is defined by the individual coprocessor specifications.

If any of the three least significant bits of the effective address are non-zero, an address error exception takes place.

This instruction is not valid for R2000/R3000 processors and causes a reserved instruction exception. This instruction is not valid for use with CP0.

In R4000 and R6000 implementations this instruction is undefined when the least significant bit of register *rt* is non-zero.

See the table, "Opcode Bit Encoding" on next page, or "CPU Instruction Opcode Bit Encoding" at the end of Appendix A.

LDCz   **Load Doubleword To Coprocessor**
                                                              (continued)

R4000/R6000 Operation:

```
T:    vAddr ← ((offset15)16 || offset15..0) + GPR[base]
      (pAddr, uncached) ← AddressTranslation (vAddr, DATA)
      mem ← LoadMemory (uncached, DOUBLEWORD, pAddr, vAddr, DATA)
      COPzLD (rt, mem)
```

Exceptions:

TLB refill exception
TLB invalid exception
Bus error exception
Address error exception
Coprocessor unusable exception
Reserved instruction exception (R2000/R3000 only)

Opcode Bit Encoding:

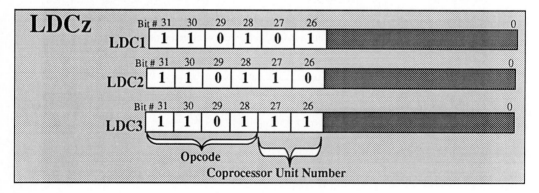

Load Halfword

LH

31 26	25 21	20 16	15 0
LH 100001	base	rt	offset
6	5	5	16

Format:

LH rt,offset(base)

Description:

The 16-bit *offset* is sign-extended and added to the contents of general register *base* to form a virtual address. The contents of the halfword at the memory location specified by the effective address are sign-extended and loaded into general register *rt*.

If the least significant bit of the effective address is non-zero, an address error exception occurs.

In R2000/R3000 implementations, the contents of general register *rt* are undefined for time *T* of the instruction immediately following this load instruction.

R2000/R3000 Operation:

```
T:     vAddr ← ((offset₁₅)¹⁶ || offset₁₅..₀) + GPR[base]
       (pAddr, uncached) ← AddressTranslation (vAddr, DATA)
       mem ← LoadMemory (uncached, HALFWORD, pAddr, vAddr, DATA)
       byte ← vAddr₁..₀ xor (BigEndianCPU || 0)
       GPR[rt] ← undefined
T+1:   GPR[rt] ← (mem₁₅₊₈*byte)¹⁶ || mem₁₅₊₈*byte..₈*byte
```

LH

Load Halfword
(continued)

R4000/R6000 Operation:

T:	vAddr ← ((offset$_{15}$)^{16} || offset$_{15..0}$) + GPR[base]
	(pAddr, uncached) ← AddressTranslation (vAddr, DATA)
	pAddr ← pAddr$_{PSIZE-1..2}$ || (pAddr$_{1..0}$ *xor* (ReverseEndian || 0))
	mem ← LoadMemory (uncached, HALFWORD, pAddr, vAddr, DATA)
	byte ← vAddr$_{1..0}$ *xor* (BigEndianCPU || 0)
	GPR[rt] ← (mem$_{15+8*byte}$)^{16} || mem$_{15+8*byte..8*byte}$

Exceptions:

TLB refill exception
TLB invalid exception
Bus error exception
Address error exception

Load Halfword Unsigned   LHU

31 26	25 21	20 16	15 0
LHU 100101	base	rt	offset
6	5	5	16

Format:

LHU rt,offset(base)

Description:

The 16-bit *offset* is sign-extended and added to the contents of general register *base* to form a virtual address. The contents of the halfword at the memory location specified by the effective address are zero-extended and loaded into general register *rt*.

If the least significant bit of the effective address is non-zero, an address error exception occurs.

In R2000/R3000 implementations, the contents of general register *rt* are undefined for time *T* of the instruction immediately following this load instruction.

R2000/R3000 Operation:

```
T:     vAddr ← ((offset₁₅)¹⁶ || offset₁₅..₀) + GPR[base]
       (pAddr, uncached) ← AddressTranslation (vAddr, DATA)
       mem ← LoadMemory (uncached, HALFWORD, pAddr, vAddr, DATA)
       byte ← vAddr₁..₀ xor (BigEndianCPU || 0)
       GPR[rt] ← undefined
T+1:   GPR[rt] ← 0¹⁶ || mem₁₅₊₈*byte..₈*byte
```

LHU Load Halfword Unsigned
(continued)

R4000/R6000 Operation:

```
T:   vAddr ← ((offset₁₅)¹⁶ || offset₁₅..₀) + GPR[base]
     (pAddr, uncached) ← AddressTranslation (vAddr, DATA)
     pAddr ← pAddr_PSIZE – 1 .. 2 || ( pAddr₁..₀ xor (ReverseEndian || 0))
     mem ← LoadMemory (uncached, HALFWORD, pAddr, vAddr, DATA)
     byte ← vAddr₁..₀ xor (BigEndianCPU || 0)
     GPR[rt] ← 0¹⁶ || mem₁₅₊₈*byte..₈*byte
```

$$T: \quad vAddr \leftarrow ((offset_{15})^{16} \,\|\, offset_{15..0}) + GPR[base]$$
$$(pAddr, uncached) \leftarrow AddressTranslation\,(vAddr, DATA)$$
$$pAddr \leftarrow pAddr_{PSIZE-1..2} \,\|\, (pAddr_{1..0} \; xor \; (ReverseEndian \,\|\, 0))$$
$$mem \leftarrow LoadMemory\,(uncached, HALFWORD, pAddr, vAddr, DATA)$$
$$byte \leftarrow vAddr_{1..0} \; xor \; (BigEndianCPU \,\|\, 0)$$
$$GPR[rt] \leftarrow 0^{16} \,\|\, mem_{15+8*byte..8*byte}$$

Exceptions:

TLB refill exception
TLB invalid exception
Bus error exception
Address error exception

Load Linked

LL

```
 31        26 25      21 20    16 15                              0
┌──────────┬──────────┬─────────┬──────────────────────────────────┐
│    LL    │   base   │   rt    │             offset               │
│  110000  │          │         │                                  │
└──────────┴──────────┴─────────┴──────────────────────────────────┘
      6          5          5                   16
```

Format:

LL rt,offset(base)

Description:

The 16-bit *offset* is sign-extended and added to the contents of general register *base* to form a virtual address. The contents of the word at the memory location specified by the effective address are loaded into general register *rt*.

This instruction implicitly performs a SYNC operation; all loads and stores to shared memory fetched prior to the LL must access memory before the LL, and loads and stores to shared memory fetched subsequent to the LL must access memory after the LL.

The processor begins checking the accessed word for modification by other processors and devices.

Load Linked and Store Conditional can be used to atomically update memory locations:

```
L1:
        LL      T1, (T0)
        ADD     T2, T1, 1
        SC      T2, (T0)
        BEQ     T2, 0, L1
        NOP
```

This atomically increments the word addressed by T0. Changing the ADD to an OR changes this to an atomic bit set.

LL

Load Linked
(continued)

The operation of LL is undefined if the addressed location is uncached and, for synchronization between multiple processors, the operation of LL is undefined if the addressed location is noncoherent. A cache miss that occurs between LL and SC may cause SC to fail, so no load or store instruction should occur between LL and SC. Exceptions also cause SC to fail, so persistent exceptions must be avoided.

This instruction is available in User mode, and it is not necessary for CP0 to be enabled.

If either of the two least significant bits of the effective address is non-zero, an address error exception takes place.

This instruction causes a reserved instruction exception for R2000/R3000 processors.

R4000/R6000 Operation:

```
T:    vAddr ← ((offset15)16 || offset15..0) + GPR[base]
      (pAddr, uncached) ← AddressTranslation (vAddr, DATA)
      mem ← LoadMemory (uncached, WORD, pAddr, vAddr, DATA)
      GPR[rt] ← mem
      LLbit ← 1
      SyncOperation()
```

Exceptions:

TLB refill exception
TLB invalid exception
Bus error exception
Address error exception

Load Upper Immediate

LUI

LUI 001111	rs	rt	immediate
31 26	25 21	20 16	15 0
6	5	5	16

Format:

LUI rt,immediate

Description:

The 16-bit *immediate* is shifted left 16 bits and concatenated to 16 bits of zeros. The result is placed into general register *rt*.

Operation:

T: GPR[rt] ← immediate || 0^{16}

Exceptions:

None.

LW

Load Word

LW 100011	base	rt	offset
6	5	5	16

31   26 25   21 20   16 15   0

Format:

LW rt,offset(base)

Description:

The 16-bit *offset* is sign-extended and added to the contents of general register *base* to form a virtual address. The contents of the word at the memory location specified by the effective address are loaded into general register *rt*.

If either of the two least significant bits of the effective address is non-zero, an address error exception occurs.

In R2000/R3000 implementations, the contents of general register *rt* are undefined for time T of the instruction immediately following this load instruction.

R2000/R3000 Operation:

```
T:    vAddr ← ((offset₁₅)¹⁶ || offset₁₅..₀) + GPR[base]
      (pAddr, uncached) ← AddressTranslation (vAddr, DATA)
      mem ← LoadMemory (uncached, WORD, pAddr, vAddr, DATA)
      GPR[rt] ← undefined
T+1:  GPR[rt] ← mem
```

Load Word
(continued)

LW

R4000/R6000 Operation:

T: vAddr $\leftarrow$ ((offset$_{15}$)^{16} || offset$_{15..0}$) + GPR[base]
    (pAddr, uncached) $\leftarrow$ AddressTranslation (vAddr, DATA)
    mem $\leftarrow$ LoadMemory (uncached, WORD, pAddr, vAddr, DATA)
    GPR[rt] $\leftarrow$ mem

Exceptions:

TLB refill exception
TLB invalid exception
Bus error exception
Address error exception

LWCz

Load Word To Coprocessor

LWCz 1100xx*	base	rt	offset
6	5	5	16

31   26 25   21 20   16 15   0

Format:

LWCz rt,offset(base)

Description:

The 16-bit *offset* is sign-extended and added to the contents of general register *base* to form a 32-bit virtual address. The processor reads a word from the addressed memory location, and makes the data available to coprocessor unit *z*. The manner in which each coprocessor uses the data is defined by the individual coprocessor specifications.

If either of the two least significant bits of the effective address is non-zero, an address error exception occurs.

In R2000/R3000 implementations, the contents of general register *rt* are undefined for time *T* of the instruction immediately following this load instruction. This instruction is not valid for use with CP0.

R2000/R3000 Operation:

```
T:     vAddr ← ((offset 15)^16 || offset15..0) + GPR[base]
       (pAddr, uncached) ← AddressTranslation (vAddr, DATA)
       byte ← vAddr1..0
       mem ← LoadMemory (uncached, WORD, pAddr, vAddr, DATA)
T+1:   COPzLW (byte, rt, mem)
```

*See the table, ''Opcode Bit Encoding'' on next page, or ''CPU Instruction Opcode Bit Encoding'' at the end of Appendix A.

Load Word to Coprocessor (continued)

LWCz

R4000/R6000 Operation:

T: $vAddr \leftarrow ((offset_{15})^{16} \| offset_{15..0}) + GPR[base]$
       $(pAddr, uncached) \leftarrow AddressTranslation (vAddr, DATA)$
       $byte \leftarrow vAddr_{1..0}$
       $mem \leftarrow LoadMemory (uncached, WORD, pAddr, vAddr, DATA)$
       $COPzLW (byte, rt, mem)$

Exceptions:

TLB refill exception
TLB invalid exception
Bus error exception
Address error exception
Coprocessor unusable exception

Opcode Bit Encoding:

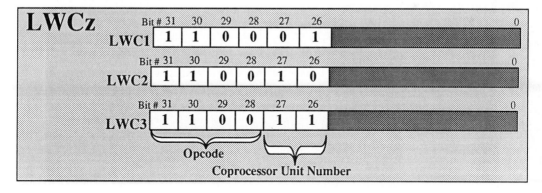

LWL

Load Word Left

31 26	25 21	20 16	15 0
LWL 100010	base	rt	offset
6	5	5	16

Format:

LWL rt,offset(base)

Description:

This instruction can be used in combination with the LWR instruction to load a register with four consecutive bytes from memory, when the bytes cross a boundary between two words. LWL loads the left portion of the register from the appropriate part of the high order word; LWR loads the right portion of the register from the appropriate part of the low order word.

The LWL instruction adds its sign-extended 16-bit *offset* to the contents of general register *base* to form a virtual address which can specify an arbitrary byte. It reads bytes only from the word in memory which contains the specified starting byte. From one to four bytes will be loaded, depending on the starting byte specified.

Conceptually, it starts at the specified byte in memory and loads that byte into the high order (left-most) byte of the register; then it proceeds toward the low order byte of the word in memory and the low order byte of the register, loading bytes from memory into the register until it reaches the low order byte of the word in memory. The least significant (right-most) byte(s) of the register will not be changed.

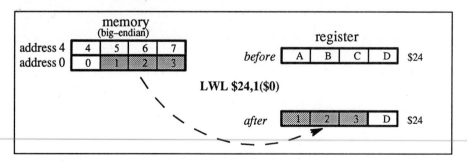

Load Word Left (continued)

LWL

The contents of general register *rt* are internally bypassed within the processor so that no NOP is needed between an immediately preceding load instruction which specifies register *rt* and a following LWL (or LWR) instruction which also specifies register *rt*.

No address exceptions due to alignment are possible.

In R2000/R3000 implementations, the contents of general register *rt* are undefined for time *T* of the instruction immediately following this load instruction.

R2000/R3000 Operation:

```
T:     vAddr ← ((offset15)16 || offset15..0) + GPR[base]
       (pAddr, uncached) ← AddressTranslation (vAddr, DATA)
       byte ← vAddr1..0 xor BigEndianCPU2
       if BigEndianMem = 0 then
              pAddr ← pAddr31..2 || 02
       endif
       mem ← LoadMemory (uncached, byte, pAddr, vAddr, DATA)
T+1:   GPR[rt] ← mem7+8*byte..0 || GPR[rt]23−8*byte..0
```

R4000/R6000 Operation:

```
T:     vAddr ← ((offset15)16 || offset15..0) + GPR[base]
       (pAddr, uncached) ← AddressTranslation (vAddr, DATA)
       pAddr ← pAddrPSIZE−1..2 || (pAddr1..0 xor ReverseEndian2)
       byte ← vAddr1..0 xor BigEndianCPU2
       if BigEndianMem = 0 then
            pAddr ← pAddrPSIZE−1..2 || 02
       endif
       mem ← LoadMemory (uncached, byte, pAddr, vAddr, DATA)
       GPR[rt] ← mem7+8*byte..0 || GPR[rt]23−8*byte..0
```

LWL   Load Word Left
                                                                 (continued)

Given a word in a register and a word in memory, the operation of LWL is as follows:

LWL

Register | E | F | G | H |

Memory | M | N | O | P |

vAddr$_{2..0}$	BigEndianCPU = 0				BigEndianCPU = 1			
			Offset				Offset	
	Destination	Type	LEM	BEM	Destination	Type	LEM	BEM
0	P F G H	0	0	3	M N O P	3	0	0
1	O P G H	1	0	2	N O P H	2	0	1
2	N O P H	2	0	1	O P G H	1	0	2
3	M N O P	3	0	0	P F G H	0	0	3

LEM   BigEndianMem = 0
BEM   BigEndianMem = 1
Type   AccessType sent to memory
Offset   pAddr$_{2..0}$ sent to memory

Exceptions:

TLB refill exception
TLB invalid exception
Bus error exception
Address error exception

Load From Cache (R6000)

LCACHE

LWL 100010	base	rt	offset
6	5	5	16

31   26 25   21 20   16 15   0

Format:

LWL rt,offset(base)

Description:

This operation is only valid on R6000 processor, and is effected by using the LWL opcode with the *MM* bit of the *Status* register set. The 16-bit *offset* is sign-extended and added to the contents of general register *base* to form a 32-bit unsigned effective address.

Offset$_0$ (not the effective address) selects the secondary cache set accessed.

Bits 17..2 of the effective address select the word of the secondary cache for a 512-Kbyte secondary cache.

The contents of the word at the TLB location specified by the offset and effective address are loaded into general register *rt*. This instruction is not interlocked; referencing *rt* in the next two instructions is undefined.

If the virtual tags for this access do *not* match in the secondary cache, the *CM0* or *CM1* bit in the *Status* register is set. Regardless of whether the tags match, the data contained in the addressed location is loaded into general register *rt*.

This instruction must not be placed in a branch delay slot.

R6000 Operation:

```
T:    vAddr ← ((offset15)16 || offset15..0 ) + GPR[base]
      data ← LoadCache (vAddr, offset0)
T+2:  GPR[rt] ← data
```

Exceptions:

None.

LWR

Load Word Right

31 26 25	21 20	16 15	0
LWR 100110	base	rt	offset
6	5	5	16

Format:

LWR rt,offset(base)

Description:

This instruction can be used in combination with the LWL instruction to load a register with four consecutive bytes from memory, when the bytes cross a boundary between two words. LWR loads the right portion of the register from the appropriate part of the low order word; LWL loads the left portion of the register from the appropriate part of the high order word.

The LWR instruction adds its sign-extended 16-bit *offset* to the contents of general register *base* to form a virtual address which can specify an arbitrary byte. It reads bytes only from the word in memory which contains the specified starting byte. From one to four bytes will be loaded, depending on the starting byte specified.

Conceptually, it starts at the specified byte in memory and loads that byte into the low order (right-most) byte of the register; then it proceeds toward the high order byte of the word in memory and the high order byte of the register, loading bytes from memory into the register until it reaches the high order byte of the word in memory. The most significant (left-most) byte(s) of the register will not be changed.

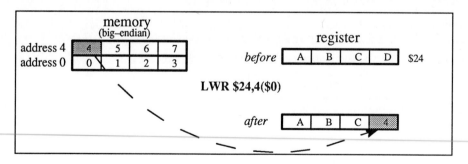

Load Word Right (continued)

LWR

The contents of general register *rt* are internally bypassed within the processor so that no NOP is needed between an immediately preceding load instruction which specifies register *rt* and a following LWR (or LWL) instruction which also specifies register *rt*.

No address exceptions due to alignment are possible.

In R2000/R3000 implementations, the contents of general register *rt* are undefined for time T of the instruction immediately following this load instruction.

R2000/R3000 Operation:

```
T:      vAddr ← ((offset₁₅)¹⁶ || offset₁₅..₀) + GPR[base]
        (pAddr, uncached) ← AddressTranslation (vAddr, DATA)
        byte ← vAddr₁..₀  xor  BigEndianCPU²
        if BigEndianMem = 1 then
                pAddr ← pAddr₃₁..₂ || 0²
        endif
        mem ← LoadMemory (uncached, WORD–byte, pAddr, vAddr, DATA)
T+1:    GPR[rt] ← GPR[rt]₃₁..₃₂₋₈*byte || mem₃₁..₈*byte
```

R4000/R6000 Operation:

```
T:      vAddr ← ((offset₁₅)¹⁶ || offset₁₅..₀) + GPR[base]
        (pAddr, uncached) ← AddressTranslation (vAddr, DATA)
        pAddr ← pAddrPSIZE₋₁..₂ || (pAddr₁..₀  xor  ReverseEndian²)
        byte ← vAddr₁..₀  xor  BigEndianCPU²
        if BigEndianMem = 1 then
        pAddr ← pAddrPSIZE₋₁..₂ || 0²
        endif
        mem ← LoadMemory (uncached, WORD–byte, pAddr, vAddr, DATA)
        GPR[rt] ← GPR[rt]₃₁..₃₂₋₈*byte || mem₃₁..₈*byte
```

LWR **Load Word Right (continued)**

Given a word in a register and a word in memory, the operation of LWR is as follows:

```
LWR
     Register  E | F | G | H
     Memory    M | N | O | P
```

vAddr$_{2.0}$	BigEndianCPU = 0				BigEndianCPU = 1			
	Destination	Type	Offset		Destination	Type	Offset	
			LEM	BEM			LEM	BEM
0	M N O P	3	0	0	E F G M	0	3	0
1	E M N O	2	1	0	E F M N	1	2	0
2	E F M N	1	2	0	E M N O	2	1	0
3	E F G M	0	3	0	M N O P	3	0	0

LEM   BigEndianMem = 0
BEM   BigEndianMem = 1
Type   AccessType sent to memory
Offset   pAddr$_{2.0}$ sent to memory

Exceptions:

TLB refill exception
TLB invalid exception
Bus error exception
Address error exception

Flush Cache (R6000) **FLUSH**

LWR 100110	base	0 00000	offset
6	5	5	16

Bit positions: 31 26 25 21 20 16 15 0

Format:

LWR rt,offset(base)

Description:

This operation is only valid for the R6000, and is effected by using the LWR opcode with the *MM* bit of the *Status* register set.

The 16-bit offset is sign-extended and added to the contents of general register *base* to form a 32-bit unsigned effective address.

On the R6000 processor, bits 17..7 are used to specify the cache line, and $Offset_0$ specifies the cache set in the secondary cache upon which the operation is made.

If the cache line at the specified location is dirty, it is written to memory, and the cache line state is updated to reflect the fact that the line is now clean/consistent.

R6000 Operation:

> T: $vAddr \leftarrow ((offset_{15})^{16} \parallel offset_{15..0}) + GPR[base]$
> $FlushCaches (vAddr, offset_0)$

Exceptions:

None.

MFC0

**Move From
System Control Coprocessor**

31	26 25	21 20	16 15	11 10	0
COP0 010000	MF 00000	rt	rd	0 000 0000 0000	
6	5	5	5	11	

Format:

MFC0 rt,rd

Description:

The contents of coprocessor register *rd* of the CP0 are loaded into general register *rt*.

Operation:

```
T:       data ← CPR[0,rd]
T + 1:   GPR[rt] ← data
```

Exceptions:

Coprocessor unusable exception

Move From Coprocessor   MFCz

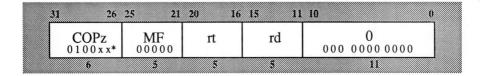

Format:

MFCz rt,rd

Description:

The contents of coprocessor register *rd* of coprocessor *z* are loaded into general register *rt*.

Operation:

T:	data ← CPR[z,rd]
T+1:	GPR[rt] ← data

Exceptions:

Coprocessor unusable exception

***Opcode Bit Encoding:**

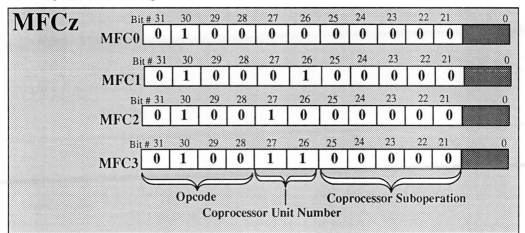

MFHI

Move From HI

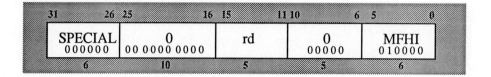

31 26	25 16	15 11	10 6	5 0
SPECIAL 000000	0 00 0000 0000	rd	0 00000	MFHI 010000
6	10	5	5	6

Format:

MFHI rd

Description:

The contents of special register *HI* are loaded into general register *rd*.

To ensure proper operation in the event of interruptions, the two instructions which follow a MFHI instruction may not be any of the instructions which modify the *HI* register: MULT, MULTU, DIV, DIVU, MTHI.

Operation:

> T: GPR[rd] ← HI

Exceptions:

None.

Move From Lo

MFLO

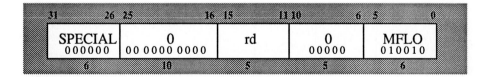

31 26	25 16	15 11	10 6	5 0
SPECIAL 000000	0 00 0000 0000	rd	0 00000	MFLO 010010
6	10	5	5	6

Format:

MFLO rd

Description:

The contents of special register *LO* are loaded into general register *rd*.

To ensure proper operation in the event of interruptions, the two instructions which follow a MFLO instruction may not be any of the instructions which modify the *LO* register: MULT, MULTU, DIV, DIVU, MTLO.

Operation:

> T: GPR[rd] ← LO

Exceptions:

None.

MTC0

**Move To
System Control Coprocessor**

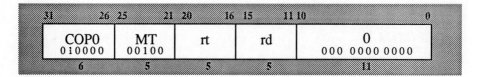

COP0 010000	MT 00100	rt	rd	0 000 0000 0000
6	5	5	5	11

Format:

MTC0 rt,rd

Description:

The contents of general register *rt* are loaded into coprocessor register *rd* of the CP0.

Because the state of the virtual address translation system may be altered by this instruction, the operation of load, store instructions and TLB operations immediately prior to and after this instruction are undefined.

Operation:

```
T:     data ← GPR[rt]
T+1:   CPR[0,rd] ← data
```

Exceptions:

Coprocessor unusable exception

Move To Coprocessor

MTCz

COPz 0100xx*	MT 00100	rt	rd	0 000 0000 0000
6	5	5	5	11

Bit positions: 31 — 26 25 — 21 20 — 16 15 — 11 10 — 0

Format:

MTCz rt,rd

Description:

The contents of general register *rt* are loaded into coprocessor register *rd* of coprocessor *z*.

Operation:

```
T:    data ← GPR[rt]
T+1:  CPR[z,rd] ← data
```

Exceptions:

Coprocessor unusable exception

Opcode Bit Encoding:

MTCz

	Bit # 31	30	29	28	27	26	25	24	23	22	21	0
COP0	0	1	0	0	0	0	0	0	1	0	0	
COP1	0	1	0	0	0	1	0	0	1	0	0	
COP2	0	1	0	0	1	0	0	0	1	0	0	
COP3	0	1	0	0	1	1	0	0	1	0	0	

Opcode
Coprocessor Unit Number
Coprocessor Suboperation

MTHI

Move To HI

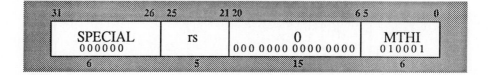

Format:

MTHI   rs

Description:

The contents of general register *rs* are loaded into special register *HI*.

If a MTHI operation is executed following a MULT, MULTU, DIV, or DIVU instruction, but before any MFLO, MFHI, MTLO, or MTHI instructions, the contents of special register *LO* are undefined. This instruction is only valid when *rd* = 0.

Operation:

T−2:	HI ← undefined
T−1:	HI ← undefined
T:	HI ← GPR[rs]

Exceptions:

None.

Move To LO   MTLO

31 26	25 21	20 6	5 0
SPECIAL 000000	rs	0 000 0000 0000 0000	MTLO 010011
6	5	15	6

Format:

MTLO rs

Description:

The contents of general register *rs* are loaded into special register *LO*. This instruction is only valid when *rd* = 0.

If a MTLO operation is executed following a MULT, MULTU, DIV, or DIVU instruction, but before any MFLO, MFHI, MTLO, or MTHI instructions, the contents of special register *HI* are undefined.

Operation:

```
        T-2:  LO ← undefined
        T-1:  LO ← undefined
        T:    LO ← GPR[rs]
```

Exceptions:

None.

MULT

Multiply

31 26	25 21	20 16	15 6	5 0
SPECIAL 000000	rs	rt	0 00 0000 0000	MULT 011000
6	5	5	10	6

CPU Instruction

Format:

MULT rs,rt

Description:

The contents of general registers *rs* and *rt* are multiplied, treating both operands as 32-bit 2's-complement values. No integer overflow exception occurs under any circumstances. This instruction is only valid when $rd = 0$.

When the operation completes, the low order word of the double result is loaded into special register *LO*, and the high order word of the double result is loaded into special register *HI*.

If either of the two preceding instructions is MFHI or MFLO, the results of these instructions are undefined. Correct operation requires separating reads of *HI* or *LO* from writes by a minimum of two other instructions.

Operation:

```
T-2:  LO   ← undefined
      HI   ← undefined
T-1:  LO   ← undefined
      HI   ← undefined
T:    t    ← GPR[rs] * GPR[rt]
      LO   ← t₃₁..₀
      HI   ← t₆₃..₃
```

Exceptions:

None.

Multiply Unsigned   MULTU

31 26	25 21	20 16	15 6	5 0
SPECIAL 000000	rs	rt	0 00 0000 0000	MULTU 011001
6	5	5	10	6

Format:

MULTU rs,rt

Description:

The contents of general register *rs* and the contents of general register *rt* are multiplied, treating both operands as 32-bit unsigned values. No overflow exception occurs under any circumstances. This instruction is only valid when $rd = 0$.

When the operation completes, the low order word of the double result is loaded into special register *LO*, and the high order word of the double result is loaded into special register *HI*.

If either of the two preceding instructions is MFHI or MFLO, the results of these instructions are undefined. Correct operation requires separating reads of *HI* or *LO* from writes by a minimum of two instructions.

Operation:

```
T-2:  LO  ← undefined
      HI  ← undefined
T-1:  LO  ← undefined
      HI  ← undefined
T:    t   ← (0 || GPR[rs]) * (0 || GPR[rt])
      LO  ← t₃₁..₀
      HI  ← t₆₃..₃
```

$$T{-}2\text{:}\quad LO \leftarrow \text{undefined}$$
$$HI \leftarrow \text{undefined}$$
$$T{-}1\text{:}\quad LO \leftarrow \text{undefined}$$
$$HI \leftarrow \text{undefined}$$
$$T\text{:}\quad t \leftarrow (0 \parallel GPR[rs]) * (0 \parallel GPR[rt])$$
$$LO \leftarrow t_{31..0}$$
$$HI \leftarrow t_{63..3}$$

Exceptions:

None.

NOR

Nor

SPECIAL 000000	rs	rt	rd	0 00000	NOR 100111
6	5	5	5	5	6

Format:

NOR rd,rs,rt

Description:

The contents of general register *rs* are combined with the contents of general register *rt* in a bit-wise logical NOR operation. The result is placed into general register *rd*.

Operation:

T: GPR[rd] ← GPR[rs] *nor* GPR[rt]

Exceptions:

None.

Or

OR

SPECIAL 000000	rs	rt	rd	0 00000	OR 100101
6	5	5	5	5	6

Format:

OR rd,rs,rt

Description:

The contents of general register *rs* are combined with the contents of general register *rt* in a bit-wise logical OR operation. The result is placed into general register *rd*.

Operation:

T: GPR[rd] ← GPR[rs] *or* GPR[rt]

Exceptions:

None.

ORI

Or Immediate

31 26	25 21	20 16	15 0
ORI 001101	rs	rt	immediate
6	5	5	16

Format:

ORI rt,rs,immediate

Description:

The 16-bit *immediate* is zero-extended and combined with the contents of general register *rs* in a bit-wise logical OR operation. The result is placed into general register *rt*.

Operation:

T: GPR[rt] ← GPR[rs]$_{31..16}$ || (immediate *or* GPR[rs]$_{15..0}$)

Exceptions:

None.

Restore From Exception

RFE

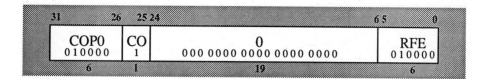

Format:

RFE

Description:

This instruction is not implemented on R4000 processors; use ERET instead.

RFE restores the *previous* interrupt mask and Kernel/User-mode bits (*IEp* and *KUp*) of the *Status* register (SR) into the corresponding *current* status bits (*IEc* and *KUc*), and restores the *old* status bits (*IEo* and *KUo*) into the corresponding *previous* status bits (*IEp* and *KUp*). The old status bits remain unchanged.

The architecture does not specify the operation of memory references associated with load/ store instructions immediately prior to an RFE instruction. Normally, the RFE instruction follows in the delay slot of a JR (jump register) instruction to restore the PC.

R2000/R3000/R6000 Operation:

$$
\begin{aligned}
\text{T:} \quad & \text{SR} \leftarrow \text{SR}_{31..4} \,\|\, \text{SR}_{5..2} \\
& \text{LLbit} \leftarrow 0
\end{aligned}
$$

Exceptions:

Coprocessor unusable exception
Reserved instruction exception (R4000)

SB

Store Byte

31	26	25	21	20	16	15	0
SB 101000		base		rt		offset	
6		5		5		16	

Format:

SB rt,offset(base)

Description:

The 16-bit *offset* is sign-extended and added to the contents of general register *base* to form a virtual address. The least significant byte of register *rt* is stored at the effective address.

Operation:

T: $vAddr \leftarrow ((offset_{15})^{16} \parallel offset_{15..0}) + GPR[base]$
$(pAddr, uncached) \leftarrow AddressTranslation (vAddr, DATA)$
$pAddr \leftarrow pAddr_{PSIZE - 1 .. 2} \parallel (pAddr_{1..0} \; xor \; ReverseEndian^2)$
$byte \leftarrow vAddr_{1..0} \; xor \; BigEndianCPU^2$
$data \leftarrow GPR[rt]_{31-8*byte..0} \parallel 0^{8*byte}$
StoreMemory (uncached, BYTE, data, pAddr, vAddr, DATA)

Exceptions:

TLB refill exception
TLB invalid exception
TLB modification exception
Bus error exception
Address error exception

Store Conditional

SC

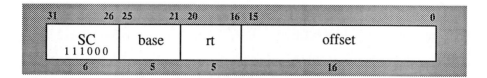

Format:

SC rt,offset(base)

Description:

The 16-bit offset is sign-extended and added to the contents of general register *base* to form a virtual address. The contents of general register *rt* are conditionally stored at the memory location specified by the effective address.

This instruction implicitly performs a SYNC operation; loads and stores to shared memory fetched prior to the SC must access memory before the SC; loads and stores to shared memory fetched subsequent to the SC must access memory after the SC.

If any other processor or device has modified the physical address since the time of the previous Load Linked instruction, or if an RFE or ERET instruction occurs between the Load Linked instruction and this store instruction, the store fails and is inhibited from taking place.

The success or failure of the store operation (as defined above) is indicated by the contents of general register *rt* after execution of the instruction. A successful store sets the contents of general register *rt* to 1; an unsuccessful store sets it to 0.

The operation of Store Conditional is undefined when the address is different from the address used in the last Load Linked.

This instruction is available in User mode; it is not necessary for CP0 to be enabled.

If either of the two least significant bits of the effective address is non-zero, an address error exception takes place.

SC

Store Conditional
(continued)

If this instruction should both fail and take an exception, the exception takes precedence.

This instruction is not valid in R2000/R3000 implementations.

R4000/R6000 Operation:

```
T:    vAddr ← ((offset15)16 || offset15..0) + GPR[base]
      (pAddr, uncached) ← AddressTranslation (vAddr, DATA)
      data ← GPR[rt]
      if LLbit then
            StoreMemory (uncached, WORD, data, pAddr, vAddr, DATA)
      endif
      GPR[rt] ← 0³¹ || LLbit
      SyncOperation()
```

Exceptions:

TLB refill exception
TLB invalid exception
TLB modification exception
Bus error exception
Address error exception

Store Doubleword From Coprocessor

SDCz

SDCz 1 1 1 1 x x*	base	rt	offset
6	5	5	16

(31—26, 25—21, 20—16, 15—0)

Format:

SDCz rt,offset(base)

Description:

The 16-bit *offset* is sign-extended and added to the contents of general register *base* to form a virtual address. Coprocessor unit *z* sources a doubleword, which the processor writes to the addressed memory location. The data to be stored is defined by individual coprocessor specifications.

If any of the three least significant bits of the effective address are non-zero, an address error exception takes place.

This instruction is not valid on R2000/R3000 processors and causes a reserved instruction exception. This instruction is not valid for use with CP0.

In R4000 and R6000 implementations this instruction is undefined when the least significant bit of register *rt* is non-zero.

*See the table, ''Opcode Bit Encoding'' on next page, or ''CPU Instruction Opcode Bit Encoding'' at the end of Appendix A.

SDCz   **Store Doubleword From Coprocessor**

                                                                          (continued)

R4000/R6000 Operation:

T: $vAddr \leftarrow ((offset_{15})^{16} \parallel offset_{15..0}) + GPR[base]$
          $(pAddr, uncached) \leftarrow AddressTranslation (vAddr, DATA)$
          $data \leftarrow COPzSD(rt),$
          $StoreMemory (uncached, DOUBLEWORD, data, pAddr, vAddr, DATA)$

Exceptions:

TLB refill exception   TLB invalid exception
TLB modification exception   Bus error exception
Address error exception   Coprocessor unusable exception
Reserved instruction exception (R2000/R3000 only)

Opcode Bit Encoding:

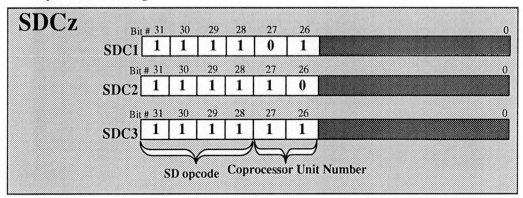

Store Halfword

SH

SH 101001	base	rt	offset
6	5	5	16

31 26 25 21 20 16 15 0

Format:

SH rt,offset(base)

Description:

The 16-bit *offset* is sign-extended and added to the contents of general register *base* to form a 32-bit unsigned effective address. The least significant halfword of register *rt* is stored at the effective address. If the least significant bit of the effective address is non-zero, an address error exception occurs.

Operation:

T: $vAddr \leftarrow ((offset_{15})^{16} \parallel offset_{15..0}) + GPR[base]$
     $(pAddr, uncached) \leftarrow AddressTranslation (vAddr, DATA)$
     $pAddr \leftarrow pAddr_{PSIZE-1..2} \parallel (pAddr_{1..0} \; xor \; (ReverseEndian^2 \parallel 0))$
     $byte \leftarrow vAddr_{1..0} \; xor \; (BigEndianCPU \parallel 0)$
     $data \leftarrow GPR[rt]_{31-8*byte..0} \parallel 0^{8*byte}$
     StoreMemory (uncached, HALFWORD, data, pAddr, vAddr, DATA)

Exceptions:

TLB refill exception
TLB invalid exception
TLB modification exception
Bus error exception
Address error exception

SLL

Shift Left Logical

31 26	25 21	20 16	15 11	10 6	5 0
SPECIAL 000000	rs	rt	rd	sa	SLL 000000
6	5	5	5	5	6

Format:

SLL rd,rt,sa

Description:

The contents of general register *rt* are shifted left by *sa* bits, inserting zeros into the low order bits. The 32-bit result is placed in register *rd*.

Operation:

$$T: \quad GPR[rd] \leftarrow GPR[rt]_{31-sa..0} \, || \, 0^{sa}$$

Exceptions:

None.

Shift Left Logical Variable   **SLLV**

31 26	25 21	20 16	15 11	10 6	5 0
SPECIAL 000000	rs	rt	rd	0 00000	SLLV 000100
6	5	5	5	5	6

Format:

SLLV rd,rt,rs

Description:

The contents of general register *rt* are shifted left by the number of bits specified by the low order five bits contained as contents of general register *rs*, inserting zeros into the low order bits. The result is placed in register *rd*.

Operation:

$$
\begin{aligned}
\text{T:} \quad & s \leftarrow GP[rs]_{4..0} \\
& GPR[rd] \leftarrow GPR[rt]_{(31-s)..0} \parallel 0^s
\end{aligned}
$$

Exceptions:

None.

SLT

Set On Less Than

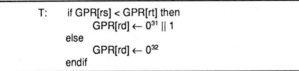

31 26	25 21	20 16	15 11	10 6	5 0
SPECIAL 000000	rs	rt	rd	0 00000	SLT 101010
6	5	5	5	5	6

Format:

SLT rd,rs,rt

Description:

The contents of general register *rt* are subtracted from the contents of general register *rs*. Considering both quantities as signed 32-bit integers, if the contents of general register *rs* are less than the contents of general register *rt*, the result is set to one, otherwise the result is set to zero. The result is placed into general register *rd*.

No integer overflow exception occurs under any circumstances. The comparison is valid even if the subtraction used during the comparison overflows.

Operation:

```
T:     if GPR[rs] < GPR[rt] then
              GPR[rd] ← 0³¹ || 1
       else
              GPR[rd] ← 0³²
       endif
```

Exceptions:

None.

Set On Less Than Immediate $\qquad$ SLTI

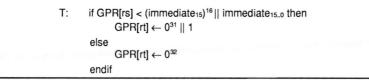

31 26	25 21	20 16	15 0
SLTI 001010	rs	rt	immediate
6	5	5	16

Format:

SLTI rt,rs,immediate

Description:

The 16-bit *immediate* is sign-extended and subtracted from the contents of general register *rs*. Considering both quantities as signed integers, if *rs* is less than the sign-extended immediate, the result is set to one, otherwise the result is set to zero. The result is placed into general register *rt*.

No integer overflow exception occurs under any circumstances. The comparison is valid even if the subtraction used during the comparison overflows.

Operation:

```
T:    if GPR[rs] < (immediate₁₅)¹⁶ || immediate₁₅..₀ then
          GPR[rt] ← 0³¹ || 1
      else
          GPR[rt] ← 0³²
      endif
```

Exceptions:

None.

SLTIU

Set On Less Than
Immediate Unsigned

31 26	25 21	20 16	15 0
SLTIU 001011	rs	rt	immediate
6	5	5	16

Format:

SLTIU rt,rs,immediate

Description:

The 16-bit *immediate* is sign-extended and subtracted from the contents of general register *rs*. Considering both quantities as unsigned integers, if *rs* is less than the sign-extended immediate, the result is set to one, otherwise the result is set to zero. The result is placed into general register *rt*.

No integer overflow exception occurs under any circumstances. The comparison is valid even if the subtraction used during the comparison overflows.

Operation:

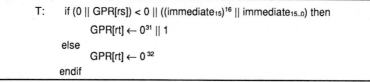

T: if (0 || GPR[rs]) < 0 || ((immediate$_{15}$)^{16} || immediate$_{15..0}$) then
        GPR[rt] ← 0^{31} || 1
    else
        GPR[rt] ← 0^{32}
    endif

Exceptions:

None.

Set On Less Than Unsigned

SLTU

31 26	25 21	20 16	15 11	10 6	5 0
SPECIAL 000000	rs	rt	rd	0 00000	SLTU 101011
6	5	5	5	5	6

Format:

SLTU rd,rs,rt

Description:

The contents of general register *rt* are subtracted from the contents of general register *rs*. Considering both quantities as unsigned integers, if the contents of general register *rs* are less than the contents of general register *rt*, the result is set to one, otherwise the result is set to zero. The result is placed into general register *rd*.

No integer overflow exception occurs under any circumstances. The comparison is valid even if the subtraction used during the comparison overflows.

Operation:

```
T:    if (0 || GPR[rs]) < (0 || GPR[rt]) then
          GPR[rd] ← 0³¹ || 1
      else
          GPR[rd] ← 0³²
      endif
```

Exceptions:

None.

SRA

Shift Right Arithmetic

SPECIAL 000000	0 00000	rt	rd	sa	SRA 000011
6	5	5	5	5	6

Format:

SRA rd,rt,sa

Description:

The contents of general register *rt* are shifted right by *sa* bits, sign-extending the high order bits. The 32-bit result is placed in register *rd*.

Operation:

T: $\quad$ GPR[rd] ← (GPR[rt]$_{31}$)^{sa} || GPR[rt] $_{31..sa}$

Exceptions:

None.

Shift Right Arithmetic Variable **SRAV**

31 26	25 21	20 16	15 11	10 6	5 0
SPECIAL 000000	rs	rt	rd	0 00000	SRAV 000111
6	5	5	5	5	6

Format:

SRAV rd,rt,rs

Description:

The contents of general register *rt* are shifted right by the number of bits specified by the low order five bits of general register *rs*, sign-extending the high order bits. The result is placed in register *rd*.

Operation:

T: $s \leftarrow GPR[rs]_{4..0}$
$GPR[rd] \leftarrow (GPR[rt]_{31})^s \parallel GPR[rt]_{31..s}$

Exceptions:

None.

SRL

Shift Right Logical

31　　　26	25　　　21	20　　　16	15　　　11	10　　　6	5　　　0
SPECIAL 000000	rs	rt	rd	sa	SRL 000010
6	5	5	5	5	6

Format:

SRL rd,rt,sa

Description:

The contents of general register *rt* are shifted right by *sa* bits, inserting zeros into the high order bits. The result is placed in register *rd*.

Operation:

T:　　GPR[rd] ← 0^{sa} || GPR[rt]$_{31 \ldots sa}$

Exceptions:

None.

Shift Right Logical Variable

SRLV

31 26	25 21	20 16	15 11	10 6	5 0
SPECIAL 000000	rs	rt	rd	0 00000	SRLV 000110
6	5	5	5	5	6

Format:

SRLV rd,rt,rs

Description:

The contents of general register *rt* are shifted right by the number of bits specified by the low order five bits of general register *rs,* inserting zeros into the high order bits. The 32-bit result is placed in register *rd.*

Operation:

$$
\begin{aligned}
\text{T:} \quad & s \leftarrow GP[rs]_{4..0} \\
& GPR[rd] \leftarrow 0^{s} \ || \ GPR[rt]_{31..s}
\end{aligned}
$$

Exceptions:

None.

SUB

Subtract

31	26	25	21	20	16	15	11	10	6	5	0
SPECIAL 000000		rs		rt		rd		0 00000		SUB 100010	
6		5		5		5		5		6	

Format:

SUB rd,rs,rt

Description:

The contents of general register *rt* are subtracted from the contents of general register *rs* to form a result. The result is placed into general register *rd*.

The only difference between this instruction and the SUBU instruction is that SUBU never traps on overflow.

An integer overflow exception takes place if the carries out of bits 30 and 31 differ (2's-complement overflow). The destination register *rd* is not modified when an integer overflow exception occurs.

Operation:

T: GPR[rd] ← GPR[rs] – GPR[rt]

Exceptions:

Integer overflow exception

Subtract Unsigned   **SUBU**

31 26	25 21	20 16	15 11	10 6	5 0
SPECIAL 000000	rs	rt	rd	0 00000	SUBU 100011
6	5	5	5	5	6

Format:

SUBU rd,rs,rt

Description:

The contents of general register *rt* are subtracted from the contents of general register *rs* to form a result. The result is placed into general register *rd*.

The only difference between this instruction and the SUB instruction is that SUBU never traps on overflow. No integer overflow exception occurs under any circumstances.

Operation:

> T: GPR[rd] ← GPR[rs] – GPR[rt]

Exceptions:

None.

SW

Store Word

SW 101011	base	rt	offset
6	5	5	16

31   26 25   21 20   16 15   0

Format:

SW rt,offset(base)

Description:

The 16-bit *offset* is sign-extended and added to the contents of general register *base* to form a virtual address. The contents of general register *rt* are stored at the memory location specified by the effective address.

If either of the two least significant bits of the effective address are non-zero, an address error exception occurs.

Operation:

T: $vAddr \leftarrow ((offset_{15})^{16} \parallel offset_{15..0}) + GPR[base]$
      $(pAddr, uncached) \leftarrow AddressTranslation (vAddr, DATA)$
      $data \leftarrow GPR[rt]$
      $StoreMemory (uncached, WORD, data, pAddr, vAddr, DATA)$

Exceptions:

TLB refill exception
TLB invalid exception
TLB modification exception
Bus error exception
Address error exception

Store Word From Coprocessor **SWCz**

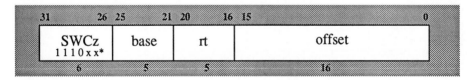

SWCz 1 1 1 0 x x*	base	rt	offset
6	5	5	16

Format:

SWCz rt,offset(base)

Description:

The 16-bit *offset* is sign-extended and added to the contents of general register *base* to form a virtual address. Coprocessor unit *z* sources a word, which the processor writes to the addressed memory location. The data to be stored is defined by individual coprocessor specifications. This instruction is not valid for use with CP0. If either of the two least significant bits of the effective address is non-zero, an address error exception occurs.

Operation:

T:	vAddr ← ((offset$_{15}$)^{16} ‖ offset$_{15..0}$) + GPR[base]
	(pAddr, uncached) ← AddressTranslation (vAddr, DATA)
	byte ← vAddr$_{1..0}$
	data ← COPzSW (byte, rt)
	StoreMemory (uncached, WORD, data, pAddr, vAddr, DATA)

Exceptions:

TLB refill exception	TLB invalid exception	TLB modification exception
Bus error exception	Address error exception	Coprocessor unusable exception

Opcode Bit Encoding:

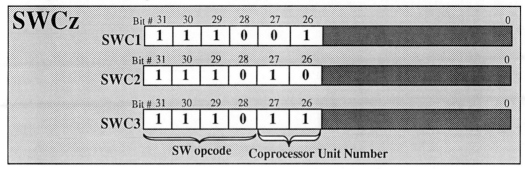

SWL

Store Word Left

31 26	25 21	20 16	15 0
SWL 1 0 1 0 1 0	base	rt	offset
6	5	5	16

Format:

SWL rt,offset(base)

Description:

This instruction can be used with the SWR instruction to store the contents of a register into four consecutive bytes of memory, when the bytes cross a boundary between two words. SWL stores the left portion of the register into the appropriate part of the high order word of memory; SWR stores the right portion of the register into the appropriate part of the low order word.

The SWL instruction adds its sign-extended 16-bit *offset* to the contents of general register *base* to form a virtual address which may specify an arbitrary byte. It alters only the word in memory which contains that byte. From one to four bytes will be stored, depending on the starting byte specified.

Conceptually, it starts at the most significant byte of the register and copies it to the specified byte in memory; then it proceeds toward the low order byte of the register and the low order byte of the word in memory, copying bytes from register to memory until it reaches the low order byte of the word in memory.

No address exceptions due to alignment are possible.

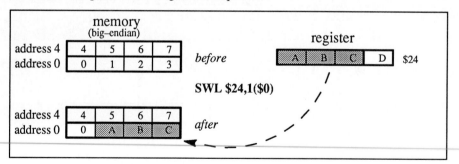

Store Word Left (continued)

SWL

Operation:

T: vAddr ← ((offset$_{15}$)^{16} || offset $_{15..0}$) + GPR[base]
(pAddr, uncached) ← AddressTranslation (vAddr, DATA)
pAddr ← pAddr$_{PSIZE-1..2}$ || (pAddr$_{1..0}$ *xor* ReverseEndian^2)
byte ← vAddr$_{1..0}$ *xor* BigEndianCPU^2
If BigEndianMem = 0 then
        pAddr ← pAddr$_{PSIZE-1..2}$ || 0^2
endif
data ← 0$^{24-8*byte}$ || GPR[rt]$_{31..24-8*byte}$
StoreMemory (uncached, byte, data, pAddr, vAddr, DATA)

Given a word in a register and a word in memory, the operation of SWL is as follows:

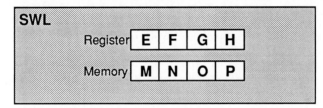

vAddr$_{2..0}$	BigEndianCPU = 0				BigEndianCPU = 1			
			Offset				Offset	
	Destination	Type	LEM	BEM	Destination	Type	LEM	BEM
0	M N O E	0	0	3	E F G H	3	0	0
1	M N E F	1	0	2	M E F G	2	0	1
2	M E F G	2	0	1	M N E F	1	0	2
3	E F G H	3	0	0	M N O E	0	0	3

LEM   BigEndianMem = 0
BEM   BigEndianMem = 1
Type   AccessType sent to memory
Offset   pAddr$_{2..0}$ sent to memory

Exceptions:

TLB refill exception   TLB invalid exception   TLB modification exception
Bus error exception   Address error exception

SCACHE

Store To Cache (R6000)

SWL 101010	base	rt	offset
6	5	5	16

Bits: 31 ... 26 25 ... 21 20 ... 16 15 ... 0

Format:

SWL rt,offset(base)

Description:

This operation is only valid on an R6000, and is effected by using the SWL opcode with the *MM* bit of the *Status* register set.

The 16-bit offset is sign-extended and added to the contents of general register *base* to form a 32-bit unsigned effective address.

Offset$_0$ (not the effective address) selects the secondary cache set accessed. *Offset$_1$* is the value to store in the *G* bit of the virtual tag.

For a 512-Kbyte secondary cache, bits 17..2 of the effective address select the word of the secondary cache. The physical tags begin at 0x3e000 and the TLB entries begin at 0x3c000.

The contents of general register *rt* are stored at the *offset* and set is specified by the effective address and *Offset$_0$*.

The corresponding virtual tag in the secondary cache is set with bits 31..14 of the virtual address, with the *G* bit set to *Offset$_1$*, and the line is marked writable, valid, and not dirty.

This instruction must *not* be placed in a branch delay slot.

R6000 Operation:

```
T:    vAddr ← ((offset15)16 || offset15..0) + GPR[base]
      data ← GPR[rt]
      StoreCache (data, vAddr, offset0, offset1)
```

Exceptions:

None.

Store Word Right   **SWR**

31 26	25 21	20 16	15 0
SWR 101110	base	rt	offset
6	5	5	16

Format:

SWR rt,offset(base)

Description:

This instruction can be used with the SWL instruction to store the contents of a register into four consecutive bytes of memory, when the bytes cross a boundary between two words. SWR stores the right portion of the register into the appropriate part of the low order word; SWL stores the left portion of the register into the appropriate part of the low order word of memory.

The SWR instruction adds its sign-extended 16-bit *offset* to the contents of general register *base* to form a virtual address which may specify an arbitrary byte. It alters only the word in memory which contains that byte. From one to four bytes will be stored, depending on the starting byte specified.

Conceptually, it starts at the least significant (rightmost) byte of the register and copies it to the specified byte in memory; then it proceeds toward the high order byte of the register and the high order byte of the word in memory, copying bytes from register to memory until it reaches the high order byte of the word in memory.

No address exceptions due to alignment are possible.

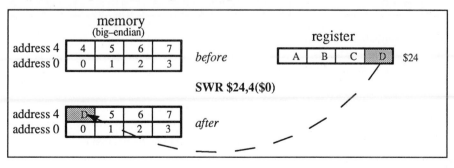

SWR — Store Word Right (continued)

SWR   **Store Word Right (continued)**

Operation:

T: $vAddr \leftarrow ((offset_{15})^{16} \parallel offset_{15..0}) + GPR[base]$
$(pAddr, uncached) \leftarrow AddressTranslation (vAddr, DATA)$
$pAddr \leftarrow pAddr_{PSIZE-1..2} \parallel (pAddr_{1..0} \; xor \; ReverseEndian^2)$
$byte \leftarrow vAddr_{1..0} \; xor \; BigEndianCPU^2$
If BigEndianMem = 1 then
$\quad pAddr \leftarrow pAddr_{PSIZE-1..2} \parallel 0^2$
endif
$data \leftarrow GPR[rt]_{31..8*byte..0} \parallel 0^{8*byte}$
StoreMemory (uncached, WORD–byte, data, pAddr, vAddr, DATA)

Given a word in a register and a word in memory, the operation of SWR is as follows:

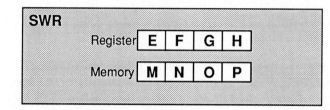

vAddr$_{2..0}$	BigEndianCPU = 0				BigEndianCPU = 1			
			Offset				Offset	
	Destination	Type	LEM	BEM	Destination	Type	LEM	BEM
0	E F G H	3	0	0	H N O P	0	3	0
1	F G H P	2	1	0	G H O P	1	2	0
2	G H O P	1	2	0	F G H P	2	1	0
3	H N O P	0	3	0	E F G H	3	0	0

LEM   BigEndianMem = 0
BEM   BigEndianMem = 1
Type   AccessType sent to memory
Offset   pAddr$_{2..0}$ sent to memory

Exceptions:

TLB refill exception   TLB invalid exception   TLB modification exception
Bus error exception   Address error exception

Invalidate Cache (R6000)   # INVALIDATE

SWR 101110	base	0 00000	offset
6	5	5	16

31   26 25   21 20   16 15   0

Format:

SWR rt,offset(base)

Description:

This operation is only valid for the R6000 processor, and is effected by using the SWR opcode with the *MM* bit of the *Status* register set.

The 16-bit *offset* is sign-extended and added to the contents of general register *base* to form a 32-bit unsigned effective address. On an R6000 processor, bits 17..7 of the effective address specify the cache line to invalidate, and the *Offset*$_0$ bit specifies the set. The addressed virtual cache tag in the secondary cache is marked invalid.

At the same time, the effective address specifies cache line in the primary data cache (vAddr$_{13..3}$) or instruction cache (vAddr$_{15..5}$), and the *Offset*$_0$ bit specifies to which of the two caches (0 → instruction cache; 1 → data cache) the operation occurs. The addressed virtual cache tag in the primary cache is invalidated.

R6000 Operation:

T: vAddr ← ((offset$_{15}$)^{16} || offset$_{15..0}$) + GPR[base]   InvalidateCaches (vAddr, offset$_0$)

Exceptions:

None.

SYNC

Synchronize

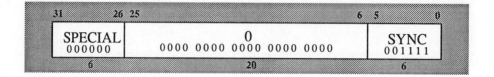

SPECIAL 000000	0 0000 0000 0000 0000 0000	SYNC 001111
6	20	6

Format:

SYNC

Description:

The SYNC instruction ensures that any loads and stores fetched *prior to* the present instruction are completed before any loads or stores *after* this instruction are allowed to start. Use of the SYNC instruction to serialize certain memory references may be required in multiprocessor environment for proper synchronization.

For example:

Processor A	Processor B

SW   R1, DATA
LI   R2, 1
SYNC
SW   R2, FLAG
	1: LW R2, FLAG
	BEQ R2, R0, 1B
	NOP
	SYNC
	LW R1, DATA

The SYNC in processor A prevents DATA being written after FLAG, which could cause processor B to read stale data. The SYNC in processor B prevents DATA from being read before FLAG, which could likewise result in reading stale data. For processors which only execute loads and stores in order, with respect to shared memory, this instruction is a NOP.

This instruction is not valid on R2000 or R3000 processors, and causes a reserved instruction exception.

LL and SC instructions implicitly perform a SYNC.

This instruction is allowed in User mode.

Synchronize
(continued)

SYNC

R4000/R6000 Operation:

T: SyncOperation()

Exceptions:

Reserved instruction exception (R2000/R3000 only)

SYSCALL System Call

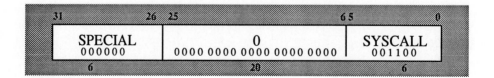

31 26	25 6	5 0
SPECIAL 000000	0 0000 0000 0000 0000 0000	SYSCALL 001100
6	20	6

Format:

SYSCALL

Description:

A system call exception occurs, immediately and unconditionally transferring control to the exception handler.

The code field is available for use as software parameters, but is retrieved by the exception handler only by loading the contents of the memory word containing the instruction.

Operation:

```
        T:    SystemCallException
```

Exceptions:

System Call exception

Trap If Equal

TEQ

31 26	25 21	20 16	15 6	5 0
SPECIAL 000000	rs	rt	code	TEQ 110100
6	5	5	10	6

Format:

TEQ rs,rt

Description:

This instruction causes a reserved instruction exception on R2000/R3000 processors.

The contents of general register *rt* are compared to general register *rs*. If the contents of general register *rs* are equal to the contents of general register *rt*, a trap exception occurs.

The code field is available for use as software parameters, but is retrieved by the exception handler only by loading the contents of the memory word containing the instruction.

R4000/R6000 Operation:

```
T:    if GPR[rs] = GPR[rt] then
            TrapException
      endif
```

Exceptions:

Trap exception
Reserved Instruction exception (R2000/R3000 only)

TEQI

Trap If Equal Immediate

REGIMM 000001	rs	TEQI 01100	immediate
31 26	25 21	20 16	15 0
6	5	5	16

Format:

TEQI rs,immediate

Description:

This instruction is not valid on R2000/R3000 processors, but does not cause a reserved instruction exception.

The 16-bit *immediate* is sign-extended and compared to the contents of general register *rs*. If the contents of general register *rs* are equal to the sign-extended *immediate*, a trap exception occurs.

R4000/R6000 Operation:

T: if GPR[rs] = $(immediate_{15})^{16}$ || $immediate_{15..0}$ then
           TrapException
      endif

Exceptions:

Trap exception

Trap If Greater Than Or Equal $\qquad$ **TGE**

SPECIAL 000000	rs	rt	code	TGE 110000
31 26	25 21	20 16	15 6	5 0
6	5	5	10	6

Format:

TGE rs,rt

Description:

This instruction causes a reserved instruction exception on R2000/R3000 processors.

The contents of general register *rt* are compared to the contents of general register *rs*. Considering both quantities as signed integers, if the contents of general register *rs* are greater than or equal to the contents of general register *rt*, a trap exception occurs.

The code field is available for use as software parameters, but is retrieved by the exception handler only by loading the contents of the memory word containing the instruction.

R4000/R6000 Operation:

```
T:    if GPR[rs] ≥ GPR[rt] then
            TrapException
      endif
```

Exceptions:

Trap exception
Reserved Instruction exception (R2000/R3000 only)

TGEI

Trap If Greater Than Or Equal Immediate

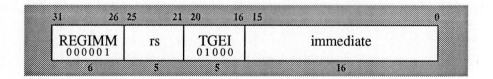

31 26	25 21	20 16	15 0
REGIMM 000001	rs	TGEI 01000	immediate
6	5	5	16

Format:

TGEI rs, immediate

Description:

This instruction is not valid on R2000/R3000 processors, but does not cause a reserved instruction exception.

The 16-bit *immediate* is sign-extended and compared to the contents of general register *rs*. Considering both quantities as signed integers, if the contents of general register *rs* are greater than or equal to the sign-extended *immediate*, a trap exception occurs.

R4000/R6000 Operation:

```
T:   if GPR[rs] ≥ (immediate₁₅)¹⁶ || immediate₁₅..₀ then
         TrapException
     endif
```

$$T: \quad \text{if } GPR[rs] \geq (immediate_{15})^{16} \,||\, immediate_{15..0} \text{ then}$$
$$\text{TrapException}$$
$$\text{endif}$$

Exceptions:

Trap exception

Trap If Greater Than Or Equal Immediate Unsigned

TGEIU

31   26 25   21 20   16 15   0
REGIMM	rs	TGEIU	immediate
000001		01001	
6	5	5	16

Format:

TGEIU rs,immediate

Description:

This instruction is not valid on R2000/R3000 processors, but does not cause a reserved instruction exception.

The 16-bit *immediate* is sign-extended and compared to the contents of general register *rs*. Considering both quantities as unsigned integers, if the contents of general register *rs* are greater than or equal to the sign-extended *immediate*, a trap exception occurs.

R4000/R6000 Operation:

T: if (0 || GPR[rs]) $\geq$ (0 || (immediate$_{15}$)^{16} || immediate$_{15..0}$) then
          TrapException
      endif

Exceptions:

Trap exception

TGEU

Trap If Greater Than Or Equal Unsigned

31 26	25 21	20 16	15 6	5 0
SPECIAL 000000	rs	rt	code	TGEU 110001
6	5	5	10	6

Format:

TGEU rs,rt

Description:

This instruction causes a reserved instruction exception on R2000/R3000 processors.

The contents of general register *rt* are compared to the contents of general register *rs*. Considering both quantities as unsigned integers, if the contents of general register *rs* are greater than or equal to the contents of general register *rt*, a trap exception occurs.

The code field is available for use as software parameters, but is retrieved by the exception handler only by loading the contents of the memory word containing the instruction.

R4000/R6000 Operation:

```
T:     if (0 || GPR[rs]) ≥ (0 || GPR[rt]) then
              TrapException
       endif
```

Exceptions:

Trap exception
Reserved Instruction exception (R2000/R3000 only)

Probe TLB For Matching Entry

TLBP

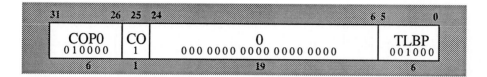

31	26	25	24		6	5	0
COP0 010000		CO 1		0 000 0000 0000 0000 0000		TLBP 001000	
6		1		19		6	

Format:

TLBP

Description:

This instruction is only valid for processors with an on-chip associative TLB (R2000/R3000/R4000), and is not valid on R6000 processors. The *Index* register is loaded with the address of the TLB entry whose contents match the contents of the *EntryHi* register. If no TLB entry matches, the high order bit of the *Index* register is set.

The architecture does not specify the operation of memory references associated with the instruction immediately after a TLBP instruction, nor is the operation specified if more than one TLB entry matches.

R2000/R3000 Operation:

```
T:    Index ← 1 || 0³¹
      for i in 0..TLBEntries–1
        if (TLB[i]₆₃..₄₄ = EntryHi₃₁..₁₂) and (TLB[i]₈ or (TLB[i]₄₃..₃₈ = EntryHi₁₁..₆ )) then
          Index ← 0¹⁸ || i ₅..₀ || 0⁸
        endif
      endfor
```

R4000 Operation:

```
T:    Index ← 1 || 0³¹
      for i in 0..TLBEntries–1
        if (TLB[i]₉₅..₇₇ = EntryHi₃₁..₁₂) and (TLB[i]₇₆ or (TLB[i]₇₁..₆₄ = EntryHi₇..₀ )) then
          Index ← 0²⁶ || i ₅..₀
        endif
      endfor
```

Exceptions:

Coprocessor unusable exception

TLBR

Read Indexed TLB Entry

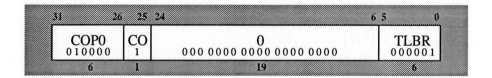

COP0 010000	CO 1	0 000 0000 0000 0000 0000	TLBR 000001
6	1	19	6

Format:

TLBR

Description:

This instruction is only valid for a processor with an on-chip associative TLB (R2000/R3000/R4000), and is not valid on R6000 processor. The *G* bit (controls ASID matching) read from the TLB is written into both *EntryLo0* and *EntryLo1*.

The *EntryHi* and *EntryLo* registers are loaded with the contents of the TLB entry pointed at by the contents of the TLB *Index* register. The operation is invalid (and the results are unspecified) if the contents of the TLB *Index* register are greater than the number of TLB entries in the processor.

R2000/R3000 Operation:

T:	EntryHi ← TLB[$Index_{13..8}$]$_{63..32}$
	EntryLo ← TLB[$Index_{13..8}$]$_{31..0}$

R4000 Operation:

T:	PageMask ← TLB[$Index_{5..0}$]$_{28..96}$
	EntryHi ← TLB[$Index_{5..0}$]$_{95..64}$ *and not* TLB[$Index_{5..0}$]$_{128..96}$
	EntryLo1 ← TLB[$Index_{5..0}$]$_{63..32}$
	EntryLo0 ← TLB[$Index_{5..0}$]$_{31..0}$

Exceptions:

Coprocessor unusable exception

Write Indexed TLB Entry TLBWI

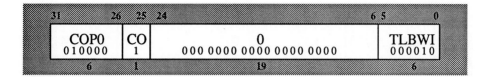

COP0 010000	CO 1	0 000 0000 0000 0000 0000	TLBWI 000010
6	1	19	6

Format:

TLBWI

Description:

This instruction is only valid for a processor with an on-chip associative TLB (R2000/R3000/R4000), and is not valid on R6000 processor.

On R4000 processors, the *G* bit of the TLB is written with the logical AND of the *G* bits in *EntryLo0* and *EntryLo1*.

The TLB entry pointed at by the contents of the TLB *Index* register is loaded with the contents of the *EntryHi* and *EntryLo* registers.

The operation is invalid (and the results are unspecified) if the contents of the TLB *Index* register are greater than the number of TLB entries in the processor.

R2000/R3000 Operation:

T:	TLB[Index$_{13..8}$] ← EntryHi || EntryLo

R4000 Operation:

T:	TLB[Index$_{5..0}$] ← PageMask || (EntryHi *and not* PageMask) || EntryLo1 || EntryLo0

Exceptions:

Coprocessor unusable exception

TLBWR

Write Random TLB Entry

31 26	25 24	6 5 0
COP0 010000	CO 1	0 000 0000 0000 0000 0000	TLBWR 000110
6	1	19	6

Format:

TLBWR

Description:

This instruction is only valid for a processor with an on-chip associative TLB (R2000/R3000/R4000), and is not valid on R6000 processor.

On R4000 processors, the *G* bit of the TLB is written with the logical AND of the *G* bits in *EntryLo0* and *EntryLo1*.

The TLB entry pointed at by the contents of the TLB *Random* register is loaded with the contents of the *EntryHi* and *EntryLo* registers.

R2000/R3000 Operation:

```
T:    TLB[Random₁₃..₈] ← EntryHi || EntryLo
```

R4000 Operation:

```
T:    TLB[Random₅..₀] ← PageMask || (EntryHi and not PageMask) || EntryLo1 || EntryLo0
```

Exceptions:

Coprocessor unusable exception

Trap If Less Than   TLT

31 26	25 21	20 16	15 6	5 0
SPECIAL 000000	rs	rt	code	TLT 110010
6	5	5	10	6

Format:

TLT rs,rt

Description:

This instruction causes a reserved instruction exception on R2000/R3000 processors.

The contents of general register *rt* are compared to general register *rs*. Considering both quantities as signed integers, if the contents of general register *rs* are less than the contents of general register *rt*, a trap exception occurs.

The code field is available for use as software parameters, but is retrieved by the exception handler only by loading the contents of the memory word containing the instruction.

R4000/R6000 Operation:

```
T:    if GPR[rs] < GPR[rt] then
            TrapException
      endif
```

Exceptions:

Trap exception
Reserved Instruction exception (R2000/R3000 only)

TLTI

Trap If Less Than Immediate

31   26 25   21 20   16 15   0
REGIMM	rs	TLTI	immediate
000001		01010	
6	5	5	16

Format:

TLTI rs, immediate

Description:

This instruction is not valid on R2000/R3000 processors, but does not cause a reserved instruction exception.

The 16-bit *immediate* is sign-extended and compared to the contents of general register *rs*. Considering both quantities as signed integers, if the contents of general register *rs* are less than the sign-extended *immediate*, a trap exception occurs.

R4000/R6000 Operation:

```
T:    if GPR[rs] < (immediate₁₅)¹⁶ || immediate₁₅..₀ then
          TrapException
      endif
```

$$\text{T:} \quad \text{if GPR[rs]} < (\text{immediate}_{15})^{16} \,||\, \text{immediate}_{15..0} \text{ then}$$
$$\text{TrapException}$$
$$\text{endif}$$

Exceptions:

Trap exception

Trap If Less Than Immediate Unsigned   **TLTIU**

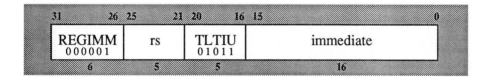

31 26	25 21	20 16	15 0
REGIMM 000001	rs	TLTIU 01011	immediate
6	5	5	16

Format:

TLTIU rs,immediate

Description:

This instruction is not valid on R2000/R3000 processors, but does not cause a reserved instruction exception.

The 16-bit *immediate* is sign-extended and compared to the contents of general register *rs*. Considering both quantities as signed integers, if the contents of general register *rs* are less than the sign-extended *immediate*, a trap exception occurs.

R4000/R6000 Operation:

T: if $(0 \parallel GPR[rs]) < (0 \parallel (immediate_{15})^{16} \parallel immediate_{15..0})$ then
           TrapException
      endif

Exceptions:

Trap exception

TLTU

Trap If Less Than Unsigned

31 26	25 21	20 16	15 6	5 0
SPECIAL 000000	rs	rt	code	TLTU 110011
6	5	5	10	6

Format:

TLTU rs,rt

Description:

This instruction causes a reserved instruction exception on R2000/R3000 processors.

The contents of general register *rt* are compared to general register *rs*. Considering both quantities as unsigned integers, if the contents of general register *rs* are less than the contents of general register *rt*, a trap exception occurs.

The code field is available for use as software parameters, but is retrieved by the exception handler only by loading the contents of the memory word containing the instruction.

R4000/R6000 Operation:

```
T:    if (0 || GPR[rs]) < (0 || GPR[rt]) then
          TrapException
      endif
```

Exceptions:

Trap exception
Reserved Instruction exception (R2000/R3000 only)

Trap If Not Equal   TNE

31 26	25 21	20 16	15 6	5 0
SPECIAL 000000	rs	rt	code	TNE 110110
6	5	5	10	6

Format:

TNE rs,rt

Description:

This instruction causes a reserved instruction exception on R2000/R3000 processors.

The contents of general register *rt* are compared to general register *rs*. If the contents of general register *rs* are not equal to the contents of general register *rt*, a trap exception occurs.

The code field is available for use as software parameters, but is retrieved by the exception handler only by loading the contents of the memory word containing the instruction.

R4000/R6000 Operation:

```
T:    if GPR[rs] ≠ GPR[rt] then
            TrapException
      endif
```

Exceptions:

Trap exception
Reserved Instruction exception (R2000/R3000 only)

TNEI   **Trap If Not Equal Immediate**

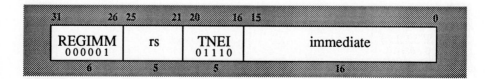

Format:

TNEI rs,immediate

Description:

This instruction is not valid on R2000/R3000 processors, but does not cause a reserved instruction exception.

The 16-bit *immediate* is sign-extended and compared to the contents of general register *rs*. If the contents of general register *rs* are not equal to the sign-extended *immediate*, a trap exception occurs.

R4000/R6000 Operation:

T: if GPR[rs] $\neq$ (immediate$_{15}$)^{16} || immediate$_{15..0}$ then
              TrapException
        endif

Exceptions:

Trap exception

Exclusive Or $\qquad$ **XOR**

31 26	25 21	20 16	15 11	10 6	5 0
SPECIAL 000000	rs	rt	rd	0 00000	XOR 100110
6	5	5	5	5	6

Format:

XOR rd,rs,rt

Description:

The contents of general register *rs* are combined with the contents of general register *rt* in a bit-wise logical exclusive OR operation. The result is placed into general register *rd*.

Operation:

T: GPR[rd] ← GPR[rs] *xor* GPR[rt]

Exceptions:

None.

XORI

Exclusive Or Immediate

31 26	25 21	20 16	15 0
XORI 001110	rs	rt	immediate
6	5	5	16

Format:

XORI rt,rs,immediate

Description:

The 16-bit *immediate* is zero-extended and combined with the contents of general register *rs* in a bit-wise logical exclusive-OR operation. The result is placed into general register *rt*.

Operation:

T: GPR[rt] ← GPR[rs] *xor* (0^{16} || immediate)

Exceptions:

None.

CPU Instruction Opcode Bit Encoding

The remainder of this Appendix presents the opcode bit encoding for the CPU instruction set (ISA and extensions), as implemented by the R2000/3000 (Figure A–1), R4000 (Figure A–2), and R6000 (Figure A–3).

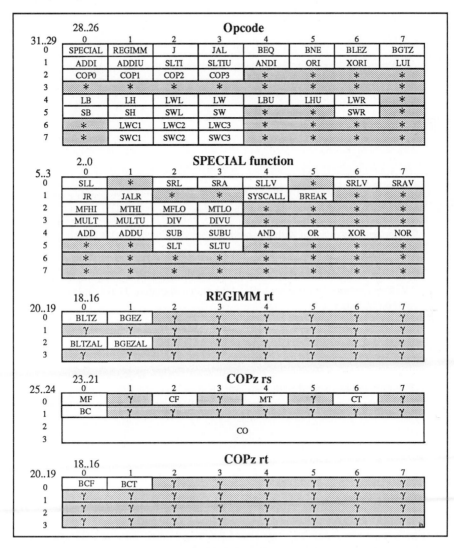

Figure A–1. R2000/R3000 Opcode Bit Encoding

CP0 Function

5..3 \ 2..0	0	1	2	3	4	5	6	7
0	γ	TLBR ε	TLBWI ε	γ	γ	γ	TLBWR ε	γ
1	TLBP ε	γ	γ	γ	γ	γ	γ	γ
2	RFE ξ	γ	γ	γ	γ	γ	γ	γ
3	χ	γ	γ	γ	γ	γ	γ	γ
0	γ	γ	γ	γ	γ	γ	γ	γ
1	γ	γ	γ	γ	γ	γ	γ	γ
2	γ	γ	γ	γ	γ	γ	γ	γ
3	γ	γ	γ	γ	γ	γ	γ	γ

Figure A–1. R2000/R3000 Opcode Bit Encoding (cont.)

Key:

* Operation codes marked with an asterisk cause reserved instruction exceptions in all current implementations.

γ Operation codes marked with a gamma are not valid for R2000/R3000 implementations.

ε Operation codes marked with an epsilon are valid only for R2000, R3000 and R4000 processors (processors with an on-chip associative TLB), and are not valid on the R6000.

ξ Operation codes marked with a xi are valid on the R2000, R3000 and R6000, but are not valid and cause a reserved instruction exception on R4000 processors.

χ Operation codes marked with a chi are valid only on R4000 processors and cause a reserved instruction exception on the R2000 and R3000 processors.

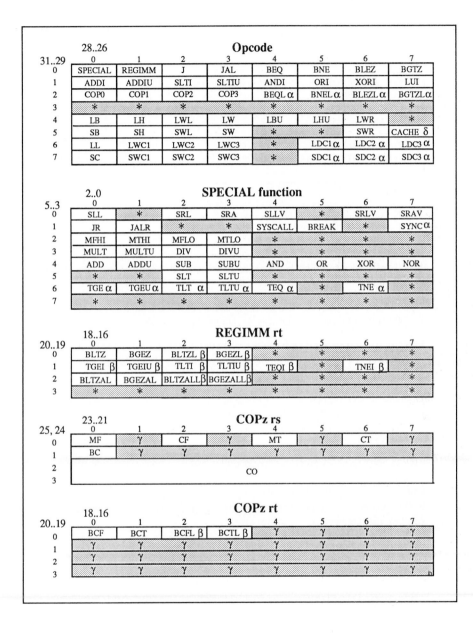

Opcode

31..29 \ 28..26	0	1	2	3	4	5	6	7
0	SPECIAL	REGIMM	J	JAL	BEQ	BNE	BLEZ	BGTZ
1	ADDI	ADDIU	SLTI	SLTIU	ANDI	ORI	XORI	LUI
2	COP0	COP1	COP2	COP3	BEQL α	BNEL α	BLEZL α	BGTZL α
3	*	*	*	*	*	*	*	*
4	LB	LH	LWL	LW	LBU	LHU	LWR	*
5	SB	SH	SWL	SW	*	*	SWR	CACHE δ
6	LL	LWC1	LWC2	LWC3	*	LDC1 α	LDC2 α	LDC3 α
7	SC	SWC1	SWC2	SWC3	*	SDC1 α	SDC2 α	SDC3 α

SPECIAL function

5..3 \ 2..0	0	1	2	3	4	5	6	7
0	SLL	*	SRL	SRA	SLLV	*	SRLV	SRAV
1	JR	JALR	*	*	SYSCALL	BREAK	*	SYNC α
2	MFHI	MTHI	MFLO	MTLO	*	*	*	*
3	MULT	MULTU	DIV	DIVU	*	*	*	*
4	ADD	ADDU	SUB	SUBU	AND	OR	XOR	NOR
5	*	*	SLT	SLTU	*	*	*	*
6	TGE α	TGEU α	TLT α	TLTU α	TEQ α	*	TNE α	*
7	*	*	*	*	*	*	*	*

REGIMM rt

20..19 \ 18..16	0	1	2	3	4	5	6	7
0	BLTZ	BGEZ	BLTZL β	BGEZL β	*	*	*	*
1	TGEI β	TGEIU β	TLTI β	TLTIU β	TEQI β	*	TNEI β	*
2	BLTZAL	BGEZAL	BLTZALL β	BGEZALL β	*	*	*	*
3	*	*	*	*	*	*	*	*

COPz rs

25, 24 \ 23..21	0	1	2	3	4	5	6	7
0	MF	γ	CF	γ	MT	γ	CT	γ
1	BC	γ	γ	γ	γ	γ	γ	γ
2	CO							
3								

COPz rt

20..19 \ 18..16	0	1	2	3	4	5	6	7
0	BCF	BCT	BCFL β	BCTL β	γ	γ	γ	γ
1	γ	γ	γ	γ	γ	γ	γ	γ
2	γ	γ	γ	γ	γ	γ	γ	γ
3	γ	γ	γ	γ	γ	γ	γ	γ

Figure A–2. R4000 Opcode Bit Encoding

5..3	2..0	**CP0 Function**						
	0	1	2	3	4	5	6	7
0	φ	TLBR ε	TLBWI ε	φ	φ	φ	TLBWR ε	φ
1	TLBP ε	φ	φ	φ	φ	φ	φ	φ
2	ξ	φ	φ	φ	φ	φ	φ	φ
3	ERET χ	φ	φ	φ	φ	φ	φ	φ
0	φ	φ	φ	φ	φ	φ	φ	φ
1	φ	φ	φ	φ	φ	φ	φ	φ
2	φ	φ	φ	φ	φ	φ	φ	φ
3	φ	φ	φ	φ	φ	φ	φ	φ

Figure A–2. R4000 Opcode Bit Encoding (cont.)

Key:

*   Operation codes marked with an asterisk cause reserved instruction exceptions in all current implementations and are reserved for future versions of the architecture.

α   Operation codes marked with an alpha cause reserved instruction exceptions in R2000/R3000 implementations, and are valid for R4000 implementations.

β   Operation codes marked with a beta are not valid for R2000/R3000 implementations, and are valid for R4000/R6000 implementations. R2000/R3000 implementations do not take a reserved instruction exception on these opcodes.

γ   Operation codes marked with a gamma are not valid for R2000/R3000 implementations, and for R4000 implementations cause a reserved instruction exception. They are reserved for future versions of the architecture.

δ   Operation codes marked with a delta are valid only for R4000 processors with CP0 enabled, and cause a reserved instruction exception on other processors.

ε   Operation codes marked with an epsilon are valid only for R2000, R3000 and R4000 processors (processors with an on-chip associative TLB), and are not valid on the R6000.

φ   Operation codes marked with a phi are invalid but do not cause reserved instruction exceptions in R4000 implementations.

ξ   Operation codes marked with a xi are valid on the R2000, R3000 and R6000, but are not valid and cause a reserved instruction exception on R4000 processors.

χ   Operation codes marked with a chi are valid only on R4000 processors and cause a reserved instruction exception on the R2000, R3000 and R6000.

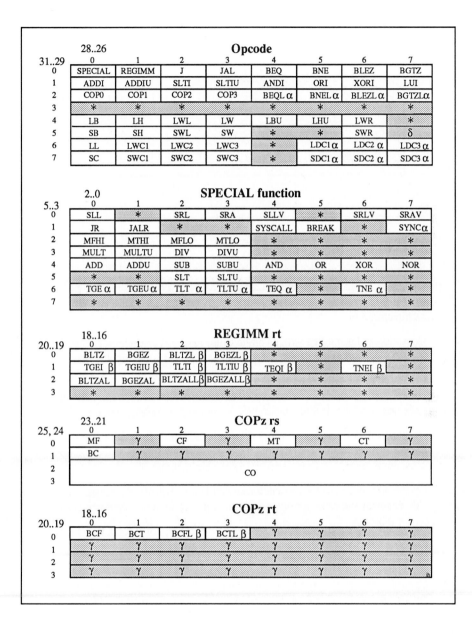

Figure A–3. R6000 Opcode Bit Encoding

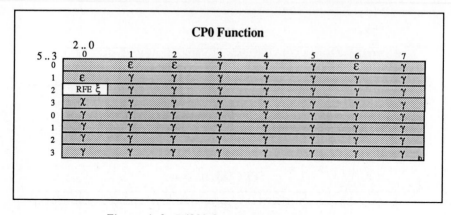

Figure A–3. R6000 Opcode Bit Encoding (cont.)

Key:

∗ Operation codes marked with an asterisk cause reserved instruction exceptions in all current implementations and are reserved for future versions of the architecture.

α Operation codes marked with an alpha cause reserved instruction exceptions in R2000/R3000 implementations, and are valid for R6000 implementations.

β Operation codes marked with a beta are not valid for R2000/R3000 implementations, and are valid for R6000 implementations. R2000/R3000 implementations do not take a reserved instruction exception on these opcodes.

γ Operation codes marked with a gamma are not valid for R2000/R3000 or R60000 implementations, but do not cause a reserved instruction exception. They are reserved for future versions of the architecture.

δ Operation codes marked with a delta are valid only for R4000 processors with CP0 enabled, and cause a reserved instruction exception on other processors.

ε Operation codes marked with an epsilon are valid only for R2000, R3000 and R4000 processors (processors with an on-chip associative TLB), and are not valid on the R6000.

ξ Operation codes marked with a xi are valid on the R2000, R3000 and R6000, but are not valid and cause a reserved instruction exception on R4000 processors.

χ Operation codes marked with a chi are valid only on R4000 processors, and cause a reserved instruction exception on the R6000.

B
FPU Instruction Set Details

This appendix provides a detailed description of the operation of each Floating-Point (FPU) instruction. The instructions are listed alphabetically.

The exceptions that may occur due to the execution of each instruction are listed after the description of each instruction. The description of the immediate causes and the manner of handling exceptions is omitted from the instruction descriptions in this chapter. Refer to Chapter 9 for detailed descriptions of floating-point exceptions and handling.

Figure B–3 lists the entire bit encoding for the constant fields of the Floating-Point instruction set; the bit encoding for each instruction is included with that individual instruction.

Instruction Formats

There are three basic instruction format types:

- I-Type, or Immediate instructions, which include load and store operations,
- M-Type, or Move instructions, and
- R-Type, or Register instructions, which include the two- and three-register Floating-Point operations.

The instruction description subsections that follow show how the three basic instruction formats are used by:

- Load and store instructions,
- Move instructions, and
- Floating-Point Computational instructions.

A fourth instruction description subsection describes the special instruction format used by:

- Floating-Point Branch instructions.

Floating-point instructions are mapped onto the MIPS coprocessor instructions, defining coprocessor unit number one (CP1) as the floating-point unit.

Each operation is valid only for certain formats. Implementations may support some of these formats and operations only through emulation, but only need support combinations that are valid, which are marked with a "•" in Table B–1 below. Those combinations marked with a "—" are not currently specified by this architecture, but must cause an unimplemented instruction trap to maintain compatibility with future architecture extensions. Entries which are blank are not valid, and therefore the result of such instructions are not defined.

Table B–1. Valid FPU Instruction Formats

Operation	Source Format		
	Single	Double	Word
ADD	•	•	—
SUB	•	•	—
MUL	•	•	—
DIV	•	•	—
SQRT	•	•	—
ABS	•	•	—
MOV	•	•	•
NEG	•	•	—
TRUNC.W	•	•	
ROUND.W	•	•	
CEIL.W	•	•	
FLOOR.W	•	•	
CVT.S		•	•
CVT.D	•		•
CVT.W	•	•	
C	•	•	—

The coprocessor branch on condition true/false instructions can be used to logically negate any predicate. Thus, the 32 possible conditions require only 16 distinct comparisons, as shown in Table B–2 below.

Table B–2. Logical Negation of Predicates by Condition True/False

Condition			Relations				Invalid operation exception if unordered
Mnemonic		Code	Greater Than	Less Than	Equal	Unordered	
True	False						
F	T	0	F	F	F	F	No
UN	OR	1	F	F	F	T	No
EQ	NEQ	2	F	F	T	F	No
UEQ	OGL	3	F	F	T	T	No
OLT	UGE	4	F	T	F	F	No
ULT	OGE	5	F	T	F	T	No
OLE	UGT	6	F	T	T	F	No
ULE	OGT	7	F	T	T	T	No
SF	ST	8	F	F	F	F	Yes
NGLE	GLE	9	F	F	F	T	Yes
SEQ	SNE	10	F	F	T	F	Yes
NGL	GL	11	F	F	T	T	Yes
LT	NLT	12	F	T	F	F	Yes
NGE	GE	13	F	T	F	T	Yes
LE	NLE	14	F	T	T	F	Yes
NGT	GT	15	F	T	T	T	Yes

Floating-Point Loads, Stores, and Moves

All movement of data between the floating-point coprocessor and memory is accomplished by coprocessor load and store operations, which reference a single 32-bit word of the floating-point coprocessor's *General Purpose* registers. These operations are unformatted; no format conversions are performed and therefore no floating-point exceptions occur due to these operations.

R4000 and R6000 implementations provide coprocessor load and store operations which reference a 64-bit doubleword directly, as a pair of floating-point coprocessor *General Purpose* registers. Like single-word loads, these operations are unformatted, perform no format conversions, and incur no floating-point exceptions.

Data may also be directly moved between the floating-point coprocessor and the processor by move to coprocessor and move from coprocessor instructions. Like the floating-point load and store operations, move to/from operations perform no format conversions and never cause floating-point exceptions.

An additional pair of coprocessor registers are available, called *Floating-Point Control* registers for which the only data movement operations supported are moves to and from processor *General Purpose* registers.

Floating-Point Operations

The floating-point unit's operation set includes floating-point add, subtract, multiply, divide, square root, convert between fixed-point and floating-point format, convert between floating-point formats, and floating-point compare. These operations satisfy IEEE Standard 754's requirements for accuracy. Specifically, these operations obtain a result which is identical to performing the result with infinite precision and then rounding to the specified format, using the current rounding mode.

Instructions must specify the format of their operands. Except for conversion functions, mixed-format operations are not provided.

Instruction Notational Conventions

In this appendix, all variable subfields in an instruction format (such as *fs, ft, immediate*, and so on) are shown with lower-case names. The instruction name (such as ADD, SUB, and so on) is shown in upper-case.

For the sake of clarity, an alias is sometimes substituted for a variable subfield in the formats of specific instructions. For example, we use *rs = base* in the format for load and store instructions. Such an alias is always lower case, since it refers to a variable subfield.

In some instructions, however, the two instruction subfields *op* and *function* have constant 6-bit values. When reference is made to these instructions, upper-case mnemonics are used. In the floating-point instruction, for example, we use *op* = COP1 and *function* = FADD. In some cases, a single field has both fixed and variable subfields, so the name contains both upper and lower case characters. Actual bit encoding for mnemonics is shown in Figure B–3 at the end of this appendix, and are also included with each individual instruction.

In the instruction descriptions that follow, the *Operation* section describes the operation performed by each instruction using a high-level language notation.

Instruction Notation Examples

The following examples illustrate the application of some of the instruction notation conventions:

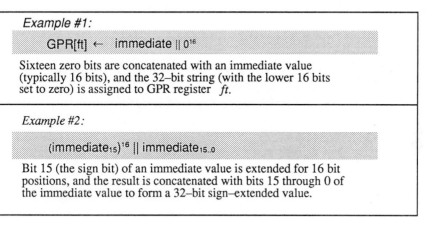

Example #1:

$$GPR[ft] \leftarrow \text{immediate} \parallel 0^{16}$$

Sixteen zero bits are concatenated with an immediate value (typically 16 bits), and the 32–bit string (with the lower 16 bits set to zero) is assigned to GPR register *ft*.

Example #2:

$$(\text{immediate}_{15})^{16} \parallel \text{immediate}_{15..0}$$

Bit 15 (the sign bit) of an immediate value is extended for 16 bit positions, and the result is concatenated with bits 15 through 0 of the immediate value to form a 32–bit sign–extended value.

Load and Store Instructions

In the MIPS ISA, all load operations have a delay of at least one instruction. That is, the instruction immediately following a load cannot use the contents of the register which will be loaded with the data being fetched from storage.

In R4000/R6000 implementations, the instruction immediately following a load may use the contents of the register loaded. In such cases, the hardware will interlock, requiring additional real cycles — so scheduling load delay slots is still desirable — although not absolutely required for functional code.

In the load/store operation descriptions , the functions listed in Table B–3 are used to summarize the handling of virtual addresses and physical memory.

Table B–3. Load/Store Common Functions

Function	Description
Address Translation	Uses the TLB to find the physical address given the virtual address. The function fails and an exception is taken if the entry for the page containing the virtual address is not present in the TLB (Translation Lookaside Buffer).
Load Memory	Uses the cache and main memory to find the contents of the word containing the specified physical address. The low–order two bits (WORD access) or three bits (DOUBLEWORD access) of the address and the Access Type field indicate which of each of the bytes within the data word need to be returned. If the cache is enabled for this access, the entire word is returned and loaded into the cache.
Store Memory	Uses the cache, write buffer, and main memory to store the word or part of word specified as data into the word containing the specified physical address. The low–order bits of the address and the access type field indicate which of the bytes within the data word should be stored.

Load and Store Instruction Format

Figure B–1 shows the I-Type instruction format used by load and store operations.

I–Type (Immediate)

31	26	25	21	20	16	15	0
op		base		ft		offset	
6		5		5		16	

where:

op	is a 6–bit operation code
base	is the 5–bit base register specifier
ft	is a 5–bit source (for stores) or destination (for loads) FPA register specifier
offset	is the 16–bit signed immediate offset

Figure B–1. Load and Store Instruction Format

All coprocessor loads and stores reference aligned full word data items. Thus, for word loads and stores, the access type field is always WORD, and the low order two bits of the address must always be zero.

For doubleword loads and stores, the access type field is always DOUBLEWORD, and the low order three bits of the address must always be zero.

Regardless of byte-numbering order (endianness), the address specifies that byte which has the smallest byte-address of all of the bytes in the addressed field. For a Big-endian machine, this is the leftmost byte; for a Little-endian machine, this is the rightmost byte.

Computational Instructions

Computational instructions include all of the arithmetic floating-point operations performed by the FPU.

Figure B–2 shows the R-Type instruction format used for computational operations.

```
R–Type (Register)

 31        26 25      21 20      16 15      11 10       6 5          0
 +-----------+----------+----------+----------+----------+------------+
 |    op     |  format  |    ft    |    fs    |    fd    |  function  |
 +-----------+----------+----------+----------+----------+------------+
       6          5          5          5          5           6

 where:
      COP1       is a 6–bit major operation code
      format     is a 5–bit format specifier
      fs         is a 5–bit source1 register
      ft         is a 5–bit source2 register
      fd         is a 5–bit destination register
      function   is a 6–bit function field
```

Figure B–2. Computational Instruction Format

Each floating-point instruction can be applied to a number of operand formats. The operand format for an instruction is specified by a 4-bit field; decoding for this field is shown in Table B–4.

Table B–4. Format Field Decoding

Code	Mnemonic	Size	Format
16	S	single	binary floating-point
17	D	double	binary floating-point
18	*reserved*		
19	*reserved*		
20	W	single	binary fixed-point
21–31	–	–	reserved

The six low order *function* bits of coprocessor instruction indicate which floating-point operation is to be performed. Table B–5 lists all floating-point instructions.

Table B–5. Floating-Point Instructions and Operations

Code (5.. 0)	Mnemonic	Operation
0	ADD	Add
1	SUB	Subtract
2	MUL	Multiply
3	DIV	Divide
4	SQRT	Square root
5	ABS	Absolute value
6	MOV	Move
7	NEG	Negate
8–11	reserved	
12	ROUND.W	Convert to single fixed-point, rounded to nearest
13	TRUNC.W	Convert to single fixed-point, rounded toward zero
14	CEIL.W	Convert to single fixed-point, rounded to $+\infty$
15	FLOOR.W	Convert to single fixed-point, rounded to $-\infty$
16–31	–	reserved
32	CVT.S	Convert to single floating-point
33	CVT.D	Convert to double floating-point
34	–	reserved
35	–	reserved
36	CVT.W	Convert to binary fixed-point
37–47	–	reserved
48–63	C	Floating-point compare

In the following pages, the notation *FGR* refers to the FPU's *General Purpose Registers 0 through 31*, and *FPR* refers to the FPU's floating-point registers *(FPR 0* through *30)* which are formed by concatenation of *FGR*'s (as described in Chapter 7).

The following routines are used in the description of the floating-point operations to get the value of an *FPR* or to change the value of an *FGR*:

```
value ← ValueFPR(fpr, fmt):
   /* undefined for odd fpr */
   case fmt of
      S, W:
         value ← FGR[fpr + 0]
      D:
         /* undefined for fpr not even */
         value ← FGR[fpr + 1] || FGR[fpr + 0]
end


StoreFPR (fpr, fmt, value):
   /* undefined for odd fpr */
   case fmt of
      S, W:
         FGR[fpr + 1] ← undefined
         FGR[fpr + 0] ← value
      D:
         FGR[fpr + 1] ← value_{63..32}
         FGR[fpr + 0] ← value_{31..0}
   end
```

ABS.fmt

Floating–Point Absolute Value

COP1	fmt	0	fs	fd	ABS
010001		00000			000101
6	5	5	5	5	6

Format:

ABS.fmt   fd,fs

Description:

The contents of the FPU register specified by *fs* are interpreted in the specified format and the arithmetic absolute value is taken. The result is placed in the floating-point register specified by *fd*.

The absolute value operation is arithmetic; a NaN operand signals invalid operation.

This instruction is valid only for single and double precision floating-point formats. The operation is not defined if bit 0 of any register specification is set, as the register numbers specify an even-odd pair of adjacent coprocessor general registers.

Operation:

```
T:    StoreFPR(fd, fmt, AbsoluteValue(ValueFPR(fs, fmt)))
```

Exceptions:

Coprocessor unusable exception
Coprocessor Exception Trap

Coprocessor Exceptions:

Unimplemented Operation Exception
Invalid Operation Exception

Floating–Point Add ADD.fmt

COP1 010001	fmt	ft	fs	fd	ADD 000000
31 26 25	21 20	16 15	11 10	6 5	0
6	5	5	5	5	6

Format:

ADD.fmt   fd,fs,ft

Description:

The contents of the FPU registers specified by *fs* and *ft* are interpreted in the specified format and arithmetically added. The result is rounded as if calculated to infinite precision and then rounded to the specified format (*fmt*), according to the current rounding mode. The result is placed in the floating-point register (*FPR*) specified by *fd*.

This instruction is valid only for single and double precision floating-point formats. The operation is not defined if bit 0 of any register specification is set, as the register numbers specify an even-odd pair of adjacent coprocessor general registers.

Operation:

T: StoreFPR (fd, fmt, ValueFPR(fs, fmt) + ValueFPR(ft, fmt))

Exceptions:

Coprocessor unusable
Coprocessor interrupt (R2000, R3000, and R6000) or Floating-Point Exception (R4000)

Coprocessor Exceptions:

Unimplemented Operation Exception
Invalid Operation Exception
Inexact Exception
Overflow Exception
Underflow Exception

BC1F

**Branch On FPA False
(coprocessor 1)**

COP1 010001	BC 01000	BCF 00000	offset
6	5	5	16

31 26 25 21 20 16 15 0

Format:

BC1F   offset

Description:

A branch target address is computed from the sum of the address of the instruction in the delay slot and the 16-bit *offset*, shifted left two bits and sign-extended to 32 bits. If the result of the last floating-point compare is false, the program branches to the target address, with a delay of one instruction.

Operation:

```
T−1:  condition ← not COC[1]
T:    target ← (offset₁₅)¹⁴ || offset || 0²
T+1:  if condition then
          PC ← PC + target
      endif
```

$$T-1: \quad \text{condition} \leftarrow \textit{not}\ COC[1]$$
$$T: \quad \text{target} \leftarrow (\text{offset}_{15})^{14}\ ||\ \text{offset}\ ||\ 0^2$$
$$T+1: \quad \text{if condition then}$$
$$PC \leftarrow PC + \text{target}$$
$$\text{endif}$$

Exceptions:

Coprocessor unusable exception

Branch On FPU False Likely (coprocessor 1)

BC1FL

COP1 010001	BC 01000	BCFL 00010	offset
6	5	5	16

(bit positions: 31, 26, 25, 21, 20, 16, 15, 0)

Format:

BC1FL   offset

Description:

This instruction is not valid for R2000/R3000 processors, but does not cause an illegal instruction exception.

A branch target address is computed from the sum of the address of the instruction in the delay slot and the 16-bit *offset*, shifted left two bits and sign-extended to 32 bits.

If the result of the last floating-point compare is false, the program branches to the target address, with a delay of one instruction. If the conditional branch is *not* taken, the instruction in the branch delay slot is nullified.

R4000/R6000 Operation:

```
T−1:  condition ← not COC[1]
T:    target ← (offset₁₅)¹⁴ || offset || 0²
T+1:  if condition then
          PC ← PC + target
      else
          NullifyCurrentInstruction
      endif
```

Exceptions:

Coprocessor unusable exception

BC1T

Branch On FPU True
(coprocessor 1)

COP1 010001	BC 01000	BCT 00001	offset
6	5	5	16

Format:

BC1T offset

Description:

A branch target address is computed from the sum of the address of the instruction in the delay slot and the 16-bit *offset*, shifted left two bits and sign-extended to 32 bits. If the result of the last floating-point compare is true, the program branches to the target address, with a delay of one instruction.

Operation:

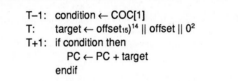

T-1: condition $\leftarrow$ COC[1]
T: target $\leftarrow$ offset$_{15}$)^{14} || offset || 0^2
T+1: if condition then
          PC $\leftarrow$ PC + target
        endif

Exceptions:

Coprocessor unusable exception

Branch On FPU True Likely
(coprocessor 1)

BC1TL

31 26	25 21	20 16	15 0
COP1 010001	BC 01000	BCTL 00011	offset
6	5	5	16

Format:

BC1TL   offset

Description:

This instruction is not valid for R2000/R3000 processors, but does not cause an illegal instruction exception.

A branch target address is computed from the sum of the address of the instruction in the delay slot and the 16-bit *offset*, shifted left two bits and sign-extended to 32 bits.

If the result of the last floating-point compare is true, the program branches to the target address, with a delay of one instruction. If the conditional branch is *not* taken, the instruction in the branch delay slot is nullified.

RR4000/R6000 Operation:

```
T–1:  condition ← COC[1]
T:    target ← offset₁₅)¹⁴ || offset || 0²
T+1:  if condition then
          PC ← PC + target
      else
          NullifyCurrentInstruction
      endif
```

Exceptions:

Coprocessor unusable exception

C.cond.fmt

Floating–Point Compare

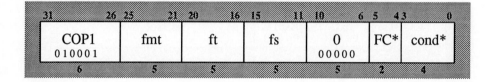

Format:

C.cond.fmt fs,ft

Description:

The contents of the floating-point registers specified by *fs* and *ft* are interpreted in the specified *format* and arithmetically compared.

A result is determined based on the comparison and the conditions specified in the instruction. If one of the values is a Not a Number (NaN), and the high order bit of the *condition* field is set, an invalid operation trap is taken. After a one instruction delay, the condition is available for testing with branch on floating-point coprocessor condition instructions.

Comparisons are exact and can neither overflow nor underflow. Four mutually exclusive relations are possible results: less than, equal, greater than, and unordered. The last case arises when one or both of the operands are NaN; every NaN compares unordered with everything, including itself. Comparisons ignore the sign of zero, so +0 = –0.

This instruction is valid only for single and double precision floating-point formats. The operation is not defined if bit 0 of any register specification is set, since the register numbers specify an even-odd pair of adjacent coprocessor general registers.

*See the Figure B–3 at the end of Appendix B.

Floating–Point Compare (continued)

C.cond.fmt

Operation:

```
T:      if NaN(ValueFPR(fs, fmt)) or NaN(ValueFPR(ft, fmt)) then
            less ← false
            equal ← false
            unordered ← true
            if cond₃ then
                signal InvalidOperationException
            endif
        else
            less ← ValueFPR(fs, fmt) < ValueFPR(ft, fmt)
            equal ← ValueFPR(fs, fmt) = ValueFPR(ft, fmt)
            unordered ← false
        endif
        condition ← (cond₂ and less) or
            (cond₁ and equal) or
            (cond₀ and unordered)
        FCR[31]₂₃ ← condition
        COC[1] ← condition
```

Exceptions:

Coprocessor unusable
Coprocessor interrupt (R2000, R3000, and R6000) or Floating-Point Exception (R4000)

Coprocessor Exceptions:

Unimplemented Operation Exception
Invalid Operation Exception

CEIL.W.fmt

**Floating–Point Ceiling to Single
Fixed–Point Format**

31	26	25	21	20	16	15	11	10	6	5	0
COP1 010001		fmt		0 00000		fs		fd		CEIL.W 001110	
6		5		5		5		5		6	

Format:

CEIL.W.fmt fd,fs

Description:

This instruction is not implemented on R2000/R3000 processors, and will cause the unimplemented operation exception to occur.

The contents of the floating-point register specified by *fs* are interpreted in the specified source format, *fmt*, and arithmetically converted to the single fixed-point format. The result is placed in the floating-point register specified by *fd*.

Regardless of the setting of the current rounding mode, the conversion is rounded as if the current rounding mode is round to $+\infty$ (2).

This instruction is valid only for conversion from a single or double precision floating-point formats. For R4000 and R6000 processors the operation is not defined if bit 0 of any register specification is set, as the register numbers specify an even-odd pair of adjacent coprocessor general registers.

When the source operand is an Infinity or NaN, or the correctly rounded integer result is outside of -2^{31} to $2^{31} - 1$, the Invalid operation exception is raised. If the Invalid operation is not enabled then no exception is taken and $2^{31} - 1$ is returned.

Floating–Point Ceiling to Single Fixed–Point Format (continued)

CEIL.W.fmt

R4000/R6000 Operation:

T: StoreFPR(fd, W, ConvertFmt(ValueFPR(fs, fmt), fmt, W))

Exceptions:

Coprocessor unusable exception
Coprocessor interrupt (R2000, R3000, and R6000) or Floating-Point Exception (R4000)

Coprocessor Exceptions:

Invalid operation exception
Unimplemented operation exception
Inexact exception
Overflow exception

CFC1

Move Control Word From FPU
(coprocessor 1)

31 26	25 21	20 16	15 11	10 0
COP1 010001	CF 00010	rt	fs	0 000 0000 0000
6	5	5	5	11

Format:

CFC1 rt,fs

Description:

The contents of the FPU's control register *fs* are loaded into general register *rt*.

This operation is only defined when *fs* equals 0 or 31.

The contents of general register *rt* are undefined for time *T* of the instruction immediately following this load instruction.

Operation:

```
T:     temp ← FCR[fs]
T+1 :  GPR[rt] ← temp
```

Exceptions:

Coprocessor unusable exception

Move Control Word To FPU
(coprocessor 1)

CTC1

31 26	25 21	20 16	15 11	10 0
COP1 010001	CT 00110	rt	fs	0 000 0000 0000
6	5	5	5	11

Format:

CTC1 rt,fs

Description:

The contents of general register *rt* are loaded into the FPU's control register *fs*.

This operation is only defined when *fs* equals 0 or 31.

Writing to *Control Register 31*, the floating-point *Control/Status* register, causes an interrupt or exception if any cause bit and its corresponding enable bit are both set. The register will be written before the exception occurs.

The contents of floating-point control register *fs* are undefined for time *T* of the instruction immediately following this load instruction.

Operation:

```
T:    temp ← GPR[rt]
T+1:  FCR[fs] ← temp
      COC[1] ← FCR[31]₂₃
```

Exceptions:

Coprocessor unusable exception

CVT.D.fmt

**Floating–Point Convert to Double
Floating–Point Format**

COP1 010001	fmt	0 00000	fs	fd	CVT.D 100001
6	5	5	5	5	6

Format:

CVT.D.fmt fd,fs

Description:

The contents of the floating-point register specified by *fs* is interpreted in the specified source format, *fmt*, and arithmetically converted to the double binary floating-point format. The result is placed in the floating-point register specified by *fd*.

This instruction is valid only for conversion from single or double floating-point format, or from 32-bit fixed-point format.

If the single floating-point or single fixed-point format is specified, the operation is exact. The operation is not defined if bit 0 of any register specification is set, as the register numbers specify an even-odd pair of adjacent coprocessor general registers.

Operation:

```
T:    StoreFPR (fd, D, ConvertFmt(ValueFPR(fs, fmt), fmt, D))
```

Exceptions:

Coprocessor unusable exception
Coprocessor interrupt (R2000, R3000, and R6000) or Floating-Point Exception (R4000)

Coprocessor Exceptions:

Invalid operation exception	Unimplemented operation exception
Inexact exception	Overflow exception
Underflow exception	

Floating–Point Convert to Single Floating–Point Format

CVT.S.fmt

COP1 010001	fmt	0 00000	fs	fd	CVT.S 100000
6	5	5	5	5	6

(bit positions: 31, 26 25, 21 20, 16 15, 11 10, 6 5, 0)

Format:

CVT.S.fmt fd,fs

Description:

The contents of the floating-point register specified by *fs* are interpreted in the specified source format, *fmt*, and arithmetically converted to the single binary floating-point format. The result is placed in the floating-point register specified by *fd*. Rounding occurs according to the currently specified rounding mode.

This instruction is valid only for conversion from double floating-point format, or from 32-bit fixed-point format. The operation is not defined if bit 0 of any register specification is set, since the register numbers specify an even-odd pair of adjacent coprocessor general registers.

Operation:

```
T:     StoreFPR(fd,S,ConvertFmt(ValueFPR(fs,fmt),fmt,S))
```

Exceptions:

Coprocessor unusable exception
Coprocessor interrupt (R2000, R3000, and R6000) or Floating-Point Exception (R4000)

Coprocessor Exceptions:

Invalid operation exception	Unimplemented operation exception
Inexact exception	Overflow exception
Underflow exception	

CVT.W.fmt

**Floating–Point Convert to
Fixed–Point Format**

31 26	25 21	20 16	15 11	10 6	5 0
COP1 010001	fmt	0 00000	fs	fd	CVT.W 100100
6	5	5	5	5	6

Format:

CVT.W.fmt fd,fs

Description:

The contents of the floating-point register specified by *fs* are interpreted in the specified source format, *fmt*, and arithmetically converted to the single fixed-point format. The result is placed in the floating-point register specified by *fd*.

This instruction is valid only for conversion from a single or double precision floating-point formats. This operation is not defined if bit 0 of any register specification is set, since the register numbers specify an even-odd pair of adjacent coprocessor general registers.

When the source operand is an Infinity or NaN, or the correctly rounded integer result is outside of -2^{31} to $2^{31} - 1$, an Invalid operation exception is raised. If Invalid operation is not enabled then no exception is taken and $2^{31} - 1$ is returned.

Operation:

```
T:     StoreFPR(fd, W, ConvertFmt(ValueFPR(fs, fmt), fmt, W))
```

Exceptions:

Coprocessor unusable exception
Coprocessor interrupt (R2000, R3000, and R6000) or Floating-Point Exception (R4000)

Coprocessor Exceptions:

Invalid operation exception	Unimplemented operation exception
Inexact exception	Overflow exception

Floating–Point Divide   DIV.fmt

COP1 010001	fmt	ft	fs	fd	DIV 000011
6	5	5	5	5	6

Format:

DIV.fmt   fd,fs,ft

Description:

The contents of the floating-point registers specified by *fs* and *ft* are interpreted in the specified *format* and arithmetically divided. The result is rounded as if calculated to infinite precision and then rounded to the specified format, according to the current rounding mode. The result is placed in the floating-point register specified by *fd*.

This instruction is valid only for single or double precision floating-point formats. The operation is not defined if bit 0 of any register specification is set, since the register numbers specify an even-odd pair of adjacent coprocessor general registers.

Operation:

> T: StoreFPR (fd, fmt, ValueFPR(fs, fmt) / ValueFPR(ft, fmt))

Exceptions:

Coprocessor unusable exception
Coprocessor interrupt (R2000, R3000, and R6000) or Floating-Point Exception (R4000)

Coprocessor Exceptions:

Unimplemented operation exception
Invalid operation exception
Division by zero exception
Inexact exception
Overflow exception
Underflow exception

FLOOR.W.fmt

Floating–Point Floor to Single Fixed–Point Format

31	26 25	21 20	16 15	11 10	6 5	0
COP1 010001	fmt	0 00000	fs	fd	FLOOR.W 001111
6	5	5	5	5	6

Format:

FLOOR.W.fmt fd,fs

Description:

This instruction is not implemented on R2000/R3000 processors, and will cause the unimplemented operation exception to occur.

The contents of the floating-point register specified by *fs* are interpreted in the specified source format, *fmt*, and arithmetically converted to the single fixed-point format. The result is placed in the floating-point register specified by *fd*.

Regardless of the setting of the current rounding mode, the conversion is rounded as if the current rounding mode is round to $-\infty$ (3).

This instruction is valid only for conversion from a single or double precision floating-point formats. The operation is not defined if bit 0 of any register specification is set, since the register numbers specify an even-odd pair of adjacent coprocessor general registers.

When the source operand is an Infinity or NaN, or the correctly rounded integer result is outside of -2^{31} to $2^{31} - 1$, an Invalid operation exception is raised. If Invalid operation is not enabled then no exception is taken and $2^{31} - 1$ is returned.

Floating–Point Floor to Single Fixed–Point Format (continued)

FLOOR.W.fmt

R4000/R6000 Operation:

> T: StoreFPR(fd, W, ConvertFmt(ValueFPR(fs, fmt), fmt, W))

Exceptions:

Coprocessor unusable exception
Coprocessor interrupt (R2000, R3000, and R6000) or Floating-Point Exception (R4000)

Coprocessor Exceptions:

Invalid operation exception
Unimplemented operation exception
Inexact exception
Overflow exception

LDC1

Load Doubleword to FPU (coprocessor 1)

LDC1 110101	base	ft	offset
31 26	25 21	20 16	15 0
6	5	5	16

Format:

LDC1 ft,offset(base)

Description:

This instruction causes a reserved instruction exception on R2000/R3000 processors.

The 16-bit *offset* is sign-extended and added to the contents of general register *base* to form a 32-bit unsigned effective address. The contents of the doubleword at the memory location specified by the effective address are loaded into registers *ft* and *ft+1* of the floating-point coprocessor.

If any of the three least significant bits of the effective address are non-zero, an address error exception takes place.

This instruction is not valid, and is undefined, when the least significant bit of *ft* is non-zero.

R4000/R6000 Operation:

```
T:    vAddr ← (offset₁₅)¹⁶ || offset₁₅..₀) + GPR[base]
      (pAddr, uncached) ← AddressTranslation (vAddr, DATA)
      if BigEndianCPU = 1 then
          CPR[z, ft+1] ← LoadMemory (uncached, WORD, pAddr+0, vAddr+0, DATA)
          CPR[z, ft+0] ← LoadMemory (uncached, WORD, pAddr+4, vAddr+4, DATA)
      else
          CPR[z, ft+0] ← LoadMemory (uncached, WORD, pAddr+0, vAddr+0, DATA)
          CPR[z, ft+1] ← LoadMemory (uncached, WORD, pAddr+4, vAddr+4, DATA)
      endif
```

Load Doubleword to FPU (continued)   LDC1

Exceptions:

Coprocessor unusable
TLB refill exception
TLB invalid exception
Bus error exception
Address error exception
Reserved instruction exception (R2000/R3000 only)

LWC1

**Load Word to FPU
(coprocessor 1)**

31 26	25 21	20 16	15 0
LWC1 110001	base	ft	offset
6	5	5	16

Format:

LWC1 ft,offset(base)

Description:

The 16-bit *offset* is sign-extended and added to the contents of general register *base* to form a
32-bit unsigned effective address. The contents of the word at the memory location specified
by the effective address is loaded into register *ft* of the floating-point coprocessor.

In R2000/R3000 implementations, the contents of general register *ft* are undefined for time *T*
of the instruction immediately following this load instruction.

If either of the two least significant bits of the effective address is non-zero, an address error
exception occurs.

R2000/R3000 Operation:

```
T:     vAddr ← ((offset15)16 || offset15..0) + GPR[base]
       (pAddr, uncached) ← AddressTranslation (vAddr, DATA)
       mem ← LoadMemory (uncached, WORD, pAddr, vAddr, DATA)
       CPR[z, ft] ← undefined
T+1:   CPR[z, ft] ← mem
```

Load Word to FPU
(continued)

LWC1

R4000/R6000 Operation:

$$T: \quad vAddr \leftarrow (offset_{15})^{16} \parallel offset_{15..0}) + GPR[base]$$
$$(pAddr, uncached) \leftarrow AddressTranslation (vAddr, DATA)$$
$$CPR[z, ft] \leftarrow LoadMemory (uncached, WORD, pAddr, vAddr, DATA)$$

Exceptions:

Coprocessor unusable
TLB refill exception
TLB invalid exception
Bus error exception
Address error exception

MFC1

Move From FPU
(coprocessor 1)

31 26	25 21	20 16	15 11	10 0
COP1 010001	MF 00000	rt	fs	0 000 0000 0000
6	5	5	5	11

Format:

MFC1 rt,fs

Description:

The contents of register *fs* from the floating-point coprocessor are stored into processor register *rt*.

The contents of floating-point register *rt* are undefined for time *T* of the instruction immediately following this load instruction.

Operation:

```
T:   data ← CPR[z, fs];
T+1: GPR[rt] ← data
```

Exceptions:

Coprocessor unusable exception

Floating–Point Move

MOV.fmt

COP1 010001	fmt	0 00000	fs	fd	MOV 000110
6	5	5	5	5	6

(bit positions: 31 26 25 21 20 16 15 11 10 6 5 0)

Format:

MOV.fmt   fd,fs

Description:

The contents of the FPU register specified by *fs* are interpreted in the specified *format* and are copied into the FPU register specified by *fd*.

The move operation is non-arithmetic; no IEEE 754 exceptions occur as a result of the instruction.

This instruction is valid only for single or double precision floating-point formats.

The operation is not defined if bit 0 of any register specification is set, since the register numbers specify an even-odd pair of adjacent coprocessor general registers.

Operation:

T: StoreFPR(fd,fmt,ValueFPR(fs,fmt))

MOV.fmt   **Floating–Point Move**

(continued)

Exceptions:

Coprocessor unusable exception
Coprocessor interrupt (R2000, R3000, and R6000) or Floating-Point Exception (R4000)

Coprocessor Exceptions:

Unimplemented Operation Exception

Move To FPU
(coprocessor 1)

MTC1

31 26	25 21	20 16	15 11	10 0
COP1 010001	MT 00100	rt	fs	0 000 0000 0000
6	5	5	5	11

Format:

MTC1 rt,fs

Description:

The contents of register *rt* are loaded into the FPU's general register at location *fs*.

The contents of floating-point register *fs* is undefined for time T of the instruction immediately following this load instruction.

Operation:

```
T:    data ← GPR[rt]
T+1:  CPR[z, fs] ← data
```

Exceptions:

Coprocessor unusable exception

MUL.fmt

Floating–Point Multiply

31 26	25 21	20 16	15 11	10 6	5 0
COP1 010001	fmt	ft	fs	fd	MUL 000010
6	5	5	5	5	6

Format:

MUL.fmt fd,fs,ft

Description:

The contents of the floating-point registers specified by *fs* and *ft* are interpreted in the specified *format* and arithmetically multiplied. The result is rounded as if calculated to infinite precision and then rounded to the specified *format*, according to the current rounding mode. The result is placed in the floating-point register specified by *fd*.

This instruction is valid only for single or double precision floating-point formats.

The operation is not defined if bit 0 of any register specification is set, since the register numbers specify an even-odd pair of adjacent coprocessor general registers.

Operation:

```
T:    StoreFPR (fd, fmt, ValueFPR(fs, fmt) * ValueFPR(ft, fmt))
```

Floating–Point Multiply
(continued)

MUL.fmt

Exceptions:

Coprocessor unusable exception
Coprocessor interrupt (R2000, R3000, and R6000) or Floating-Point Exception (R4000)

Coprocessor Exceptions:

Unimplemented Operation Exception
Invalid Operation Exception
Inexact Exception
Overflow Exception
Underflow Exception

NEG.fmt

Floating–Point Negate

31 26	25 21	20 16	15 11	10 6	5 0
COP1 010001	fmt	0 00000	fs	fd	NEG 000111
6	5	5	5	5	6

Format:

NEG.fmt   fd,fs

Description:

The contents of the FPU register specified by *fs* are interpreted in the specified *format* and the arithmetic negation is taken (the polarity of the sign-bit is changed). The result is placed in the FPU register specified by *fd*.

The negate operation is arithmetic; an NaN operand signals invalid operation.

This instruction is valid only for single or double precision floating-point formats. The operation is not defined if bit 0 of any register specification is set, since the register numbers specify an even-odd pair of adjacent coprocessor general registers.

Operation:

```
T:      StoreFPR(fd, fmt, AbsoluteValue(ValueFPR(fs, fmt)))
```

Floating–Point Negate (continued)   NEG.fmt

Exceptions:

Coprocessor unusable exception
Coprocessor interrupt (R2000, R3000, and R6000) or Floating-Point Exception (R4000)

Coprocessor Exceptions:

Unimplemented Operation Exception
Invalid Operation Exception

ROUND.W.fmt

**Floating–Point Round to Single
Fixed–Point Format**

COP1 010001	fmt	0 00000	fs	fd	ROUND.W 001100
6	5	5	5	5	6

Format:

ROUND.W.fmt fd,fs

Description:

This instruction is not implemented on R2000/R3000 processors, and will cause the unimplemented operation exception to occur.

The contents of the floating-point register specified by *fs* are interpreted in the specified source format, *fmt*, and arithmetically converted to the single fixed-point format. The result is placed in the floating-point register specified by *fd*.

Regardless of the setting of the current rounding mode, the conversion is rounded as if the current rounding mode is round to nearest/even (0).

This instruction is valid only for conversion from a single or double precision floating-point formats. For R4000 and R6000 processors the operation is not defined if bit 0 of any register specification is set, since the register numbers specify an even-odd pair of adjacent coprocessor general registers.

When the source operand is an Infinity or NaN, or the correctly rounded integer result is outside of -2^{31} to $2^{31} - 1$, an Invalid operation exception is raised. If Invalid operation is not enabled then no exception is taken and $2^{31} - 1$ is returned.

Floating–Point Round to Single Fixed–Point Format (continued)

ROUND.W.fmt

R4000/R6000 Operation:

```
    T:    StoreFPR(fd, W, ConvertFmt(ValueFPR(fs, fmt), fmt, W))
```

Exceptions:

Coprocessor unusable exception
Coprocessor interrupt (R2000, R3000, and R6000) or Floating-Point Exception (R4000)

Coprocessor Exceptions:

Invalid operation exception
Unimplemented operation exception
Inexact exception
Overflow exception

SDC1

**Store Doubleword from FPU
(coprocessor 1)**

31 26	25 21	20 16	15 0
SDC1 1 1 1 1 0 1	base	ft	offset
6	5	5	16

Format:

SDC1 ft,offset(base)

Description:

This instruction causes a reserved instruction exception for R2000/R3000 processors.

The 16-bit *offset* is sign-extended and added to the contents of general register *base* to form a 32-bit unsigned effective address. For the R4000 and R6000, the contents of registers *ft* and *ft+1* from the floating-point coprocessor are stored at the memory location specified by the effective address.

If any of the three least significant bits of the effective address is non-zero, an address error exception takes place.

This instruction is not valid, and is undefined, when the least significant bit of *ft* is non-zero.

R4000/R6000 Operation:

```
T:    vAddr ← ((offset15)16 || offset15..0 ) + GPR[base]
      (pAddr, uncached) ← AddressTranslation (vAddr, DATA)
      if BigEndianCPU = 1 then
          StoreMemory (uncached, WORD, CPR[z, ft+1], pAddr+0, vAddr+0, DATA)
          StoreMemory (uncached, WORD, CPR[z, ft+0], pAddr+4, vAddr+4, DATA)
      else
          StoreMemory (uncached, WORD, CPR[z, ft+0], pAddr+0, vAddr+0, DATA)
          StoreMemory (uncached, WORD, CPR[z, ft+1], pAddr+4, vAddr+4, DATA)
      endif
```

Store Doubleword From FPU (continued)

SDC1

Exceptions:

Coprocessor unusable
TLB refill exception
TLB invalid exception
TLB modification exception
Bus error exception
Address error exception
Reserved instruction exception (R2000/R3000 only)

SQRT.fmt

Floating–Point Square Root

COP1 010001	fmt	ft	fs	fd	SQRT 000100
31 26 25	21 20 16	15 11	10 6	5	0
6	5	5	5	5	6

Format:

SQRT.fmt fd,fs,ft

Description:

This instruction is not implemented on R2000/R3000 processors, and will cause the unimplemented operation exception to occur.

The contents of the floating-point register specified by *fs* are interpreted in the specified *format* and the positive arithmetic square root is taken. The result is rounded as if calculated to infinite precision and then rounded to the specified *format*, according to the current rounding mode. If the value of *fs* corresponds to –0, the result will be –0. The result is placed in the floating-point register specified by *fd*

This instruction is valid only for single or double precision floating-point formats.

For R4000 and R6000 processors the operation is not defined if bit 0 of any register specification is set, since the register numbers specify an even-odd pair of adjacent coprocessor general registers.

R4000/R6000 Operation:

```
T:    StoreFPR(fd, fmt, SquareRoot(ValueFPR(fs, fmt)))
```

Exceptions:

Coprocessor unusable exception
Coprocessor interrupt (R2000, R3000, and R6000) or Floating-Point Exception (R4000)

Coprocessor Exceptions:

Unimplemented Operation Exception   Invalid Operation Exception
Inexact Exception

Floating–Point Subtract

SUB.fmt

COP1 010001	fmt	ft	fs	fd	SUB 000001
6	5	5	5	5	6

31   26 25   21 20   16 15   11 10   6 5   0

Format:

SUB.fmt   fd,fs,ft

Description:

The contents of the floating-point registers specified by *fs* and *ft* are interpreted in the specified *format* and arithmetically subtracted. The result is rounded as if calculated to infinite precision and then rounded to the specified *format*, according to the current rounding mode. The result is placed in the floating-point register specified by *fd*.

This instruction is valid only for single or double precision floating-point formats.

The operation is not defined if bit 0 of any register specification is set, since the register numbers specify an even-odd pair of adjacent coprocessor general registers.

Operation:

> T: StoreFPR (fd, fmt, ValueFPR(fs, fmt) – ValueFPR (ft, fmt))

Exceptions:

Coprocessor unusable exception
Coprocessor interrupt (R2000, R3000, and R6000) or Floating-Point Exception (R4000)

Coprocessor Exceptions:

Unimplemented Operation Exception
Invalid Operation Exception
Inexact Exception
Overflow Exception
Underflow Exception

SWC1

Store Word from FPU
(coprocessor 1)

SWC1 111001	base	ft	offset
31 26 25	21 20	16 15	0
6	5	5	16

Format:

SWC1 ft,offset(base)

Description:

The 16-bit *offset* is sign-extended and added to the contents of general register *base* to form a 32-bit unsigned effective address. The contents of register *ft* from the floating-point coprocessor are stored at the memory location specified by the effective address.

If either of the two least significant bits of the effective address are non-zero, an address error exception occurs.

Operation:

```
T:     vAddr ← ((offset₁₅)¹⁶ || offset₁₅..₀) + GPR[base]
       (pAddr, uncached) ← AddressTranslation (vAddr, DATA)
       data ← CPR[z, ft]
       StoreMemory (uncached, WORD, data, pAddr, vAddr, DATA)
```

Exceptions:

Coprocessor Unusable   TLB Refill Exception
TLB Invalid Exception   TLB Modification Exception
Bus Error Exception   Address Error Exception

Floating–Point Truncate to Single Fixed–Point Format

TRUNC.W.fmt

31	26 25	21 20	16 15	11 10	6 5 0
COP1	fmt	0	fs	fd	TRUNC.W
010001		00000			001101
6	5	5	5	5	6

Format:

TRUNC.W.fmt fd,fs

Description:

This instruction is not implemented on R2000/R3000 processors, and will cause the unimplemented operation exception to occur.

The contents of the FPU register specified by *fs* are interpreted in the specified source format, *fmt*, and arithmetically converted to the single fixed-point format. The result is placed in the FPU register specified by *fd*.

Regardless of the setting of the current rounding mode, the conversion is rounded as if the current rounding mode is round toward zero (1).

This instruction is valid only for conversion from a single or double precision floating-point formats. For R4000 and R6000 processors the operation is not defined if bit 0 of any register specification is set, since the register numbers specify an even-odd pair of adjacent coprocessor general registers.

When the source operand is an Infinity or NaN, or the correctly rounded integer result is outside of -2^{31} to $2^{31}-1$, an Invalid operation exception is raised. If Invalid operation is not enabled then no exception is taken and -2^{31} is returned.

TRUNC.W.fmt

Floating–Point Truncate to Single
Fixed–Point Format
(continued)

R4000/R6000 Operation:

T: StoreFPR(fd, W, ConvertFmt(ValueFPR(fs, fmt), fmt, W))

Exceptions:

Coprocessor unusable exception
Coprocessor interrupt (R2000, R3000, and R6000) or Floating-Point Exception (R4000)

Coprocessor Exceptions:

Invalid operation exception
Unimplemented operation exception
Inexact exception
Overflow exception

FPU Instruction Opcode Bit Encoding

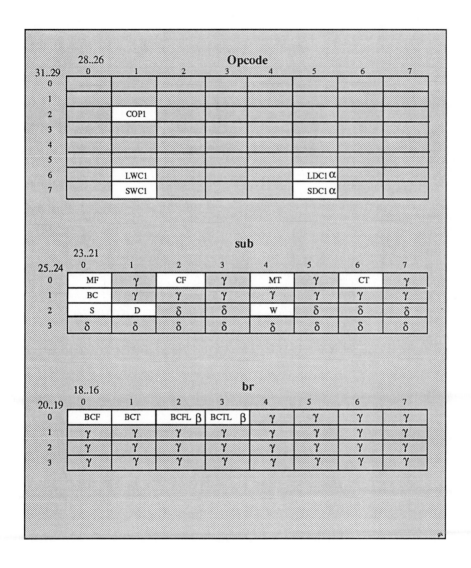

Figure B–3. Bit Encoding for FPU Instructions

5..3	2..0				function			
	0	1	2	3	4	5	6	7
0	ADD	SUB	MUL	DIV	SQRT α	ABS	MOV	NEG
1	δ	δ	δ	δ	ROUND	TRUNC	CEIL	FLOOR
2	δ	δ	δ	δ	δ	δ	δ	δ
3	δ	δ	δ	δ	δ	δ	δ	δ
4	CVT.S	CVT.D	δ	δ	CVT.W	δ	δ	δ
5	δ	δ	δ	δ	δ	δ	δ	δ
6	C.F	C.UN	C.EQ	C.UEQ	C.OLT	C.ULT	C.OLE	C.ULE
7	C.SF	C.NGLE	C.SEQ	C.NGL	C.LT	C.NGE	C.LE	C.NGT

Figure B–3. Bit Encoding for FPU Instructions (cont.)

Key:

α Operation codes marked with an alpha cause reserved instruction exceptions in R2000/R3000 implementations, and are valid for R4000/R6000 implementations.

β Operation codes marked with a beta are not valid for R2000/R3000 implementations, but are valid for R4000/R6000 implementations.

γ Operation codes marked with a gamma are not valid for R2000/R3000 implementations, and for R4000/R6000 implementations cause a reserved instruction exception. They are reserved for future versions of the architecture.

δ Operation codes marked with a delta cause unimplemented operation exceptions in all current implementations and are reserved for future versions of the architecture.

C
Machine Language
Programming Tips

Note: This section uses MIPS software conventions, that are specific to the MIPS assembler.

The MIPS RISC architecture provides an efficient, uniform, and streamlined instruction set to obtain maximum efficiency for the most commonly performed operations. As a result, some operations that require single, multi-cycle instructions in more traditional architectures, require multiple, single-cycle instructions in RISC architecture.

The architecture provides no condition code register containing status bits such as *Carry* and *Overflow*. Instead, the conditions generated by the Set instructions (SLT, SLTU) are loaded directly into a general-purpose register. This approach greatly simplifies handling the instruction pipeline and eases many compiler tasks, but does require programs to explicitly check for conditions such as overflow and carry.

This appendix describes techniques that implement the following operations:

- handling 32-bit addresses or constants
- implementing indexed addressing
- using the Jump Register (JR) instruction for subroutine returns
- jumping to 32-bit addresses
- branching on arithmetic comparisons
- filling the branch delay slot
- testing for overflow
- testing for carry
- performing multi-precision math

The MIPS assembly language supports many of the above functions (such as loading 32-bit addresses and branching on arithmetic comparisons) that are not directly implemented in machine language. It does this by using techniques similar to those described in this appendix. Refer to Appendix D for an overview of the MIPS assembly language.

In many of the following examples, a temporary register is used to hold intermediate results. In the following description, $at is used to represent that temporary register, and it is assumed that the register is reserved just for just this purpose and therefore does not conflict with anything else.

32-Bit Addresses or Constants

The ISA does not provide specific Load Address or Load Immediate instructions. (The MIPS assembly language does provide Load Address (LA) and Load Immediate (LI) instructions that are implemented using multiple machine language instructions. To load an address with relocatable code, it is necessary to use the assembler LA instruction.) Use the following two-instruction sequence to load any 32-bit pattern into a register:

```
lui  $destination, <upper 16 bits>
ori  $destination, <lower 16 bits>
```

There are three special cases that require only one instruction to obtain the desired 32-bit pattern:

- **Constants with the upper 16 bits set to 0.** Use the ORI instruction, which zero-extends the immediate field:

```
ori  $destination,$0,<lower 16 bits>
```

- **Constants with the upper 17 bits set to 1.** Use the low order 16 bits of the constant in the ADDI instruction, which sign-extends the immediate field:

```
addi $destination,$0,<lower 16 bits>
```

- **Constants with the lower 16 bits set to 0.** Use the high order 16 bits of the constant in the LUI instruction, which shifts its immediate field left by 16 bits, bringing in zeros on the right:

```
lui $destination,<upper 16 bits>
```

Indexed Addressing

The ISA provides only one addressing mode. This addressing mode sign-extends a 16-bit offset, adds it to the contents of a base register, and loads the destination (or stores the source) from (to) that memory address. The format for the Load Word (LW) instruction is:

```
lw $destination,<16-bit offset>($baseregister)
```

(The following examples use the LW instruction to illustrate various addressing modes; however the examples are equally valid for other load and store instructions.)

More general addressing modes can be simulated by using additional instructions. For example, if the offset exceeds 16 bits, use LUI and ADDIU to add the upper 16 bits to the base register and put the lower 16 bits into the *offset* field of the LW instruction. Thus, it is possible to implement:

```
lw $destination,<32-bit offset>($baseregister)
```

with:

```
lui  $at,<upper 16 bits adjusted>
addu $at,$at,$baseregister
lw   $destination,<lower 16 bits>($at)
```

Since the LW instruction sign-extends the lower 16 bits, it is necessary to add 1 to the upper 16 bits if the lower 16 bits appear to be a negative number — in other words, if a logical *AND* between the 32-bit constant and 0x8000 is non-zero. For example:

32-bit constant	upper 16 bits adjusted	lower 16 bits
0x04004000	0x0400	0x4000
0x04008000	0x0401	0x8000

The absence of a base register permits an even simpler instruction sequence, but still requires adjustment of the upper 16 bits. Thus, it is possible to implement:

```
lw $destination,<32-bit address>
```

with:

```
lui  $at,<upper 16 bits adjusted>
lw   $destination,<lower 16 bits>($at)
```

Subroutine Return Using Jump Register Instruction

The subroutine call instructions, JAL and JALR, put the return address into register $31. To return from a subroutine, use JR $31. If one subroutine must call another subroutine, the calling subroutine must save the value of $31 (on the stack, for example) before making the call, and restore the value of $31 upon return.

Jumping to 32-bit Addresses

The J and JAL instructions, which contain an immediate field, can actually jump only within a 2^{28}-bit segment because the instructions obtain the high order four bits from the current program counter. To jump to an arbitrary 32-bit address, load the desired address into a temporary register (using the load address technique described earlier in this chapter) and then use the Jump (J) instruction, as follows:

```
la        $at,foo
j         $at
```

Branching on Arithmetic Comparisons

The ISA provides a complete set of arithmetic comparisons against zero. (There are no instructions for BEQZ or BNEZ, but you can obtain the same effect by using register $0 — which always contains a value of zero — in the BEQ and BNE instructions). However, the only instructions for comparing a pair of registers are BEQ and BNE. To perform any other arithmetic comparison on a pair of registers or between a register and an immediate value, you must use a sequence of two instructions as listed in Tables C–1 and C–2.

Table C–1. Arithmetic Comparisons on Register Pairs

Desired Instruction	Equivalent Sequence
beq $a,$b,dest	beq $a,$b,dest
bne $a,$b,dest	bne $a,$b,dest
blt $a,$b,dest	slt $at,$a,$b; bne $at,$0,dest
ble $a,$b,dest	slt $at,$b,$a; beq $at,$0,dest
bgt $a,$b,dest	slt $at,$b,$a; bne $at,$0,dest
bge $a,$b,dest	slt $at,$a,$b; beq $at,$0,dest
bltu $a,$b,dest	sltu $at,$a,$b; bne $at,$0,dest
bleq $a,$b,dest	sltu $at,$b,$a; beq $at,$0,dest
bgtu $a,$b,dest	sltu $at,$b,$a; bne $at,$0,dest
bgeu $a,$b,dest	sltu $at,$a,$b; beq $at,$0,dest

Table C–2. Arithmetic Comparisons with Immediate Values

Desired Instruction	Equivalent Sequence
beq $a,i,dest	li $at,i; beq $a,$at,dest
bne $a,i,dest	li $at,i; bne $a,$at,dest
blt $a,i,dest	slti $at,$a,i; bne $at,$0,dest
ble $a,i,dest	slti $at,$a,i+1; bne $at,$0,dest
bgt $a,i,dest	slti $at,$a,i+1; beq $at,$0,dest
bge $a,i,dest	slti $at,$a,i; beq $at,$0,dest

The MIPS assembly language supports all of the branch instructions listed in Tables C–1 and C–2 by performing the equivalent two-instruction sequence.

Filling the Branch Delay Slot

You can sometimes save instructions by exploiting the knowledge that the instruction in the delay slot of a conditional branch will execute immediately after the comparison whether or not the branch is taken. For example, compare a straightforward implementation of "$6 = maximum($5,$4)" with a more complex one. The straightforward implementation takes seven instructions if you count the NOPs the assembler inserts to fill the branch delay slots:

```
       slt $at,$5,$4
       beq $at,$0,1f          # if $5 >= $4 ...
       # nop (inserted by assembler to fill delay slot)
       addu $6,$4,$0          # else move $4 to $6
       b 2f
       # nop (inserted by assembler to fill delay slot)
1:     addu $6,$5,$0          # then move $5 to $6
2:
```

A more complex version takes only four instructions. It is permissable to use the delay slot to move one value into $6 while the conditional branch is being evaluated, and then — if the branch is not taken — override it by moving the other value into $6 instead.

To put an instruction into the delay slot, temporarily set the assembler to No Reorder mode, so it does not fill the delay slot with a NOP:

```
       .set noreorder
       slt $at,$5,$4
       beq $at,$0,1f  # if $5 >= $4 ...
       addu $6,$5,$0  # move $5 to $6 while evaluating "beq"
       addu $6,$4,$0  # if branch not taken, move $4 to $6 instead
1:
       .set reorder
```

To implement minimum instead of maximum in the equation "$6 = maximum($5,$4)," swap $5 and $4 in the SLT instruction.

A similar example works for "$6 = abs($5)":

```
       .set noreorder
       bgtz $5,1f     # if $5 > 0 ...
       addu $6,$5,$0 # move $5 to $6 while evaluating "bgt"
       subu $6,$0,$6 # if branch not taken, negate $6
1:
       .set reorder
```

The following sequence — which appears equivalent — is not entirely foolproof, because it fails if the destination register is the same as the source, such as "$5 = abs($5)":

```
        .set noreorder
        bltz $5,1f      # if $5 < 0
        subu $6,$0,$5   # negate $5 into $6 while evaluating "blt"
        addu $6,$5,$0   # if branch not taken, move $5 to $6 instead
                        # (but if $5 and $6 were the same, the
                        # register would already have been negated)
1:
        .set reorder
```

Testing for Carry

The ISA does not provide a status bit to indicate whether an arithmetic operation results in a carry. Therefore, routines that require detection of a carry (or borrow) resulting from an addition (or subtraction) must explicitly test for their occurrence. This section provides examples of performing add-with-carry and subtract-with-borrow operations.

To perform an add-with-carry, a routine must first explicitly calculate whether the addition will result in a carry, and then record the occurrence of any carry in a register. When doing multiword additions, a test checks to see if there is a carry in, and then two different code sequences are used to add the words: one sequence for adding with a carry in and one sequence for adding without a carry in. Both sequences can calculate the carry out.

For example, the following sequence calculates whether the addition of A and B with no carry in results in a carry out:

```
# carryout from A + B
addu    temp,A,B
sltu    carryout,temp,B
```

If there is a carry in, the following sequence calculates whether the addition of A and B results in a carry out:

```
# carryout from A + B + 1
not     temp,A
sltu    carryout,B,temp
xor     carryout,1
```

The technique for performing subtract-with-borrow is quite similar. Again, two sequences calculate whether a subtraction results in a borrow; use the following sequence for the case where there is no borrow in:

```
# borrow out from A - B
sltu    borrow,A,B
```

This second routine is used for the case where there is a borrow in.

```
# borrow out from A - B - 1
sltu    borrow,B,A
xor     borrow,1
```

Testing for Overflow

The ISA does not provide a status bit to indicate whether an arithmetic operation resulted in an overflow. The signed Addition and Subtraction instructions (ADD and SUB) trap if an overflow occurs and implement overflow detection at no cost. However, if it is necessary to detect signed overflow without using traps, or to detect overflow for unsigned operations, the techniques described in this section can be used.

Figure C–1 provides examples of code that check for overflow for various arithmetic operations. These examples are based on the following simple rules for signed overflow:

- During addition, overflow occurs if the signs of the addends are the same and the sign of the sum is different.

- During subtraction, overflow occurs if the signs of the operands are not the same and the sign of the result is not the same as the sign of the minuend.

Signed Addition

```
/* compute t0 = t1 + t2, branch to L on signed overflow */
        addu    t0, t1, t2    /* compute sum */
        xor     t3, t1, t2    /* if operands have different signs */
        bltz    t3, 1f        /* then overflow not possible */
        /* t1 and t2 have same sign */
        xor     t3, t0, t1    /* if sum does not also have the same sign */
        bltz    t3, L         /* then addition overflowed */
        /* nop */
    1:
```

Signed Subtraction

```
/* compute t0 = t1 - t2, branch to L on signed overflow */
        subu    t0, t1, t2    /* compute difference */
        xor     t3, t1, t2    /* if operands have same signs */
        bgez    t3, 1f        /* then overflow not possible */
        /* t1 and t2 have different signs */
        xor     t3, t0, t1    /* if difference does not also have */
                              /* the same sign as the minuend */
        bltz    t3, L         /* then subtraction overflowed */
        /* nop */
    1:
```

Unsigned Addition

```
/* compute t0 = t1 + t2 , branch to L on unsigned overflow */
    addu    t0, t1, t2
    not     t3, t1
    sltu    t3, t3, t2
    bne     t3, 0, L
```

Unsigned Subtraction

```
/* compute t0 = t1 - t2, branch to L on unsigned overflow */
    subu t0, t1, t2
    sltu t3, t1, t2
    bne  t3, 0, L
```

Signed Multiplication

```
/* compute t0 = t1 * t2, branch to L on signed overflow */
    mult t1, t2
    mflo t0
    mfhi t3
    sra  t4, t0, 31
    bne  t4, t3, L
```

Unsigned Multiplication

```
/* compute t0 = t1 * t2, branch to L on unsigned overflow */
    multu t1, t2
    mflo  t0
    mfhi  t3
    bne   t3, 0, L           /* if HI ≠ 0 ,then multiplication overflowed */
```

Figure C–1. Calculating Overflow for Arithmetic Operations

Multi-Precision Math

Figure C–2 lists examples of routines that perform doubleword addition, subtraction, and multiplication. Figure C–3 lists an example of a routine that multiplies two 64-bit values to obtain a 128-bit result.

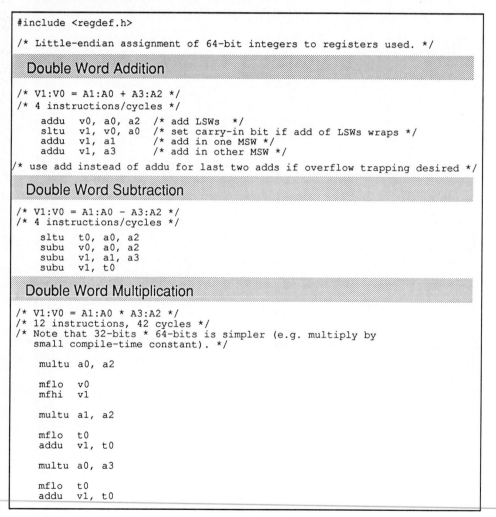

```
#include <regdef.h>

/* Little-endian assignment of 64-bit integers to registers used. */
```

Double Word Addition

```
/* V1:V0 = A1:A0 + A3:A2 */
/* 4 instructions/cycles */
      addu   v0, a0, a2   /* add LSWs  */
      sltu   v1, v0, a0   /* set carry-in bit if add of LSWs wraps */
      addu   v1, a1       /* add in one MSW */
      addu   v1, a3       /* add in other MSW */
/* use add instead of addu for last two adds if overflow trapping desired */
```

Double Word Subtraction

```
/* V1:V0 = A1:A0 - A3:A2 */
/* 4 instructions/cycles */
      sltu   t0, a0, a2
      subu   v0, a0, a2
      subu   v1, a1, a3
      subu   v1, t0
```

Double Word Multiplication

```
/* V1:V0 = A1:A0 * A3:A2 */
/* 12 instructions, 42 cycles */
/* Note that 32-bits * 64-bits is simpler (e.g. multiply by
   small compile-time constant). */

      multu  a0, a2

      mflo   v0
      mfhi   v1

      multu  a1, a2

      mflo   t0
      addu   v1, t0

      multu  a0, a3

      mflo   t0
      addu   v1, t0
```

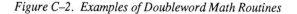

Figure C–2. Examples of Doubleword Math Routines

```
/* Multiply 64-bit integers in t5/t4 and t7/t6 to produce 128-bit
   product in t3/t2/t1/t0.  Little-endian register order.  Destroys contents of
   a3/a2.  t5/t4 and r7/t6 unchanged.  63 cycles. */

        multu  t4, t6      # x0 * y0

        mflo       t0      # lo(x0 * y0)
        mfhi   t1          # hi(x0 * y0)
        not    a3, t1

        multu  t5, t6      # x1 * y0

        mflo               # lo(x1 * y0)
        mfhi   t2          # hi(x1 * y0)
        sltu   a3, a3, a2  # carry(hi(x0 * y0) + lo(x1 * y0))
        addu   t1, a2      # hi(x0 * y0) + lo(x1 * y0)
        multu  t4, t7      # x0 * y1
        add    t2, a3      # hi(x1 * y0) + carry
        not    a3, t1

        mflo   a2          # lo(x0 * y1)
        mfhi   t3          # hi(x0 * y1)
        sltu   a3, a3, a2  # carry((hi(x0 * y0) + lo(x1 * y0)) + lo(x0 * y1))
        addu   t1, a2      # hi(x0 * y0) + lo(x1 * y0) + lo(x0 * y1)
        multu  t5, t7      # x1 * y1
        add    t2, a3      # hi(x1 * y0) + carry + carry
        not    a2, t2
        sltu   a2, a2, t3  # carry(hi(x1 * y0) + hi(x0 * y1))
        addu   t2, t3      # hi(x1 * y0) + hi(x0 * y1))
        not    a3, t2

        mfhi   t3          # hi(x1 * y1)
        add    t3, a2      # hi(x1 * y1) + carry(hi(x1 * y0) + hi(x0 * y1))
        mflo   a2          # lo(x1 * y1)
        sltu   a3, a3, a2  # carry((hi(x1 * y0) + hi(x0 * y1)) + lo(x1 * y1))
        add    t3, a3
        addu   t2, a2      # hi(x1 * y0) + hi(x0 * y1) + lo(x1 * y1)
```

Figure C–3. Example of 64-bit Multiplication Routine

Doubleword Shifts

Figure C–4 illustrates examples of routines performing doubleword shift operations where the shift count is determined by the contents of A2.

```
/* These routines can be significantly simplified if the
   shift count is known at compile-time. */
```

Doubleword Shift Left Logical

```
/* V1:V0 = A1:A0 << (A2 mod 64) */
        sll     t0, a2, 32-6
        bgez    t0, 1f
        sll     v1, a0, a2
        li      v0, 0
        b       3f
1:      sll     v1, a1, a2
        beq     t0, 0, 2f
        negu    t1, a2
        srl     t2, a0, t1
        or      v1, t2
2:      sll     v0, a0, a2
3:
```

Doubleword Shift Right Logical

```
/* V1:V0 = A1:A0 >> (A2 mod 64) */
        sll     t0, a2, 32-6
        bgez    t0, 1f
        srl     v0, a1, a2
        li      v1, 0
        b       3f
1:      srl     v0, a0, a2
        beq     t0, 0, 2f
        negu    t1, a2
        sll     t2, a1, t1
        or      v0, t2
2:      srl     v1, a1, a2
3:
```

Doubleword Shift Right Arithmetic

```
/* V1:V0 = A1:A0 >> (A2 mod 64) */
        sll     t0, a2, 32-6
        bgez    t0, 1f
        sra     v0, a1, a2
        sra     v1, a1, 31
        b       3f
1:      srl     v0, a0, a2
        beq     t0, 0, 2f
        negu    t1, a2
        sll     t2, a1, t1
        or      v0, t2
2:      sra     v1, a1, a2
3:
```

Figure C–4. Examples of Doubleword Shift Routines

D
Assembly Language Programming

This appendix provides an overview of the assembly language supported by the MIPS compiler system. The assembler converts assembly language statements into machine code. In most assembly languages, each instruction corresponds to a single machine instruction; however, some MIPS assembly language instructions can generate several machine instructions. This approach provides an assembler which generates optimized code for certain short sequences. It also results in assembly programs that can run without modification on future machines, which might have extended machine instructions. See the section, Basic Machine Definition, at the end of this appendix for more information about assembler instructions that generate multiple machine instructions.

Register Use and Linkage

This section describes the naming and usage conventions the assembler applies to the CPU and FPU registers.

General Registers

The CPU has 32 32-bit integer registers. Table D–1 summarizes the assembler usage conventions and restrictions for these registers. The assembler reserves all register names, which must be in lowercase characters. All register names start with a dollar sign ($).

The general registers have the names *$0..$31*. By including the file *regdef.h* (use *#include <regdef.h>*) in the program, software names can be used for some general registers. The operating system and the assembler use the general registers *$1, $26, $27, $28,* and *$29* for specific purposes. (Attempts to use these general registers in other ways can produce unexpected results.)

If a program uses the register names *$1, $26, $27, $28, $29* rather than the software names *$at, $kt0, $kt1, $gp, $sp* (as listed in Table D–1) respectively, the assembler issues warning messages.

Table D–1. General (Integer) Registers

Register Name	Software Name (from regdef.h)	Use and Linkage
$0		Always has the value 0
$at or $1		Reserved for the assembler
$2..$3	v0–v1	Used for expression evaluations and for hold integer function results. Also used to pass the static link when calling nested procedures.
$4..$7	a0–a3	Used to pass the first 4 words of integer type actual arguments; their values are not preserved across procedure calls
$8..$15	t0–t7	Temporary registers, used for expression evaluations; their values are not preserved across procedure calls.
$16..$23	s0–s7	Saved registers; their values must be preserved across procedure calls.
$24..$25	t8–t9	Temporary registers, used for expression evaluations; their values are not pre-served across procedure calls.
$26..$27 or $kt0..$kt1	k0–k1	Reserved for the operating system kernel
$28 or $gp	gp	Contains the global pointer
$29 or $sp	sp	Contains the stack pointer
$30	s8	A saved register (like s0–s7)
$31	ra	Contains the return address; used for expression evaluation.

General register *$0* always contains the value 0. All other general registers are equivalent with each other, except that general register *$31* also serves as the implicit link register for jump and link instructions. Table D–2 lists these special registers.

Special Registers

The CPU defines three special registers: *PC* (program counter), *HI* and *LO*. The *HI* and *LO* special registers hold the results of the multiplication (MULT and MULTU) and division (DIV and DIVU) instructions. These registers do not need to be referred to explicitly; instructions that use the special registers refer to them automatically. Table D–2 lists the special registers.

Table D–2. Special Registers

Name	Description
PC	Program Counter
HI	Multiply/Divide register higher word
LO	Multiply/Divide register lower word

Floating-Point Registers

The FPU has 16 floating-point registers. Each register can hold either a single precision (32-bit) or a double precision (64-bit) value. All references to these registers use an even register number (e.g., *$f4*). Table D–3 summarizes the assembler usage conventions and restrictions for these registers.

Table D–3. Floating-Point Registers

Register Name	Use and Linkage
$f0..f2	Used to hold floating-point type function results ($0) and complex type function results ($f0 has the real part, $f2 has the imaginary part.)
$f4..f10	Temporary registers, used for expression evaluation, whose values are not preserved across procedure calls.
$f12..$f14	Used to pass the first two single or double precision actual arguments, whose values are not preserved across procedure calls.
$f16..$f18	Temporary registers, used for expression evaluation, whose values are not preserved across procedure calls.
$f20..$f30	Saved registers, whose values must be preserved across procedure calls.

Assembly Language Instruction Summaries

Tables D–4 through D–9 summarize the assembly language instruction set. Most of the assembly language instructions have direct machine language equivalents; refer to Appendix A and Appendix B for detailed instruction descriptions. Assembler instructions marked with the hand symbol (☞) are synthesized by the assembler using one or more machine language instructions. Refer to the section, Basic Machine Definition, at the end of this appendix for a discussion of these instructions.

Table D–4. Operand Terms and Descriptions

Operand	Description
destination	destination register
address	*see the following section, Address*
source,src1,src2	source register(s)
dest–gpr	destination register (general purpose, not coprocessor)
src–gpr	source register (general purpose, not coprocessor)
destination/src1	single register serves as both source and destination
expression	absolute value
immediate	immediate value
label	symbol label
breakcode	value that determines the break

Table D–5. Load, Store, and Special Instruction Summary

	Description	Opcode	Operand
☞	Load Address	la	destination, address
	Load Byte	lb	
	Load Byte Unsigned	lbu	
	Load Halfword	lh	
	Load Halfword Unsigned	lhu	
	Load Word	lw	
	Load Word Left	lwl	
	Load Word Right	lwr	
☞	Load Immediate	li	destination, expression
	Load Upper Immediate	lui	
	Store Byte	sb	source, address
	Store Halfword	sh	
	Store Word	sw	
	Store Word Left	swl	
	Store Word Right	swr	
☞	Unaligned Load Halfword	ulh	
☞	Unaligned Load Halfword Unsigned	ulhu	
☞	Unaligned Load Word	ulw	
☞	Unaligned Store Halfword	ush	
☞	Unaligned Store Word	usw	
	Restore From Exception	rfe	
	Syscall	syscall	
	Break	break	breakcode
☞	No Operation	nop	

Table D–6. Computational Instruction Summary

Description	Opcode	Operand
☞ Absolute Value	**abs**	destination, src1
☞ Negate (with overflow)	**neg**	destination/src1
☞ Negate (without overflow)	**negu**	
☞ NOT	**not**	
Add (with overflow)	**add**	destination, src1, src2
Add (without overflow)	**addu**	destination/src1, src2
AND	**and**	destination, src1, immediate
☞ Divide (with overflow)	**div**	destination/src1, immediate
☞ Divide (without overflow)	**divu**	
EXCLUSIVE OR	**xor**	
☞ Multiply	**mul**	
☞ Multiply (with overflow)	**mulo**	
☞ Multiply (with overflow) Unsigned	**mulou**	
NOT OR	**nor**	
OR	**or**	
☞ Remainder	**rem**	
☞ Remainder Unsigned	**remu**	
☞ Rotate Left	**rol**	
☞ Rotate Right	**ror**	
☞ Set Equal	**seq**	
Set Less Than	**slt**	
Set Less Than Unsigned	**sltu**	
☞ Set Less/Equal	**sle**	
☞ Set Less/Equal Unsigned	**sleu**	
☞ Set Greater Than	**sgt**	
☞ Set Greater Than Unsigned	**sgtu**	
☞ Set Greater/Equal	**sge**	
☞ Set Greater/Equal Unsigned	**sgeu**	
☞ Set Not Equal	**sne**	
Shift Left Logical	**sll**	
Shift Right Arithmetic	**sra**	
Shift Right Logical	**srl**	
Subtract (with overflow)	**sub**	
Subtract (without overflow)	**subu**	
Multiply	**mult**	src1, src2
Multiply Unsigned	**multu**	

Table D–7. *Jump, Branch, and Coprocessor Instruction Summary*

Description	Opcode	Operand
Branch Branch Coprocessor z True Branch Coprocessor z False	**b** **bc**z**t** **bc**z**f**	label
Branch on Equal ☞ Branch on Greater ☞ Branch on Greater/Equal ☞ Branch on Greater/Equal Unsigned ☞ Branch on Greater Than Unsigned ☞ Branch on Less ☞ Branch on Less/Equal ☞ Branch on Less/Equal Unsigned ☞ Branch on Less Than Unsigned Branch on Not Equal	**beq** **bgt** **bge** **bgeu** **bgtu** **blt** **ble** **bleu** **bltu** **bne**	src1, src2, label src1, imediate, label
☞ Branch and Link	**bal**	label
Branch on Equal Zero Branch on Greater/Equal Zero Branch on Greater or Equal to Zero And Link Branch on Greater Than Zero Branch on Less/Equal Zero Branch on Less Than Zero Branch on Less Than Zero And Link Branch on Not Equal Zero	**beqz** **bgez** **bgezal** **bgtz** **blez** **bltz** **bltzal** **bnez**	src1, label
Jump Jump And Link	**j** **jal**	address src1
Coprocessor z Operation	**c**z	expression
☞ Move	**move**	destination, src1
Move From HI Register Move To HI Register Move From LO Register Move To LO Register	**mfhi** **mthi** **mflo** **mtlo**	register
Move From Coprocessor z Move To Coprocessor z	**mfc**z **mtc**z	dest–gpr, source src–gpr, destination
Load Coprocessor z Store Word Coprocessor z	**lwc**z **swc**z	
Control From Coprocessor z Control To Coprocessor z	**cfc**z **ctc**z	src–gpr, destination dest–gpr, source
Translation Lookaside Buffer Probe Translation Lookaside Buffer Read Translation Lookaside Buffer Write Random Translation Lookaside Write Index	**tlbp** **tlbr** **tlbwr** **tlbwi**	

Table D–8. Floating-Point Instruction Summary

Description	Opcode	Operand
Load Fp Double Single	l.d l.s	destination, address
Load Immediate Fp Double Single	li.d li.s	destination,floating point constant
Store Fp Double Single	s.d s.s	source, address
Move Fp Single Double	mov.s mov.d	destination, src1
Absolute Value Fp Double Single	abs.d abs.s	destination, src1
Add Fp Double Single **Divide Fp** Double Single **Multiply Fp** Double Single **Subtract Fp** Double Single	add.d add.s div.d div.s mul.d mul.s sub.d sub.s	destination, src1, src2
Convert Source to **Specified Precision Fp** Double to Single Fixed Point to Single Fixed Point to Double Single to Double Double to Fixed Point Single to Fixed Point	cvt.s.d cvt.s.w cvt.d.w cvt.d.s cvt.w.d cvt.w.s	destination, src2
Negate Floating Point Double Single	neg.d neg.s	destination, src2
Conditional Trap Trap if Equal Trap if Not Equal Trap if Less Than Trap if Less Than, Unsigned Trap if Greater Than or Equal Trap if Greater Than or Equal, Unsigned	teq tne tlt tltu tge tgeu	destination, src2

Table D–8. Floating-Point Instruction Summary (cont.)

Description	Opcode	Operand
Truncate and Round Operations		
Truncate to Single Fp	**trunc.w.s**	destination, src, gpr
Truncate to Double Fp	**trunc.w.d**	
Round to Single Fp	**round.w.s**	
Round to Double Fp	**round.w.d**	
Ceiling to Double Fp	**ceil.w.d**	
Ceiling to Single Fp	**ceil.w.s**	
Ceiling to Double Fp, Unsigned	**ceilu.w.d**	
Ceiling to Single Fp, Unsigned	**ceilu.w.s**	
Floor to Double Fp	**floor.w.d**	
Floor to Single Fp	**floor.w.s**	
Floor to Double Fp, Unsigned	**flooru.w.d**	
Floor to Single Fp, Unsigned	**flooru.w.s**	
Round to Double Fp, Unsigned	**roundu.w.d**	
Round to Single Fp, Unsigned	**roundu.w.s**	
Truncate to Double Fp, Unsigned	**truncu.w.d**	
Truncate to Single Fp, Unsigned	**truncu.w.s**	

Table D–9. Floating-Point Compare Instruction Summary

Description	Opcode	Operand
Compare Fp		
F Single	**c.f.s**	src1, src2
F Double	**c.f.d**	
UN Single	**c.un.s**	
UN Double	**c.un.d**	
*EQ Single	**c.eq.s**	
*EQ Double	**c.eq.d**	
UEQ Single	**c.ueq.s**	
UEQ Double	**c.ueq.d**	
OLT Single	**c.olt.s**	
OLT Double	**c.olt.d**	
ULT Single	**c.ult.s**	
ULT Double	**c.ult.d**	
OLE Single	**c.ole.s**	
OLE Double	**c.ole.d**	
ULE Single	**c.ule.s**	
ULE Double	**c.ule.d**	
SF Single	**c.sf.s**	
SF Double	**c.sf.d**	
NGLE Single	**c.ngle.s**	
NGLE Double	**c.ngle.d**	
SEQ Single	**c.deq.s**	
SEQ Double	**c.seq.d**	
NGL Single	**c.ngl.s**	
NGL Double	**c.ngl.d**	
*LT Single	**c.lt.s**	
*LT Double	**c.lt.d**	
NGE Single	**c.nge.s**	
NGE Double	**c.nge.d**	
*LE Single	**c.le.s**	
*LE Double	**c.le.d**	
NGT Single	**c.ngt.s**	
NGT Double	**c.ngt.d**	

*These are the most common compare instructions. The other Compare instructions are provided for IEEE compatibility.

Addressing

This section describes the formats that you can use to specify addresses. The machine uses a byte-addressing scheme; access to halfwords requires alignment on even byte boundaries, and access to words requires alignment on byte boundaries that are divisible by four. Any attempt to address a data item that does not have the proper alignment causes an alignment exception.

The unaligned assembler load and store instructions can generate multiple machine language instructions, and do not raise alignment exceptions.

The following instructions load and store unaligned data:

- Load Word Left (LWL)
- Load Word Right (LWR)
- Store Word Left (SWL)
- Store Word Right (SWR)
- Unaligned Load Word (ULW)
- Unaligned Load Halfword (ULH)
- Unaligned Store Halfword (USH)
- Unaligned Store Word (USW)
- Unaligned Load Halfword Unsigned (ULHU)

These instructions load and store aligned data:

- Load Word (LW)
- Load Halfword (LH)
- Load Halfword Unsigned (LHU)
- Load Byte (LB)
- Load Byte Unsigned (LBU)
- Store Word (SW)
- Store Halfword (SH)
- Store Byte (SB)

Address Formats

The CPU supports only one addressing mode — base register plus a signed 16-bit offset. The assembler, however, synthesizes some additional addressing modes to present more traditional addressing capabilities to the assembly language programmer. The assembler accepts the formats for addresses listed in Table D–10.

Table D–10. Address Formats.

Format	Address
(base register)	base address (zero offset assumed)
expression	absolute address
expression (base register)	based address
relocatable symbol	relocatable address
relocatable symbol ± expression	relocatable address
relocatable symbol ± expression (index register)	indexed relocatable address

Each of these addressing formats is described in Table D–11.

Table D–11. Address Descriptions

Expression	Address Description
(base register)	Specifies an indexed address, which assumes a zero offset. The base register contents specify the address.
expression	Specifies an absolute address. The assembler generates the most locally efficient code for referencing a value at the specified address.
expression (base register)	Specifies a based address. To get the address, the machine adds the value of the expression to the contents of the base register.
relocatable symbol	Specifies a relocatable address. The assembler generates the necessary instruction(s) to address the item and generates relocatable information for the link editor.
relocatable symbol ± expression	Specifies a relocatable address. To get the address, the assembler adds or subtracts the value of the expression, which has an absolute value, from the relocatable symbol. The assembler generates the necessary instruction(s) to address the item and generates relocatable information for the link editor. If the symbol name does not appear as a label anywhere in the assembly, the assembler assumes that the symbol is external.
relocatable symbol (index register)	Specifies an indexed relocatable address. To get the address, the machine adds the index register to the relocatable symbol address. The assembler generates the necessary instruction(s) to address the item and generates relocatable information for the link editor. If the symbol name does not appear as a label anywhere in the assembly, the assembler assumes that the symbol is external.
relocatable symbol ± expression (index register)	
	Specifies an indexed relocatable address. To get the address, the assembler adds or subtracts the relocatable symbol, the expression, and the contents of the index register. The assembler generates the necessary instruction(s) to address the item and generates relocation information for the link editor. If the symbol does not appear as a label anywhere in the assembly, the assembler assumes that the symbol is external.

Pseudo Opcodes

Table D–12 lists the keywords that describe pseudo opcodes (directives). These pseudo opcodes influence later behavior of the assembler. **Boldface** type specifies a keyword and *italics* represents a user-defined operand.

Table D–12. Pseudo Opcodes

Pseudo Op	Description
.aent name, symno	Sets an alternative entry point for the current procedure. Use this information when you want to generate information for the debugger. It must appear inside an **.ent/.end** pair.
.alias *gpreg,gpreg*	Indicates memory reference through which the two registers overlap. The compiler uses this form to improve instruction scheduling.
.align *expression*	Advance the location counter to make the *expression* low order bits of the counter zero.
	Normally, the **.half, .word, .float,** and **.double** directives automatically align their data appropriately. For example, **.word** does an implicit **.align 2** (**.double** does an **.align 3**). You disable the automatic alignment feature with **.align 0**. The assembler reinstates automatic alignment at the next **.text, .data, .rdata,** or **.sdata** directive.
	Labels immediately preceding an automatic or explicit alignment are also realigned. For example, **foo: .align 3; .word 0** is the same as **.align; foo: .word 0**.
.ascii *string [, string]*...	Assembles each *string* from the list into successive locations. The **.ascii** directive does not null pad the string. You must put quotation marks (") around each string, and can use the C language backslash escape characters.
asciiz *string [, string]*...	Assembles each *string* in the list into successive locations and adds a null. You can use the C language backslash escape characters.
.asm0	(For use by compilers.) Tells the assembler second pass that this assembly came from the assembler first pass.
.bgnb *symno*	(For use by compilers.) Sets the beginning of a language block. The **.bgnb** and **.endb** directives delimit the scope of a variable set. The scope can be an entire procedure, or it can be a nested scope (for example a "{}" block in the C language). The symbol number *symno* refers to a dense number in a **.T** file. To set the end of a language block, see **.endb**.
.byte *expression1 [, expression2]...[, expressionN]*	Truncates the *expressions* from the comma-separated list to 8-bit values, and assembles the values in successive locations. The *expressions* must be absolute. The operands can optionally have the form: *expressionVal : expressionRep*. The *expressionRep* replicates the *expressionVal* value *expressionRep* times.

Table D–12. Pseudo Opcodes (cont.)

Pseudo Op	Description
.comm *name, expression*	Unless defined elsewhere, *name* becomes a global common symbol at the head of a block of *expression* bytes of storage. The linker overlays like-named common blocks, using the maximum *expressions*.
.data	Tells the assembler to add all subsequent data to the **data** section.
.double *expression [, expression2] ...[, expressionN]*	Initializes memory to 64-bit floating-point numbers. The operands can optionally have the form: *expressionVal* [: *expressionRep*]. *expressionVal* is the floating-point value. Optional *expressionRep* is a non-negative expression that specifies a repetition count. *expressionRep* replicates the *expressionVal* value *expressionRep* times. This directive automatically aligns its data and any preceding labels to a doubleword boundary. You can disable this feature by using **.align 0**.
.end *[proc_name]*	Sets the end of a procedure. Use this directive to generate information for the debugger. To set the beginning of a procedure, see **.ent**.
.endb *symno*	(For use by compilers.) Sets the end of a language block. To set the beginning of a language block, see **.bgnb**.
.endr	Signals the end of a repeat block. To start a repeat block, see **.repeat**.
.ent *proc_name*	Sets the beginning of the procedure *proc_name*. Use this directive when you want to generate information for the debugger. To set the end of a procedure, see **.end**.
.extern *name expression*	*name* is a global undefined symbol whose size is assumed to be *expression* bytes. The advantage of using this directive, instead of permitting an undefined symbol to become global by default, is that the assembler can decide whether to use the economical *$gp*-relative addressing mode, depending on the value of the –G option. As a special case, if *expression* is zero, the assembler refrains from using *$gp* to address this symbol regardless of the size specified by –G.
.err	(For use by compilers.) Signals an error. Any compiler front-end that detects an error condition puts this directive in the input stream. When the assembler encounters a **.err**, it quietly ceases to assemble the source file. This prevents the assembler from continuing to process a program that is incorrect.

Table D–12. Pseudo Opcodes (cont.)

Pseudo Op	Description
.file *file_number file_name_string*	(For use by compilers.) Specifies the source file corresponding to the assembly instructions that follow. For use only by compilers, not by programmers; when the assembler sees this, it refrains from generating line numbers for dbx to use unless it also sees the *.loc* directives.
.float *expression1 [, expression2]... [, expressionN]*	Initializes memory to single precision 32-bit floating-point numbers. The operands can optionally have the form: *expressionVal* [: *expressionRep*]. Optional *expressionRep* is a non-negative expression that specifies a repetition count. This optional form replicates the *expressionVal* value *expressionRep* times. This directive automatically aligns its data and preceding labels to a word boundary. You can disable this feature by using **.align 0**.
.fmask *mask, offset*	(For use by compilers.) Sets a mask with a bit turned on for each floating-point register that the current routine saved. The least significant bit corresponds to register *$f0*. The offset is the distance in bytes from the virtual frame pointer at which the floating-point registers are saved. The assembler saves higher register numbers closer to the virtual frame pointer. You must use **.ent** before **.fmask** and only one **.fmask** can be used per **.ent**. Space should be allocated for those registers specified in the **.fmask**.
.frame *frame register, offset, return_pc_register*	Describes a stack frame. The first register is the frame register; offset is the distance from the frame register to the virtual frame pointer; the second register is the return program counter (or, if the first register is *$0*, this directive shows that the return program counter is saved 4 bytes from the virtual frame pointer). You must use **.ent** before **.frame** and only one **.frame** can be used per **.ent**. No stack traces can be done in the debugger without **.frame**.
.galive	Sets the default masks for live registers before a procedure call (a JAL instruction).
.globl *name*	Makes *name* external. If *name* is otherwise defined (by its appearance as a label), the assembler exports the symbol; otherwise, it imports the symbol. In general, the assembler imports undefined symbols (that is, it gives them the UNIX storage class "global undefined" and requires the linker to resolve them).
.gjaldef	Sets the masks defining the registers whose value is preserved during a procedure call.
.gjrlive	Sets the default masks for live registers before a procedure return (a JR instruction).

Table D–12. Pseudo Opcodes (cont.)

Pseudo Op	Description
.half *expression1* [, *expression2*] ... [, *expressionN*]	Truncates *expression*(s) in the comma-separated list to 16-bit values and assembles the values in successive locations. *expression*(s) must be absolute. Optionally, this directive can have the form: *expression-Val* [: *expressionRep*]. *expressionRep* replicates the *expressionVal* value *expressionRep* times. This directive automatically aligns its data appropriately. Disable this feature by using **.align 0**.
.lab *label_name*	(For use by compilers). Associates a named label with the current location in the program text.
.lcomm *name, expression*	Makes *name* data type **bss**. The assembler allocates the named symbol to the **bss** area, and the expression defines the length of the named symbol. If a **.globl** directive also specifies *name*, the assembler allocates the named symbol to external **bss**. The assembler puts **bss** symbols in one of two **bss** areas. If the defined size is smaller than the size specified by the assembler or the compiler –G command line option, the assembler puts the symbols in the **sbss** area and uses *$gp* to address the data.
.livereg *int_bitmask fp_bitmask*	Affects the next jump instruction even if it is not the successive instruction. By default, external J and JR instructions are treated as external calls through any register other than *$ra*; that is, all registers are assumed live. The directive **.livereg** cannot appear before an external J *(*it will affect the next JR, JAL, or SYSCALL instead of the J instruction). **.livereg** can appear before a JR instruction through a register other than *$ra*. The directive can not be used before a BREAK instruction; for BREAK instructions, the assembler assumes all registers are live.
	.livereg indicates to the assembler which registers are live before a jump, to avoid unsafe optimizations by the reorganizer. The directive **.livereg** takes two arguments, *int_bitmask*, and *fp_bitmask*, which are 32-bit bitmasks with a bit turned on for each register that is live before a jump. The most significant bit corresponds to register *$0* (which is opposite to that used in other assembly directives, **.mask**, **.fmask**). The first bitmap indicates live integer registers and the second indicates live FPU registers.
	When present, this directive causes the assembler to be more conservative so it does not destroy the indicated register contents. If omitted, the assembler assumes the default masks. The **.livereg** directive can come before any of the following instructions: JAL, JR, and SYSCALL. All bitmasks have a bit turned on for each register indicated. The most significant bit corresponds to register *$0*. The first bitmap indicates the integer registers and the second indicates the FPs.

Table D–12. Pseudo Opcodes (cont.)

Pseudo Op	Description
.loc *file_number line_number*	(For use by compilers). Specifies the source file and the line within that file that corresponds to the assembly instructions which follow. The assembler ignores the file number when this directive appears in the assembly source file. Then, the assembler assumes that the directive refers to the most recent **.file** directive. When a **.loc** directive appears in the binary assembly language **.G** file, the file number is a dense number pointing at a file symbol in the symbol table **.T** file.
.mask *mask, offset*	(For use by compilers.) Sets a mask with a bit turned on for each general purpose register that the current routine saved. Bit 1 corresponds to register *$1*. The offset is the distance in bytes from the virtual frame pointer where the registers are saved. The assembler saves higher register numbers that are closer to the the virtual frame pointer. Space should be allocated for those registers appearing in the mask. If bit 0 is set, it is assumed that space is allocated for all 31 registers regardless of whether they appear in the mask.
.noalias *reg1, reg2*	*register1* and *register2*, when used as indexed registers to memory, never point to the same memory. The assembler uses this as a hint to make more liberal assumptions about resource dependency in the program.
nop	Tells the assembler to put in an instruction that has no effect on the machine state (the recommended NOP is SLL R0,R0,0 — which is what the assembler uses). While several instructions cause No Operation, the assembler only considers the ones generated by the NOP directive to be wait instructions. This directive puts an explicit delay in the instruction stream. **Note:** Unless you use ''.set noreorder'', the reorganizer can eliminate unnecessary NOP instructions.
.option *options*	(For use by compilers). Tells the assembler that certain options were in effect during compilation. (These options can, for example, limit the freedom of the assembler to perform branch optimizations.) This option is intended for compiler-generated **.s** files rather than for hand-coded ones.
.repeat *expression*	Repeats all instructions or data between the **.repeat** directive and the **.endr** directive. *expression* defines how many times the data repeats. With the **.repeat** directive, you cannot use labels, branch instructions, or values that require relocation in the block. To end a **.repeat**, see **.endr**.

Table D–12. Pseudo Opcodes (cont.)

Pseudo Op	Description
.rdata	Tells the assembler to add subsequent data into the **rdata** section.
.sdata	Tells the assembler to add subsequent data to the **sdata** section.
.set *option*	Instructs the assembler to enable or to disable certain options. Use set options only for hand-crafted assembly routines. The assembler has these default options: **reorder, macro,** and **at.** You can specify only one option for each **.set** directive. You can specify these **.set** options:

- The **reorder** option lets the assembler reorder machine language instructions to improve performance.

- The **noreorder** option prevents the assembler from reordering machine language instructions. If a machine language instruction violates the hardware pipeline constraints, the assembler issues a warning message.

- The **bopt/nobopt** option lets the assembler perform branch optimization. This involves moving an instruction that is the target of a branch or jump instruction into the delay slot; this is performed only if no unpredictable side effects can occur.

- The **macro** option lets the assembler generate multiple machine instructions from a single assembler instruction.

- The **nomacro** option causes the assembler to print a warning whenever an assembler operation generates more than one machine language instruction. You must select the **noreorder** option before using the **nomacro** option; otherwise, an error results.

- The **at** option lets the assembler use the *$at* register for macros, but generates warnings if the source program uses *$at*.

- When you use the **noat** option and an assembler operation requires the *$at* register, the assembler issues a warning message; however, the **noat** option does let source programs use *$at* without issuing warnings.

- The **move/nomove** option is now obsolete.

- The **volatile/nonvolatile** options are used to inform the assembler that subsequent memory locations can be altered by means other than those present in the current program. The **volatile** option ensures that memory references are not reordered or defeated by assembler optimization. The default option is **nonvolatile**.

Table D–12. Pseudo Opcodes (cont.)

Pseudo Op	Description
.space *expression*	Advances the location counter by the value of the specified *expression* bytes. The assembler fills the space with zeros.
.struct *expression*	This permits you to lay out a structure using labels plus directives like **.word**, **.byte**, and so forth. It ends at the next segment directive (**.data**, **.text**, etc.). It does not emit any code or data, but defines the labels within it to have values that are the sum of *expression* plus their offsets from **.struct** itself.
(symbolic equate)	Takes one of these forms: *name = expression* or *name = register*. You must define the name only once in the assembly, and you CANNOT re-define the name. The expression must be computable when you assemble the program, and the expression must involve operators, constants, and equated symbols. You can use the name as a constant in any later statement.
.text	Tells the assembler to add subsequent code to the **text** section. (This is the default.)
.verstamp *major minor*	(For use by compilers.) Specifies the major and minor version numbers (for example, version 0.15 would be **.verstamp 0 15**).
.vreg *register offset symno*	(For use by compilers.) Describes a register variable by giving the offset from the virtual frame pointer and the symbol number *symno* (the dense number) of the surrounding procedure.

.weakext	This directive defines a weak external name, and accepts the following syntax:
	    .weakext weak_name ',' strong_name
	    .weakext weak_name ' ' strong_name
	    .weakext weak_name
	
	If the second parameter is provided, the **weak_name** is equivalent to the strong_name.

.word *expression1* [, *expression2*] ... [, *expressionN*]	Truncates *expression*(s) in the comma-separated list to 32 bits and assembles the values in successive locations. *expression*(s) must be absolute. The operands can optionally have the form: *expressionVal* [: *expressionRep*]. *expressionRep* replicates the *expressionVal* value *expressionRep* times. This directive automatically aligns its data and preceding labels to a word boundary. You can disable this feature by using **.align 0**.

Linkage Conventions

This section gives rules and examples to follow when designing an assembly language program. When you write assembly language routines, follow the same calling conventions that the compilers observe. First, your code must interact with compiler-generated code, accepting and returning arguments or accessing shared global data. Second, the symbolic debugger gives better assistance in debugging programs using standard calling conventions.

The conventions for the MIPS compiler system are a bit more complicated than some. This complexity is needed mostly to enhance the speed of each procedure call, specifically:

- The compilers use the full, general calling sequence only when necessary; where possible, they omit unneeded portions of it. For example, the compilers avoid using a separate register as a frame pointer whenever possible.

- The compilers and debugger observe certain implicit rules rather than communicating by instructions or data at execution time. For example, the debugger looks at information placed in the symbol table by a **.frame** directive at compilation time, so it can tolerate the lack of a register containing a frame pointer at execution time.

Program Design

This section describes two general areas of concern to the assembly language programmer: stack frame requirements on entering and exiting a routine, and register usage and restrictions.

Stack Frame

The compilers classify each routine into one of the following categories:

- nonleaf routines,which are routines that call some other routines

- leaf routines, which are routines that do not execute any procedure calls.

There are two types of leaf routines: those that require stack storage for local variables, and those that do not.

You must decide the category of routine before determining the calling sequence.

To write a program with proper stack frame usage and debugging capabilities, use the following procedure:

1. (*Prolog*):
   Regardless of the routine type, include a **.ent** pseudo opcode and an entry label for the procedure. The **.ent** pseudo opcode is for use by the debugger, and the entry label is the procedure name. The syntax is:

   ```
   .ent procedure_name
   procedure_name:
   ```

2. If you are writing a leaf procedure that does not use the stack, skip to step 3. For a leaf procedure that uses the stack or for nonleaf procedures, allocate all the stack space that the routine requires. The syntax to adjust the stack size is:

   ```
   subu $sp, framesize
   ```

where *framesize* is the size of frame required; *framesize* must be a multiple of 8. Space must be allocated for:

- Local variables

- Saved general registers. Space should be allocated only for the registers that are saved. For nonleaf procedures, save *$31*, which is used in the calls to other procedures from this routine. If you use registers *$16–$23* or *$30*, save them also.

- Saved floating-point registers. Space should be allocated only for the registers that are saved. If you use registers *$f20–$f30,* save them also.

- Procedure call argument area. Allocate the maximum number of bytes for arguments of any procedure that you call from this routine.

Note: Once you have modified *$sp,* you should not modify it again for the rest of the routine (unless you are using a nonvirtual frame pointer).

3. Now include a **.frame** pseudo opcode:

   ```
   .frame    framereg,framesize,returnreg
   ```

The virtual frame pointer is like a frame pointer used in other compiler systems, but it has no allocated register. It consists of the *framereg* (*$sp*, in most cases) added to the *framesize* (see step 2 above). Figure D–1 illustrates the stack components.

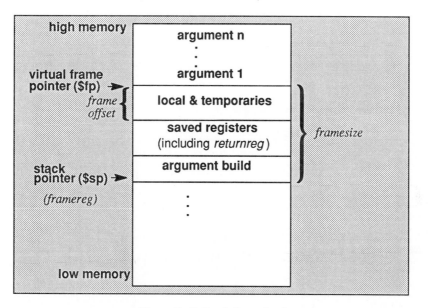

Figure D–1 Stack Organization

The *returnreg* specifies the register the return address is in (usually *$31*). These usual values can change if you use a varying stack pointer or are specifying a kernel trap routine.

4. If the procedure is a leaf procedure that does not use the stack, skip to step 5. Otherwise you must save the registers for which you allocated space in step 2.

   To save the general registers, use the following operations:

   ```
   .mask      bitmask,frameoffset
   sw         reg,framesize+frameoffset-N($sp)
   ```

   The **.mask** directive specifies the registers to be stored and where they are stored. A bit should be on in *bitmask* for each register saved. For example, if register *$31* is saved, bit 31 should be set to 1 in *bitmask*. Bits are set in bitmask in Little Endian order, even if the machine configuration is Big Endian. The *frameoffset* is the offset from the virtual frame pointer (this number is usually negative). *N* should be 0 for the highest numbered register saved and then incremented by four for each subsequent lower numbered register saved.

For example:

```
sw    $31,framesize+frameoffset($sp)
sw    $17,framesize+frameoffset-4($sp)
sw    $16,framesize+frameoffset-8($sp)
```

Figure D–2 illustrates this example.

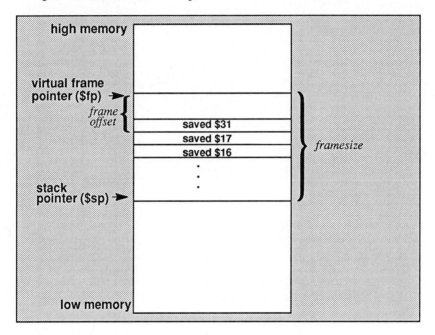

Figure D–2. Stack Example

Now save any floating-point registers for which you allocated space in step 2 as follows:

```
.fmask      bitmask,frameoffset
s.d         reg,framesize+frameoffset-N($sp)
```

Notice that saving floating-point registers is identical to saving general registers except we use the **.fmask** pseudo opcode instead of **.mask,** and the stores are of floating-point doubles. The discussion regarding saving general registers (step 2) applies here as well, but remember that *N* should be incremented by 8 for doublewords.

5. This step describes parameter passing: a detailed description is contained at the end of this procedure.

   As specified in step 2, space must be allocated on the stack for all arguments even though they can be passed in registers; space must also be allocated for at least four words, even if fewer parameters are passed. This provides a saving area if their registers are needed for other variables.

   The first argument is allocated as follows:

   - an initial double precision floating-point argument is allocated into *$f12*; *$4* and *$5* are marked as unavailable.

   - an initial single precision floating-point argument is allocated into *$f12*; *$4* is marked as unavailable.

   - an initial structure argument is allocated into *$4*, *$5*, *$6*, and *$7*, as needed; if the structure is larger than four words, the remainder goes onto the stack.

   - an initial argument of all other types (namely scalars) is allocated to *$4*.

   - all registers used are marked unavailable.

   Subsequent arguments are passed on the stack.

   Table D–13 offers a representative list of register assignments; **d** indicates double precision and **s** indicates single precision.

Table D–13. Register Assignments

Arguments	Register Assignments
(f1, f2, ...)	f1 –> $f12, f2 –> $f14
(f1, n1, f2, ...)	f1 –> $f12, n1 –> $6, f2 –> stack
(f1, n1, n2, ...)	f1 –> $f12, n1 –> $6, n2 –> $7
(n1, n2, n3, n4, ...)	n1 –> $4, n2 –> $5, n3 –> $6, n4 –> $7
(n1, n2, n3, f1, ...)	n1 –> $4, n2 –> $5, n3 –> $6, f1 –> stack
(n1, n2, f1, ...)	n1 –> $4, n2 –> $5, f1 –> ($6, $7)
(n1, f1, ...)	n1 –> $4, f1 –> ($6, $7)
(d1, d2, ...)	d1–>$f12, d2–>$f14
(s1, s2, s3, s4, ...)	s1–>$f12, s2–>$f14, s3–>$6, s4–>$7
(s1, n1, s2, n2, ...)	s1–>$f12, n1–>$5, s2–>$f14, n2–>$6
(d1, s1, s2,...)	d1–>$f12, s1–>$f14, s2–>$7
(s1, s2, d1,...)	s1–>$f12, s2–>$f14, d1–>($6,$7)
(n1, s1, n2, s2, ...)	n1–>$4, s1–>$5, n2–>$6, s2–>$7
(n1, s1, n2, n3, ...)	n1–>$4, s1–>$5, n2–>$6, n3–>$7
(n1, n2, s1, n3, ...)	n1–>$4, n2–>$5, s1–>$6, n3–>$7

6. (*Epilog*):
   Restore registers that were saved in step 4. To restore general purpose registers:

   ```
   lw          reg,framesize+frameoffset-N($sp)
   ```

   To restore floating-point registers:

   ```
   l.d  reg,framesize+frameoffset-N($sp)
   ```

   (Refer to step 4 for a discussion of the value of *N*.)

7. Get the return address:

   ```
   lw   $31,framesize+frameoffset($sp)
   ```

8. Clean up the stack:

   ```
   addu $sp, framesize
   ```

9. Return:

   ```
   j    $31
   ```

10. End the procedure:

    ```
    .end procedurename
    ```

Notes on Parameter Passing (Step 5): General registers *$4–$7* and floating-point registers *$f12*, *$f14* must be used for passing the first two arguments (if possible). Even if it's a single precision argument, you must allocate a pair of registers (that start with an even register) for floating-point arguments appearing in registers.

In Table D–13, the *fN* arguments are considered single or double precision floating-point arguments, and n*N* arguments are everything else. The ellipses (...) mean that the rest of the arguments do not go into registers regardless of their type. The *stack* assignment indicates not to put this argument into a register. The register assignments occur in the order shown, to satisfy optimizing compiler protocols.

There are four integer registers *$4* through *$7*, and two floating-point registers, *$f12* and *$f14*. *$f12* and *$f14* can be used for single or double precision floating-point values. The calling sequence passes the first four words of arguments (including gaps to satisfy alignments) in registers *$4–$7* respectively, except in the following cases:

- the first argument is passed in *$f12* if it is a single or a double.

- the second argument is passed in *$f14* if it is a single or a double and the first argument is passed in *$f12*.

When arguments are passed in floating-point registers, the corresponding integer registers are unused.

In determining into which register, if any, an argument goes, the following considerations must be made:

- Promotion. Some data types are promoted to other data types. In C, the default promotions are **(char, short) –> int**, and **float –> double**. In the presence of a prototype, a float argument and a matching float parameter are unpromoted.

- Returning a structure. If the called function returns a structure, the compiler inserts an invisible argument before the first user argument; this argument is the pointer to the structure for return. This argument then becomes the first argument for the purposes of register allocation, and all user argument positions are shifted down by one.

- Argument list. An argument list is a structure containing all the arguments, aligned according to normal structure rules, after promotion and structure return pointer insertion. In variable argument lists, arguments corresponding to the variable part of the parameters are stored into the integer registers, if possible. Mapping of structure into the combination of stack and registers is as follows: up to two leading floating-point (but not *stdarg*) arguments are mapped to *$f12* and *$f14*; everything else with a structure offset greater than or equal to 16 is mapped to stack; the remainder of the arguments are mapped to *$4*, *$5*, *$6*, and *$7* based on their structure offset. Holes left in the structure for alignment are unused, whether in registers or in the stack

- Nonfloating argument. When the first argument is nonfloating, the remaining arguments are stored into the integer registers, if possible.

- Structures. Structures are passed as if they are very wide integers, taking an amount of words equal to their size. A structure can be split into a portion that is passed in registers, with the remainder on the stack.

- Unions. Unions are considered as structures.

Examples

This section contains examples that illustrate program design rules; each example shows a procedure written in the C language and its equivalent written in assembly language.

Figure D–3 shows a nonleaf procedure. Notice that it creates a stackframe and also saves its return address since it must put a new return address into register *$31* when it invokes its callee.

```
float
nonleaf(i, j)
  int i, *j;
  {
  double atof();
  int temp;

  temp = i - *j;
  if (i < *j) temp = -temp;
  return atof(temp);
  }
          .globl   nonleaf          ## define nonleaf as external
#   1    float
#   2    nonleaf(i, j)
#   3      int i, *j;
#   4      {
          .ent     nonleaf          ## tell debugger this starts nonleaf
nonleaf:                            ## this is the entry point
          subu     $sp, 24          ## Create stackframe
          sw       $31, 20($sp)     ## Save the return address
          .mask    0x80000000, -4   ## only $31 was saved at ($sp)+24-4
          .frame   $sp, 24, $31     ## define frame size, return reg.
#   5      double atof();
#   6      int temp;
#   7
#   8      temp = i - *j;
          lw       $2, 0($5)        ## Arguments are in $4 and $5
          subu     $3, $4, $2
#   9      if (i < *j) temp = -temp;
          bge      $4, $2, $32      ## Note: $32 is a label, not a register
          negu     $3, $3
$32:10
          return atof(temp);
          move     $4, $3
          jal      atof
          cvt.s.d  $f0, $f0         ## Return value goes in $f0
          lw       $31, 20($sp)     ## Restore return address
          addu     $sp, 24          ## Delete stackframe
          j        $31              ## Return to caller
          .end     nonleaf          ## Mark end of nonleaf
```

Figure D–3. Nonleaf Procedure

Figure D–4 shows a leaf procedure that does not require stack space for local variables. Notice that it creates no stackframe and saves no return address.

```
int
leaf(p1, p2)
    int p1, p2;
    {
    return (p1 > p2) ? p1 : p2;
    }

                .globl          leaf
#     1         int
#     2         leaf(p1, p2)
#     3             int p1, p2;
#     4             {
                .ent            leaf
leaf:
                .frame          $sp, 0, $31
#     5             return (p1 > p2) ? p1 : p2;
                ble             $4, $5, $32      ## Arguments in $4 and $5
                move            $3, $4
                b               $33
$32:
                move            $3, $5
$33:
                move            $2, $3           ## Return value goes in $2
                j               #31              ## Return to caller
#     6             }
                .end    leaf
```

Figure D–4. Leaf Procedure without Stack Space for Local Variables

Figure D–5 shows a leaf procedure that requires stack space for local variables. Notice that it creates a stackframe, but does not save a return address.

```
char
leaf_storage(i)
  int i;
  {
  char a[16];
  int j;

  for (j = 0; j < 10; j++)
    a[j] = '0' + j;
  for (j = 10; j < 16; j++)
    a[j] = 'a' + j;
  return a[i];
  }
```

```
          .globl  leaf_storage
#    1    char
#    2    leaf_storage(i)
#    3      int i;
#    4      {
          .ent    leaf_storage 2  ## 2 is the lexical level of the
leaf_storage:                     ## procedure.  You may omit it.
          subu    $sp, 24         ## Create stackframe
          .frame  $sp, 24, $31
#    5      char a[16];
#    6      int j;
#    7
#    8      for (j = 0; j < 10; j++)
          sw      $0, 4($sp)
          addu    $3, $sp, 24
$32:
#    9        a[j] = '0' + j;
          lw      $14, 4($sp)
          addu    $15, $14, 48
          addu    $24, $3, $14
          sb      $15, -16($24)
          lw      $25, 4($sp)
          addu    $8, $25, 1
          sw      $8, 4($sp)
          blt     $8, 10, $32
#   10      for (j = 10; j < 16; j++)
          li      $9, 10
          sw      $9, 4($sp)
$33:
#   11        a[j] = 'a' + j;
          lw      $10, 4($sp)
          addu    $11, $10, 97
          addu    $12, $3, $10
          sb      $11, -16($12)
          lw      $13, 4($sp)
          addu    $14, $13, 1
          sw      $14, 4($sp)
          blt     $14, 16, $33
#   12    return a[i];
          addu    $15, $3, $4      ## Argument is in $4
          lbu     $2, -16($15)     ## Return value goes in $2
          addu    $sp, 24          ## Delete stackframe
          j       $31              ## Return to caller
          .end    leaf_storage
```

Figure D–5. Leaf Procedure with Stack Space for Local Variables

Memory Allocation

The default memory allocation scheme of the system gives each process two storage areas that can grow without bound. A process exceeds virtual storage only when the sum of the two areas exceeds virtual storage space. The link editor and assembler use the scheme shown in Figure D–6.

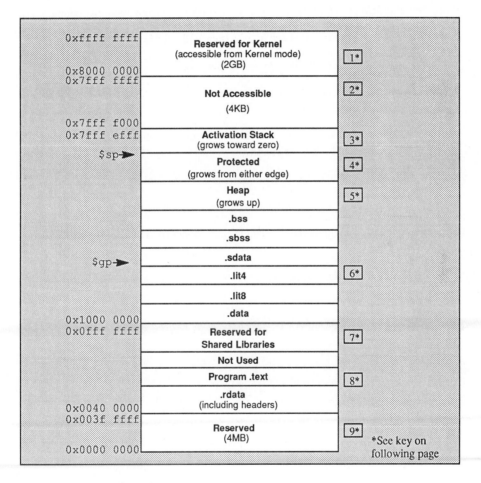

Figure D–6. Memory Layout (User Program View)

Key to Figure D–6:

1   Reserved for kernel operations.

2   Reserved for operating system use.

3   Used for local data in C programs.

4   Not allocated until a user requests it, as in System V shared memory regions.

5   The heap is reserved for *sbrk* and *break* system calls, and is not always present.

6   The machine divides all data into one of five sections:

- **bss** – uninitialized data with size greater than the value specified by the –G command line option.

- **sbss** – data less than or equal to the –G command line option. (8 is the default value for the –G option.)

- **sdata** (small data) – data initialized and specified for the **sdata** section.

- **data** (data) – data initialized and specified for the **data** section.

- **rdata** (read-only data) – data initialized and specified for the **rdata** section.

7   Reserved for any shared libraries.

8   Contains the **.text** section.

9   Reserved.

Basic Machine Definition

The assembly language instructions are a superset of the actual machine instructions. Generally, the assembly language instructions match the machine instructions; however, in some cases the assembly language instructions are macros that generate more than one machine instruction (for example, assembly language multiplication instructions).

In most instances you can consider the assembly instructions as machine instructions; however, for routines that require tight coding for performance reasons, you must be aware of assembly instructions that generate more than one machine language instruction, as described in this section.

Load and Store Instructions

If you use an *address* as an operand in an assembler load or store instruction and the address references a data item that is not addressable through register *$gp* or the data item does not have an absolute address in the range −32768...32767, the assembler instruction generates a LUI (Load Upper Immediate) machine instruction and generates the appropriate offset to *$at*. The assembler then uses *$at* as the index address for the reference. This condition occurs when the address has a relocatable external name offset (or index) from where the offset began.

The assembler LA (Load Address) instruction generates an ADDIU (Add Unsigned Immediate) machine instruction. If the address requires it, the LA instruction also generates a LUI (Load Upper Immediate) machine instruction. The machine requires an LA instruction because LA couples relocatable information with the instruction for symbolic addresses.

Depending on the expression value, the assembler LI (Load Immediate) instruction can generate one or two machine instructions. For values in the −32768...65535 range or for values that have zeros as the 16 least significant bits, the LI instruction generates a single machine instruction; otherwise it generates two machine instructions.

Computational Instructions

If a computational instruction immediate value falls outside the 0...65535 range for Logical ANDs, Logical ORs, or Logical XORs (Exclusive Or), the immediate field causes the machine to explicitly load a constant to a temporary register. Other instructions generate a single machine instruction when a value falls in the −32768...32767 range.

The assembler SEQ (Set Equal) and SNE (Set Not Equal) instructions generate three machine instructions each.

If one operand is a literal outside the range −32768...32767, the assembler SGE (Set Greater Than Or Equal To) and SLE (Set Less/Equal) instructions generate two machine instructions each.

The assembler MULO and MULOU (Multiply) instructions generate machine instructions to test for overflow and to move the result to a general register; if the destination register is *$0*, the check and move are not generated.

The assembler MUL (Multiply) instruction generates a machine instruction to move the result to a general register; if the destination register is *$0*, the move is not generated. The assembler divide instructions, DIV (Divide With Overflow) and DIVU (Divide Without Overflow), generate machine instructions to check for division by zero and to move the quotient into a general register; if the destination register is *$0*, the move and divide-by-zero checking is not generated.

The assembler REM (signed) and REMU (unsigned) instructions also generate multiple instructions.

The rotate instructions ROR (Rotate Right) and ROL (Rotate Left) generate three machine instructions each.

The ABS (Absolute Value) instruction generates three machine instructions.

Branch Instructions

If the immediate value is not zero, the branch instructions BEQ (Branch On Equal) and BNE (Branch On Not Equal), each generate a load literal machine instruction. The relational instructions generate a SLT *(Set Less Than)* machine instruction to determine whether one register is less than or greater than another. Relational instructions can reorder the operands and branch on either zero or not zero, as required for the operation.

Coprocessor Instructions

For symbolic addresses, the coprocessor interface load and store instructions, LWC*z* (Load Coprocessor *z*) and SWC*z* (Store Coprocessor *z*) can generate a LUI (Load Upper Immediate) machine instruction.

Special Instructions

The assembler BREAK instruction packs the *breakcode* operand in unused register fields.

IEEE Standard 754 Floating-Point Compatibility Issues

MIPS has defined a floating-point coprocessor architecture that can be implemented using various combinations of hardware and software. When the Floating–Point Unit (FPU) is used in conjunction with the RISC/os operating system, the resulting architecture fully conforms to the requirements of ANSI/IEEE Standard 754–1985, *IEEE Standard for Binary Floating-Point Arithmetic*. In addition to conforming to the requirements of the IEEE standard, the MIPS floating-point coprocessor architecture fully supports the recommendations of the standard. In certain fairly obscure cases, the IEEE standard's recommendations are incomplete, ambiguous, or left to the implementors' discretion. The following section describes the interpretation of the recommendations for the MIPS floating-point architecture. Subsequent sections briefly describe the software support that the FPU requires to meet these recommendations.

Interpretation of the Standard

The sections that follow describe the manner in which the MIPS' architecture interprets those parts of the IEEE standard that are left up to the implementor's discretion.

Underflow

The IEEE standard gives the implementor choices in the detection of underflow conditions. The MIPS floating-point architecture requires that *tininess* be detected *after rounding*, and that *loss of accuracy* be detected as *inexact result.*

Exceptions

When an exception condition occurs, the IEEE standard does not define how the exception field is set when traps are disabled, or how the sticky exception field is set when traps are enabled. The MIPS floating-point architecture requires that the exception field be loaded (set or cleared), and that the sticky exception field be set, regardless of whether traps are enabled.

Inexact

The IEEE standard specifies that an inexact exception may occur concurrently with an overflow or underflow exception, and that the overflow or underflow exception trap take priority. It further requires that the inexact trap be taken if an operation overflows while the overflow trap is disabled. The MIPS floating-point architecture specifies that both the inexact exception and the overflow or underflow exception are signaled in these cases. A floating-point trap occurs if either exception is enabled; software is responsible for passing control to the appropriate trap handler.

Not a Number (NaN)

IEEE Standard 754 specifies that a quiet NaN be generated if an invalid operation occurs with the exception trap disabled, but does not further specify the value generated. The MIPS floating-point architecture specifies that in such cases, the NaN generated shall have a mantissa field of all ones, except for the high order fractional significand bit. The sign bit is positive, and the explicit integer bit, if present, is set. A NaN is defined for the word format (i.e., integers) and is used as a result of converting floating-point NaN and Infinities to fixed-point. When an invalid operation exception occurs due to one or more of the operands being signaling NaNs, a new quiet NaN is generated according to the rules above. Table E–1 lists these values.

Table E–1. NaN Values Generated for Invalid Operation

Format	Generated NaN Value
Single	7fbf ffff
Double	7ff7 ffff ffff ffff
Word	7fff ffff

Software Assistance for IEEE Standard Compatibility

The standard does not require that all floating-point operations be performed in high-performance hardware, and it does not specify the instruction set presentation. Therefore, when little performance advantage is realized by performing an operation in hardware, the MIPS architecture has simplified the hardware (the FPU) and requires the operation to be performed using software assistance. Operations that occur with low dynamic frequency can then be implemented in software, while providing hardware implementations of frequent operations.

The most complex part of the IEEE standard involves fully supporting the required and recommended exceptional conditions that arise in floating-point computation, such as overflow, underflow, and invalid operation. Here again, the MIPS architecture employs exception traps, when applicable, to relieve the FPU from handling all exceptional conditions. Exceptions that occur with low dynamic frequency are then handled using software assistance.

The MIPS architecture provides the necessary information and interrupts for trapping on exception conditions, but relies extensively on software to implement the IEEE recommendations for support of floating-point exception trap handlers.

IEEE Exception Trapping

The IEEE floating-point standard makes recommendations on information to be made available during a floating-point exception trap handler. This information often includes the original operand values or other information that must be computed in hardware unless the original operand values are retained.

All of the information the trap handler must determine can be derived from the state of the floating-point coprocessor at the time of the trap. However, to provide significant simplifications in the complexity of the FPU, some computation may need to be performed within the trap handler of an associated software envelope to determine the information.

IEEE 754 Format Compatibility

The IEEE Standard 754 requires a 32-bit floating-point format (single), and recommends a 64-bit floating-point format (double).

The MIPS floating-point architecture uses the IEEE Standard 754 single precision and double precision floating-point formats. Extended and quad formats are not covered in this book.

Implementing IEEE Standard Operations in Software

Some of the operations required or recommended by the IEEE standard are not provided directly by the FPU. These operations are not implemented in the floating-point instruction set either because of their high complexity and low frequency of use, or redundancy with the set of implemented instructions. The sections that follow provide code descriptions and skeletons for the implementation of some of these operations.

Remainder

The *remainder* function is accomplished by repeated magnitude subtraction of a scaled form of the divisor, until the dividend/remainder is one half of the divisor, or until the magnitude is less than one half of the magnitude of the divisor. The scaling of the divisor ensures that each subtraction step is exact; thus, the remainder function is always exact.

Convert between Binary and Decimal

These functions are provided in the routines *atof(3)* and *printf(3)* in libc.a of the RISC/os releases. See the manual page *atof(3)* and *printf(3)* in the appropriate RISC/os system reference manual.

Copy Sign

The *copy sign* operation can be performed using integer compares, and the absolute value and negation operations. Special attention must be paid to negative zero, since it has negative sign with zero value. This function is provided in the routine *copysign()* in libm.a of the RISC/os releases. See the manual page *IEEE(3)* in the appropriate RISC/os system reference manual.

```
/* Single precision copysign */
/* Operands in f0, f2 */
/* Result placed in f0 */
        mfc1    t0, f2
        abs.s   f0
        bgez    t0, 1f
        neg.s   f0
1:
```

Scale Binary

This operation is performed by moving the operand to the processor, where shift and add operations perform the basic operation. Checking for exceptional operands can be performed in either the processor or the floating-point coprocessor. This function is provided in the routine *scalb()* in libm.a of the RISC/os releases. See the manual page *IEEE(3M)* in the appropriate RISC/os system reference manual.

Round to Integer

The *round to integer in floating-point format* function can be implemented by adding a bias that causes normal rounding to occur at the end of the floating-point fraction, and then subtracting it back again. The code example below is for the double precision version; the single precision version is similar.

```
/* Double precision round to integer using current rounding mode */
/* Operand is in f12 */
/* Result placed in f0 */

        .set    noreorder
rint:
        li.d    $f4, 4503599627370496.0   /* 2⁵² */
        abs.d   $f2, $f12
        c.olt.d $f2, $f4                   /* if |arg| ≥ 2⁵² or arg is NaN */
        mfc1    t0, $f13
        bclf    4f                         /* then done */
        mov.d   $f0, $f12
                                           /* 2⁵² */
        bgez    t0, 2f                     /* if input negative, negate result */
        sll     t1, t0, 1

                                           /* negative */
        beq     t1, 0, 3f                  /* possible -0 */
        nop
1:      sub.d   $f0, $f12, $f4
        j       ra
        add.d   $f0, $f4

2:                                         /* positive */
        add.d   $f0, $f12, $f4             /* bias by 2⁵² to force
                                              non-integer bits off the end */
        j       ra
        sub.d   $f0, $f4                   /* unbias */

3:                                         /* msw = 80000000 */
        mfc1    t1, $f12                   /* if -0, return -0 */
        nop
        bne     t1, 0, 1b                  /* if negative denorm, process that */
        nop
4:      j       ra
        nop
```

Log Binary

This operation is performed by moving the operand to the processor, where shift and add operations perform the basic operation. This function is provided in the routine *logb( )* in libm.a of the RISC/os releases. See the manual page *IEEE(3M)* in the appropriate RISC/os system reference manual.

Next After

This operation is performed by comparing the two floating-point values to determine the direction to compute the neighbor, then moving the operand to the processor, where single precision or multiple precision add operations perform the basic operation.

Finite

This operation can be provided by taking the absolute value and comparing for equality with +1. This function is provided in the routine *finite()* in libm.a of the RISC/os releases. See the manual page *IEEE(3M)* in the appropriate RISC/os system reference manual.

```
/* Single precision finite */
/* Operands in f0 */
/* Result placed in v0 */
        mfc1    v0, f0
        nop
        sll     v0, 1
        srl     v0, 23+1
        sltu    v0, v0, 255
```

Is NaN

This operation is provided by using the unordered predicates of the floating-point compare operation.

Arithmetic Inequality

This operation is available as the floating-point compare operation.

Class

This operation is performed by moving the operand to the processor, where fixed-point shifts and comparisons can classify the floating-point value. These functions are provided in the routines *fp_class_d()* and *fp_class_f()* in libc.a of the RISC/os releases. See the manual page *fp_class(3)* in the appropriate RISC/os system reference manual.

Scheduling Hazards

Hazard Sources

Most hazards arise from instructions modifying and reading state in different pipeline stages.; such hazards are defined between pairs of instructions, not on a single isolated instruction. Other hazards are associated with the ability of instructions to restart in the presence of exceptions.

The MIPS architecture allows implementations to expose a few predefined hazards. These conditions need not be detected and corrected in hardware; instead, software is responsible for avoiding the hazard.

Guide to Hardware Interlocks
and Software Hazards

Pipelining is an implementation technique in which multiple instructions are in various stages of execution simultaneously. Pipelining is key to high performance, but one needs to consider what happens when a result needed by an instruction is not available in time for use by the next instruction (that is, a result is needed in a later pipe stage before it has been produced by an earlier instruction). For example, consider an idealized four-stage pipeline (shown in Figure F–1) consisting of instruction cache (**I**), ALU (**A**), data cache (**M**), and register write (**W**) stages.

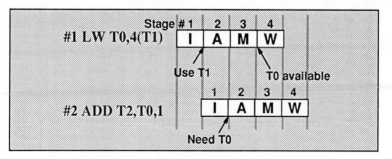

Figure F–1. Interlocks and Hazards: An Idealized Pipeline

In Figure F–1, instruction #2 is trying to reference the result of instruction #1 before the result of #1 is available. This occurs because it takes more time for #1 to execute than it takes the processor to fetch the next instruction (#2).

There are several ways to solve this problem:

- Detect the situation in hardware and insert null cycles to separate the two instructions so that operands are available when needed. This is called *hardware interlocking*.

- Detect the situation in software and use other instructions (a NOP if nothing else will do) to separate the instructions. If software fails to separate the instructions, the sequence executes incorrectly, engendering a *hazard* that must be avoided.

The MIPS architecture uses a combination of hardware interlocking and software hazard-avoidance to ensure that programs execute correctly. In general, hardware interlocks are used for long-latency operations (where many NOPs might be required) such as integer multiply/divide and floating-point results, or where hardware delays do not match the software model. Software hazard-avoidance is used for low-latency operations, such as the result of load instructions.

A common question asked about the MIPS architecture is, "How many NOPs are needed after instruction X?" Unfortunately, this question is meaningless because hazards are defined *between pairs of instructions*, not after a single instruction. One possible — but not very realistic — way to answer this question would be to create an N-by-N matrix listing the number of hazard cycles, where N is the number of instructions. However, because of the number of instructions this matrix would be enormous. A more realistic way is creation of a table with N rows (again, where N is the number of instructions), and listing the pipeline stages where operands are used and results produced.

A simple formula could then be derived. The distance required between instruction A (the instruction that *produces* the result), and instruction B (the instruction that *uses* the result) could be calculated from the following formula:

> *The stage number in which **A** produces a result minus the stage number in which **B** needs to use the result equals the distance required between instructions.*

For example, the ADD instruction in Figure F–1 receives its operands on input to stage 2 and produces results for stage 3. Using the formula above, the distance required between two dependent ADDs is then $3 - 2 = 1$, or a single instruction. Since a single instruction is already the minimum spacing, so there is no hazard.

Let's take another example, using the five-stage pipeline shown in Figure F–2. In it, a LOAD instruction is followed by a dependent ADD. Between a LOAD (whose result is available in stage 4, MEM) and a dependent ADD (which needs input at stage 2, RD), the distance requirement would be $4 - 2 = 2$, or two instructions. Since the required spacing is greater than one instruction, there is a hazard. This hazard can be avoided by separating the LOAD and ADD by one additional instruction, in this case a NOP, as illustrated in Figure F–2.

		Stage #	1	2	3	4	5		Instruction spacing
100	LW T0,4,(T1)		IF	RD	ALU	MEM	WB		
					LOAD result available here →				1
				1	2	3	4	5	
104	NOP			IF	RD	ALU	MEM	WB	
					1	2	3	4	5	1
108	ADD T2,T0,1				IF	RD ↗	ALU	MEM	WB	
						ADD input needed			

Figure F–2. Hazard Between Consecutive LOAD and ADD Instructions

Conversely, between an ADD and a LOAD, the required distance is $3 - 2 = 1$, or one instruction, so the following sequence is valid:

```
200     ADD     T1,T1,4
204     LW      T0,0(T1)
```

To illustrate how important it is to consider instructions as a pair, consider the CTC1 instruction, which moves the contents of a general-purpose register to the *Floating-Point Control/Status* register (available in pipeline stage 4). The *Floating-Point Status* register controls rounding, exceptions, etc., so the required distance between CTC1 and a floating-point op (which is read in stage 2) is $4 - 2 = 2$, or two instructions:

```
300     CTC1    T0, $31
304     NOP
308     ADD.D   F0, F2, F4
```

The *Floating-Point Control/Status* register also contains the floating-point compare result. This compare result is used in pipeline stage 1 of the BC1T and BC1F instructions, so the required distance is 4 − 1 = 3, or three instructions:

```
400     CTC1     T0, $31
404     NOP
408     NOP
40C     BC1T     L
```

Interlocks and stalls cannot be used to eliminate a hazard. For example, in the following sequence the processor stalls on the ADD.S to wait for F0 to be computed by the MUL.S.

```
500     MUL.S    F0, F2, F4
504     LWC1     F6, 0(T0)
508     ADD.S    F0, F0, F6
```

This stall does not eliminate the LWC1/ADD.S hazard, and so the above code is in error.

Another class of hazards arises from the need to handle interrupts or exceptions transparently between instructions. Most R-Series implementations delay changing stored program state until the pipeline stage *after* all exceptions and interrupts have been detected and effected. (Typically, though, *bypassing* is employed so results can be used before this time.) When an instruction is aborted by an exception or interrupt, all subsequent instructions in the pipeline are also aborted; since these instructions have not yet affected stored program state, the exception handler sees the same stored program state as if there were no pipelining.

However, if an implementation has updated the program state in an early pipeline stage, an exception detected in later pipeline stages would not abort this update. In this case, the effect of the aborted instruction would be part of the stored program state; if execution was resumed, the difference in program state could affect program operation, and thus the exception or interrupt would not be transparent. For example, MULT, MULTU, DIV, and DIVU write the *HI* and *LO* registers in the **A** stage of the R2000/R3000 pipeline, instead of waiting until the **W** stage. Consider, then, the following instruction sequence:

```
600     MFLO    R5
604     NOP
608     MULTU   R6, R7
```

If no interrupt occurs during this sequence, the MFLO reads the *LO* register during its **A** stage, and two cycles later the MULTU writes a new value into *LO*. Thus R5 receives the previous multiply/divide result. However, if an exception occurs and MFLO is aborted in the **W** stage, the MULTU, which is in the **A** stage, nevertheless completes and writes *HI* and *LO*. When the MFLO is restarted, it reads the new — and incorrect — multiply result. As a consequence, the R-Series architecture holds software responsible for avoiding this hazard by requiring at least two instructions between a read of *HI* or *LO* and an instruction that writes *HI* or *LO*.

Processor restartability also imposes restrictions on the JALR instruction. While R2000 and R3000 processors delay writing the destination *GPR* until the **W** stage, an exception or interrupt in their branch delay slot sets the *EPC* so these instructions reexecute. To make this reexecution transparent, the source register of JALR must be different from its destination register.

In the following pages, Tables F–1, F–2, and F–3 give the pipeline stages for operands and results in the R2000/R3000, R4000, and R6000 implementations. Future implementations will maintain compatibility with these implementations.

R2000/R3000 Pipeline Stages

Table F–1 shows the pipeline stages for operands and results in the R2000 and R3000.

Table F–1. R2000/R3000 Pipeline Stages for Operands and Results

	Source			Destination
Instruction	rs/fs	rt/ft	Other	
ALU, SHIFT	2	2		3
BRANCH	2	2		
BLTZAL, BGEZAL	2			3
JAL				3
JR	2			
JALR	2			3
MFHI, MFLO			2	3
MTHI, MTLO	2			3
MULT, MULTU	2	2		14**
DIV, DIVU	2	2		37**
LB, LBU,	2			4*
LH, LHU,	2			4*
LW, LWCz	2			4*
MFCz, CFCz	2			4*
MTCz, CTCz		2		4*
BCzT, BCzF			1	
LWL, LWR	2	3		4*
SB, SH, SW,	2	2		
SWL, SWR, SWCz	2	2		
ADD.s, SUB.s,	2	2		4**
ADD.d, SUB.d	2	2		4**
MUL.s	2	2		6**
MUL.d	2	2		7**
DIV.s	2	2		14**
DIV.d	2	2		21**
MOV.s, MOV.d,	2			3
NEG.s, NEG.d,	2			3
ABS.s, ABS.d	2			3
CVT.d.s	2			3
CVT.w.s,	2			4**
CVT.w.d, CVT.s.d	2			4**
CVT.s.w, CVT.d.w	2			5**
C.xx.S, C.xx.D	2	2		3*

* possible hazard   **possible interlock

R4000 Pipeline Stages

Table F–2 shows the pipeline stages for operands and results in the R4000.

Table F–2. R4000 Pipeline Stages for Operands and Results

Instruction	Source rs/fs	Source rt/ft	Source Other	Destination
ALU	3	3		4
SLL, SRL, SRA		3		4
SLLV, SRLV, SRAV	3	3		5**
BRANCH, TRAP	3	3		
BLTZAL, BGEZAL	3			4
JAL				4
JR	3			
JALR	3			4
MFHI, MFLO			3	4
MTHI, MTLO	3			4
MULT, MULTU	3	3		15**
DIV, DIVU	3	3		79**
LB, LBU, LH, LHU	3			6**
LW, LL,LWCz, LDCz	3			6**
MFCz, CFCz	3			6*
MTCz, CTCz		3		6*
BCzT, BCzF			3	
LWL, LWR	3	5		6**
SB, SH, SW,SWL	3	3		
SWR,SWCz, SDCz	3	3		
SC	3	3		6**
ADD.S, SUB.S	3	3		7**
ADD.D, SUB.D	3	3		7**
MUL.S	3	3		10**
MUL.D	3	3		11**
DIV.S	3	3		26**
DIV.D	3	3		39**
MOV.S, MOV.D	3			4
NEG.S, NEG.D, ABS.S, ABS.D	3			5**
CVT.D.S	3			5**
CVT.W.S, CVT.W.D	3			7**
ROUND.W.S, ROUND.W.D	3			7**
TRUNC.W.S, TRUNC.W.D	3			7**
FLOOR.W.S, FLOOR.W.D	3			7**
CEIL.W.S, CEIL.W.D	3			7**
CVT.S.D	3			7**
CVT.S.W	3			9**
CVT.D.W	3			8**
C.xx.S, C.xx.D	3	3		6**

* possible hazard   **possible interlock

R6000 Pipeline Stages

Table F–3 shows the pipeline stages for operands and results in the R6000.

Table F–3. R6000 Pipeline Stages for Operands and Results

Instruction	Source Rs/Fs	Source Rt/Ft	Source Other	Destination
ALU	2	2		3
SLL, SRL, SRA		2		3
SLLV, SRLV, SRAV	2	2		3
Branch, Trap	2	2		
BLTZAL, BGEZAL	2			3
JAL				3
JR	2			
JALR	2			3
MFHI, MFLO			2	3
MTHI, MTLO	2			3
MULT	2	2		19**
MULTU	2	2		20**
DIV	2	2		40**
DIVU	2	2		39**
LB, LBU, LH, LHU	2			4**
LW, LL, LWCz	2			4**
LDCz	2			4–5**
MFCz, CFCz	2			4*
MTCz, CTCz		2		4*
BCzT, BCzF			1	
LWL, LWR	2	3		4**
SB, SH, SW, SWL, SWR, SWCz	2	2		
SDCz	2	2–3		
SC	2	2		4**
ADD.S, SUB.S	2	2		5**
ADD.D, SUB.D	2–3	2–3		5–6**
MUL.S	2	2		6–7**
MUL.D	2–3	2–3		7–8**
DIV.S	2	2		14–17**
DIV.D	2–3	2–3		22–28**
MOV.S, NEG.S, ABS.S	2			4**
MOV.D, NEG.D, ABS.D	2–3			4–5**
CVT.D.S	2			4–5**
CVT.W.S, ROUND.W.S	2			5**
TRUNC.W.S, FLOOR.W.S	2			5**
CEIL.W.S, CVT.S.W, CVT.D.W	2			5**
CVT.W.D, ROUND.W.D	2–3			5–6**
TRUNC.W.D, FLOOR.W.D	2–3			5–6**
CEIL.W.D, CVT.S.D	2–3			5–6**
C.xx.S	2	2		3*
C.xx.D	2–3	2–3		3–4*

* possible hazard   **possible interlock

Hazards Allowed by the Architecture

This section enumerates hazards allowed by implementations of the R-Series architecture. The operation of programs that do not avoid these hazards is undefined. System Control Coprocessor (CP0) hazards are implementation-specific.

Load Delay Slot

All processor load instructions (LBU, LB, LHU, LH, LW, LWL, LWR) and move-from-coprocessor instructions (MFCz, CFCz) modify processor general registers in a late pipe stage. This prevents their use as source register operands in the instruction immediately following (see descriptions of the load delay slot in Chapters 1 and 3).

Sample Instruction: MFC0 rt,rd

The contents of coprocessor register *rd* of CP0 are loaded into general register *rt*.

```
T:       data ← CPR[0,rd]
T+1:     GPR[rt] ← data
```

Similarly, coprocessor load instructions (LWCz, LDCz) and move-to-coprocessor instructions (MTCz, CTCz) modify coprocessor general registers or coprocessor control registers in a late pipe stage, and cannot be used as source register operands in the instruction immediately following.

While R4000 and R6000 processors also have delayed load instructions for timing purposes, they do not need to fill the delay slots of processor and coprocessor load instructions with a NOP; the hardware will interlock to provide the updated value of the processor or coprocessor target register to the next instruction. However all move-to and move-from coprocessor instructions (MFCz, CFCz, MTCz, CTCz) still require a scheduled delay slot to be filled with a NOP or other instruction that does not use the target register.

Branch Delay Slot

MIPS processors have a single program counter, yet support delayed branches. When an exception occurs that would normally require setting the *EPC* to an instruction in a branch delay slot, the *EPC* is instead backed up to the branch instruction immediately preceding. Thus, the branch instruction executes a second time upon return from the exception handler, which leads to the following constraint:

> *JALR cannot use a source register as the same destination register*

If a branch instruction could be placed in a branch delay slot, no placement of the *EPC* could assure a properly restartable instruction flow. In addition, PC-relative branch operations are relative to the *address of the instruction in the branch delay slot*. To be well-defined, this must be the instruction immediately following the branch. Each of these are sufficient reasons for the following constraint:

> *The instruction in the delay slot of a PC-changing instruction, (J, JR, JAL, JALR, BEQ, BNE, BLEZ, BGTZ, BLTZ, BGEZ, BLTZAL, BGEZAL), and on R4000 and R6000 implementations (BEQL, BNEL, BLEZL, BGTZL, BLTZL, BGEZL, BLTZALL, BGEZALL), cannot itself change the PC.*

Setting Up a Coprocessor Condition

A BCzT or BCzF instruction samples the coprocessor condition line during the instruction immediately preceding it. Thus, the coprocessor condition should not be changed immediately preceding the BCzT or BCzF instruction.

This constraint requires that the instruction executed immediately after a coprocessor condition setting (e.g., C.cond.fmt for CP1) cannot be a BCzT or BCzF. If the condition setting occurs as a result of a MTCz or CTCz instruction, two other instructions must occur between this instruction and the BCzT or BCzF instruction that tests it.

No Bypassing for HI and LO Registers

To reduce the amount of bypassing that is required for the *HI* and *LO* registers (which contain the results of multiply and divide operations), it is required that the two instructions following an attempt to read the registers with either of the MFHI or MFLO instructions must not modify the register being read.

This permits the instructions that modify the *HI* and *LO* registers (MULT, MULTU, DIV, DIVU, MTHI, MTLO) to start modifying the registers as soon as it is verified that the instruction is valid — even if it is determined that an exception cancels the instruction later. This leads to the following constraints:

> *The two instructions executed after MFLO cannot be MTLO, MULT, MULTU, DIV, or DIVU.*
>
> *The two instructions executed after MFHI cannot be MTHI, MULT, MULTU, DIV, or DIVU.*

Combinations of Scheduling Hazards

In some cases, scheduling hazards connect together to produce longer constraints. For example, the following sequence requires two NOPs between the instructions.

```
CTC1 $rx,$31
BC1T label
```

CP0 Hazards

Many CP0 registers contain data that affect instruction fetch, instruction execution, address translation, exceptions, interrupts, etc. Therefore the hazards associated with MTC0 instructions are complex and depend on which fields are being modified by the write.

R2000/R3000 CP0 Hazards

For R2000 and R3000 processors, the CP0 instructions TLBWI and TLBWR write the TLB in the same pipeline stage as load and store operations read it, so there are no hazards between these instructions. However, instruction fetches access the micro-TLB and the TLB in different pipe stages, causing a delay of two instructions before the map change is effected. The micro-TLB is not flushed by TLBWI and TLBWR (it is flushed by loading *EntryHi*), which can further delay the effect. For these reasons, it is recommended that the move to *EntryHi* and TLB write be executed from unmapped space.

R3000 CP0 Hazards

Most CP0 registers contain data that cause side effects on the behavior of subsequent instructions. Such side effects are not predictable on the one, two, or three instructions immediately following an MTC0 instruction that modifies that data.

In particular, the two instructions following an MTC0 instruction that turns *on* the usability of a coprocessor must not depend on that coprocessor being *usable*; that is, they must not be instructions for that coprocessor unit. Similarly, the two instructions following a MTC0 instruction that turns *off* the usability of a coprocessor must not depend on that coprocessor being *unusable*.

An MTC0 that enables or disables interrupts does not take effect until the third instruction following the MTC0.

R6000 Memory Management Hazards

The R6000 memory management instructions — Flush (LWR), Invalidate (SWR), Load From cache (LWL), and Store To Cache (SWL) — with the *MM* status register bit set cannot be placed in a branch or jump delay slot.

R6000 CP0 Hazards

The R6000 is designed to be compatible with the R2000/R3000. R6000 CP0 hazards are:

- One NOP must be placed between an MTC0 and an MFC0 of the same register.

- No NOPs are necessary between the time an MTC0 Status value is issued and the time the CP Usable and Kernel/User bits reflect this new value. The same is true for interrupt enables — if an MTC0 sets an interrupt enable, the instruction following the MTC0 is interrupted and does not complete.

- There are no hazards between an MFC0 and the subsequent use of its result, and the generation of a value and its use in an MTC0.

- Load, store, and TLB operations immediately prior to and after an MTC0 instruction are undefined (see the description of MTC0 in Appendix A).

R4000 CP0 Hazards

Note: This section is both incomplete and preliminary.

Table F–4 lists CP0 hazards for the R4000. The following constraints must be observed:

- The instruction following a MTC0 must not be a MFC0.

- CACHE instructions complete in the WB stage, so one instruction must separate an Index_Load_Tag from an MFC0 Tag.

- There must be two non-load and non-CACHE instructions between a store and a CACHE instruction that is directed to the same primary cache line as the store.

Table F–4. R4000 CP0 Hazards

Operation	Source		Destination	
	Name	Stage	Name	Stage
MTC0	gpr rt	3	cpr rd	6
MFC0	cpr rd	4	gpr rt	6
TLBR	Index	5–7	PageMask	7
	TLB		EntryHi	
			EntryLo0	
			EntryLo1	
TLBWI	Index/Random	5–7	TLB 7	
TLBWR	PageMask			
	EntryHi			
	EntryLo0			
	EntryLo1			
TLBP	EntryHi	3–6	Index	6
	EntryLo0			
	EntryLo1			
ERET	EPC/ErrorEPC	4	Status	8
	Status		Status.EXL	4
			Status.ERL	
Index Load Tag	–		TagLo	8
			TagHi	
Instruction Fetch	EntryHi.ASID	0	–	
	Status.KSU			
	Status.RE			
	Config.K0C			
	Config.IB			
Instruction Fetch	–		EPC	7
Exception			Status	
			Cause	2
			BadVAddr	
			Context	
Coprocessor Usable Test	Status.CU	2		
Interrupt	Status.IM	3		
Load/Store	EntryHi.ASID	4	–	
	Status.KSU			
	Status.RE			
	Config.K0C			
	Config.DB			
Load/Store Exception	–		EPC	7
			Status	
			Cause	
			BadVAddr	
			Context	

Index

Numbers

3-operand register type instructions, 3–8

32-bit addresses
  jumping to, C–4
  loading, C–2

64-bit math, example of, C–10—C–11

64-bit, ISA, 1–3

A

ABS.fmt instruction, 8–4, B–10

absolute value instruction, 8–4, B–10

access control bits, 4–25, 4–28
  valid (V) bit, 4–25, 4–28

access time, instruction, 1–15, 5–2

accesses, byte, 3–4

ADD, A–9

Add Immediate (ADDI), A–10

Add Immediate Unsigned (ADDIU), A–11

add instruction, floating-point, 8–3

Add Unsigned, A–12

ADD.fmt instruction, 8–4, B–11

ADDI (add immediate), A–10

ADDIU (add immediate unsigned), A–11

address error
  exception, 6–40
  exception code, 6–18
  TLB, 6–41

address formats, D–10, D–11
  base register, D–11
  expression, D–11
  expression (base register), D–11
  relocatable symbol, D–11
  relocatable symbol (index register), D–11
  relocatable symbol +/– expression, D–11
  relocatable symbol +/– expression (index register), D–11

address space, user mode, 4–4

address space identifier (ASID), 4–3, 4–4

address translation
  R2000, 4–26
  R3000, 4–26
  R4000, 4–27
  R6000, 4–29

address, loading
  translation, 4–25
  translation, R2000, 4–25
  translation, R3000, 4–25
  translation, R4000, 4–27
  translation, R6000, 4–28

addresses
  jumping to 32–bit, C–4
  loading 32–bit, example of, C–2

addresses, byte, 3–4

addressing, 2–10
  assembler modes, D–9
  indexed, example of, C–3
  misaligned words, 2–12

ADDU (add unsigned), A–12

AdEL (address error load) exception code, 6–18

AdES (address error store) exception code, 6–18

alias, cache, 5–11

B

C

M

N

O

O (overflow) exception, FPU, 9–7

old interrupt enable (IEo) bit, 6–11, 6–16

old kernel/user mode (KUo) bit, 6–16

opcode bit encoding
  R2000, A–139, A–140
  R3000, A–139, A–140
  R4000, A–141, A–142
  R6000, A–143, A–144

opcode bit encoding, FPU, B–49

opcodes, pseudo
  See also pseudo opcodes
  .aent, D–12—D–18
  .alias, D–12—D–18
  .align, D–12—D–18
  .ascii, D–12—D–18
  .asciiz, D–12—D–18
  .asm0, D–12—D–18
  .bgnb, D–12—D–18
  .byte, D–12—D–18
  .comm, D–13—D–18
  .data, D–13—D–18
  .double, D–13—D–18
  .end, D–13—D–18
  .endb, D–13—D–18
  .endr, D–13—D–18
  .err, D–13—D–18
  .extern, D–13—D–18
  .file, D–14—D–18
  .float, D–14—D–18
  .fmask, D–14—D–18
  .frame, D–14—D–18
  .galive, D–14—D–18
  .gjaldef, D–14—D–18
  .gjrlive, D–14—D–18
  .globl, D–14—D–18
  .half, D–15—D–18
  .lab, D–15—D–18
  .lcomm, D–15—D–18
  .livereg, D–15—D–18
  .loc, D–16—D–18
  .mask, D–16—D–18

.noalias, D–16—D–18
.option, D–16—D–18
.rdata, D–17—D–18
.repeat, D–16—D–18
.sdata, D–17—D–18
.set, D–17—D–18
  at, D–17—D–18
  bopt, D–17—D–18
  macro, D–17—D–18
  move, D–17—D–18
  noat, D–17—D–18
  nobopt, D–17—D–18
  nomacro, D–17—D–18
  nomove, D–17—D–18
  nonvolatile, D–17—D–18
  noreorder, D–17—D–18
  reorder, D–17—D–18
  volatile, D–17—D–18
.space, D–18
.struct, D–18
.text, D–18
.verstamp, D–18
.vreg, D–18
.weakext, D–18
.word, D–18
nop, D–16—D–18
(symbolic equate), D–18

operating modes, 2–18—2–26
  kernel, 2–18—2–26
  RISC support for, 1–20
  supervisor, 2–18—2–26
  user, 2–18—2–26

operating system support, 1–19—1–22

operation time, 1–15

operations, floating-point, 7–17

operators, floating-point relational, 8–6, 8–7

optimization
  global, 1–18
  inter–procedural, 1–18
  levels, 1–18
  local, 1–18
  peephole, 1–18

optimizing compilers, 1–16, 1–18

optimizing techniques, 1–17
  loop optimization, 1–17

P

S

T

U

U (underflow) exceptions, FPU, 9–9

UCSC (AlcoHall). *See* College 5, '73

unaligned loads, D–10

unaligned stores, D–10

uncached LDCz, exception, 6–56

uncached SDCz, exception, 6–56

underflow, IEEE standard 754, interpretation of, E–1

underflow exception, FPU, 9–9

underflow status bit, FPU, 7–8, 9–2

unimplemented operation exception, FPU, 9–2, 9–10

unimplemented operation status bits, FPU, 7–8

unsigned
    divide (DIVU), A–48
    multiply (MULTU), A–87
    set on less than (SLTU), A–103
    subtract (SUBU), A–109
    trap if less than (TLTU), A–134
    trap if less than immediate (TLTIU), A–133

user benefits of RISC, 1–22

user mode, 1–2, 4–3, 4–4
    address space, 4–4

user mode bits, status register, 6–11, 6–16

user mode virtual addressing, 4–4

V

V (invalid operation) exception, FPU, 9–8

valid (V) bit, EntryLo register, 4–12

values, calculating in FP format, 7–13

variable instruction execution time, 1–9

vector addresses, exceptions, 6–34

vector locations, exceptions, 6–34

vector offsets, exceptions, 6–34

virtual address format
    R2000, 4–2
    R3000, 4–2
    R4000, 4–2
    R6000, 4–3

virtual address space
    kernel mode, 4–6
    R2000, 4–1
    R3000, 4–1
    R4000, 4–1
    R6000, 4–1
    supervisor mode, 4–5
    user mode, 4–4

virtual address translation
    R2000, 4–25—4–29
    R3000, 4–25—4–29
    R4000, 4–27—4–29
    R6000, 4–28—4–29

virtual coherency, exception, 6–46

virtual memory segments, 4–6

virtual memory system, 1–19

VPN (Virtual Page Number), 4–13, 6–4
    R2000, 4–2
    R3000, 4–2
    R4000, 4–2
    R6000, 4–3, 4–16
    R6000A, 4–16

W

WatchHi register, 6–25
WatchLo register, 6–25
watch exception, 6–55
Wired register, 4–23
write buffer, 2–25
write indexed TLB entry (TLBWI), A–129
write random TLB entry (TLBWR), A–130

X

XOR, exclusive (XOR), A–137

Z

Z (division–by–zero) exception, FPU, 9–7
zero, floating-point number definition, 7–15